THE CIVILIZATION OF THE AMERICAN INDIAN SERIES

THE FLATHEAD INDIANS

▲▲▲▲▲▲▲▲▲▲▲▲▲▲▲▲▲▲▲▲▲

THE FLATHEAD INDIANS

▼▼▼▼▼▼▼▼▼▼▼▼▼▼▼▼▼▼▼▼▼

by John Fahey

UNIVERSITY OF OKLAHOMA PRESS : Norman

By JOHN FAHEY

Inland Empire: D. C. Corbin and Spokane (Seattle, 1965)
Ballyhoo Bonanza: Charles Sweeny and the Idaho Mines (Seattle, 1971)

Library of Congress Cataloging in Publication Data

Fahey, John.
  The Flathead Indians.
  (The Civilization of the American Indian series)
  Bibliography: p.
  1. Salish Indians.   I. Title.   II. Series.
E99.S2F24   970.3   73–7420
ISBN 0–8061–1126–7

▲▲▲▲▲▲▲▲▲▲▲▲▲▲▲▲▲▲▲▲▲▲▲▲▲▲▲▲▲▲▲▲

For my own three "Indians"—
JOHN, KATE, and MIKE

▼▼▼▼▼▼▼▼▼▼▼▼▼▼▼▼▼▼▼▼▼▼▼▼▼▼▼▼▼▼▼

▲▲▲▲▲▲▲▲▲▲▲▲▲▲▲▲▲▲▲▲▲▲▲▲▲▲▲▲

PREFACE

▼▼▼▼▼▼▼▼▼▼▼▼▼▼▼▼▼▼▼▼▼▼▼▼▼▼▼

THIS STUDY of the Flathead Indians begins with a chapter that deals briefly with the Flatheads before their meeting with Lewis and Clark in 1805. In ten additional chapters it surveys political, social, and economic changes among them between 1805 and the opening of their reservation in 1910.

The first chapter is a general and somewhat conjectural summary of Flathead prehistory. It is intended as a starting point for outlining a century of rapid and momentous change. Two anthropologists who read the manuscript politely indicated skepticism here and there. I hereby thank John A. Ross and C. Thomas Brockmann for their valued suggestions (many adopted) and absolve them from complicity in my hypothesizing.

I expect that this book will be neither Indian enough for our Indian apologists nor novel enough for those to whom the perversion of Indian peoples seems old hat. With due respect for both views, I feel that the frontier experience—the conflict of cultures, the one shared experience of Indian and white—provides a useful place to begin. For the Flatheads, the century depicted here represents a benchmark from which old ways may be traced back into time, and new ways, forward toward the future. The Flatheads, as various investigators among them have found, really do not have an unbroken, sacrosanct cultural link with some ancient period; they tend to adopt what white men say about them as legitimately their story.

As author I have made a few ground rules for you as reader. You will see that I tell the story through participants as far as practical with some modernizing of punctuation, spelling, and grammar, although in taking Salish terms from the 1879 *Dictionary of the Kalispel or Flat Head Language* I preserve its spellings and diacritical markings.

The flaw in my dependence on contemporary accounts is common to studies of Indian peoples—no Indian version exists. But I do not feel secure, and I don't think you would, with an inferential history—a mirror history, if you will, in which the story is deduced by reversing or reading from the back accounts by men of an alien culture. Therefore, I have used the letters, journals, diaries, and reports available, recognizing their shortcoming.

Under the Indian Reorganization Act of 1934, the confederation of Flathead, Kutenai, and Pend Oreille Indians formed by treaty in 1855 was chartered as the Confederated Salish and Kootenai tribes. Flatheads and Pend Oreilles both are Salish peoples, and the Flatheads have always preferred to be called the Salish. But Salish is a linguistic classification, referring to Indians who speak Salish. Because there are a good many Salish speakers in this book, I resort to the less acceptable name of Flatheads.

As Father Lawrence B. Palladino explained in *Indian and White in the Northwest*, the Salish language has no consonants *b, d, f, r,* or *v.* The name of the chief Victor was therefore spoken Mitto, and Henry, Alee, although the war chief of historical times somehow got an *r* in his written name and is known as Arlee. I necessarily use a uniform spelling. But, as an example, there are as many who spell Charlot one way as another—Charlot, Charlos, or Charlo. The *t* in Charlot is silent.

You will see that Flatheads refers both to a people who lived in the Bitterroot Valley and to a nation formed by treaty, but I think the context will make its meaning clear where the term appears. Occasionally I call the Bitterroot people the Flatheads proper. I also call the Kalispels the Lower Pend Oreilles because it saves frequent bracketed interpolations in quoted letters and reports.

Furthermore, I use plural forms of tribal names that seem more suited than antiquarian forms to general readership.

As a perceptive reader, you will discover a lack of consistency in estimates of Indian populations. Counting Indians in early days was difficult. I let the figures stand as reported, but call attention to discrepancies in the narrative when they seem important to interpretation.

It is evident to me that the Flatheads expected to play a satisfactory role in a bicultural civilization when white men first invaded their territory. They were ready to be schooled; they wanted to share white technology. Their anticipation of equal treatment did not endure long. The Flatheads underestimated the numbers of potential white settlers, and the tribe's governance by council could not cope with the complexities of speedy change.

My assumptions are that the Flathead way of life, discovered by white men in 1805, was neither stable nor durable, but a culture in transition, fragile, and out of equilibrium with its environment. The Flatheads' adoption of ancient Blue Jay rites as late as 1898 seems to support this view.

As their involvement with white men's affairs deepened, the Flatheads lost management of events that affected them. The account moves to political emphasis, therefore, to summarize political, military, juridical, and economic activities that altered their lives. Not only are there no satisfactory Indian versions, but, as time passes in the story, the Flatheads participate less in decisions. Their contact with white men becomes ritualistic and symbolic, and their capability to influence the course of events diminishes.

The aging chief, Charlot, recognized the situation but found no way to insert himself into the process of governance by bureaucracy. He simply resisted. I trust that when I don't focus sharply on the Flatheads here and there, you will agree that many processes and events bear on their acculturation. In sum the events produce an impression of continuity.

Anyone who writes about Indians must be humbled by the vastness of archival holdings in public, religious, and merchant collections, and by the likelihood that archeological discoveries will upset his best guesses about the past. I regard this account of the Flatheads as a compendium—the sort of historical frame that others will find useful for their own studies of the Flatheads of Montana. The book does not contain all of the information I collected and certainly does not contain all that is to be known about the Flatheads.

Anthropologists classify the Flatheads as Plateau Indians. By this, they mean the Indians of a cultural area approximately bounded on the north by the McKenzie Basin drainage, on the south by the California-Oregon border, on the west by the Cascades, and on the east by the Rocky Mountains. This, with the buffalo ranges of the Upper Missouri, is the geographic setting of my narrative.

The confederated tribes won a judgment on August 5, 1966, against the United States of America for $4,431,622.18, representing the fair market values in 1859 of an estimated 12,806,000 acres they forfeited under their 1855 treaty. Two groups of attorneys pursued this claim for twenty-five years, dating from a contract with the tribal council entered March 19, 1941. The original attorneys were George M. Tunison, a veteran of Indian claims suits, and Charles J. Kappler, the noted compiler of Indian laws and treaties. Kappler died in 1946 and Tunison in 1954, whereupon the tribe contracted in 1955 with Wilkinson, Boyden, Cragun and Barker to continue. Twenty-one partners or associates of this firm took part in the proceedings at one time or another.

About two-thirds of the land surrendered by the Flatheads has been set aside as forest preserves: the Flathead and Bitterroot national forests created in 1897; the Missoula, Kootenai, and Lolo in 1906; a portion of the Cabinet, 1907; and the Blackfoot, 1908.

Many scholars, librarians, and friends helped me gather and interpret the material for the narrative that follows. I thank them and regret that they are not all identified here. The bibliography and notes indicate the breadth of my debt to them. I express my gratitude especially to the late Father William L. Davis, S.J., who was wise and generous with his collection of De Smet, Hudson's Bay, Catholic, and related materials; Mrs. Edith M. Shaw, my reliable resource for scarce volumes and manuscripts, who retired in June, 1972, from the library staff at Eastern Washington State College; and Father Wilfred P. Schoenberg, S.J., archivist of the Oregon Province of the Society of Jesus, who opened his files, guided me through them in a search for manuscripts and photographs, and made a number of useful suggestions.

The maps were drawn by Carol Bellinger of the Eastern Washington State College cartographic laboratory.

The Flatheads have been a preoccupation of my household for some years, and with the encouragement and interest of my wife, Peggy, to whom I give special thanks, I have written here what I think is important to know about their first century of contact with white civilization.

JOHN FAHEY

Cheney, Washington
June, 1973

CONTENTS

ILLUSTRATIONS AND MAPS

THE FLATHEAD INDIANS

▲▲▲▲▲▲▲▲▲▲▲▲▲▲▲▲▲▲▲▲▲▲▲▲▲▲

CHAPTER 1

THE DESCENDANTS OF COYOTE

▼▼▼▼▼▼▼▼▼▼▼▼▼▼▼▼▼▼▼▼▼▼▼▼▼▼

IN THE BEGINNING the Sun created the heavens and the earth. And the earth was void and empty. And the Sun created every living and moving creature. And he gave them power according to their kind, commanding: Increase and multiply, fill the waters, and the earth, and the air. But the Sun perceived that many creatures were evil. And he created Coyote, saying to him: Behold, the earth is a dwelling place for monsters. And he sent Coyote to change earth into a place of cool mountains, forests with game, and streams with fish. And Coyote caught the wild gale and tamed it, and he cooled the hot and warmed the cold winds. And as he traveled over the earth, his wives bore him children who begat Indian tribes.

As time passed, Coyote roamed the land. Where he found wayward Indians, he transformed them into animal, wood, or stone. Their shapes remain in trees and rocks. Monsters he turned into mountains and valleys. The Coriacan Defile (O'Keefe Canyon) north of Missoula, Montana, was a monster that swallowed unsuspecting travelers until Coyote killed it. Although he played many tricks, Coyote also gave the Indians useful gifts such as fire and taught them to make weapons and utensils. Many times Coyote died at the hands of enemies, but Fox revived him by jumping over him.

The Flathead Indians of Montana descended from Coyote. Although common in the folktales of many peoples, Coyote remained the Flatheads' particular friend; he howled to warn of enemies nearby; he yipped three times to signal approaching strangers. By origin, the Flatheads are *skéligu*, their own word for angels and Indians that is loosely translated as "human beings."

Coyote is central in the mythical heritage of the Flatheads, a tradition passed from old to young around winter campfires where venerable men told stories. The old women talked among themselves and recited tales for young children. Formal storytelling was taboo in summer. Generally members of the tribe agreed on an approved version of the stories known best. A number of the Flatheads' tales occur in a time before *skéligu*; they portray animals acting with human motives, talking, sometimes wearing clothing, and possessing magical powers. When Coyote stories were intended to be comic, the narrator might use a high-pitched tone, while his listeners laughed uproariously. When the speaker was serious and faithful to an accepted version, listeners interjected approving remarks.

Traditional tales, often spun in contests to determine the best storytellers, suited the Flatheads to explain natural phenomena and to illustrate moral principles for children. All but the youngest knew the fabulous elements were only good stories. The narratives served well enough to explain his world to the Flathead, to amuse him, and to illumine his relationship to unseen forces—the spirit world around him.

As depicted in tales, and as the Flatheads knew from experience, animals exercised supernatural powers. Disturbed robins could cause rainfall; ants could stop it; eggs found by chance were an omen of rain. Certain spirits—those of eagle, grizzly, and elk— were most powerful. Animal relics representing these powers served the Flatheads as talismans to influence forces that decided human fates.

Certain trees and rocks, as well as animals, possessed strong powers. On the plain of the Bitterroot River stood a pine more than three hundred years old with a ram's horn imbedded in it seven feet from the ground. Wishes spoken to this tree were fulfilled, and the Flathead who hung a wisp of his hair on it was assured long life. An isolated tree, or one deformed by wind or lightning, also frequently possessed powers that the Indians discovered by experience.

Thus the Flatheads' affinity for the land and its creatures was spiritual. Indians did not conquer earth or bring it under their sway; they regarded earth as a mother, nurturing and sustaining them. The Flatheads thought of their homeland as a broad area they could never use for farming. In early times they did not think of farming the land at all. The unfortunate estimate that each Indian required eighty square miles of wild country to sustain his natural mode of living eventually convinced white men of the impracticality of the Indians' concept of land.

As earth was eternal, time was the present. Until the advent of white men among them, the Flatheads recognized no historical continuity, although they kept short chronological records by memory, tying knots in cords, or notching sticks to mark events and passage of time. The Flathead past, except as expressed in their folk tales, ended with the recollections of the oldest men and women. Virtually all stories about the past concerned events the teller saw himself or heard from a participant. "It would be most interesting and intriguing to learn about the Flathead traditions and legends regarding the creation of the world," remarked an early missionary. "Except among the elders . . . these traditions are now unknown. Since the native is concerned neither with the past nor the future, the younger generation completely ignores these stories."[1]

When the white man demanded to know the history of the Flatheads, however, the Indians obliged him. In the earliest times they could recall, the Flatheads migrated from an older home to the Bitterroot Valley of western Montana, finding it already occupied by fabulous bands of giants, dwarves, and a small tribe of dirty, stupid Indians regarded as the Foolish people—very useful for moralistic stories.

An outline of the Flatheads' real past may emerge some day from archeological research and further studies of Salish dialects. Salish is the Indian language family that the Flatheads share with such peoples of the interior Pacific Northwest as Shuswaps, Thompsons,

5

Wenatchis, Columbias, Okanogans, Sanpoils, Nespelims, Colvilles, Lakes, Lower Pend Oreilles (Kalispels), Upper Pend Oreilles, Spokanes, and Coeur d'Alenes, and with more than twenty tribes on the coasts of Washington and British Columbia. Salish is also the name by which the Flatheads prefer to be known. It means simply, "The people who speak Salish."

Despite the presence of the Foolish people, who disappeared in a way unknown, the Flatheads settled in the enveloping Bitterroot where high mountains and narrow passes partially protected them from pestilence carried up the Missouri and Columbia rivers and from Blackfoot raiders skulking from the buffalo plains of the Upper Missouri and the Saskatchewan. How long ago this may have been, none of the Flatheads seemed to know. Some Pend Oreilles who lived near Flathead Lake assert their people shifted northward to give the Flatheads room, and that at least one band of the newcomers flattened infants' heads by binding. Several tribes identify the Flatheads with terms signifying the flattening of heads.

Flatheads deny that their ancestors flattened heads but accept the theory that they are called Flatheads because sign language identified them by pressing both sides of the head with the hands. Misinterpreting this sign, white explorers moving westward across North America expected to come upon people with flattened heads beyond the Rocky Mountains. The same sign, with an additional gesture indicating Flathead Lake, identified the Salish north of the Flatheads until French trappers found this tribe wearing dentalium earrings and called them Pend Oreilles.[2]

Linguistic evidence indicates the various Salish speakers lived together in the interior of British Columbia several thousand years ago before separating into bands that preserved the language and some of the folk tales. Some bands remained inland; others migrated to the ocean shores. Probably their separation was friendly, for interior bartered with coastal Salish for slaves, sea-shell ornaments, small utensils such as bone needles, and other goods, trading a few of these in turn to other peoples east of them. Approximately four thousand years before Christ, by European reckoning, the Pacific Northwest interior turned drier, requiring its inhabitants to borrow tools and methods of the desert people to their south, probably by progressive trading along the western slopes of the continental divide, a route that grew in importance as sections of the interior plateau turned to desert and as, centuries later, horses became the prime item of barter.

By two thousand years before Christ, Athabascan-speaking peoples north of the Salish began to edge southward in migrations of varying intensity. Some Athabascans stalled after penetrating Salish areas, but others continued to move, generation after generation, for perhaps six hundred years. Under the pressure of this migration, a number of Salish were jostled from position.

Some Salish consequently drifted through the Okanogan Valley onto the Columbia Plateau, but possibly others, including the Flatheads, crossed the Rockies eastward before turning south. Confined by unfamiliar plains to a narrow corridor of mountain parklands and river systems, these Salish withstood the rip current of Athabascan migration flowing into the American southwest about 1000 A.D., but felt its vigor, traded with its people, and bobbed in its periphery until they encountered Sahaptin speakers who slowed the Flatheads' drift southward and bent their course into the Bozeman River valley. Perhaps the Flatheads stayed close to their mountain valleys, venturing onto the plains in comparatively recent times.

The Flatheads adopted social forms as well as manufacturing techniques and weapons from peoples they encountered in these early times. Other borrowings seem relatively recent. A pure Flathead tradition, if one existed, was progressively diluted by cultural borrowings, intermarriages, and adoptions, so that the Flatheads as a society combined features of the original Plateau and adopted Plains cultures. So lively was the cultural infusion, in fact, that older Blackfeet consider the Flatheads a Plains people.

Due to movement and adaptation, the Flatheads underwent continual change in habitat and social organization in the half millenium preceding European settlement in their homelands. In that five hundred years, change accelerated for the Flatheads, first with their own migration, then with acquisition of horses, and finally at its most rapid pace when they encountered white civilization. Modifications that once took centuries soon occurred in one generation. Aware of the process, and of the peril of extinction if they did not adapt, the Flatheads accommodated or fled each new circumstance thrust on them. When white men asked the Flatheads to tell about old times, however, the Indians could not assess their experience because of the constant process of alteration. They had been buffeted in a manner mysterious and beyond recounting.

By perhaps 1700 A.D. the Flatheads' gateway position between the Plains tribes and those of the plateau enhanced use of Salish as a common tongue. The first literate white men among the Flatheads observed that with Salish alone "one can converse from the United States to the Willamette . . . without the necessity of an interpreter. . . . [Also] he will find many among the Blackfeet, the Crows, and the Crees who speak the Flathead language." About 1823 a Hudson's Bay Company trader said, "Throughout this vast extent of country there is but one language spoken . . . if we except the Kutanee nation who understand the general language . . . although they have a distinct language of their own."[3]

Utilization of the Flathead dialect as a universal tongue indicates widespread trading and also suggests considerable shifting of position among Salish-speaking bands over an area which, from archeological evidence, stretched from Canyon Ferry, twenty-five miles east of modern Helena, westward to the present Grand Coulee Reservoir in north central Washington, and from The Dalles on the south to the Fraser on the north, during the several hundred years immediately before white men reached western Montana. The pattern of Indian settlement in this region lay in river valleys where bands located as string communities along waterways.[4]

The movement of Salish and neighboring peoples reflects not only pressures of migration but their roving searches for food and raw materials. Despite abundant game, there was not enough in one area to feed the Flathead population. They moved to find more. Indians of the intermontane region relied on Mother Earth to replenish roots and berries which they gathered seasonally, but, wherever game existed in small quantities, the Flatheads soon depleted the supply. No faunal balance between supply and demand allowed the Flatheads to remain in one place; they sought meat beyond their immediate residence as long as they depended on wild foods.

For these reasons the Flatheads established an annual cycle of gathering and hunting that followed the seasons. From the time of their arrival in modern western Montana until approximately 1840, the Flatheads hunted buffalo west of the Rocky Mountains. Describing the Flathead country—the Bitterroot Valley—as about two hundred and sixty miles long and fifty miles wide, the Hudson's Bay Company clerk, Alexander Ross, remarked in 1825 that "in the southern parts, beaver are considerable plenty, & but there only. Buffalo are there also in great numbers."[5]

While hunting methods were primitive, the western bison survived, but as the Indians' destructive capability grew with acquisition of horses and guns, buffalo rapidly disappeared. Until these western bison were virtually exterminated, the Flatheads ventured onto the plains to hunt mainly in spring. Within twenty years of Ross's comment, however, the western herds would be so reduced that the Flatheads would depend on hunts on the plains entirely for meat and materials to subsist and trade.

Before they had horses and guns, the Flatheads hunted by surrounding a few buffalo or stampeding animals over cliffs to be dashed to death. A man with powerful spiritual assistance lured buffalo to places where they could be killed. Occasionally in winter a lone buffalo could be driven into a snowdrift and, mired, dispatched with spears and arrows. The Flatheads on occasion used cliffs ("buffalo kills") near Thompson Falls and the present Martinsdale forest ranger station. Near such sites, discarded arrow and lance heads, shards, and other debris indicate considerable economic activity. The time spent to skin and butcher animals and to conduct thanksgiving rites made buffalo kills important locations for intertribal trading.

Despite dwindling herds west of the Rockies, the Flatheads considered the buffalo inexhaustible; when the herds eventually thinned, they regarded the cause as supernatural and complained that "buffalo are not close or plenty as they were before the white man came among us."[6]

With buffalo products among their trade goods, the Flatheads bartered manufactured items and seasonal surpluses. This trading differed from the exchange of reciprocal gifts, which was customarily limited to friends and relatives. The trade covered a broad area. Incised dentalium and abalone earrings from southern Oregon (and perhaps from California, brought north to coastal tribes by Spanish seamen) reached northward to the Fraser and eastward to Plains tribes. Watertight bags and baskets made by the Nez Percés, flat wallets, bows, and similar goods passed through Salish hands to the plains in return for pipestone, manufactured pipes, and molded Blackfoot pottery.

Goods occasionally moved surprising distances. For example, in 1789 a Siouan battle-ax reached Indians of the lower Columbia. Flatheads also traded for obsidian points (arrow heads) with the Shoshonis and Thompsons, who used them in burial ceremonies. From the Thompsons, the Flatheads received dressed moose skins, painted hide bags, and fish products.

By the eighteenth century blue glass beads appeared among the Shoshonis and Klamaths, who passed them to Flatheads. Soon afterward a trickle of iron knives, white trade beads, and assorted European items reached western Montana from the east. (Common butcher knives came without handles because the Indians preferred to fashion their own from bone or wood.) Only horses and guns at first were commodities the Flatheads did not possess in some form. The other goods in trade circulated on the basis of superior quality, representing access to raw materials or better manufacturing techniques. For example, beads, an Indian favorite, were used generally to replace dyed quills to decorate clothing—the beads glittering in sunlight and casting colored beams in shadows. Trading occurred at established meeting places or where Indians gathered to dig, fish, or hunt.[7] Although much of the Flatheads' trading stock came from buffalo, among Spokanes and Coeur d'Alenes whitened deerskin clothing made by Flatheads was popular.

Despite intertribal warfare, periods of peace allowed hunting and trading with enemies. Blackfeet and Flatheads, characterized as unrelenting foes, concluded truces for barter. An old tale says Flatheads defeated Bannocks in a battle to use a mountain pass between the Big Hole Basin and Ross's Hole and thereafter passed uncontested. As the easternmost of the Plateau tribes, the Flatheads bore the first fury of Blackfoot retaliation for offenses during the hunt, while the Flathead land served as the collecting place for western tribes bound for buffalo plains.

Not all Flatheads hunted buffalo. Customarily the youngest children, some women, and the elderly remained in camp in the Bitterroot Valley while the hunters and able members of families went to the buffalo grounds, and certain small bands are said to have eschewed the bison hunt. Hunter or not, the Flathead economy included useful tasks for each person, according to age and sex, from making and repairing equipment to teaching skills and tradition, this last the contribution of the aged. The instruction by the elders in food gathering, weaponry, and ritual was a foundation of Flathead survival in a world where the wisdom of an experienced warrior or fetish of a shaman might prove the tribe's most important resource.

The mode of life that the Flatheads evolved in the Bitterroot Valley was the last phase in their swiftly changing aboriginal culture. Their tribal ceremonies relating to conflict and food were simple, consisting mainly of dances and prayers to sun and earth for success and abundance. Flatheads occasionally offered bits of their flesh to the sun. A culture of longer duration would have developed more complex rites and, perhaps, select orders for its men. But men and women participated together in rites. The word *chines-uénshi* means, "I dance the war dance, where only men should dance, although women are also admitted, and marriages often publicly concocted there." This, from an 1879 dictionary compiled by priests. Patently, what should have been a fierce dance sometimes was a social occasion.

Despite their brief tenure in the Bitterroot Valley, the Flatheads appeared to dominate their intermontane territory when white men arrived. The geographer-explorer David Thompson in 1787 confidently asserted the Salish claim to past dominion over a larger area, reporting that a region east of the Rockies also had been "in full possession" of the Flatheads, Pend Oreilles, Kutenais, and Shoshonis at one time. The Pend Oreille chief, Alexander, would make the same assertion sixty-two years later at a treaty council, and Victor, chief of the Flatheads, would advise his son, Charlot, to retreat toward that eastern ground if he were driven from the Bitterroot Valley.[8]

Flathead community life was mobile due to its seasonal migrations to hunt, gather, dig, and fish. White trappers and traders reported this life as they saw it, but Indian lives through the eyes of an alien culture often seem to lack motivation beyond food or war, and the traits of one or several individuals easily become generalized as those of a band or a nation. We can be sure, however, that the Flatheads were a geographic grouping of highly individualistic persons, many born into other tribes and adopted by the Flatheads, who drew together for security and society.

Except in winter, the Flatheads rarely camped more than ten or fifteen days in one location. The women prepared and preserved foods, made clothing, and maintained the households, which included moving the lodges of poles and skins. The men procured meat and hides, guarded the camp, and made weapons.

In spring the Flatheads hunted buffalo. The hunters returned in time to accompany the camp to camas, bitterroot, and onion fields, judging the season by a "bitterroot moon," where women dug with paddle-shaped sticks or elk-horn diggers while the root was tender before flowering. Bitterroot, which grows abundantly on gravel terraces flooded in spring, pushes shoots above ground under the snow, and in late June blooms with pink petals. It occurred in the Bitterroot Valley, at places along the Clark's Fork, in Grass Valley, in the Big Hole, and near Philipsburg. Dried by baking three days in pits or steamed in skin bags, stored in parfleches (skin bags), and pounded into flour for small cakes or boiled with berries, bitterroot was a Flathead staple.

Camas, also cooked in pits, served as a sweetener prized by many tribes. With light blue flowers so thick that fields of camas sometimes resembled lakes, it grew near Potomac, Darby, Lake Como, and Rock Creek, where Nez Percés and Pend Oreilles joined Flatheads to dig; on occasion, even Plains bands participated under tenuous compacts supposed to guarantee the Flatheads safe passage on the plains. A favorite meeting place to council was a spirit tree twelve miles south of Darby. Visiting tribes scrupulously observed the customs of the host tribe as they dug. In turn the Flatheads respected the practices of a host tribe when some of them fished for salmon with the Nez Percés, Colvilles, or Spokanes. In later times, when Indians owned horses, a short summer hunt was held by agreement among bands that joined for camas digging.

As occasion offered, Flatheads also dug sunflower roots; stripped the bark of pine, larch, and fir for sap and the edible cambium layer; gathered black moss from pine trees to be washed and baked into cakes; pulled wild carrots and parsnips; fished the local streams; and snared or shot fowl and small game. Raw meats and roots usually were boiled in woven or skin bags containing water heated by dropping hot stones into it. Cakes were baked over open fires. In winter, foods were cooked inside the tipis in stone-lined pits or by boiling in bags sunk into the ground. For seasoning and supplemental foods, Flathead women gathered choke, service, and huckleberries in bark baskets.

To be sure they would find enough wild foods, Flatheads observed rituals marking the passage of seasons. Both in tribal and individual prayers, the number of supernatural beings was indefinite. The Flatheads agreed on no hierarchy of spirits, and the male sun approached most nearly their notion of a supreme being. Individual prayers to the sun were occasional; tribal prayers to the sun were seasonal. Long ago in their past, Flatheads had occasionally sacrificed captives to the sun by fastening them cruciform to trees. In a society subject to caprices of nature, prayer offered reassurance that all was being done that could be done, and the supernatural provided a useful social control of individuals.

The Flatheads' individual communication with the supernatural centered on visions and special powers conferred by spirit helpers. For access to spirits, Flatheads relied on practices and charms which the white men called "medicine." Medicine involved the intervention of personal helpers. Charms might be talismans, potions, powders, or private songs used to promote supernatural help in achieving success in warfare, hunting, courting, seduction, or gambling. Charms also offered protection against someone else's power.

Power was demonstrated by luck and wealth. The poor were believed to have ineffectual powers. An individual Flathead carried a small leather pouch, usually hung by a thong around his neck, containing relics of a highly personal nature connected with his *sumesh*, his power. Special songs summoned his spirit ally—songs usually learned in adolescence by a youngster sent alone into the forests or mountains to fast and await a vision of a spirit guardian from whom he obtained influence. Boys nearly always went on such spirit quests; girls often did, but were guarded. Spirit helpers might also come in unsought visions and dreams. Formal quests were preceded by fasting, sweating, and ritual bathing. The pragmatic Flatheads, even if impressed by the questor's report of his spirit vision, waited to see a demonstration of power before believing in it.

Certain men and women who showed unusual powers as seers, prophets, and physicians came to be regarded as shamans. Missionaries would call them "jugglers," signifying the manipulation, sleight-of-hand, and incantations commonly used in shamanistic performances. These special people were respected but did not act as full-time medicine men. Shamans forewarned of raids, located and summoned bison, cured illnesses, and were forever being asked to find lost articles. While Flathead shamans apparently did not engage in public contests of power, feuds between strong ones were not unknown. Ghosts played a minor role in spiritual beliefs; they ordinarily were souls seeking to redress earthly wrongs or warn the living. The dwarves who lived in volcanic craters and showed themselves only to a few Flatheads possessed extremely powerful medicine. Fortunate the Flathead who knew a dwarf as his protector.

Doctoring included natural plant remedies for minor ailments as well as ritual. Shamans and herb doctors borrowed techniques from each other, although most herb doctors were women, some of whom specialized in a single illness. Flatheads learned herb medicine in dreams or exchanged remedies with other tribes. Sweating, the universal tonic and curative, was both therapeutic and ceremonial purifier. Flatheads built hollow mounds of sticks covered with grass mats or turf as sweat lodges, heated by hot rocks dashed with water.

Among common remedies the Flatheads employed carrot roots

to relieve headaches, a yellow-flowered herb (probably agrimony) of the rose family to stop diarrhea or cure a sore throat, and a woodpecker's beak or rattlesnake fang thrust into caries to allay toothache. They made teas of Oregon grape to assist delivery of the placenta, prevent conception, or treat venereal disease; yarrow tea to aid colds; wormwood, applied lukewarm from boiling, to reduce swelling. They used the dried leaves of the common evergreen plant, kinnickinick, to promote rapid healing of burns; inhaled powdered false hellebore roots to induce sneezing or relieve nasal congestion; and covered open sores with herb, dung, mud, or pitch poultices. The doctors also splinted broken arms or legs, and occasionally amputated. They pried out infected teeth.[9] If the patient cried out or moaned, he was jeered.

Ritual physicians blew upon affected parts of the body, uttering incantations, shaking rattles, dancing, and wearing costumes for the purpose because Flatheads realized that major illness or injury resulted from the stronger power of a rival or invasion of the body by an unfriendly spirit which must be driven out. The successful shaman expected payment; one who failed might be killed by survivors of the patient. When dogs barked all night, the Flatheads understood sickness was coming and burned juniper to purify their lodge interiors with smoke.

Flatheads used herbs and plants for purposes other than medicinal. Oregon grape root and pine moss colored quills yellow; berries supplied red dyes; clay, requiring a hard trip east, also was used for red coloring; and black came from beds of natural asphalt. The Flatheads made perfumes and insect repellants from grasses and shrubs, employing yarrow as an aromatic body deodorant and strands of sweetgrass, folded into clothing, as a garment deodorant. Meadow-rue seeds, chewed and rubbed over the body, served as perfume. A shampoo of orange honeysuckle grew longer hair, and the sap of western larch held it in place. Fir needles could be ground for baby powder. Paint was also part of the Indian's toilet. "Paint is like anything else of an Indian's dress or fancy; and feathers likewise. . . . Paint is part of his dress," observed a white who lived among the Flatheads.

Far from libertine, the Flathead lived within bounds imposed

15

by his spiritual world, tangible and unpredictable. Yet no somber mood prevailed. He enjoyed jokes and laughter. Inconsequential activities of each day required no supernatural assistance, but the Flathead prudently summoned his guardian's aid for important ventures, including play.

Favorite games among the Flatheads were common to many tribes. They included the hand game, or stick game, in which opposing teams, facing each other, concealed bones—one decorated —which they passed from one player to another by hand, using feints and distractions, singing lucky songs. Players and bystanders wagered, and colored sticks were used to tally the score when the decorated bone was located by an opponent. Another popular game required contestants to throw arrows or small spears at rolling hoops with colored spokes, attempting to hit a chosen color, and again betting against each other and with spectators. The games not only supplied recreation but functioned as practical exercises in hand and eye skills, although no Flathead thought of them in this way.

Spiritual influences affected a Flathead from birth. In order to protect her child from namelessness, a Flathead mother named him for the first object she saw after his birth. He might be Dry Wood or Old Moccasin until he earned a name by deeds or received one from his father or an uncle. The gift of a name from a relative was not uncommon, and the name often recalled an incident of the hunt or war. To make him placid in later life, a child's mother would rub heart of a fool-hen, mashed with white clay, over his chest. Ants mixed with white clay as a poultice made him energetic, and heart of eagle or hawk conferred courage. The heart of mouse assured him stealth to steal horses.[10]

Many facets of Flathead life changed when the Indians acquired horses. The horse extended the tribe's range and recast its values. Caravans with horses to carry their loads might travel thirty miles in one day; mounted warriors could ride one hundred if necessary. The manner and date of acquiring horses, according to Flathead timekeeping and recollection, was from the Shoshonis by theft about 1600. Probably they actually obtained horses by peaceful exchange with the Shoshonis sometime between 1700 and 1730.

The plausible source lay in the established trade route to the Flatheads' south along which Spanish goods trickled for a century or more. The Spanish forebade selling guns to Indians or allowing them even to ride horses, but stories of both came northward, and by 1659 the Spanish reported Apache raids for horses. About the same time, the Apaches traded slaves for horses from the Pueblos. By 1692 the Utes were mounted, and then the Comanches. When the Utes and Comanches acquired horses, they turned into bison-hunting nomads, foreshadowing the Flatheads' conversion to Plains bison hunters.

The Comanches, Utes, and Kiowas—all of Shoshoni linguistic stock—formed a chain of commerce from New Mexico to Montana by way of the Colorado, Grand, Green, and Snake river courses. Not only had these tribes provided a pathway for native and European bartered wares, but the Salish, when mounted, would consider them allies against the Blackfeet. By 1705 Kiowas appeared in Comanche raiding parties at Spanish ranches near Amarillo, and a few years later occasional Flatheads joined them. The chain thus passed horses northward from one tribe to the next, west of the continental divide, until they reached the Shoshonis, the funnel for horses into the interior Pacific Northwest. The exchange of horses for guns owned by northern tribes doubtless speeded the spread of horse bands.

As a result of this route, the Flatheads adopted the Spanish saddle, bridle, and handling, modified to suit Indian life. As they adapted, the Flatheads fashioned rawhide bridles (the Nez Percés preferred braided hair) and devised a pad saddle, a soft pillow of animal skin stuffed with hair or grass, without stirrups. For a time, Plains and mountain tribes armored their horses in the Spanish manner with several thicknesses of leather. In 1806 Meriwether Lewis would watch Flatheads castrate a stallion with Spanish technique and declare their way better than those of Americans or British.

About 1700 the Flatheads discarded quartzite, basalt, and slate for making weapon points in favor of flint, chalcedony, jasper, and chert—rock materials from central Montana. Possibly this marks the date of widened trade relations introduced by the horse which served both as transportation and unit of barter. Flathead trade goods appear to have changed markedly about the same time; matting, basketry, and pottery were discarded for robes, skin bags, and hide products as more suited to a mounted population.[11] But commerce was only one aspect of the equine revolution. The horse transformed the Flatheads' military and hunting practices so wholly that the Salish expression for going to war came to mean literally "stealing horses." Profound psychological changes involved wealth, ritual, and food gathering—the foundations of Flathead life.

The Flatheads within a decade converted from pedestrians to horsemen. Guarding and caring for horses became the central occupation of males not at hunt or war.

Over their years of observing buffalo, the Indians discovered no pattern to herd movements, but with horses they widened their searches and killed more bison. Running with a moving herd, the mounted hunter aimed his arrows to strike within an area two feet in diameter behind the buffalo's forelegs. Internal bleeding brought the stricken buffalo slowly to a halt, then to his knees, and finally to the earth in death. The successful Flathead hunter who once prized his hard-won robe and his tipi of twelve to twenty-four hides now collected more skins than he could use. He killed wantonly and discarded less desirable buffalo products. In this way, the horse contributed to destruction of the bison. The Flathead man, needing additional women in his lodge to clean and tan a growing accumulation of hides, often took several wives. To please a favored one, a Flathead hunter might trade a horse for sixty or seventy elks' teeth to decorate her dress.

The hunt for bison, and warfare with competing tribes on the plains, molded an increasingly hazardous life for the Indian hunter. But hunting and warfare afforded the man almost his only opportunities to demonstrate prowess, daring, and courage, and thus to advance socially. In time, Flathead hunting produced an elite group among its own men and attracted ambitious men from other tribes. The Flatheads acknowledged leading and wealthy families —wealth measured in horses, which led, in turn, to ample robes, food, and clothing, all considered reasonable rewards for intelligence and hard work. An obligation of the prestigious was generosity; it was reprehensible not to feed, house, and share with worthy visitors and one's family.

Of Plateau tribes the Flatheads and Kutenais alone appear to have ranked war honors: a coup (a blow struck with a special decorated stick) on a living enemy, killing, taking weapons, and stealing enemy horses. Flathead warriors also counted as coup being one of the first four to strike a fallen enemy in battle. To be the first to lay hands on an enemy or to strike him with a weapon was a special feat of bravery.

Knowing a war or hunting party on the plains might be forced to retreat, the Flatheads erected wood or stone fortifications at strong points near the mountains to which they retired when possible. Their favored routes to buffalo took them up the Blackfoot River, over the Lewis and Clark Pass, and down the Sun River, or, if by southern trails, through Gibbons Pass and the Big Hole Country. The membership of the hunting party often dictated the route. If they were traveling with Pend Oreilles, the Flathead hunters would take a central route; if with Nez Percés, a southern. When they could, they camped in coves on streams where fallen timber and the defile afforded natural fortification. When too far from home to run for their barricades, the Flatheads, like Plains tribes, fled under attack into thickets or dug shallow pits for protection, hoping to hold off an assault until dark, when they might escape.

Flathead men at war or hunting wore only breechcloth, charms, and paint, and carried weapons. On the attack each warrior acted individually, dashing toward the enemy, usually leaping from side to side to unsettle defenders' aims or riding partially concealed by his horse.

Although bison were hunted year around, the Flathead ahorse exerted his major economic effort on the winter buffalo hunt, for one buffalo provided as much meat as ten deer, and hides were at their best in winter. An observer of an Indian hunt wrote that, after killing bison and scattering the herd:

> The hunters rode back and fell to work skinning and cutting up the killed. . . . The fat on the back and loins was taken off in great sheets

known as "depuyee" [*depouille*]; then the flesh was cut off in large masses from the rump, haunches, and shoulders, and all the ribs, neck, lower legs, were left to the wolves. The Indians were very fond of certain parts of the entrails and of the liver which they would devour hot and raw.[12]

Estimated meat yields of dressed animal carcasses were: bison, 1,000 pounds; moose, 800; elk, 350, and deer, 100 pounds. Moose provided good meat, but elk hide resisted tanning.[13] The Flatheads' concentration on bison was by preference because hunting for other animals was seasonably good in their montane homeland.

As hunting depended more and more on horses, the Flatheads placed horses high in ceremonies; they decorated their best horses with fringes trailing to the ground, feathers, beaded trappings, and intricate designs painted on the horse; they designated a notable horse, often white, to carry the calumet on the march and an honored woman to lead it. The Flatheads gelded horses in rituals supposed to develop speed, endurance, or sturdiness. Some Flathead men received advice or warnings from favorite dead horses in dreams. Pack animals were separated from hunters, for bad luck in the chase resulted from loading bison meat on a hunting horse. The Indian horse was a type; it averaged a little under fourteen hands high, weighed about seven hundred pounds, possessed a large head, good eyes, and a neck and head joined like parts of a hammer. Indian ponies came in a wide assortment of solid and mixed colors.[14] The Flatheads prized horses with flowing tails.

On the hunt the Flatheads rose before sunrise and usually skipped breakfast as part of the ritual in which shamans sought visions to locate buffalo or assure success. While the women broke camp, the men guarded their grazing horses and rode out in scouting parties, as directed by shamans, to find buffalo. A scout signaled bison by spreading open a blanket or, if no enemy was near, firing his gun into the air. A missionary later mentioned "the ingenious telegraphic signs" used in hunting. If the hunters were successful, the women were summoned with pack horses. They cut the meat into thin strips to be dried in the sun on a framework of boughs over a small fire to drive away flies. To preserve stored meat and keep insects from it, Flathead women put it in hide bags with wild bergamot, peppermint, or pineapple weed. The hides were softened by scraping and rubbing with compounds of brain and sagebrush, but this was a slow process that waited until the return home. On the night of a good hunt, the camp feasted on meat. Otherwise, they nibbled roots and went to sleep.

Predictably, the scope of trade expanded when the Indians secured horses. Nez Percés, Spokanes, and Cayuses—doubtless joined by Flatheads—bartered in California in the early nineteenth century. The Flatheads became considerable merchants of horse-flesh. The Crows, pushing westward across the plains of the Yellowstone River valley, bartered directly with the Flatheads, Shoshonis, and Nez Percés for horses, Spanish riding gear, blankets, and horn bows, for which they exchanged knives, awls, and iron points of European manufacture. For a time the Crow nation convened each summer expressly to trade for Flathead horses.

Tribes going from the plateau to the plains commonly carried commodities to trade: salmon oil and salmon pemmican mixed with oil and put up in fish-skin bags, camas cakes, berries, Indian hemp and twine, woven bags, horn bows, shells, seashell beads, and greenstone pipes. For these, Plains tribes offered bonnets of Sioux style, robes tanned and ornamented, leather shirts, catlinite or catlinite pipes, and similar goods.

The mass hunt and warfare drew Flatheads into bands large enough to defend themselves. To meet the challenge of rivalry on the plains, indeed, the Flatheads copied a tribal political structure common among Plains Indians consisting of a council of headmen to decide questions of general import. From the council, influential leaders emerged to be designated chiefs, usually for specific ventures such as war or a hunt.

Governance remained extremely flexible, nevertheless, and a person, lodge, or band often moved away from the tribe rather than obey a decision of the council. Because Flatheads intermarried much with other tribes, the political system did not stand on kinship. Neither did chiefs exercise authority binding on the individual except during a crisis, in war, or on the march, for, although the Flatheads recognized and ranked their leaders, the chief's function "consisted of marching at the head of the rest when hunting and making inspirational comments each morning and evening," reported a white among them.[15] The chief might chastise a malingerer, or direct others to help a family whose equipment scattered on the march, but this was considered for common good rather than a display of primacy. The chief also acted as group conscience and might scold a malefactor publicly. In the final determination of his affairs, however, each Flathead was master of himself.

The core unit within the tribe was, of course, the family, in which cousins to the fourth degree were addressed as brothers and sisters. Beyond the seventh, cousins might marry. The family constituted an economic as well as a kinship unit. With few barriers to intertribal marriages, a range of variations arose in the behavior, size, and composition of the Flathead family. No distinct pattern appeared other than a patriarchal society exploiting a geographic area. Flatheads married freely among contiguous Pend Oreilles, Nez Percés, and Spokanes; less often among Kutenais, Shoshonis, and others regarded as inferior; and even sometimes a Blackfoot. A Flathead husband married his wife's sisters if he could support them. A Flathead daughter might remain in the family into which she was born and trace her lineage through her mother. A son often married into another band but received his name and his training from his natural father and uncles.

It was said that by 1844 there were no Flatheads of unmixed ancestry, so common were intermarriages. These produced a web of kinship and social intercourse with tribes immediately west of the Flatheads on whose peaceful demeanor the Flatheads relied.

Even more important than family might be friendship. "The Flatheads place so great a store upon friendship . . . that to secure it they often give you the shirts from their backs without being asked," it was said.[16] *Szokoi* denotes a war companion "dearer than a brother." The bond of true friendship held to death and his friend could lead a Flathead to do anything.

Within the family system, the economic role of women expanded after acquisition of the horse. Cowives and other additional women for work grew more important in the bison economy. Women moved with a large hunting camp to take part as closely as possible, and as soon as the man killed a buffalo, the women took part in butchering and skinning. Excepting the horses, weapons, and *sumesh*, the wife owned everything: clothing, food, and even the lodge. Her possessions were hers to dispose. Apparently women did not hunt but sometimes served as auxiliaries in battles, picking up arrows and other weapons for reuse, and occasionally they participated as warriors.

One Kutenai known as "Bundosh" acted as a frequent messenger between the Flatheads, Kutenais, and Blackfeet to arrange trading truces. The Flatheads considered this person a woman with strong medicine.[17]

Despite their importance, women were often treated harshly by Flathead men, and lazy or nagging wives were casually put aside before Catholic missionaries came among them. A Salish term denotes the woman who had a horse placed at her door by a man who abandoned her. A Flathead man, visiting a man at his lodge and finding only women there, remarked, "Your lodge was empty." But the Flathead woman was far from subservient or meek. "The ancient custom of female despotism . . . continues without cease," wrote a missionary. He observed that a wife, displeased by her husband, refused to feed him and denied him admittance to the lodge. Women were known to interrupt councils of the chiefs. An insulted woman thrust her index and middle fingers into a man's face as a gesture of contempt.[18]

Women's attitudes were passed from one generation to the next by assigning girls, at first menstruation, to older, respected women for social instruction. Girls usually looked forward to menstruation as marking the time of their entry into adult tribal life. Girls were marriageable after puberty. Boys married after they established themselves as hunters and warriors.

According to tradition, sometime after they obtained horses the Flatheads were driven from homes on the plains into the Rocky Mountains by Blackfeet, who were more numerous and armed with guns. The Blackfoot onslaught continued past the middle of the nineteenth century. The Blackfeet had lived on the Saskatoon plains near Eagle Hills, four hundred miles east of the Rockies, early in the eighteenth century. That the Salish and Kutenais traded with Blackfeet during this period is evident. The Blackfeet obtained their

23

first horses from the tribes west of them by exchange, and added to their herds by theft. Horses induced the Blackfeet to leave their forest homes and migrate onto the plains. With mounts, the Blackfeet pushed southwestward into the Upper Missouri buffalo preserve, inevitably colliding in their hunts with Flatheads.

The Flatheads said later that the Blackfeet pursued them relentlessly from the buffalo ranges. This is probably only a convenient explanation, for one segment of the Blackfeet, the Little Robes, remained friendly with the Flatheads. The story assumes a central organization of the Blackfeet which did not exist. Even though Blackfoot attackers owned some guns, these muskets were slow to reload and inaccurate beyond fifty yards. A good bowman could launch a dozen arrows while his opponent reloaded such a firing piece and, as a participant in an Indian battle remarked, the Indian bow "is a more terrific weapon of war than a musket."[19] Yet the noise and striking power of the musket afforded a psychological advantage. The Flatheads recognized the potential superiority of guns and resolved to obtain them.

A deadlier enemy—smallpox—decimated the Flatheads, Nez Percés, Blackfeet, and nearly all the tribes mingling in the Montana buffalo lands between 1760 and 1770. One epidemic in that decade, and perhaps another in 1781, swept from the plains into the Rockies and the Columbia Plateau, wiping out small bands and reducing large ones.

The Flatheads had never been numerous. Estimates of their prehistoric population range from a likely four thousand to an unlikely fifteen thousand. Hunting and gathering societies are small. Early white travelers saw that women outnumbered Flathead men and concluded that warfare had reduced the male population. It is likely that more males died as children, that ambitious young men left their home bands, and that extra women were added for economic reasons. Pregnancy in Flathead society was as dangerous as war and, because a pregnant wife might not be able to work hard, her husband took other wives to maintain the level of labor.

The smallpox epidemic struck while Flathead and Nez Percé hunting parties camped together on the plains. When the Nez Percés from Walla Walla took fresh horses to meet their hunters in the spring, they found the lodges standing in order but nearly all the occupants dead. Many bands fled to escape the disease. In 1781, Blackfeet were known to carry the deadly infection, contracted while looting a Shoshoni camp exterminated by smallpox.[20]

Probably the smallpox drove the Flathead remnants into the isolated, sheltered Bitterroot Valley, protected by high, sharp mountains thick with pines, fir, spruce, and cedar, where the Blackfeet followed to raid for horses. The Bitterroot's grassy pastureland was ideal for raising horses, and it is not unlikely that the Flatheads chose it as a refuge for its temperate climate, good forage, and protection for their horses. Once the Flatheads retreated behind the mountains, the Blackfeet with superior numbers and guns remained on the Flathead frontier, a deadly menace to wealth and survival.

No more than a generation later, white men penetrated the Flatheads' country. In the grassy valley of sweet roots and herbs known as Ross's Hole, the Flathead chieftain, Three Eagles, sighted an armed party approaching. Because they were not wearing blankets, he thought them a war party, and alerted his camp. When the visitors came on peaceably, however, the chief went out to meet them, carrying a white buffalo robe to throw over the shoulders of their leader. The date was September 4, 1805, and the travelers were William Clark, Meriwether Lewis, and the men of the Corps of Volunteers for North-Western Discovery, explorers from the United States of America.

These *séme* (a Salish word meaning not human, an old word for bogeymen) from the United States identified the Flatheads in their journals as Ootlashoots, possibly from the Salish word for red willow, the Indians' name for the Bitterroot River. When Lewis recopied his journal at the end of the journey, however, he called these Indians the Flatheads. A renowned painting by Charles M. Russell depicting this meeting hangs behind the speaker's desk in the Montana state capitol at Helena.

Sharing the Flatheads' berries (virtually their only food at this season) the *séme* admired the Indians' horses and traded for nine of them. Communication was awkward, as Clark recorded: "What we said had to pass through several languages before it got to theirs." One member of the American force thought the Flatheads might be long lost Welshmen, and on this possibility Lewis wrote down their names for objects to compare later with Welsh terms. After a brief stay, the explorers moved north to Lolo Creek (Travelers' Rest, of which Clark drew a rough sketch) and then over a mountain trail marked by trees the Indian pack horses had scraped, using a Flathead guide. The Flatheads went on to a rendezvous with Shoshonis at the three forks of the Missouri. Lewis and Clark also returned by way of Travelers' Rest. On their homeward journey, Lewis saw bands of wild horses along the Blackfoot River, where Salish had turned loose their less desirable animals.[21]

Apparently the Flatheads impressed the exploring party as similar to many other Indians they encountered, for Lewis and Clark commented mainly on the Flatheads' language and "very fine horses," estimating that each man owned from twenty to one hundred. For their part, the Flatheads told the explorers about other bands of their nation living on the headwaters of the Missouri and Columbia rivers, thus sustaining their idea of themselves as a far-flung people who traded often among others. The arrival of American explorers set in motion a new series of great and rapid changes for the Flatheads.

CHAPTER 2

▲▲▲▲▲▲▲▲▲▲▲▲▲▲▲▲▲▲▲▲▲▲▲▲▲▲▲▲

THE RISE AND DECLINE OF FUR TRADING

▼▼▼▼▼▼▼▼▼▼▼▼▼▼▼▼▼▼▼▼▼▼▼▼▼▼

THE SIGNIFICANCE OF 1805 for the Flatheads lies in their emergence through the Lewis and Clark reports as a people with a precise character and location in documented history. A number of explorers flattered themselves the first white men the Rocky Mountain Indians saw, but earlier figures move like shadows through Flathead memory. Legends recall Chinese on the Columbia six or seven hundred years before Lewis and Clark, trading wax tablets. Could the seer, Shining Shirt, have been a lost armored Spaniard? Some Salish remember tales of four or five wandering red-haired strangers wearing fur clothing and horned helmets who perished of natural causes near Rock Lake in Spokane country. Coastal Indians could have brought white men inland when they came to trade. In any case, the Flatheads depended on trade routes that connected them, albeit indirectly, with French, British, and Spanish communities before 1805.

If the trader René Jessaume reached the Mandans in 1793, the Flatheads probably met him. Another trader, Pierre-Antoine Tabeau, in 1795 named Flatheads among the tribes that visited the Mandans to barter peltries every year. As the fur trappers moved westward across North America, Peter Fidler of the Hudson's Bay Company traded with Flathead neighbors, the Kutenais, in 1793. In the winter of 1800–01 David Thompson of the North West

Company, a Canadian fur company based in Montreal, sent two men to winter with the Kutenais and report on the tribes associating with them. They discovered that the Kutenais owned some guns. Possibly a North West party under James Hughes who found the Flat Bows also learned of the Flatheads. A trader named Alexander Henry heard that a party from the United States crossed the Rockies and "had a misunderstanding with the Snake Indians, the Flatheads, and the Pierced Noses."[1]

John Colter, a former member of the Lewis and Clark expedition, while trading in the summer of 1808 encountered a band of Flatheads in the Beaverhead region, took part on their side in a skirmish with Blackfeet, and after the fray induced the Flatheads to accompany him to Fort Raymond, operated by the St. Louis fur company headed by Manuel Lisa.

To the north at Kootenay House near Lake Windermere, David Thompson heard that Flatheads and Nez Percés, attempting to reach his camp, were cut off by raiding Blackfeet and went instead to an unidentified American "military post." In the fall of 1807 Thompson dispatched the huge clerk, Finan McDonald, to trade southward along the Kootenai River. McDonald ascended the stream to a place near present Libby, Montana, set up two leather lodges for his party, erected a log shanty warehouse, and with James McMillan, another Nor'wester, wintered there in 1808–09, collecting furs from Flatheads and Pend Oreilles.

Relying on McDonald's information, Thompson himself moved southward in 1809, exploring the Kootenai region, although he had been charged by his company with following the Columbia River straightway to the sea, a task at which he unaccountably dallied. With him Thompson carried Patrick Gass's published journal of the Lewis and Clark enterprise as a guide to the country and the Indians.

The David Thompson advancing to trade with the Flatheads was an obstinate, cantankerous Welshman nearing his fortieth year. He was not wholly unaware of Flatheads, for as a former employee of the Hudson's Bay Company he had seen Blackfeet, Piegans, and Bloods setting out in 1787 to steal horses from the Salish and Kutenais. Thompson was one of the few men of the North West

Company who troubled himself to learn Indian dialects. He got on well with Indians, but his aggressive morality and irresolution diminished his leadership of white men. On occasion the discomfort of a badly set broken leg made him irascible. Trained as a surveyor, Thompson was to be recognized as the outstanding geographer of his time, the mapper of the wilderness.

As he followed an Indian road near the eastern shore of Lake Pend Oreille, Thompson chanced upon fifty-four Flatheads, twenty-three Pend Oreilles, and four Kutenais. "Our arrival rejoiced them very much," Thompson said, "for except the four Kootanaes their only arms were a few rude lances, and flint-headed arrows. Good bowmen as they are, these arrow heads broke against the shield of tough bison hide, or even against thick leather could do no harm."[2] Thompson traded these Flatheads some guns, probably the English trade musket of .59 caliber, a three- to four-foot octagonal barrel, incised with the fox-in-the-circle trademark of the North West Company. He also sold them some iron arrowheads.

Not long after, when Piegans appeared, Thompson noted the eagerness with which the Flatheads rode to attack, "proud of their guns and iron-headed arrows." Other Indians came to barter. "Even the women preferred an awl or needle to blue beads, the favorite of the sex for ornament."[3] Thompson's remark depicts the Flatheads as practical traders.

On a point extending into Lake Pend Oreille, Thompson built Kulyspell House, a post of two log buildings. Then he moved upstream to winter among the Flatheads, on whom he proposed to rely for horses. Thompson traded for horses, berries, and fish with the Indians en route to the site he selected for a second post, Saleesh [Salish] House, erected on the north bank of the Clark Fork during the mild November and December of 1809. Three log structures were built as warehouse, office, and living quarters.

Thompson referred to the Salish here as "an intelligent race of men," hospitable, proud of "their industry and their skill in doing anything, and [who] are as neat in their persons as circumstances will allow." He was perhaps not so favorably impressed with their delicacy when he saw them cook unskinned beaver or eat lice from their clothing.

During the winter, Thompson sold the Flatheads twenty guns and several hundred iron arrowheads, "with which they thought themselves a fair match for the Piegans," and on their summer buffalo hunt, accompanied by McDonald, the Flatheads fought Piegans in a day-long battle. McDonald shot two of the seven Piegans killed, and the Flatheads lost five men, "the first time the Piegans were in a manner defeated," remarked Thompson, "and they determined to wreck their vengeance on the white men who . . . furnished arms and ammunition to their enemies."[4] Thompson thereafter detoured widely to avoid Piegans, as a rule, but in 1811 nonetheless tried to arrange peace between the Piegans and Flatheads. After consulting their Nez Percé and Spokane allies, the Salish declined a truce because the Piegans could not guarantee that other Blackfoot bands would observe it.

Thompson was not the only trader in the unfamiliar Flathead country. Possibly Americans visited the Flatheads in 1807. A party of forty-two, two formerly with Lewis and Clark, were reported in the area under command of Charles Courtin, trading briefly near present Missoula and on the Columbia. Jacques (Jocko) Finlay, a free trapper outfitted by the Hudson's Bay Company, lived among the Indians near Flathead Lake in 1808–10, giving the Jocko River his name, and in 1810 the Bay dispatched John Howse (who gave a mountain pass his name) to trade and explore for one year among the Kutenais and the Flatheads.

The St. Louis entrepreneur, Lisa, placed his man, Andrew Henry, at the three forks of the Missouri, from where Henry moved to the Snake, near present St. Anthony, Idaho, before abandoning the district as barren. Henry proposed rallying northern Shoshonis and Flatheads to war on the Blackfeet to minimize the peril to trappers. Pierre Menard, a prosperous Lisa partner from Kaskaskia, Illinois, also connived to set Flatheads against Blackfeet "so we may take some prisoners, and send one back with propositions of peace. . . . Unless we can have some peace with these [Blackfeet] or unless they can be destroyed, it is idle to think of maintaining an establishment" at Three Forks. Another trapper, Reuben Lewis, brother of Meriwether, suggested working with the Flatheads to diminish the hazards of Rocky Mountain commerce.[5]

The fur patrols of John Jacob Astor appeared in the area, sending men inland from the mouth of the Columbia River. Two young clerks of Astor's Pacific Fur Company, Ross Cox and Russell Farnham, paused at Saleesh House before setting up their own camp at a Flathead village near present Heron, Montana. "On the tenth [of November, 1810] we came to a small village of the Flathead nation, chiefly consisting of old men, women, and children," wrote Cox later. "We were quite charmed with their frank and hospitable reception, and their superiority in cleanliness over any of the tribes we had seen hitherto."[6] His tiny log post, closed in the summer, was reopened by Cox late in 1811, then abandoned with the collapse of Astor's Pacific venture in the War of 1812 and sale of its assets to the North West Company in 1813.

From the surrender of Astor's posts until approximately 1825, the Flatheads' dealings with white men were confined to British traders in fur. The signal achievement of the fur business in this time was mapping the country. So little was known of the region that Thompson's maps of 1813–14 were taken to remote Fort William to deny them to competitors.

In their early relationships the Flatheads regarded white men as courageous, if not otherwise admirable, for "the natives learned to curse in French and English and to cheat in the other [languages]," a missionary soon would remark.[7] Finding the Flatheads friendly, trappers made no overt attempt to change the Indians' style of life other than providing them goods and encouraging the Flatheads to trap beyond their requirements. Even though it had no competition, or perhaps because there was none, the North West Company did not maintain a regular trade but encouraged the Indians to bring furs to its posts; it did not send its own trappers into the field until dependence on Indians failed to sustain a profitable volume of peltries.

For nearly forty years the fur trade in the Flathead country centered at Saleesh House, generally known after 1812 as Flathead Post or occasionally as Fort Flathead. The post was never fortified, rarely manned out of season; its location changed three times and it was secondary to Spokane and Colville in the pattern of fur and trade.

Flatheads seemed unenthusiastic beaver trappers. "Their common safety will not admit of their separating for the purpose of procuring furs, otherwise they would soon become first rate beaver hunters," the trader Alexander Ross observed.[8] He said that only in spring did Blackfoot raids abate so the Flatheads would trap. When the Indians trapped, they were instructed and outfitted by white traders, who employed a five-pound steel trap, chained underwater to a stake and baited with castoreum, ordinarily visited once a day. The Pend Oreilles and Kutenais, regarded as indolent by whites, produced more than half the annual beaver catch for Flathead Post.

To encourage the Indians to trap, Finan McDonald, who succeeded James McMillan in charge at the Flathead, extended them credit in winter to be repaid with pelts in the summer. The trading stock of the post was not limited to necessities. Thompson's inventory included four cotton shirts, two bottles of peppermint, one of lavender, seven gross of hawk bells, eleven hundred plain rings, more than one hundred buttons, and seven and one-half yards of blue calico. The Flatheads were eager for bells and buttons as decorations. Remote, off the main routes of fur trade, Flathead Post nevertheless afforded British merchants a foothold in Flathead country that they would not relinquish until they closed Fort Connah, yet another post among Flatheads and Pend Oreilles, in 1871.

As a result of the American withdrawal in 1812, the written versions of Flathead customs and history consist of correspondence, journals, and the books of British and occasional free trappers. The erstwhile Astor trader, Ross Cox, joined the North West Company, served in the fur commerce until 1818, retired to Ireland, and in 1831 published *Adventures on the Columbia,* intending his descriptions of Indian life to attract the growing middle-class readership for science and exploration. Thompson's *Narrative,* written from the geographer's journals near the end of his life for the purpose of recouping his estate, added to a small collection of literature that mentioned the Flatheads, and the journals of such traders as Alexander Ross and Peter Skene Ogden, published by editors in the twentieth century, as well as references to the Flatheads by other contemporaries, sketch a Flathead culture and history that the Indians recounted as theirs by the middle of the nineteenth century. Typically the story ran, as Cox put it, that the Flatheads, once numerous, had been decimated by wars with the Blackfeet: "The only cause assigned by the natives . . . for their perpetual warfare is their love of buffalo."[9]

Ross, counting 110 warriors among 304 Flathead men and boys, wrote:

> The Flatheads are but few in numbers and their country often subject to invasion.... War is therefore their trade, hunting their pastime only; yet being solely dependent on their trader for the means of defence, they are assiduous to please, peaceable, unassuming, and much attached to the whites.[10]

Ross and Cox both described Flathead deerskin clothing, whitened with clay. The men's dress consisted of long leggings (unlike white men's trousers, Indian pants were not joined at the torso) from waist to ankle and a loose shirt falling to the knees; that of women, a loose robe to the ankles, ornamented with fringes, quills, and feathers. The robes were fastened at the breast with a small stick. The clothing was manufactured by women using dehaired deerskin cut with a stone knife to patterns memorized in childhood and sewn with twisted sinew. Flatheads usually owned more than one change. Almost twenty-five years later, the missionaries would confirm these descriptions of clothing and observe that Flathead men rubbed red grease on their faces to protect against sunburn and flies. Women wore a woven bark hat which served as a bowl at meals.

Despite such descriptions, the journals and letters of fur trappers, unless intended for future publication, often contain little more than notes on the weather, distances, and furs. By contrast to the hostile Blackfeet, the Flatheads were amiable toward trappers, who naturally took the side of the Salish and fought for them. But most tribes, including the Blackfeet, had their white apologists. Few cared for the Kutenais, but of them T. W. Blakiston, a British lieutenant, wrote, "They are honest and do not beg, qualities which I have never met with yet in any Indians."[11] Despite biases in early accounts, the concensus stands that the Flatheads accepted white men hospitably, shared food, lodge, and women with them, and hunted and fought courageously. By standards of white mountain men and fur hunters, the Flatheads were clean, generous, trustworthy, and brave; by those of the genteel East or Europe, the Flatheads would have seemed unwashed, coarse, impulsive, and dreadfully primitive. Unfortunately for an understanding of Indian life, the trappers considered the Flathead religion as superstition; they ignored or treated as merely curious the spiritual designs that directed the material.

In its business, the North West Company proposed to control the Columbia River and its tributaries as a source of furs and a transportation network. The Snake River was important in this scheme. Following a reconnoiter far up the Snake in 1817, North West trapping shifted southward from Flathead into Shoshoni country. The Shoshonis consented to trap, beaver were plentiful, and the company's brigade under Donald McKenzie pushed farther south in 1819–20 and again in 1820–21. The United States had not lost its interest in the area, for the federal government continued to negotiate with the British for possession.

For their part, St. Louis traders poked cautiously up the Missouri after the War of 1812, but a slow recovery of European markets and fractious Indians deterred them. In 1818 the Anglo-American Commission declared Oregon jointly occupied for a ten-year period, and a U.S. military expedition under Major Stephen H. Long rode from St. Louis to the Rockies of Colorado in 1820 as a gesture toward enforcing Congress' ban on foreign traders. In a report that was widely publicized, Long said the Upper Missouri was "almost wholly unfit for cultivation," thus erecting a paper barrier against farm immigration that preserved the country temporarily for trappers and Indians.

Buoyed by an empty promise of military protection, St. Louis companies once more dispatched well-equipped fur squadrons up the Missouri toward the Rocky Mountains, but while the strongest of these, Lisa's former associates under Joshua Pilcher, delayed, the North West and Hudson's Bay Companies merged in 1821, placing Hudson's Bay in the Columbia region where it had not operated previously. Pilcher reached the Yellowstone in 1822, then withdrew below the Mandans' villages in 1823 after Blackfeet slaughtered a trading party of seven.

Two other St. Louis merchants, William H. Ashley and Andrew Henry, continued trading on the Upper Missouri, using white trappers recruited through newspaper advertisements. Never free of danger from the Blackfeet, these Americans accused the British of inciting the Indians against them; their accusations prompted two military flourishes, the visit of Colonel Henry Leavenworth's troop to the Upper Missouri in 1823 and that of General Henry Atkinson two years later.

The continuing threat of Indian attack on the plains and the richness of Oregon fur streams persuaded Ashley and Henry to transfer their operations west of the continental divide, setting down American trappers in the Snake River drainage which the Hudson's Bay Company, using former North West posts and men, considered its chief source of peltries in the Columbia district. The Bay enjoyed good relations with the Indians; company men were comparatively few, many married Indian women, and the company took only the land necessary for posts and small farms. The Bay met the American incursion with competitive prices and heavy trapping in areas open to both British and Americans.

The Bay's woolen goods were among the most popular items in Indian trade, but the company feared that Americans would offset this advantage by generous distribution of whiskey and rum among Indians. "We would wish to avoid a collision with the Americans if possible, and direct that no intrusion be made on their territory," the Bay's governor and committee notified its manager in North America, George Simpson. Simpson felt the continuing negotiations between Great Britain and the United States for partition of the Oregon country threatened the company, mentioning "our present uncertain tenure on the Columbia," but the Bay maintained seven interior stations: the Flathead, Spokane, Okanogan, Nez Percé, Thompson River, Fort George, and Canoe River posts.[12]

The Bay's concentration on competitive trapping in the Snake area restored Flathead Post to prominence for three years as the outfitting station for Snake brigades. "Since the Flatheads have become the general rendezvous for the Snake trappers," commented Alexander Ross, "their land has been greatly ruined."[13] Flathead Post was moved at this time downstream on the Clark Fork to Bad Rock. The 1823 Snake expedition under Finan McDonald set out from Flathead Post, and the 1824 party under Ross also outfitted there, including three Flatheads among its thirty-six Indian men from twelve tribes—accompanied by twenty-five women and sixty-four children. The company equipped each trapper with a gun, ammunition, two to four horses, six to ten steel traps, and clothing. As Ross's party started southward, John Work of the Hudson's Bay Company entered Flathead territory to trade with the Indians. Ross was snowed in in the Bitterroot Valley for nearly one month. When finally he moved again, one of his subparties, robbed of furs and guns by Indians, was rescued by Americans under Jedediah S. Smith, an Ashley-Henry lieutenant, who then traveled with the Bay brigade, to Ross's dismay.

From this time, Americans joined the wintering Bay and free trappers at Flathead Post, precisely the circumstance the Hudson's Bay Company had hoped to avoid, and spied on company routes and Indian trade. The Flatheads themselves also visited Spokane House to trade and race horses on its five-mile course. Spokanes wore leather leggings and buffalo robes purchased from Flatheads, according to the Bay's Spokane House report of 1822–23, which described the Spokanes as lazy by comparison and demanding of the company because of the occupation of their lands.[14]

A change in Hudson's Bay administration, however, soon returned Flathead Post to its familiar subordinate status. With the appointment in 1824 of a former wintering partner of North West, Dr. John McLoughlin, as chief Bay factor in the Columbia district, and a personal inspection of the region by Simpson, Spokane House was closed for a new interior entrepôt, Fort Colville, named for Simpson's mentor, Andrew Colvile. Outfitting the Snake brigade was moved from Flathead to Fort Nez Percés as more economical and efficient, and the trapping seasons were inverted; rather than trap through the summer, company parties now trapped through the winter when beaver were glossiest. These changes ended company wintering among the Flatheads, although there remained those freemen whom Simpson considered "a worthless and motley crew . . . the very scum of the country . . . outcasts."[15]

Alexander Ross, regarded as "empty headed" by Simpson, was relegated with eight men to Flathead Post, and the bold, combative veteran, Peter Skene Ogden, placed in charge of Snake trapping brigades. The brigades included a number of Iroquois who had migrated or been brought into the Oregon country as trappers. On his return to the East from the Pacific, Simpson met headmen of the Flatheads, Nez Percés, Kutenais, and Spokanes at Spokane House, gave each tobacco and ammunition, took sons of two chiefs for schooling at Red River Mission, and acknowledged the requests of all the chieftains for missionaries to teach their tribes.

When his 1825 brigade set out on December 20, Ogden left the Flatheads behind, although William Kittson, the clerk at Kootenay Post, used them as couriers to Ogden. But Ogden could not rid himself of Jedediah Smith's American patrol. After accompanying Ross to Flathead Post in October, Smith traveled with or near the Bay brigade. Neither could Ogden, or any other Bay leader, trust Iroquois trappers, because they had so often defected, and McLoughlin attempted to apportion Iroquois among various brigades. John W. Dease of Hudson's Bay wintered from 1825 to 1829 at Flathead mainly because he exercised some influence over Iroquois.[16]

Shadowed by Smith, Ogden met other American brigades as he moved southward into modern Utah and lost much of his catch when Iroquois joined American groups for higher pay. He notified Simpson of a projected American post on the Marias River: "If [it is] carried into effect we shall soon lose our Flathead and Kutenai trade." With the appearance of more Americans, the Bay embarked on deliberate exhaustion of the Snake, "to hunt as bare as possible all the country south of the Columbia and west of the [Rocky] mountains." By 1831, John Work found the Snake no longer productive enough to support a brigade.

Ogden's 1826–27 brigade again encountered Americans, and Flathead Post was dominated that season by traders from the United States, who used John Gray, an Ogden deserter, as their spokesman among the Indians. Gray, a native of New York who came from the Iroquois known as "praying Indians," reached Flathead country in 1816 with his wife, acquired a fearsome reputation as a knife fighter, and exerted considerable influence among Indians of the Rocky Mountains for twenty years. Piegans who customarily carried their peltries to Edmonton bartered now with Americans, including Robert Campbell and David E. Jackson of the Ashley company, and Ogden himself moved contrary to instructions onto U.S. territory on the Upper Missouri, where he met Bloods and Piegans from Fort des Prairies on the Saskatchewan en route to trade with Americans at Flathead Post. McLoughlin permitted Ogden to adjust prices to meet this competition and sent inland a larger supply of green beads and brass kettles to attract the Indians.

The declining Flathead Post consisted of six huts under a single roof (Ross described them as "deserted booths"), customarily closed during the spring while traders moved among the bands, reopened in the fall for formal trading with Indians, and used to shelter those trappers' families that did not accompany the brigade. During winter months aged and infirm Indians also camped about the post while the able-bodied hunted buffalo. Ross reported in March, 1825:

> The number of whites with their families who have usually wintered at Flathead house are, one gentleman, eight labouring men, five women and ten children. . . . The Kootenay post having been thrown up this winter, the people fell upon this post, which together with the Iroquois outcasts from Snake expedition, augmented the number from seven to fourteen.[17]

The number would grow in succeeding years.

During the Christmas season, Ross had counted one hundred and twenty-eight lodges of Flatheads, Pend Oreilles, Kutenais, and Nez Percés gathered to trade, remarking that the Flatheads and Kutenais now owned more than one gun for each man and boy. For formal commerce, Ross appointed a day for each tribe. On their day, said he, the mounted Flatheads moved toward the post about ten o'clock in the morning, chanting a peace song, halting a short distance off to fire rifle salutes. Ross replied with his cannon. The head chief then advanced, welcomed the white men to Flathead territory, and apologized for the small catch of beaver. When Ross invited the headmen into his hut to smoke, it was the signal for the entire caravan to enter the camp, women leading horses loaded with Indian goods. Brisk bartering occupied the remainder of the day, the Flatheads trading pelts, baled buffalo meat, buffalo tongues, and other native products. The foodstuffs were sent to Colville as post supplies.

Another trader, John Work, identified such native products as dried roots, venison, dressed skins, robes, saddles, rawhide cord, and dogs, which the whites took in exchange for axes, awls, thimbles, files, copper and brass kettles, knives, fishhooks, guns, ammunition, flints, cloth, mirrors, bells, red paint, and tobacco. On the Sabbath, Ross required his men in Bay fashion to dress neatly and rest; on Christmas he smoked with the chiefs and gave each a dram of rum. While the Bay men deserted Flathead Post for the summer, the Indians broke doors and windows, tore up flooring to hunt for small treasures, and burned parts of the huts.

Once re-established west of the Rockies, Americans soon significantly changed the fur system. In the same year (1824) that McLoughlin took command of the Columbia, William Ashley of St. Louis abandoned fixed stations for fur collection and outfitting. Instead, he named a place and time for itinerant trapping brigades to meet his supply caravans and exchange their catches for new outfits. With this arrangement, Ashley sent his trains through the valley of the Platte River and over South Pass rather than shipping by boat on the Missouri. Most St. Louis companies soon joined Ashley in this scheme. Thus began the legendary rendezvous of the fur trade. To the rendezvous flocked Indians, trappers, freemen, and mountain vagrants of every ilk for the next fifteen years. Eventually a few wealthy men, some from Britain and Scotland, visited for adventure.

Rendezvous sites were moved annually within the Green River drainage to afford plentiful pasture for horses and to avoid troublesome tribes. British company trappers rarely participated, but Hudson's Bay inquired assiduously each season (especially among the Nez Percés) about the success of the rendezvous. Although it was an economical system for fur companies, the rendezvous—an occasion for drinking, gambling, whoring with Indian women, and carefree conviviality—often stripped the trapper of his year's wages, returning him to the beaver streams outfitted on credit.

The Flatheads took part in the annual rendezvous from its beginning; they trekked to it in large caravans, and once there delighted in arraying their horses in bright trappings to gallop through the white camps or, as did one chief, drive buffalo through the camp-grounds. White trappers identified approaching Flatheads at a distance by their tribal martial music, chromes chanted to drumbeats.[18] About 1825 a colony of Flatheads, Nez Percés, and others presumably went with a returning St. Louis train to settle near the mouth of the Kaw [Kansas] River at its confluence with the Missouri.[19]

Following the 1827 rendezvous at Bear Lake on the present Idaho-Utah border, Ashley was said to have realized a 70 per cent profit that established his fortune in one year. While the tale kindled wider interest in fur trading, Ashley sold his company to Jedediah Smith, William Sublette, and David E. Jackson, contracting to supply them from St. Louis, and Sublette obtained a federal license specifically to trade with the Flatheads.

From this time, however, a sinister competition hampered American fur companies. Rivals did not pause at murder, subversion, inciting Indians against other traders, or free distribution of whiskey and rum to the natives. New outfits spied on older ones to find the best beaver preserves. Smith, Jackson, and Sublette in 1830 brought wagons into the Wind River country but, in view of the antagonism in the trade, sold their firm to younger men: Milton Sublette, Thomas Fitzpatrick, and James Bridger. Sublette and Bridger pursued an erratic course of four hundred miles simply to elude John J. Astor's revitalized brigades, ending their chase by wintering in 1830–31 among the Flatheads. McLoughlin advised his people there to buy the Americans' furs if they could. Some Flatheads, in the meantime, traveled regularly down the Columbia to buy at Fort Vancouver, occasionally carrying home scalps, women, and horses purloined from tribes along the way.[20]

Two other parties of Americans had wintered at Flathead Post in 1827–28, and Joshua Pilcher himself, caught by snow and commercial disaster, stayed at Flathead Lake in the winter of 1828–29.

Although he described Flathead Post as "a mere wintering establishment," Pilcher wrote a report published by the federal government that contradicted the earlier impression that the West was a great desert. Pilcher said the Flatheads' valley would support a considerable farming population. He was desperate enough that winter to offer to turn against American traders and work for the Hudson's Bay Company, but the company declined his proposal. Echoing Ross's impression that the trade destroyed the Flatheads' country, Pilcher observed, "In the absence of game and fish, they [the Indians] are driven to every extremity to sustain life—devouring every bird, beast, insect and creeping thing they can get hold of, and tearing up ground for roots."[21]

With an increasing number of Americans coming, John Work at Colville remarked, "Indian trade at the Flatheads is declining." To offset the decline, McLoughlin suggested that Flathead Post be "the wintering station of the person in charge of the Spokane or Colville district." In contrast to flagging trade for the Bay, Robert Campbell, directing a brigade for Smith, Jackson, and Sublette, succeeded well enough among the Flatheads that Simpson personally authorized Dease to meet American fur prices and to stock luxuries at Flathead Post to entice Americans to sell the Bay their furs. McLoughlin wrote Work to give Campbell the same bartering terms afforded Pilcher, adding, "It is not our interest to induce fur men to remain about the Flatheads."[22]

To evade Astor's men, Fitzpatrick moved the 1831 and 1832 rendezvous sites to Pierre's Hole. Between these meetings, one large party of Flatheads and Nez Percés wintered with Americans at the junction of the Lemhi and Salmon rivers, gambling and regaling each other with adventure stories. Another band of Flatheads and Nez Percés in Beaverhead country sold their horses to Americans for inflated prices, then walked to the Bitterroot on snowshoes, carrying fine colored blankets. They reported that Americans planned to build a post on Flathead lands in the spring. Work met a Flathead party who told him Americans under Andrew Drips of the American Fur Company were three days behind them and, when Drips came up, recognized in the group an Iroquois who had deserted Ogden several years earlier.

The 1832 rendezvous was remembered as unusually lively: Indian belles wore skins decorated with shells, beads, feathers, and quills; there was plenty to eat and drink; Sublette organized a trappers' parade to amuse the Indians; and a Flathead chief harangued from horseback on morals and honesty. An estimated one hundred and twenty lodges of Nez Percés and eighty of Flatheads attended.

The location proved ill chosen because, as parties under Sublette and Nathaniel J. Wyeth departed on July 18, 1832, they discovered several hundred Blackfeet nearby, apparently trying to pass the rendezvous without being seen. The Blackfeet seem to have entered Pierre's Hole without realizing the rendezvous was in progress. The Flatheads, Nez Percés, and trappers—perhaps euphoric from their romp—saw an opportunity to humble their fiercest enemies, while Sublette declared the whites could not afford to lose face with the Rocky Mountain Indians by avoiding a fight at the start of the season. He called reinforcements from the main rendezvous camp.[23]

When the Blackfeet realized they had been detected, they sent forward a chief bearing a peace pipe. He was met on open ground by a trapper and a Flathead, who murdered him and snatched his crimson blanket. The Blackfeet thereupon retreated to a thicket, threw up breastworks, and defended themselves during an attack directed by Sublette, who doubtless hoped to revenge their murder of his brother four years earlier. Twenty-six Blackfeet were killed before the band slipped away at night. If nothing else, the 1832 rendezvous further provoked the Blackfeet against the Flatheads, their allies, and white friends. The Blackfeet retaliated, running off five hundred Nez Percé horses and wiping out a Flathead and Nez Percé horse-stealing party of fifty men during the next year.

Trapping through the winter of 1832–33, Wyeth eventually reached Flathead Post, then in charge of François Rivet, a former member of Ogden's brigade and Ogden's relative by marriage. The hungry Indian dogs damaged Wyeth's fur packs by eating sinew thongs and flesh left on furs during the night, and the Indians said there were few beaver in the area. Wyeth wrote in his journal:

This valley is the most romantic place imaginable. Above and below the valley the mountains of each range close upon the river so as apparently to afford no outlet either way. About two hundred horses feeding upon the green plain and perhaps fifteen Indian lodges and numerous barking dogs, with now and then a half-breed on horseback galloping gracefully with plenty of jingling bells attached to all parts of himself and horse—it really is a scene for a poet.[24]

The 1833 rendezvous, returned to Green River, attracted Captain Benjamin L. E. Bonneville, on leave from the United States Army, and a group of sportsmen guided by the Scot, Captain William Drummond Stewart, whose party included Dr. Benjamin Harrison, an adventuresome son of William Henry Harrison. Bonneville subsequently spent part of one year among the Nez Percés and Flatheads, writing of the latter that they numbered about one hundred warriors and, an honest and religious people, observed every festival of the Roman Church. He fancied himself peacemaker between Blackfeet and Flatheads but, when he broached peace to the Flatheads, they smoked and talked for two days, then answered that warfare kept their people alert, they would become soft and lazy without it, and they did not trust the Blackfeet. During the same time, Wyeth was writing his associates in the East praising the Snake country. "Into this section I have been, and have myself taken a pack of beavers in less than a month, and the furs of this region are excellent."[25]

Despite pervasive hostility, the Blackfeet now traded with Americans on the Upper Missouri, seeking not only guns, utensils, and whiskey, but also woolens imported from France, Belgium, and England. Woolens were light and warm and dried more rapidly than skin clothing. American commercial strength thus grew among the Indians. (By the 1830's, American mills had entered the international competition among woolens manufacturers.) The Piegans often befriended American merchants and arranged periods of peace with the Flatheads; they were the beaver trappers of the Blackfoot nation, for other Blackfeet stole most of the furs they offered in trade.

The awesome ascent of the side-wheel steamer, the *Yellowstone*, to Fort Union on the Missouri in 1832 opened a new period in Indian commerce, because it offered a water route that could deliver

43

freight in volume to a region that would not be penetrated by suitable roads until after the Civil War. To the Flatheads, the advent of steamers meant an end to the comparatively safe rendezvous; they now met American trade at river ports, passing en route through Blackfoot country.

Moreover, changes in European fashions about 1830 from beaver to silk hats, with the rising popularity of nutria as a decorative fur, greatly diminished the world market for beaver pelts. (The beaver hat was actually made of a felt into which fine inner hairs of beaver fur were pressed, held by their natural barbs, to make a durable, attractive headpiece.) In 1842 the beaver headdress of the British army gave way to a cloth cap, depressing the market further. Within a few years, consequently, beaver trapping declined, and for perhaps four decades buffalo robes and meats dominated the market, shifting the geographic center of Indian commerce from the Columbia and tributaries to the buffalo prairies—Blackfoot country.

Both the Hudson's Bay and St. Louis companies for some years experimented with cloths manufactured from buffalo hair. An American firm had been formed as early as 1821, and the Bay authorized a trial shipment of buffalo wool in 1824, but sufficient raw material could not be obtained.

Except for increased danger from Blackfeet, the change to buffalo pleased the Flatheads. They far preferred chasing buffalo to trapping beaver; their women prepared robes well, and the Missouri River routes lay nearer bison country where they wanted to roam.

The rendezvous did not expire for another decade and beaver trapping never wholly ended, but Hudson's Bay's role slowly shifted from fur trader to that of supplier for Indians, immigrants, and U.S. military expeditions. The changes in trade and the increased number of Americans west of the Rockies persuaded the Bay to further conciliatory measures with competitors; the company bought furs directly from Americans at higher prices than did their own U.S. firms, or outfitted Americans, as it did Warren A. Ferris, a trapper who wintered at Colville in 1833–34. Ferris was supplied at Flathead Post in April, 1834, by the trader there, Francis Ermatinger, and bartered his goods to Flatheads on the Bitterroot

River, enduring their customary ceremony of shaking hands with the entire camp on his departure. Then he set out for Green River, pursued by Ermatinger seeking payment.

While Ferris reported that American interest in the beaver trade was waning perceptibly, Wyeth advised his associates that he had

> sent messengers to the Pawnacks [Bannocks], Shoshones, Snakes, Nez Perces, and Flatheads to make [buffalo] robes and come and trade.... I am under the impression that these Indians will make a good quantity of robes whenever they find that they can sell them.[26]

The buffalo robe constituted a risky item in world commerce for many years, as its popularity fluctuated in European and Oriental markets. But the robe trade brought Flathead Post again into temporary prominence as the Hudson's Bay Company's easternmost site in the Columbia district, a place where bison-hunting Indians congregated seasonally. Ermatinger accompanied Flathead expeditions (apparently at McLoughlin's suggestion) to hunt buffalo in 1833, 1834, 1835, and 1837 to dissuade them from falling in with American traders en route. By going with the Flatheads, he also hoped to do away with the necessity of opening the post in winter. To maintain his friendly relationship, Ermatinger entered into the Flatheads' recreation at home. A level stretch of the Jocko Valley known as the Course des Femmes is supposed to preserve the memory of foot races among Indian women for prizes offered by Ermatinger.

An 1837 visitor to Flathead Post called it "a common log hut, covered with poles and dirt, about 16 by 20 . . . an old Frenchman [Rivet] in charge with a small supply of goods, and about two packs of beaver which he had collected during the winter." The visitor reported that the Flatheads of that time paused on their way to the Missouri to dig bitterroot, met their allies in the Big Hole, and moved at a rate of ten to fifteen miles a day, packing their goods on horses.[27] Encountering Blackfeet, the Flatheads killed five, whose scalps they dangled from ramrods. Because Ermatinger was with them, Blackfeet nevertheless approached Flatheads to trade, flying a red Hudson's Bay flag. As a precaution the Flatheads dug rifle pits before the Blackfeet arrived.

By the middle thirties some river valleys of the Columbia district had been trapped nearly barren of beaver and American trappers extended their routes, making their return for the rendezvous less convenient. Then an economic panic in 1837 seriously depressed the dwindling markets for beaver pelts and buffalo robes. Pratte, Chouteau & Company of St. Louis, a leading American firm, heard that Hudson's Bay attracted no bids for beaver pelts that season and advised its own agents to restrain Indians from hunting, because sales of buffalo robes would be unlikely. The Indians could not comprehend these conditions; they suspected the traders of colluding to lower prices.

In 1838, however, a smallpox epidemic scattered Indian hunters, reduced the number of furs and robes offered, and killed large proportions of several tribes. While Flathead buffalo parties were in the field, smallpox claimed everyone in their Bitterroot camp except fifteen children. Disease and flagging markets reduced attendance at the 1838 rendezvous. But in the following year, Pratte, Chouteau & Company delivered forty-five thousand robes to St. Louis for processing and marketing, and during the next twenty years upward of one hundred thousand robes passed through St. Louis annually. Such sweeping changes in demand and routes brought only a solemn patrol to the rendezvous in 1841. Many familiar faces were missing. Pleased by this turn, Hudson's Bay increased trapping in the Columbia district, while many Americans moved southward to New Mexico. Pratte, Chouteau & Company learned from agents that trappers were fighting for the few peltries in the Rockies.[28]

Each year now the Indians killed thousands of buffalo beyond their needs, offering as much as one-fourth of their total kill for market. Raw green hides stretched over the frames of poles, scraped on the prairie, and then baled until the hunt ended—the product of this industry flowed into St. Louis by tons. Among the Flatheads the robe commerce raised female status because of the need for hide dressers. Deaths of men from smallpox and warfare and the usefulness of women in the burgeoning bison trade rapidly increased the proportion of females among the Flatheads. In 1825 Alexander Ross had counted "304 men and lads, 153 women, 162

Flathead sweatlodge, made of a frame of sticks over which canvas and soil were placed. (Rebecca Lesher collection, Gonzaga University)

Two women on horses, tipi in background. The Flatheads obtained horses in the early eighteenth century. (Montana Historical Society)

Flathead man, wearing a warrior's headdress. (Montana Historical Society)

Flathead man, holding a pipe tomahawk. The white skin clothing, beaded pouch, and hair are typically Flathead. The feathered bonnet is of the Sioux type, acquired by trade with Plains tribes, but common among Flatheads as a result of barter. (Montana Historical Society)

Flathead mother and daughters. The pattern of these dresses is traditional and was memorized in childhood. Skin clothing, and later cloth, was cut to these memorized patterns. The beadwork and braided hair are typical of Flathead women. (Montana Historical Society)

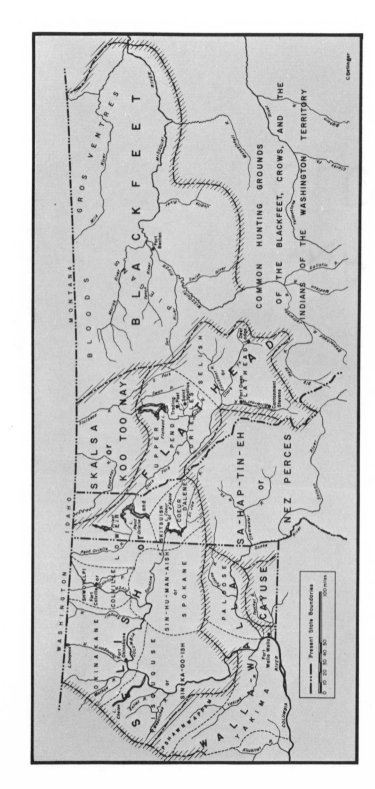

The geographic locations of tribes in eastern Washington Territory, based on a map prepared under the direction of Governor Isaac I. Stevens and transmitted by him September 16, 1854, with his report to the Commissioner of Indian Affairs. Some typographical corrections have been made. (National Archives)

Father Nicholas Point's sketch of John Gray, an Iroquois who migrated to the Flathead country early in the fur trapping period and was a leader among the Indians. The sketch is among DeSmet letter books in the Washington State University Archives.

Trader's store on Flathead Lake, photographed by F. Jay Haynes. The store is typical of cabins dignified with the names of Post or Fort. (Montana Historical Society)

Michel, par son frère François de Gillar

Michel, Red Feather, or Insula, a popular chief of the Flatheads and friend of white trappers. (P. J. DeSmet collection, Washington State University Archives)

A drawing by Gustav Sohon of Flatheads crossing a river by wrapping their possessions in tipi skins which trapped enough air to serve as rafts. From records of the Chief Signal Officer, U.S. Army. (National Archives)

Eneas, chief of the Dayton Creek Kutenais, undated. (Dr. A. A. Sallquist collection, Gonzaga University)

Ste Marie Village des Têtes-Plates.
St Mary's among the Flat Heads

Nº 23

Father Nicholas Point's sketch of the construction of the original St.
Mary's in 1841 in the Bitterroot Valley. A woodcut, somewhat changed,
was made from this sketch to accompany Letter 23 in DeSmet's *Letters
and Sketches.* (P. J. DeSmet collection, Washington State University
Archives)

Father Nicholas Point's sketch of the chief reporting to his council that buffaloes have been sighted. (P. J. DeSmet collection, Washington State University Archives)

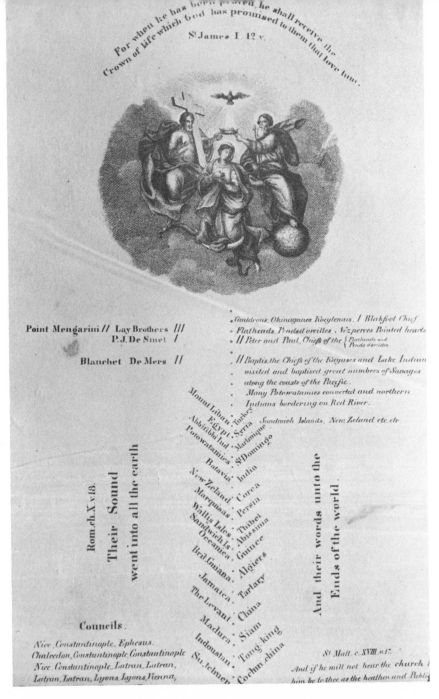

A portion of DeSmet's Catholic ladder, showing the Flatheads, Pend Oreilles, Kutenais, and the Blackfoot chief, Nicolas, in their places in the Christian chronology. Father DeSmet had a number of these printed in Paris as foldouts in religious books. (P. J. DeSmet collection, Washington State University Archives)

Fathers Adrian Hoecken, S.J., and Pierre Jean DeSmet (right), S.J. DeSmet founded the Flathead mission and sent Hoecken to organize St. Ignatius mission among the Pend Oreilles. (Gonzaga University)

VICTOR OU LA PERCHE DE LOGE.
Chef de la Tribu Tête-Plate.
Pages 216 & 235.

An idealized sketch of Victor, chief of the Flathead nation, published in DeSmet's *Oregon Missions*, 1847. (P. J. DeSmet collection, Washington State University Archives)

children. Of said numbers are six chiefs and 100 warriors."[29] In 1840, within fifteen years of Ross's census, Flathead women out-numbered men. The additional females included captives, slaves, and the wives of polygamous marriages.

In conducting the robe trade, the business amenities of the beaver days lingered: white men trading with Flatheads continued to provide feasts and gifts, endure long sessions with the pipe, listen to speeches, and watch horse parades before trading could begin. Robes cost buyers not more than one dollar's worth of trade goods (sugar and coffee were in special demand), but expensive trans-portation required that purchases be culled before the robes were sent down river.

The fur trade, without intending it, largely destroyed the Indian way of life by depleting small game and speeding extermination of the buffalo; it mapped the West and estimated the locations and sizes of native populations; it demonstrated the agricultural promise of large areas previously unknown or discounted as desert. The zenith of the fur trade immediately preceded a period in the United States when white men moved westward in numbers to escape crowding on older frontiers, to evade political or military obliga-tions, to hunt gold, or simply to regain lost confidence in individual worth.

By 1849 immigration to Oregon numbered thousands each year, and Peter Ogden wrote Sir George privately, "The fur trade and civilization can never blend together and experience teaches us that the former invariably gives way to the latter." He gloomily pre-dicted that the Indians and whites would never be one people. Three years after this, the Bay's James Douglas, governor of Van-couver Island, advised an interior trader, "Times are changed, and we have now no other object in the Columbia but to secure our actual property and possessory rights, making money in the mean-time by general trade, if possible."[30]

▲▲▲▲▲▲▲▲▲▲▲▲▲▲▲▲▲▲▲▲▲▲▲▲▲▲▲▲▲▲

CHAPTER 3

THE MEDICINE OF BLACKROBES

▼▼▼▼▼▼▼▼▼▼▼▼▼▼▼▼▼▼▼▼▼▼▼▼▼▼▼▼

JESUIT MISSIONARIES were the first white men who intentionally altered the Flathead way of life, using methods annealed by experience with other tribes of North and South America. The missionaries intended to show the Indians the virtues of piety and toil, to teach them "not to pray only, but also to work, toil being next to godliness, and after piety, the best aid to good living for fallen man."

The Jesuits built a mission among the Flatheads in 1841 as the effect of two causes: appeals for religious teachers by the Indians of the Rocky Mountains, and designation of the Society of Jesus by the Catholic Church as its mission arm to western Indians. The Salish thus realized the prophecies of Shining Shirt, who predicted that men in black robes would come to teach them, change their lives, and help them survive when the game was gone. Shining Shirt, said to have worn a metal cross, warned the Flatheads and Pend Oreilles not to resist the blackrobes.

The impetus for missionary work among the heathen Indians of the plateau came from the appearance in St. Louis in 1831 of four natives "who live across the Rocky Mountains, near the Columbia River," as the Catholic bishop of St. Louis described them. Two of these Indians died and were buried in St. Louis, their names recorded as Paul and Narcisse, and their tribes as Nez Percé and

Flathead, in the cathedral parish *Liber Mortuorum*. A short time later, a Canadian traveler to St. Louis told the bishop that the Flatheads and Blackfeet had "received some notion of the Catholic religion from two Indians who had been to Canada."[1] The identity of the four Indians and fates of the two survivors is uncertain. The painter George Catlin claimed to have met the survivors on a river steamer; he drew them in Sioux dress, identified them as Nez Percés, and apparently inquired later about them from General William Clark, the explorer, now Indian superintendent at St. Louis.

The composition of this 1831 delegation has been warmly debated, but that is not as important as the religious fervor fostered by reports of their appeal for Christian teachers. A Wyandot half-breed interpreter, William Walker, wrote about the Indians to his friend George P. Disoway, who submitted an article including Walker's letter to the *Christian Advocate*, which published the item March 1, 1833. The newspaper commented editorially on March 22, and printed other letters on the subject May 10. That Walker's letter was embroidered hearsay is certain, but its entreaty fell upon Christians in the eastern United States and Canada as a "Macedonian cry," a compelling summons from little known tribes located vaguely in a region beyond the Rocky Mountains.[2]

The bishop, Joseph Rosati, described the Indians' visit in a letter to the *Annals of the Association for the Propagation of the Faith* on December 31, 1831. In its concern for pagan aborigines, the second provincial council of Baltimore on October 27, 1833, petitioned Rome to place the western Indians of the United States in the care of the Society of Jesus, a request approved on July 26, 1834. The Jesuits began recruiting and training young European novices for the Rocky Mountain mission field.

Flatheads probably visited St. Louis in 1831 because they knew the way. As early as 1825, one of the Iroquois among them, Ignace, took his young son, Baptiste, to St. Louis en route to Canada to visit an older son. Entrusted to General Clark, Baptiste was delivered to Father Charles F. Van Quickenborne and enrolled in St. Regis Seminary at Florissant, fifteen miles north of St. Louis, where he remained two years. The spartan discipline there apparently offended the Indian students, for the school, teaching morals, letters, and manual training, closed in 1831.[3]

In that year, 1831, a dozen or more mixed-blood families from the Flatheads, Kutenais, and Iroquois migrated from the Rocky Mountains to the mouth of the Kaw River, settling on the bottoms near the Missouri. Others would follow them; in 1836 twelve families, including the formidable John Gray, would "come down from the Rocky Mountains . . . with the intention of not returning and of looking to the salvation of their souls."[4]

According to tribal memory, four Flatheads and three Nez Percés started for St. Louis in 1831 to seek missionaries, but two Flatheads and two Nez Percés died at Independence, the others turned back, and another died before they reached home.[5]

It is evident that long before 1831 the Flatheads—and all other interior Indians—learned a good deal about the Christian religion. Such men as David Thompson, an adherent of the Church of England, and the Bible-quoting Jedediah Smith, an aggressive Methodist, practiced their convictions openly in camp. Russell Farnham was Catholic and so was François Rivet, the free trapper living among the Flatheads as early as 1809 and assigned by the Hudson's Bay Company to Flathead Post, where he spent most of the years between 1813 and 1839. The majority of trappers were nominally Catholics, but often poor examples, the kind described by Father Gregory Mengarini as "low Canadians . . . equal to, if not more ignorant, superstitious, and stupid than many children of the forest." Yet one of these, Jean Baptiste Gervais, was specifically identified by missionaries as having taught the Flatheads about the Catholic religion. If nothing else brought white men's religion to their attention, the Indians could not have failed to see the Hudson's Bay men observing the Sabbath at the trading posts.

Iroquois Indians, instructed by Jesuits at Caughnawaga Mission near Sault Ste. Louis and employed as fur company trappers, deserted the brigades to live among western tribes. Some of these may have been remnants of an independent hunting party decimated about 1799 by Gros Ventres enraged by their superior airs. These Indians, who came from a large area of upper New York, had seen Dutch settlements at first hand; their knowledge of white men and white medicine made them influential among Plateau tribes—yet the mystery is: why did they not teach the Flatheads more about the skill of warfare? Thompson mentioned six Iroquois he encountered in 1810 in Flathead country "who had come this far to trap beaver." God-fearing these Indians may have been, but Alexander Ross remarked, "The singing of hymns of these hypocritical wretches is a sure sign of disaffection."[6]

Doubtless some Flatheads heard about Christian religion in 1829 from Garry, the Spokane youth educated at the Red River school, who preached Sunday homilies during a visit to his band.

Because they generally regarded white men as brave, and because these men had been places and seen things the Flatheads had not, the Indians felt the trappers were protected by powerful supernatural guardians. The Iroquois probably heightened the sense of mystery by refusing to teach the Flatheads their Christian prayers "for fear they would get them wrong." From the various instructions and examples, the Flatheads concocted a mixture of their own and Christian practices that lingered for a century. Many trappers later admitted their surprise at hearing the savages singing and reciting Christian hymns and prayers. It is difficult to know how much doctrine the Flatheads absorbed, but they gave their concept of Christianity a naturalistic cast—the soul they conceived as a lining of the body. "I have always found it very difficult to learn their real opinion on . . . religious subjects," David Thompson said. "Asking them questions . . . is to no purpose; they will give the answer best suited to avoid other questions, and please the enquirer."[7]

A year or more after the unfortunate attempt by the seven to reach St. Louis, the Flatheads met a white man in the Nez Percés' camp who represented himself as a minister. He gathered the Indians around him in a circle and announced he would serve whichever tribe chose him. Noting the Flatheads' and Catholic Iroquois' hesitation, the Nez Percés accepted him, but this man here drops from view. In the following year, Garry visited the Flatheads to preach. To offset his son's handicap of youth, Garry's father, Illim-Spokanee, delivered the words, among them an assertion that Catholic priests ate the dead.[8] Old Ignace, living for a time among the Snakes, returned to the Bitterroot shortly after this, accompanied by a half-breed, Gabriel Prudhomme; both declared Garry's statement false, but a schism formed, dividing the Flatheads on the subject of Christian practices. Many simply gave up Christianity. There arose among the Flatheads a prophet dance which spread to other tribes—a blend of Christian and aboriginal rites that reflected their confusion.

The first missionaries commissioned to serve the Flatheads were Jason Lee and his nephew, Daniel Lee, sent by the New England Conference of the Wesleyan church. Before setting out for the Rocky Mountains, Jason discussed the western country with the trader Nathaniel Wyeth at Wyeth's home in Cambridge, Massachusetts, and the Lees joined Wyeth's supply train bound for the 1834 rendezvous. To the Lees, as to nearly all Christians of eastern states, the term "Flatheads" referred to the tribes of a large, ill-defined area west of the Rocky Mountains.

As they traveled with the train, however, the Lees discovered that the name signified a specific tribe in the Bitterroot Valley. They also realized that the traders opposed missionary endeavors among the Indians as destructive to the fur trade. The men of the supply train were barely civil to the Lees. (The Hudson's Bay Company believed that "men of desperate character" followed the missions.)

At the Green River rendezvous, someone told the Flatheads and Nez Percés that missionaries had come to them. The Indians called on the Lees to shake hands, and asked to talk to Jason, but—experiencing doubts when he saw these men—Jason told them he was busy. The Indians inquired whether he planned to come home with them and Lee asked, instead, that they meet him at Wyeth's post, Fort Hall. Then Jason Lee prayed, "Lord, direct us in our choice of a location."[9]

Thomas McKay of the Hudson's Bay Company and the Scot adventurer Sir William Drummond Stewart described the Flatheads to the Lees as a small tribe poorly situated for a mission. When the Lees eventually reached Fort Vancouver to meet their supply ship, John McLoughlin "observed to them that it was too dangerous [in Flathead country] to establish a mission; that to do good to the Indians, they must establish themselves where they could collect them around them," and offered the two missioners "the same assistance as settlers."[10] The Lees remained on the Willamette River, although Jason felt that the Flatheads' interest in Christianity was genuine.

At the 1835 rendezvous, the Flatheads met Dr. Marcus Whitman and the Reverend Samuel Parker, a Presbyterian, and impressed both men with their desire for Christian teaching. Parker apparently attracted the Flatheads, for in company with Nez Percés they traveled with him toward Walla Walla until they turned off to hunt buffalo. He saw Flatheads again at a religious meeting in the Nez Percés' camp and reported to his mission board that both of these tribes seemed promising mission fields. According to Flathead timekeeping, sometime in 1835 another unidentified minister called them together in the Bitterroot Valley to talk and sing hymns, but left when he learned that the Catholic Iroquois gainsaid him.[11]

After these meetings with Protestant missionaries, Old Ignace (Ignatius Francis or Ignace La Moose) volunteered to go to St. Louis to ask a Catholic priest to come as a missionary. Taking two sons, Charles and Francis, aged ten and fourteen, whom he intended to have baptized and schooled, Ignace reached St. Louis late in 1835. There, speaking in French, he told Father Helias d'Huggeghem, a Belgian Jesuit, that he had worked for the Jesuits at Caughnawaga before migrating westward between 1812 and 1820, and that he had come to St. Louis representing the Flatheads, Nez Percés, Spokanes, Kutenais, Cayuses, and two tribes the priest could not identify, to seek a Catholic missionary.[12] This conversation is the basis for statements that the Iroquois among the Flatheads came from Caughnawaga Mission; this was the story most likely to ingratiate Ignace to Father Helias. Ignace's story was regarded as confirmation that the 1831 delegation had, indeed, been composed of Flatheads and Nez Percés. Ignace got the idea that priests would come to the Flatheads immediately, and returned to the Bitterroot to announce the blackrobes were on their way. As Samuel Parker remarked, the Indians did not comprehend the difference between a possibility and a promise. The Flatheads watched anxiously for the blackrobe they expected.

When no priest appeared, another delegation of three Flatheads and one Nez Percé set out in 1837 for St. Louis, guided by Old

Ignace, in the company of W. H. Gray, an impetuous Methodist layman returning to the East from his mission service. Ignoring plague among the Plains Indians, and without waiting for the fur caravan, Gray started with a small train from the rendezvous, heedless of warnings that his horses would draw Indian thieves. At Ash Hollow (Nebraska) on the North Platte River, Sioux halted the party, separated the Indians from it, and killed them. Ignace might have been spared because he wore white men's clothing, but he volunteered to die with the Indians. When the story spread, Gray was censured by traders for his rashness; four drunken trappers at the 1838 rendezvous threatened him, but Gray escaped their chastisement by hiding in the Reverend Cushing Eels's tent while Eels calmed the mountain men.

When the Flatheads learned the fate of their delegates, they sent two young French-speaking Iroquois, Pierre Casaveta (or Gauche) and Ignace Chapped Lips (or Young Ignace), by American Fur Company boat in 1839, perhaps expedited by a fearful defeat in 1838 by Blackfeet on the Lavelle Creek trail, where the Flatheads' rock breastworks and the battle-scarred trees could be seen half a century later.

For some reason the Blackfeet withdrew from their accustomed prairie haunts shortly after the affray, allowing the two Iroquois to reach St. Joseph Mission among the Potawatomies at Council Bluffs without incident. There the two met a stocky Jesuit priest, Father Peter John De Smet, who wrote his brother:

> With tears in their eyes, they begged me to return with them. If only my health would permit it, I might have the luck this time to get further up the Missouri, and should God deem me worthy of the honor I would willingly give my life to help these Indians.[13]

As Father De Smet could promise them nothing, the delegates went on to St. Louis. There they appealed to Bishop Rosati, who was so moved by their zeal that he wrote the Jesuit father general in Rome, John Roothaan, describing four Indian delegations dispatched by the Flatheads, his favorable impressions of three that arrived (including the 1831 Indians), and closing with the words, "For the love of God, my Very Reverend Father, do not abandon these souls!" Father Peter J. Verhaegen, the Jesuit superior, also wrote the father general, confessing that he had been so touched by the Flathead delegates that he had rashly promised two priests would visit them the following spring. Thus the commitment was made.

Casaveta returned to the Bitterroot with his happy tidings, and Ignace wintered at Fort Leavenworth to await the missionaries and guide them to the Flatheads. Now Father De Smet advanced his wish to serve the Indians of the Rocky Mountains and was selected. He set out for New Orleans to solicit funds from wealthy patrons to pay for the journey. In the meantime, during 1838, Fathers Francis N. Blanchet and Modeste Demers had reached Fort Vancouver from Montreal, stopping en route to preach and baptize Indians. They did not enter the Bitterroot but spent some time with the Pend Oreilles.

Although he did not raise enough money to take a companion, Father De Smet started for the Rockies on March 27, 1840, carrying letters-patent from Bishop Rosati describing his task as being "to visit and evangelize the various tribes of aborigines living beyond the Rocky Mountains, some of whom, in particular those called the Flatheads, have, through deputies dispatched repeatedly to St. Louis, signified a most ardent desire for the Catholic faith."[14] At Westport, the sturdy missionary joined the annual trading expedition of the American Fur Company commanded by Andrew Drips, and—almost immediately beset by malaria—went with the train to Green River, reaching the rendezvous on June 30. His arrival was timely, for the Flatheads recognized that the trapping trade was closing and their lives were changing again.

The Flatheads and Pend Oreilles, under the medicine man Chalax, met Father De Smet. (Chalax, by prayer, could predict the time and magnitude of Blackfoot attacks.) They remained at the rendezvous less than a week, while Father De Smet celebrated mass daily in the open air, preaching in French and English, and the Indians sang the hymns they knew. Father De Smet encountered an old Flemish soldier turned trapper, Jean Baptiste de Velder, who volunteered to be his companion.

At Pierre's Hole approximately sixteen hundred Indians waited

71

to greet the blackrobe. The Flathead chief, Bear Looking Up, whom De Smet called Big Face, welcomed the priest with the words, "From time to time, good white men have given us advice and we have followed it. . . . Blackrobe, we will follow the words of your mouth." Satisfied that the dispositions of six hundred Indians were sufficient, Father De Smet baptized them, including the aging head chiefs Big Face and Walking Bear. He explained that he had come only to visit, and would return to stay the following spring. Appointing "for their spiritual head a very intelligent Indian, whom I had taken pains to instruct," and requesting the Flatheads to choose a permanent site for a mission in their country, Father De Smet turned back toward St. Louis.[15]

Meanwhile the Jesuit superior at St. Louis had chosen Fathers Nicholas Point and Gregory Mengarini as missionaries to the Rocky Mountain Indians. On his return, Father De Smet again went to New Orleans and addressed letters to clergy in Philadelphia begging money to send missionaries and farm implements to the Flatheads. He raised eleven hundred dollars, of which New Orleans contributed one thousand.

Before the priests' departure for the Rockies, Father Verhaegen appointed De Smet as superior of the mission with authority to establish two locations, although he counseled the group to concentrate in one. He also reminded them that the Missouri Province was already in debt more than five thousand dollars as a result of its expenditures on Indian missions. Three coadjutor brothers, William Claessens, Joseph Specht, and Charles Huet, were sent along as blacksmith, tinner, and carpenter. This party set out for Oregon country with their goods in carts drawn by mules.

Father De Smet, forty years old, was the strong member of this band; Father Mengarini, in Verhaegen's view, at twenty "has but little experience in the ministry and should be applied to the study of the language," in which, with medicine, he was trained; Father Point, forty-two, a native of France and a primitive artist, suffered periods of delusion that made him disagreeable occasionally despite his devotion to the missions.

The missioner band gathered at Westport to join John Bidwell's train, piloted by Thomas Fitzpatrick, a mountain man who, with

Robert Campbell, had been adopted as a blood brother by the Flathead chieftain, Insula. John Gray was with the train as hunter. Another member of the caravan, Joseph Williams, a Methodist missionary bound for Oregon, passed the days on the road discussing philosophy with Father De Smet. Fathers Mengarini and Point (but not De Smet) took their turns as night guards. Bidwell would describe De Smet as saintly, "a man of great kindness and affability," and De Smet would say the missionaries "relieved our traveling companions of a heavy load of prejudice against our holy religion."

Six influential Flathead men intercepted the train near Fort Hall (now owned by Hudson's Bay) to escort it to the adobe fort, where twenty others waited. Some of the tribe, expecting the missionaries at the rendezvous, had stayed there sixteen days before running out of food and had then left, muttering that the double-tongued priests would not come, but older men had silenced their talk.

To feed their Indian escorts at Fort Hall, the missionaries bought two bags of pemmican for one dollar each from Francis Ermatinger, all the fort could spare. This meager supply exhausted, the missionaries and Indians ate fish caught in streams en route to the Bitterroot Valley. The stingy rations foreshadowed the material life that the missioners had entered. For their first years they would, as several remarked, live like Indians. But the harsh surroundings were tempered by the enthusiasm of the Flatheads. "The tribe had the appearance of a flock crowding with eagerness around their shepherd," Father De Smet wrote the provincial at St. Louis. "The mothers offered us their little children, and so moving was the scene that we could hardly refrain from tears." His greeting encouraged De Smet to imagine "that we would soon behold the happy days of the primitive Christians among the Indians."[16]

The Flatheads reported that Christian prayer had already served them. In a five-day battle earlier in the year, seventy Flatheads had killed fifty Blackfeet of a superior force, while only one Flathead, wearing hide armor, was wounded. They believed they had won because the Flatheads knelt to pray, their war chief admonishing, "Let no one arise until he has prayed well." The wounded warrior died four months later, the day after his baptism.

On September 4, 1841, the feast of Our Lady of Mercy, four and one-half months after leaving Westport, the missionaries reached the mission site chosen by the Flatheads, a grassy meadow shaded by cottonwood and pine trees, on the right bank of the Bitterroot River. Around the site were grassy hillocks dotted with bushes and, not far off, sharper hills covered with trees. There the Jesuits planted a wooden cross, naming the spot St. Mary's. Father Point's painting of their arrival shows fifteen undecorated tipis in a semicircle, a two-wheeled mule cart, and, among horses gamboling on the riverbank, the white steed that Big Face, selecting his finest, had given Father De Smet. The missionaries sent Flathead messengers to other Indian camps to report their coming, started to build shelters, and began translating prayers and hymns into Salish with the aid of Prudhomme.

Word of their arrival soon reached the Whitman mission among the Cayuses. Narcissa Whitman complained that the Jesuits had taken "the same language that part of our missionaries are occupying. Now we have Catholics on both sides of us."[17]

The Flatheads proved eager to organize the tribe into a religious hierarchy. Big Face tried to give his place as chief to Father De Smet, who naturally declined. Nevertheless, to administer their work among the Indians, the Jesuits depended on strong chiefs. These they found in Big Face among the Flatheads and Loyola (as they christened him) among the Pend Oreilles. When Big Face, christened Paul, died and was buried in the red drapery that he had hung on his lodge to mark the Sabbath, his son, Victor, as prefect of the Flathead men's congregation called the Society of the Sacred Heart, was elevated to chief. Later the missionaries would rely on Eneas (Ignace), an Iroquois from New York, among the Kutenais.

They found that sometime earlier, under the influence of Christianity, some Flathead headmen had begun to judge their people's actions as good or evil—a relatively new notion among Indians—and exercised social controls on this basis. The main instruments of control were tribal ridicule and ostracism. The missionaries readily turned the Flatheads' dawning recognition of evil deeds to the Catholic concepts of confession and penance.[18]

Father Mengarini's translation of catechism into Salish was not easy:

> The Flathead language is truly very difficult and complicated. Furthermore, it is in no way related to European languages. One might say that brevity of expression is carried to excess. For them, one word is really a complete phrase. Often the Salish closely combine two, three, or four words with the singular result that the word composed is shorter than the ... words which made it. This ... constitutes a richness in vocabulary unequalled by other languages.

With white men, the priest noticed, the Flatheads spoke slowly, but among themselves, laconically, and sometimes with gestures alone.[19]

Shortly after the priests reached St. Mary's, a delegation of Coeur d'Alenes visited to ask for a missionary. Father De Smet, sensible to his letters-patent, determined to visit as many tribes as practical, and consequently was to range far from the Flatheads in the coming years, expecting to convert even the Blackfeet. De Smet went to see the Coeur d'Alenes while the brothers built temporary huts, a chapel, and a stockade. "Our good brothers and Canadians are engaged ... in erecting around our establishment a strong palisade, fortified with bastions, to shelter us from incursions of the Blackfeet," the mission superior wrote of the rude cottonwood shelters, roofed with split shingles, chinked with dirt and grass, and lighted during the day by dim windows of scraped deerskin.[20] In these the missionaries would live for seven years.

The Jesuits, whose ministries among the Potawatomies and Osages had not been entirely happy, were pleased with the Flatheads. Father De Smet called them "a chosen people; ... it would be easy to make this tribe a model for other tribes." Point, writing later to Jesuit countrymen, compared the Flatheads to ingenuous low Britons, and the Indians of the plains to Parisians, cunning and deceitful. "They are characterized by the greatest simplicity, docility, and uprightness," De Smet declared of the Flatheads on one occasion. "Yet, to the simplicity of children is joined the courage of heroes." Throughout his mission service, Father De Smet would not substantially alter this view of the Flatheads.[21] The Flatheads apparently were equally delighted with the missionaries, for they delayed their departure on the winter hunt of 1841–42 to linger near the mission so long that they nearly starved.

Because the Flatheads, in company with the Pend Oreilles and Nez Percés, would be gone to hunt buffalo for approximately six months, Father Point went with them to continue their religious instruction. But the teaching could not be done on the plains. The hunt alone, declared Father Mengarini, after going on one, "is enough to negate all the efforts of a missionary." The Flathead men were too busy guarding horses and hunting to pay attention to priests. Some were killed or injured; others stole women from passing bands; and warfare "keeps them barbarous and takes their attention from their faith."[22]

During the 1841–42 hunt, the Nez Percés of the combined party killed a dozen Blackfeet. The Pend Oreilles, surprised and facing annihilation, rallied behind a woman, Kuilix (or Red for the color of her robe), and killed twenty-eight enemies. The Blackfeet fought no more that winter, believing the Flatheads, Pend Oreilles, and Nez Percés divinely protected by the medicine of the blackrobes.

For the Flatheads, the "finger of God" moved helpfully in hunting as in war. It was a good hunt and, on a single day when one hundred and fifty-three buffalo fell to the Flatheads, Father Point considered the kill miraculous. In momentary enthusiasm for the hunt, the priest attempted to pursue buffalo:

> I urged my horse to a herd of fugitives, and . . . had no difficulty in getting up to them. I even succeeded in getting the foremost to abandon his position but, enraged, he stopped short, and presented such a terrible aspect that I thought it more prudent to open a passage and let him escape.[23]

Father Point nevertheless thought the Blackfeet the greatest danger of the hunt. During the 1841–42 winter, the aging Nicolas, a Blackfoot chief supposedly baptized by Father De Smet, came to the Flathead camp, giving Father Point hope that Nicolas would become the Christian apostle of his people. Nicolas' son had lived among the Flatheads for some years. But the priests' concern for Blackfoot souls angered the Flatheads. On one occasion when Flatheads had surrounded Blackfeet, Father Point insisted that the enemy be spared. The Flatheads obeyed "most reluctantly, and became highly incensed against the priest for meddling."[24]

Clearly the winter buffalo hunt reduced the missionaries' effect on the Flatheads. The Indians regarded the fathers as bearers of strong medicine; they opposed extending this power to unfriendly tribes. Father Point accompanied the Flatheads once more on a winter hunt and Father Mengarini went once, also incurring the Flatheads' disapproval by rescuing Blackfeet from them. The Flatheads threatened to abandon Mengarini on the plains.

Meanwhile, Father Blanchet, vicar general in Oregon of the archbishop of Quebec, had written Father De Smet a letter of welcome in which he described the prospects for rewarding missionary work on the lower Columbia. "We are really overwhelmed with business," he said. "The savages apply to us from all sides." In April, 1842, De Smet visited Fort Vancouver to buy clothes and agricultural implements for the Flathead mission from the Hudson's Bay Company. He and Father Blanchet met and between them laid plans for a broader cooperative Catholic effort, including a college in the Willamette Valley.[25]

Here Father De Smet saw Blanchet's "Catholic ladder," a large colored drawing depicting the major events of Catholic doctrine from the creation to the present day. Aware of Point's success in instructing Indians by sketching and encouraged by Blanchet's work among the Indians, Father De Smet carried the ladder back to the Bitterroot. Later he commissioned a Paris publisher to print quantities of ladders for Indian missions, and the Flatheads learned to whittle their own: a long stick on which forty short parallel lines marked forty centuries of world history, thirty-three notches for the years of Christ's life, three crosses to show the manner of His death, carved churches, twelve notches for apostles, and eighteen more marks for the centuries since Christ's crucifixion.

The mission field envisioned by Fathers Blanchet and De Smet stretched from the mouth of the Columbia eastward to include the Blackfeet, and the two men agreed that De Smet should canvas Europe to recruit additional priests. The Jesuit father general, hearing of this plan, observed that "the domesticated Indians, the Flatheads, and the surrounding tribes are quite enough . . . and may

God grant that we find it possible to keep up what has been started without taking on new and far-reaching engagements." He added that the missions were always in debt and that extending the work to the Blackfeet would accentuate fiscal problems. Nevertheless, Father De Smet went to Europe. When he left them, the Flatheads lost their beloved priest forever.[26] In October he sent directions for Father Point and a brother to open a mission among the Coeur d'Alenes.

In their first years among the Flatheads, the missionaries challenged the spiritual core of Indian life, preaching an eternity ruled by one all-powerful God in contrast to the native concept of a present influenced by erratic supernaturals. Many Flatheads embraced the Catholic religion fully. There remained a number of skeptics who feared abandoning the old beliefs, or thought that they might offend their spirit guardians. Others had been confused by conflicting claims of Protestant and Catholic missioners, some disillusioned by trappers' disdain for affairs of the soul, and some were hot-blooded, ambitious young men interested mainly in war and hunting. Shamans continued to be important, among them Bear Track (baptized Alexander), who possessed power from a white buffalo calf and who declined to humble himself by living near the mission. The Flatheads heard all kinds of opinions, because their country was crossed constantly by white men and other Indian tribes and they themselves ranged far. It was common, for example, to go to the Great Salt Lake for salt.

Their conduct shows, however, that many accepted and held the Catholic faith. On one occasion, hearing Father De Smet recite persecutions of the church in Europe, Victor asked the priest to invite Pope Gregory XVI to live in safety among the Flatheads. (A similar invitation would be sent to Pius IX in 1875.) Father Mengarini optimistically reported that shamanism was declining and the hand game losing favor; he said that some Indian men were becoming skilled workmen, and even children did chores, such as gathering firewood.

The Flatheads had no choice but to continue their annual cycle to procure food: the winter buffalo hunt, the spring dig for camas and bitterroot, summer hunting and fishing, and fall gathering of berries and roots. On the other hand, their daily routine settled into a religious schedule: Rise for prayers at daybreak, instructions in the faith during the morning, camp chores until noon, catechism in the early afternoon, and then labor in the fields until sundown. For children, Father De Smet "adopted the system of instruction and bestowing rewards in usage in the schools of the brothers," giving tickets of approbation for good recitations. Some of the tickets found currency as charms of blackrobe medicine.

The Flatheads carefully and fervently used the external signs of the Catholic faith, such as the rosary, prayers, and hymns, but Father Mengarini declared them impatient for immediate answers to prayers; he had to rotate the order for confessions or all the Flatheads would confess every day. On Sunday a first mass was celebrated for the general community and a second for those who had been on guard. The Sabbath afternoon passed in children's games before and after the benediction. A musician as well as linguist and physician, Mengarini taught the Flatheads traditional church hymns in Latin and adapted tribal chants to religious themes.

The Flatheads understood that warfare, hunting, and constant guarding deterred their full religious life. Certain old practices gave ground. When a man died, for example, the Flatheads continued their customary all-night vigil in his lodge, and his widow often dressed in old, dirty clothes as a sign of mourning, but the practices of surrounding his grave with his goods, slaughtering horses at graveside, and an occasional wifely suicide were given up.

A number of Flatheads wished to live quietly, and a few sold their horses and peltries to buy a cow or two for farming, but often could not support a family from the land. Wrote Father Mengarini:

The soil [of the Bitterroot Valley] is naturally dry and filled with large rocks . . . and we cannot find arable spots except along the creeks which are often located at great distances from each other. To cultivate one hundred acres of land the Flatheads are forced to make five different camps within a sixteen-mile area. In addition the large rocks hidden beneath the surface of the ground frequently break the plows.[27]

Frosts limited crops to wheat, barley, oats, potatoes, and peas. In the name of religion, Victor tried without success to establish lasting peace with the Blackfeet, Bannocks, Crows, and Sioux.

In addition to farming, which was alien to them, the Flatheads adopted incongruous symbols of white civilization. By 1843 Father Mengarini had formed a military band among Indian children, consisting of two clarinets, two accordians, three ottoviani, and three flutes. "It would be appreciated if he [the father general] would send some military instruments, some trombones, some tympanies, etc., etc., with the orchestration for each instrument, and several pieces of music composed for this type of group," he advised the father general. "It is incredible how the natives like music."[28] In the mission chapel, an organ hauled by pack horses from St. Louis played Gregorian accompaniment to services until visiting Nez Percés accidentally crushed the pipes by leaning on them. American flags flew on holidays, and Indian patrols, no matter what their purposes, flew the Stars and Stripes.

Despite these trappings of civilization, the mission life at St. Mary's "was nearly as the Indian life, and our ordinary fare was buffalo meat and tallow, and roots and berries," Father Anthony Ravalli recalled some years later.

A thing which marred our tranquility was the continual infestation of Blackfeet, and of Bannock Indians, who rendered dangerous our going out a short distance from our palisade, named with the pompous title of fort. . . . Nearly every other day there was stealing of horses from our camp, and murdering of our people. The valley was then interspersed with many bushes, giving a ready cover to the hostiles.[29]

Among Jesuits the Rocky Mountain missions were regarded as "loca vastissima, aspera, pleraque" (a most desolate, rugged, and harsh place). The missions were also noted for an abundance of mosquitoes. Indeed, after the curious habits of the natives, visitors nearly always wrote home about mosquitoes. They could not be overlooked.

Recruiting in the Jesuit houses of Europe provided additional missioners for the field. For its first two years, St. Mary's Mission served as destination for all Jesuits assigned to the Rocky Mountain Indians. In 1842 Fathers Peter De Vos and Adrian Hoecken reached it; in the next year, Joseph Joset and Peter Zerbinatti arrived. In 1844, however, the Society of Jesus adopted the Columbia River route, disembarking its people and supplies from ocean vessels at Fort Vancouver and sending those destined for the interior by canoe or horseback along the Hudson's Bay paths. By this way Fathers Ravalli, John Nobili, and Louis Vercruysse reached the Flatheads, leaving Michael Accolti on the Willamette. Three years later Father Gregory Gazzoli, Anton Goetz, and Joseph Menetrey took the Columbia route to mission stations. Their arrivals demonstrated Father De Smet's success in recruiting in Italy, Germany, and the Low Countries, where he often addressed a religious community during the mandatory silence of its meal.

As the corps of Jesuit missionaries grew, so did the number of missions. Father Point established Sacred Heart among the Coeur d'Alenes in 1842. In 1844 Father Hoecken, with Brother John McGean, opened a mission among the Upper Pend Oreilles. Some of this tribe had been baptized in 1841 by Father Demers. Others of the Pend Oreilles were baptized by De Smet and, during the winter buffalo hunt of 1841–42, by Point.

With the opening of St. Ignatius Mission among the Pend Oreilles in November, 1844, this band's chieftain, Loyola, forswore buffalo hunting, thus "reducing himself to poverty," and each evening gathered his headmen to teach them the lessons Father Hoecken taught him during the day. Loyola knew that many of his people derided his conversion, but declared, "The rascals may kill me, but as long as I am breathing they must go straight." The chief held his band accountable for their behavior and, until his death in 1846, the Pend Oreilles followed his example, like it or not. He urged the band to hold onto its land, telling them, "God gave us this land. We must keep it."[30]

In 1845 Father Nobili was sent to the Okanogans, and Father Ravalli

received orders from Father De Smet to go near Fort Colville and there construct a small log chapel in order to prevent two [Protestant] ministers residing not far from the place from taking possession of the intended Colville mission. Such was the beginning of that mission which was really opened several years after.[31]

Later in the same year, Ravalli came to St. Mary's among the Flat-heads to succeed Zerbinatti, who drowned while bathing.

Of the missions, St. Mary's was most comfortable. In 1846 Father Mengarini, returning from Fort Vancouver, brought with him a Canadian, Peter Biledot, an artisan who built a small grist- and sawmill for the mission, using buhrstones imported from Belgium by Father Ravalli. The saw was fashioned by filing notches in iron wagon tires. The mission farm was planted to wheat, oats, and barley from seeds Father De Smet had brought from Colville four years earlier, and its livestock numbered forty head of cattle, hogs, and many fowls. De Smet thought that with little effort two rivulets could be diverted from the river to irrigate the priests' garden. Around the chapel stood twelve frame houses for Indians and mission employees.

Many tribes visited St. Mary's, including Blackfeet, who approached flying the flag of the United States to indicate peaceful intentions. Father De Smet wrote the provincial in St. Louis, naming as visitors also the Shoshonis, Bannocks, Nez Percés, and Pend Oreilles, "who are as fervent in their Christianity as the Flatheads." He recorded that Flathead men no longer capriciously abandoned wives, fathers no longer sold their daughters for horses, and the Flatheads had begun to treat enemies with mercy.[32]

During 1845 the Blackfeet suffered a series of battle disasters. Flatheads and Pend Oreilles killed twenty-one in two encounters; Crees took twenty-seven Blackfoot scalps; and Crow raiders virtually wiped out the Little Robes, driving one hundred and sixty women into captivity and slaughtering the men and children. With these defeats, and the victory of the Flatheads over a Bannock force that outnumbered them three to one, Father De Smet observed that the Indians had reason "to fear the medicine of the blackrobes." The Blackfeet told the missionary they knew the Flatheads possessed powerful protection, because "we saw their old men, their women and children, on their knees, imploring the aid of heaven." The Blackfeet begged the priest to take pity on them with his terrible power.

Another opportune time seemed to have come to attempt a permanent peace between the Flatheads and the Blackfeet. This would be done by extending the Catholic faith to the Blackfeet. Fathers De Smet and Point visited the Blackfeet in their hunting camp in the Judith Basin, using Hugh Monroe, a white trader adopted by Piegans, as interpreter, and the council was so satisfactory that in the fall of 1846 Point went to Fort Lewis (Benton) to open the Blackfoot mission. His Gros Ventre interpreter spoke the dialect imperfectly, but the priest captivated the Indians with his sketches. Some Blackfeet soon claimed the crucifix's power saved them from annihilation by Crows who surrounded their camp in the night.

Establishing a mission among the Blackfeet was one of Father De Smet's last works in the Rocky Mountain missions. He was reassigned to St. Louis as treasurer of the Missouri Province of the society, and, although he continued his intense concern for the Indian missions, he did not serve in them again. Father Joset succeeded him as superior in the Rocky Mountains.[33]

When he left the Flatheads, Father De Smet promised to send them ammunition, knives, and other things they asked for. Before these arrived in the Bitterroot, however, he wrote them a letter vigorously scolding the chiefs for whipping, a punishment they favored. The letter was "a great disappointment to the Indians," remarked Father Mengarini, but the chiefs stopped whipping and thereby lost some of their control.[34]

The year 1846 marked the high point of St. Mary's influence among the Flatheads. The mission remained in peril from Blackfoot attacks, although the Jesuits hoped conversion of the Indians would reduce warfare. Some even imagined that the Flatheads might be the agents of Christianizing the Blackfeet, the "saviors rather than the conquerors," as Father Point expressed it. Instead, the Flatheads resisted sharing Christian power with the Blackfeet, and a series of misfortunes showed that their own Christian power was waning. A number of Flatheads reverted to shamanism.

As buffalo herds receded under Indian killings with guns and horses, the Flatheads were absent from the mission for longer periods. On their return from the 1846–47 winter hunt, half-breeds reintroduced the hand game openly among them, luring young men across the river from the mission to play. One told Father Mengarini, "They behaved even worse than they did before you

83

came." White transients, including a trader, Angus McDonald, and the Nez Percés, who brought their shamans, disparaged the priests to the Flatheads and, at last, one Indian interrupted holy services to condemn the missionaries and the chiefs publicly. A number of Flatheads withdrew from the services without protesting. For days the chiefs took no action, despite an outbreak of smallpox that claimed eighty-six lives and which the priests regarded as a sign of God's displeasure with the Flatheads. Only under interdict and the cancellation of religious services did the older men agree to intervene on behalf of the missionaries, and the division of the Flatheads subsided. The Flatheads heard about the murder of Whitman. They knew no avenging bolt from heaven had struck down his killers. During the 1847–48 winter hunt, many Flatheads sickened and some died from drinking polluted water. Father Mengarini purged those who returned.[35]

St. Mary's now faced two stern threats—money and apostasy. Father Mengarini predicted the mission could not last two more years. Consultation with the superior and fellow missionaries was difficult. Father Joset heard from St. Mary's by Flathead couriers only three or four times a year. Father Roothaan wrote mission patrons, "Our allocations have been less and less, although our needs are greater and greater." All the missions were understaffed, and financial support dwindled. Appealing for more brothers, Father Joset reported, "Our men are discouraged and the evil is becoming contagious. They think themselves abandoned." Without more men, "nothing remains but to close all the [Rocky Mountain] missions, one after the other."[36] The political turbulence in France and depression in Europe reduced funds for the missions.

The Society for the Propagation of the Faith, which in 1844–45 allocated the Rocky Mountain missions 41,120 francs, did not actually raise that much money for them. "These missions have not previously received a portion more or less approaching that amount," a church official remonstrated, "and how will the remainder be paid them?" Father Roothaan inquired, "Our allocations have been less and less. . . . Why is this?"[37] But the Society supplied only 32,549 francs in 1848, and no more than 20,000 the following year, despite Roothaan's appeal to its president in Paris on behalf of twelve priests and thirteen coadjutor brothers in the Rocky Mountains. Roothaan gloomily forecast collapse of the missions unless 100,000 francs could be advanced in 1848 and 1849.

While support decreased, gold discoveries in California drove prices higher in 1848–49, and Father Accolti, the new superior for the Rockies, advanced a plan that was seriously considered to assign priests and brothers to prospect for gold to finance the missions. The missionaries were denied discounts on their purchases from the Hudson's Bay Company, which, dealing with a bursar in London, considered the Jesuits wealthy. Nevertheless, by 1848 company correspondence described the resources of the Jesuit missions in Oregon as "very precarious" and in 1849 the company temporarily cut off credit to Accolti to avoid possible losses.

The discomforts of mission life were debilitating. The winters of 1846–47 and 1848–49 were extremely cold. Father Joset said the thermometer indoors registered 14 degrees below zero. The missionaries at St. Mary's remained in temporary dwellings and chapel, now held from falling down by twenty-two supporting beams. "We have been at various times forced to escape quickly to avoid the rats," Mengarini advised the father general. "When it rains, if the snow deepens, we cannot say mass."[38] Delivery of supplies often took two years. The priests, wearing threadbare black, improvised garb from blue cloth sold to the Indians for leggings by the Hudson's Bay Company.

Within the Society of Jesus, disagreements surfaced on conduct of the missions. Some criticized Father De Smet's popular books about Indian life as fanciful, and claimed that they caused "bitter disappointment to missionaries" entering the field. One superior remarked that De Smet "compromised the future of the missions by giving too generously to the Indians, and in making them promises he was unable to keep."[39] Other men thought that, by contrast to De Smet, Fathers Mengarini and Ravalli impressed the Flatheads as niggardly. A few declared that, as superior, Joset displeased the Flatheads by failing to understand their temperament, and Ravalli concluded that Joset thought St. Mary's troubles were imaginary. In the new superior, Accolti, the missionaries at St. Ignatius, St. Mary's, and the other isolated stations recognized a greater concern for the burgeoning California field than for the Rocky Mountain Indians.

Finally the church and dwellings at St. Mary's were moved from the riverside to flat land and there constructed as a quadrangle with walls of adobe, a fortress to offer better protection from Blackfeet and Bannocks, but the underbrush afforded a prowler cover where he might lie concealed for several days waiting his opportunity to steal horses. The Jesuits fired a few shots at random each night to maintain the illusion of watchfulness.

Meanwhile, the overland trail to the south of the Flathead country carried more traffic as immigrant trains en route to Oregon and California passed the important supply station of Fort Hall. New visitors reached the Bitterroot, among them Carl A. Geyer, the German botanist who accompanied some Jesuits to St. Mary's and spent the summer there gathering specimens. The population of Oregon was estimated to have doubled with the migration of 1845 alone, and when in 1846 Mormon trains appeared on the trail, traffic increased. In 1847 a few Mormons quit Salt Lake, dissatisfied, moving north to Fort Hall, from which they went on to California or into western Montana to range cattle herds. Hudson's Bay experienced a rising number of desertions of men who chose to live among the Indians.

Flatheads began, by the early forties, to accompany white trappers to Fort Hall to barter with immigrants. (The smallpox of 1848 apparently was contracted from a wagon train.) Inevitably the Indians brought back white men with them, who usually took Flathead women and often encouraged the Indians to ignore their priests. The missionaries could "see the influence of such malcontents . . . in the behavior of our Indians, growing less affectionate and [more] indifferent, and showing pretensions before unknown to them."[40]

As the mission alone raised farm produce, eight or ten men from immigrant trains came in 1847 with cattle, intending to winter at St. Mary's, but were turned away because there was not enough food for them. They protested that they were Catholics. "Alas! What is their religion?" Mengarini asked, calling them "Canadians of low extraction, who had for many years neglected . . .

religion."[41] But these newcomers spoke Salish and talked against the missionaries.

The Flatheads, who once had stayed near the mission, now absented themselves for long periods and pitched their tipis farther from the adobe compound. "The majority gave up private prayer and vented insult and injury every day upon the missionary," Ravalli told Roothaan. A critical incident occurred when a Blackfoot horse thief, caught near the Flathead village, was executed on the spot, and another Blackfoot who had been living among the Flatheads ran away in fright. He was also shot and died three days later, after Father Ravalli instructed and baptized him. Word of these killings reached the Blackfeet, who resolved to avenge them by murdering the missionaries. Although the Flatheads knew of this resolve, they went on their winter buffalo hunt in 1849–50 without warning the priests, leaving only an indigent old chief and some women and children in their village. Father Mengarini had gone to confer with Father Joset at the Coeur d'Alene mission when, on September 12, 1849, a war party of fifty Blackfeet approached St. Mary's. Father Ravalli was the only missionary there; he was concerned about running out of food to feed the Indians in his care. The Blackfeet did not attack the adobe mission because they did not know the strength of its occupants, but when the mission horses were released from the compound to graze, the Blackfeet showed themselves. They ran off the horses and killed the Indian boy with the herd.[42]

When the news reached him, Father Mengarini went on to the Willamette to appeal to the superior, Accolti. The following spring the superior visited Sacred Heart among the Coeur d'Alenes, where he listened to more reports of attacks and Flathead apostasy. On one occasion, he was told, Indians of neighboring tribes had threatened missionaries with pistols. Father Accolti ordered St. Mary's closed, and sent Joset to help in removing its religious articles and records. He sadly concluded that among the Flatheads, "The old generation of that once-brave nation is passed away. . . . What now remains is nothing but a handful of undisciplined and corrupted youth which cares nothing about priests and religion, and who have no respect at all, even for their chieftains."[43]

Father Joset found a trader, John Owen, camped near the mission with goods and cattle, on his second visit and now intending to settle in the Bitterroot Valley. To Owen he sold the mission's buildings and fences for two hundred and fifty dollars with the understanding that, if the mission were reestablished before the beginning of 1852, the Society of Jesus could buy them back. Then in November, 1850, the missionaries departed from this first mission among the Rocky Mountain Indians. Joset and Brother Claessens wintered on Horse Plains and in the spring went to the Lower Pend Oreilles; Ravalli moved to St. Ignatius, where the Flathead headman, Victor, and many of his band joined him, helping Ravalli prepare for another move in the spring. Father Mengarini was transferred to the Willamette, and then to California, for which he had embarked before Victor came down to Portland to beseech him to return to the Bitterroot.

Where the mission had been, John Owen opened business in competition with the Hudson's Bay Company. Taking notice, Richard Grant at Fort Hall wrote Sir George Simpson, "Mr. McDonald, in charge of the Flathead company post, will be required to be better supplied than the Snake country has been for years past; otherwise he will not be able to cope with opposition, which I fear will be a drawback on his returns." Grant heard that Owen prospered. At his adobe post, "The whiskey keg stands just where the Rev'd Father did when saying mass, and the measures on the altar. If this is the case, I am inclined to the opinion that religion and the fur trade in these parts are hand in hand declining as civilization is increasing."[44]

▲▲▲▲▲▲▲▲▲▲▲▲▲▲▲▲▲▲▲▲▲▲▲▲▲▲▲▲

CHAPTER 4

STEVENS: "Un homme a doubles bouches"

▼▼▼▼▼▼▼▼▼▼▼▼▼▼▼▼▼▼▼▼▼▼▼▼▼▼▼▼

IN THE YEARS immediately following the Jesuits' withdrawal from the Bitterroot Valley, the United States negotiated a formal treaty with the Flatheads and sent them its agents. The Flatheads adapted only slightly to white civilization, but an onrush of white settlers, displaying their superior airs of permanence and proprietorship, disrupted the accustomed pursuits of the Indians, usurped their lands, and turned their soil to farming. Harbingers of these changes had been visible for a decade. "Since wild life becomes more scarce each year, the Flatheads are forced to break into bands to search it out," Father Mengarini noted in 1848. "Often these bands are joined by natives of other tribes for mutual protection."[1] Thus the Flatheads, whose bands had joined together for protection, now broke apart again to survive.

During 1853 Major Isaac I. Stevens, thirty-five, the newly appointed governor of Washington Territory, passed through Flathead country en route to the Pacific Coast. He was met at St. Mary's —now Fort Owen—by a supply train of eighteen men under Lieutenant Rufus Saxton, Jr., which carried provisions for Stevens' troop eastward from the Columbia. As Saxton's party approached St. Mary's, they met John Owen and his brother Francis, who had abandoned their adobe fort to escape the Blackfeet. Bolstered by the presence of soldiers, the Owens turned back to the Bitterroot.

The majority of the Flatheads were absent hunting buffalo, while older Iroquois tended fields near a village of log cabins around the old mission site.

Stevens' purpose on his westward journey was threefold: to map a northern route for a transcontinental railroad, to explore, and to learn the disposition of the natives. On his way, he sounded out influential chiefs on sharing their land peaceably with white men. The Indians seemed willing. When he reached Fort Owen, Stevens issued a proclamation dated September 29, 1853, declaring himself governor and territorial superintendent of Indian affairs. (He published a similar proclamation November 28 at Olympia, the territorial capital.) Near the old mission the governor found Victor with nine lodges, preparing to join the Flathead camp on the plains.

Stevens wrote James Doty, his secretary, several letters from Fort Owen, commending one of his two Piegan guides to Doty at Fort Benton, inquiring about the attitude of the Blackfeet toward farming (noting that the commissioner of Indian affairs instructed him especially to list agricultural implements needed and to name prospective interpreters), stating his intent to establish a bimonthly express from Fort Owen to Puget Sound, and directing that his Piegan guides each be paid one blanket, leggings, shirt, knife, mirror, some paint, powder, and balls—nothing more. The governor intended to change affairs in the Pacific Northwest; he was, wrote Stevens, "determined to be independent of the fur companies."[2]

Before leaving, Stevens formed a party of fifteen men commanded by Lieutenant John Mullan to survey the region, find mountain passes, and record meteorological observations. The squadron built Cantonment Stevens, a cluster of huts on the Bitterroot River fourteen miles from Fort Owen, where it wintered 1853–54. Flathead headmen came to ask Mullan to intercede for return of the missionaries. The barometric observer, Private Gustav Sohon, drew portraits of Indians, learned Salish well enough to interpret, and passed some of his time compiling a Salish-English dictionary.

From Olympia, Stevens addressed the commissioner of Indian affairs recommending that Indian titles be extinguished to the land in Washington Territory east of the Cascade Mountains to the

Missouri River. Stevens reported some "retired servants" of the Hudson's Bay Company and John Owen well settled among the Flathead Indians. The tribes he met along his way impressed the governor as amenable to negotiations; he therefore recommended councils east and west of the Cascades during the summer of 1854. He wrote:

> There is much valuable land and an inexhaustible supply of timber east of the Cascades. I consider its speedy settlement so desirable that all impediments should be removed.... There is a population of about 6,000 Indians in about twelve different tribes east of the Cascades.... The amount that will be required to negotiate treaties with these Indians will be not less than $13,000.[3]

In his message to the territorial legislature, Stevens reiterated these concerns:

> The Indian title has not been extinguished, nor even a law passed to provide for its extinguishment east of the Cascade Mountains. Under the land law of Congress it is impossible [for settlers] to secure titles to land, and thus the growth of towns and villages is obstructed.

Stevens also notified the legislature that he had directed the Hudson's Bay Company to halt its trading with Indians on United States soil by the middle of 1854, a stricture the company politely ignored while its management corresponded with the governor about his interpretation of the 1846 treaty setting a border between United States and British possessions.[4]

Soon Stevens advised the commissioner of Indian affairs that Mullan at Fort Owen had written him

> a report of outrages committed by the Blackfeet Indians since the period of my passing through their country. . . . I consider that the convening of the council [with the Indians] at Fort Benton during next summer, which I recommended . . . is become a matter of necessity.[5]

For administration, Stevens divided the territory into Indian districts, naming the one occupied by the Flatheads the "eastern district," although it continued to be known as the Flathead Agency, and he assigned agents and public employees to the tribes.

The half-breed free trapper living among the Flatheads, Gabriel Prudhomme, was appointed tribal interpreter on November 10, 1853. The following January, Stevens named the assistant artist of his expedition, Thomas Adams, as agent to the Flatheads, Kutenais, and Pend Oreilles.

Stevens sent James Doty, accompanied by Dr. Richard H. Lansdale, a pioneer physician of the Puget Sound country, to schedule a series of treaty councils with the Indians. Mullan broached the plan for a council to the Flatheads and Pend Oreilles, probably relaying to them Stevens' assurance that "the Great Father appreciates their services and understands their merits; that he will hereafter protect them from incursions of the Blackfeet," and emphasizing, as Stevens ordered, the hope for "lasting peace."

The governor's policy called for cession of aboriginal lands, placing the Indians on reservations, and paying them by annual shipments of goods, the mode of removal practiced by the United States since the early years of the nineteenth century. Doty and Lansdale found the Indians eager for the council. Based on their reports, Stevens scheduled major treaty councils at Walla Walla, Hellgate (near Missoula), and Fort Benton, proposing to assemble all the tribes under his jurisdiction east of the Cascades at one or another of these sites.

Between the Doty-Lansdale visits and the time for councils, the Jesuit missionaries moved St. Ignatius Mission eastward to a place south of Flathead Lake and about ten miles from the Course des Femmes, where the Flatheads, Pend Oreilles, and other tribes frequently passed. Father Joset, the superior, agreed to the relocation only after Father Menetrey's repeated entreaties and several appeals from Hoecken; the superior then provided two thousand dollars to assist in re-establishing St. Ignatius. The Upper Pend Oreilles moved en masse with the missionaries, and, while the Flatheads did not patronize the new mission in numbers, its placement afforded the territorial governor a tangible clustering of the Indians of the Bitterroot Valley and Flathead Lake, and its location was to be a factor in selecting their reservation.[6] The mission lay on the gravelly floor of one of several valleys separated by bread-loaf hills covered with grasses and shrubs, cut by thin streams marked by growths of cottonwood and birch trees along their banks.

The blackrobes' influence with the Indians prompted Stevens to request their assistance: Father Hoecken would attend the council scheduled for Hellgate in Flathead country; Father Ravalli was to suggest to the Coeur d'Alenes that they accept a reservation jointly with the Flatheads, Kutenais, and Pend Oreilles; and Father Menetrey would arrange to have the Flatheads meet Stevens at St. Ignatius for the Hellgate negotiations.

In the meantime, the governor concluded treaties with tribes west of the Cascades during 1854. His conduct at these councils did not reassure the Indians, for Stevens relied on promises, threats, and humiliation of strong chiefs to obtain the land cessions he had written into draft treaty documents before leaving Olympia. His first council east of the Cascades convened on May 29, 1855, at Walla Walla with the Nez Percés, Umatillas, Cayuses, Walla Wallas, and Yakimas. Although the bargaining was difficult, Stevens obtained his concessions in a paper signed June 11, and set out for the Flatheads' country. En route the governor stopped at the Coeur d'Alene mission, but did not attempt a negotiation. As chief territorial officer, he naturalized the Jesuit priests there as American citizens.

After a difficult crossing of the high, swift Bitterroot River on July 4, the Stevens caravan on July 7 met a welcoming troop of three hundred men and chiefs of the Flatheads, Kutenais, and Pend Oreilles. Among the leaders was Victor, possessor of vaunted rabbit power, whose skill as a negotiator remained to be tested; he recently had lost standing among the Flatheads by the Christian act of allowing a rival to strike him without reprisal. A subchief, Moses, asked if Victor were his chief, replied, "Yes, but I never listen to him." On the basis of their earlier talks with Mullan, Victor and the other headmen believed that Stevens' central purpose in the approaching council was to assist the Flatheads in their strife with the Blackfeet.

The Indians escorted the Stevens party to their village on the Hellgate River, and the whites pitched their own camp about one mile away, while Stevens, himself, chatted with the chiefs. A little later, the head chiefs Victor, Alexander, and Michel returned the visit in Stevens' tent, where they smoked and talked while Stevens sized up the Indian leaders. He intended to impose not only a treaty but a political regimen in which one leader would speak for all the assembled tribes, and for this head chief Stevens settled on Victor, although privately he regarded the Flathead as simple-minded and lethargic. The governor's choice could not have been based on numerical superiority of the Flatheads, because he esti-mated the populations of the tribes as 450 Flatheads, 350 Kutenais, and 600 Pend Oreilles—figures he regarded as possibly low, because several hundred Indians were absent hunting buffalo.[7]

The selection of a supreme chief to represent a nation of tribes in the manner of a European head of state differed fundamentally from the Indian conception of a chief's office. Generally the Indians chose a chief for his prowess in war or hunting or because he was a powerful shaman. Moreover, combining the Kutenais with the Flatheads and Pend Oreilles stands as geographic accident, based on the residence of one band of Kutenais at Dayton Creek on the west shore of Flathead Lake. The Kutenais' historic territory had been Tobacco Plains to the west; they did not claim Salish links; their relatives lived in villages scattered in Idaho and Canada; and in the past, Kutenais and Flatheads had often fought. Stevens in-cluded the Kutenais, however, much to the disgust of the Flatheads and Pend Oreilles.

The Hellgate treaty council met in July heat in a grove of tall (lodgepole) pines without lower limbs, where approximately twelve hundred Indians gathered with the unkempt ubiquitous covey of white traders and trappers circulating among them. Sohon sketched the scene: a council table shaded by a bower of interlaced branches supported by poles, Indians sitting on the ground, many naked with their blankets thrown aside, and several wearing jaunty visored trade caps. In a portrait about this time, he depicted Victor wearing the high European beaver hat that the chief treasured. Stevens' party of twenty-two included Doty, Lansdale, and the governor's thirteen-year-old son, Hazard; it was not a military force. Victor, Alexander, and Michel, openly jealous of one another, advanced to places of distinction at the table.

As Stevens opened the council with a speech (translated at inter-vals) arguing the advantages of a reservation, Victor doubtless showed surprise, for he had not believed that the governor would ask for his land. "The governor desired to place all three tribes, as they were really one people... on one reservation," Hazard Stevens recalled. Very likely neither the white nor the Indian negotiators understood one another well. Father Hoecken, who kept a diary of the conference, observed that Stevens' official interpreter, Ben Kiser, translated badly: *"Ben Kyser parle la langue tete platte très mal, et rend les choses en Anglais aussi très mal."* Nonetheless, the proceedings according to Kiser and transcribed by Doty stood as the official record of the council.[8]

When their turns came to speak, the Indian chiefs explained that each tribe expected to keep its own lands. Victor was interpreted as saying, "I have two places," as he pointed first toward the Bitterroot Valley to the south and then toward the Jocko Valley to the north. "I will think of it, and tell you which is better. I believe you wish to assist me to help my children here so that they may have plenty to eat, and so that they may save their souls."[9]

The Indian concensus opposed a single reservation, but the chiefs agreed to deliberate this possibility with their headmen and to meet the governor on the next day. Hazard Stevens, in his account drawn forty-six years later from public documents and his father's papers, implies that former Hudson's Bay Company traders counseled the Indians to make unreasonable demands. Quite possibly the Flatheads came to Hellgate disposed to resist the governor, because tidings of his peremptory behavior at Walla Walla had preceded him to the council. If no one else had told the Flatheads that the Yakimas disliked the Walla Walla treaty, they would have learned it from the two Nez Percé observers who accompanied Stevens to Hellgate.

On the second day, when Stevens urged the Indian headmen to speak freely, a noted Pend Oreille, Big Canoe, said he believed Indians and whites could live amicably without a written treaty, voicing the Indian concept of hospitality in their territory. Stevens waited him out but ignored his inference and, turning to the head chiefs, inquired whether they had agreed on one reservation. The chiefs answered that they had, but not on its location. Victor did not want to live on Pend Oreille land; Alexander and Michel wished to stay near St. Ignatius Mission. Hazard Stevens concluded that the Flatheads' dislike of the mission "was one cause of their unwillingness to move" from the Bitterroot Valley.[10]

Stevens designated Victor as the one representative of all the tribes at this meeting when he rejected Alexander's claim to chieftainship of Upper and Lower Pend Oreilles. The third day, however, found Victor adamant on removal. Stevens, suspecting the priests at St. Ignatius of advising the Indians against his proposal, accused Father Hoecken, but the missionary denied influencing the Indians. Stevens then tried a show of affability; he ordered the next day (Thursday, July 12) set aside for feasting, and provided the Indians with two beeves, coffee, sugar, flour, and other stores. After eating, the Indians fell to discussing a reservation. Alexander allegedly agreed to move the Pend Oreilles to the Bitterroot, but when Victor paid him no heed petulantly resolved to remain near the mission. One of his headmen, Red Wolf, laughed that if Alexander moved, his people would not go with him.

The council reconvened on Friday with Stevens eager to conclude its business. When Victor continued to resist moving from the Bitterroot, Stevens attempted to humiliate him. "*Un jour une tragedie dans la comedie,*" Father Hoecken wrote in his diary. "*Victor etant appelle une vielle femme une chien par le Governor. Du moins parler interprete, laisee la place et retourne dans la loge.*" As soon as the governor called him an old bitch, Victor left the conference, while Alexander retorted that the governor was "*un homme a doubles bouches.*" On Saturday Victor sent word that he had reached no decision. On Sunday no meetings were scheduled.

The Flathead chief returned to the conference table on Monday, which was to be the last day of the Hellgate council. Victor proposed that the president of the United States inspect the two areas and select the better as a reservation. Alexander, smarting from Victor's slight, would not agree, and neither would Michel. Stevens saw that he could achieve nothing more. He assigned the Pend Oreilles and Kutenais to lands near St. Ignatius Mission and agreed that the Flatheads should not be obliged to move until the federal government surveyed the two proposed reservations.

Thus, after eight days, a formal treaty of eleven articles was signed, virtually intact as Stevens brought it in draft to Hellgate, save article 2 describing reservation boundaries. The combined tribes ceded twenty-five thousand acres, and Victor was formally recognized as chief of a confederated nation of Flatheads, Pend Oreilles, and Kutenais. The treaty provided that other tribes might also be placed on their reservation with the Indian nation's consent, that whites might settle on lands not occupied by Indians, and that the United States would pay the confederation one hundred and twenty thousand dollars over twenty years.[11] Moses, the Flathead second chief, alone refused to make his mark on the document where Doty had written his name, saying, "My brother is buried here. I did not think you would take the only piece of ground I had." White witnesses included Lansdale, W. H. Tappan, R. H. Crosby, William Craig, and Sohon.

To the Indian commissioner, Stevens reported:

These tribes are, by the treaty, consolidated into one nation called the Flathead nation, with Victor, the chief of the Flatheads, as head chief of the nation. . . . In consequence of the refusal of the Kootenay and upper Pend d'Oreille chiefs to agree to the selection of the reservation by the President . . . I carefully explained the whole matter to Father Hocken, Jesuit missionary whose presence I had required at the treaty ground, and whose influence with these Indians is almost unbounded.[12]

Stevens appeared satisfied with the compromise at the time. He wrote the special Indian agent at Olympia, Colonel M. T. Simmons, "We are proceeding grandly. . . . Made a treaty yesterday with the Flatheads, Kootenays, and upper Pend d'Oreilles numbering some 1,400 souls." After the signing, Stevens distributed presents to the chiefs. He gave Victor a blue military coat with yellow sash which became the chief's most formal attire.

On the next day, Stevens called the chiefs together again to ask them to go with him to a council with the Blackfeet. "The Flatheads were sorry I did not bring soldiers to the Blackfoot council," Stevens recalled several months later. "I told the Flatheads we wanted no soldiers . . . [that] we had no soldiers, yet we did all our business." Despite their fears of Blackfoot treachery, fifteen chiefs of the Flathead nation consented to go with Stevens and the repre-

97

sentatives of other tribes, including the Nez Percés, Coeur d'Alenes, and Walla Wallas.

It was agreed that the Flatheads should hunt buffalo south of the Missouri River until the Blackfoot council convened at Fort Benton, and accordingly sixty-eight lodges of Flatheads, led by Victor, with a number of Pend Oreilles under Alexander, set off accompanied by Thomas Adams and Ben Kiser. The two white men were directed by Stevens to keep him posted on the tribes' location and to prevent any conflict with Blackfeet. If possible, Adams and Kiser were also to find the Crows and invite them to attend.

As the governor moved toward Fort Benton, he learned that his treaty goods had been delayed in consignment upriver from St. Louis and could not reach Fort Benton on the tentative council date. Stevens had tried to avoid a delay of this kind; visiting the national capital during the summer of 1854, he had begged the Department of the Interior to make certain of a timely shipment, and had written President Pierce directly to urge that the government charter a steamer rather than send the goods on a fur company vessel. The responsibility for delivery was delegated, however, to fat Albert Cumming, superintendent of Indian affairs at St. Louis, who opposed the council, tried to defer it for one year, and, failing this, belatedly contracted to send Stevens' goods on an American Fur Company boat.

Shortly after the Hellgate council had adjourned, Stevens directed Lansdale to inspect the two proposed Flathead reservations and to encourage the Coeur d'Alenes and Lower Pend Oreilles to move onto a preserve with the confederated nation. Father Ravalli reported the Coeur d'Alenes would cede land but would not move. Father Menetrey invited the Lower Pend Oreilles, strung in bands along the Pend Oreille River near modern Bonners Ferry, Idaho, to come to St. Ignatius to discuss relocation, and these destitute families, hampered by a lack of horses, started for the mission late in the season, encountering snow and enduring near starvation.

To comply with Stevens' order to him of September 7, 1855, Lansdale inspected the Bitterroot and Jocko valleys. Considering that the Indians were to be made farmers, he inspected only arable land, finding that of the Bitterroot poor in quality and intersected by moraines. On the west side of the valley, he reported, the

fertile spots are numerous but of small extent. . . . The amount of fertile, arable lands on the east side of the river [I estimate] at twenty-five sections or square miles. . . . The whole of the open lands in the valley, both wet and dry, afford good grazing and may be estimated at three hundred square miles.[13]

Regarding the Jocko lands of the Pend Oreilles, Lansdale declared the Jocko *ronde*

affords the best pasturage in the valley and upon the encircling hills is twenty square miles of arable land of good quality and thirty square miles of grazing lands. . . . This ronde has the reputation of being the warmest valley in all of the higher ranges of the Rocky Mountains, and is a good locality for agency buildings and desirable for pasturage, tillage, and beauty of landscape.

His report continued:

As, in your instruction, you state that it is contemplated to consolidate the Lower Pend d'Oreille and the Coeur d'Alene tribes . . . with those tribes embraced in the Bitter Root treaty . . . I would declare it as my conviction that the northern district is preferable. . . .

Besides the above considerations, upon the northern tract are located the only operations that have for their object the instruction of the ignorant but honest natives in the rudiments of the Christian religion and morals, and in some of the ruder arts; and however much a protestant people and government might desire another system of religious training—yet it is the choice of these most immediate concerned, and they should not be arbitrarily deprived of its blessings.

Although Victor and the Flatheads, hunting buffalo on the Musselshell River while they waited for the Blackfoot council, did not know of Lansdale's recommendation, their future reservation had been decided. The doctor's estimate of this land, three and one-half years before the Senate would ratify the Hellgate treaty, was not the government survey specified in the treaty, but in Stevens' opinion the Flatheads' location had been decided. By stubborn refusal to move, however, some Flatheads prolonged their tenure in the Bitterroot Valley thirty-six years.

Lansdale calculated that removing the Flatheads would cost only a small part of the thirty-six thousand dollars stipulated as first-year payment in article 4 of the treaty, because "all the federated tribes are locomotive; they have ready and sufficient means in their numerous horses for transportation of all persons, and all the lodges, provisions, and goods belonging to each family." Consequently, he suggested that three-fourths of the money be spent for farm equipment and seeds, cloth for women to sew, payment of laborers on a communal farm, and prizes to the best farmers and homemakers as the Indians settled into agrarian life. Neither would the Flatheads immediately need houses, "until the Indians are so far advanced as to feel the need of permanent abodes and to be both disposed and willing to keep such homes in some good degree of neatness and repair." Lansdale completed his inspection in time to attend the Blackfoot council.

Stevens' treaty caravan reached Fort Benton with provinder low, to find the fort on short rations until river boats arrived, and, as he sent hunting parties to replenish his food supply, the governor allowed the Indians to scatter for buffalo hunting. Hazard Stevens described the natives as "armed with very inferior smoothbore guns and bows and arrows. In hunting the buffalo, they use the latter almost exclusively, and it was not unusual for a stalwart brave to drive an arrow clear through a buffalo so that the point would stick out the farther side."[14]

The main body of Nez Percés, consisting of one hundred and eight lodges, encamped with forty lodges of Shoshonis and the Flatheads and Pend Oreilles in one large village south of the fort. Near them rose fifty-four lodges of the Gros Ventres and one Piegan band. In all, perhaps twelve thousand Indians had gathered to await the council, but as the days, and then weeks, passed without treaty goods, the buffalo herds moved and the various bands followed them, first toward the Yellowstone River, and then northward to the Judith. Finally, on September 10 Adams advised Stevens that the Flatheads must leave the vicinity of the fort in twelve or fourteen days to obtain food. Other tribes grew restive.

Faced with disintegration of his council, Stevens dispatched his packmaster, Christopher P. Higgins, to notify the Indians the meeting would begin early in October. Adams replied that by then the Flatheads would be hunting on the Judith. The Flathead camp was on the move, hunting in a wide arc around Fort Benton.

Partly to advance down river toward his dilatory supply boat and partly to meet the Indians, Stevens moved the council to the mouth of the Judith on the Missouri, where the goods were unloaded and the delayed council opened at one o'clock on the afternoon of Tuesday, October 16, 1855, bringing together traditional friends and enemies of the Upper Missouri and Rocky Mountains. Perhaps thirty-five hundred Indians remained. As interpreters to the Flatheads, Stevens assigned Kiser and Sohon, with the Indians' assent.

The reluctant Cumming spoke first, delivering a gift of tobacco from the absent Assiniboins, whom he described as eager for peace, and then Stevens enumerated the tribes represented: Bloods, Blackfeet, Piegans, Gros Ventres, Nez Percés, Kutenais, Pend Oreilles, Flatheads, Snakes, and even one Cree—Broken Arm, a chief whose mark would appear on the treaty document. Doty had been unable to induce the northern Blackfeet, above the forty-ninth parallel, to take part, and the Crows could not be located. Describing the proposed treaty, Stevens told the Indians:

> We want to establish you in your country on farms. We want you to have cattle and raise crops. We want your children to be taught, and we want you to send word to your Great Father, through us, where you want your farms to be, and what schools and mills you want.

The deliberations soon showed that the Blackfoot tribes had come prepared to accept whatever the governor offered, but the Flatheads, Pend Oreilles, Nez Percés, and Snakes were uncommitted beyond wanting peace. The treaty did not emerge from mutual consents, but like Stevens' other treaties was drafted in advance for approval unless the Indians rejected specific provisions. In brief, Stevens proposed that the tribes promise to live in peace, stay at home when not hunting or trading, and share the common hunting ground in Blackfoot territory that had been defined in the Laramie treaty of 1851.

The Pend Oreilles, through Alexander, offered the sole objection:

They considered the common hunting ground too small to support their numbers and opposed the proposed closure of northern passes, Cut Bank and Marias, which they were accustomed to use. Little Dog, a noted Piegan warrior who (realizing Indian days were ending) had served as a messenger to northern Blackfeet for the governor, replied, "Since he [Alexander] speaks so much of it, we will give him liberty to come out in the north."

In this friendly spirit, peace was arranged and the treaty made. The council opened a benign period of Indian relationships, although François Saxa, a Flathead, claimed Blackfeet stole twenty horses from him twenty days after the council adjourned. The treaty contained some curious provisions, for article 1 recognized the tribes as sovereign entities capable of treating with the United States, while article 11 confirmed the dependence of the Indians on the federal government. Cumming declared the compact would hold Indian lands inviolable for ninety-nine years. On the other hand, article 7 provided that whites might move through and live in Indian territory, and article 8 gave them the right to build roads, telegraph lines, and military posts. The overriding attraction of the Blackfoot council had been the widespread Indian desire for peace, and the Indians either ignored the implications of other provisions or regarded them as inevitable. The gifts were distributed, the chiefs made their marks on the document, and at four in the afternoon of the second day the council adjourned.

During the next week the various tribes mingled near the council site, one band and then another breaking away to start homeward or return to hunting. Such was the amity that the Flatheads remained on the Musselshell undisturbed through the winter, returning to the Bitterroot in April of the following year. Stevens stayed four days after the council before leaving for Olympia, only to be met near the Teton River by his express rider, who reported that tribes on both sides of the Cascades were at war with the whites, settlers and miners murdered, Major Haller defeated by Yakimas, and a large force waiting to intercept and kill Stevens near Walla Walla. In a warning letter the acting governor, Charles H. Mason, urged Stevens to go eastward and return to Olympia by ocean vessel from New York. Stevens instead, with a guide and one man, set out for the capital overland, arriving without incident.

Once in the capital, Stevens prohibited settlers, traders, and missionaries from entering the interior and ordered that those already there deal with Indians under military surveillance. He deferred further treaty making.

On November 10, 1855, Stevens appointed Lansdale agent to the Flathead nation and in his notification said that he would recommend to the president that the Jocko be designated the Flatheads' reservation. Lansdale reached the wintry Jocko twelve days later, finding it no longer the temperate valley described in his report; he brought four workmen, an interpreter, and the interpreter's Indian wife as cook. Near the mouth of the Jocko River they completed three cottonwood log huts, chinked with mud and covered by a communal roof, just in time to be confined for two weeks by a howling winter storm into which they ventured only for fuel.

Most of the Indians were gone. The Flatheads remained hunting on the Musselshell; the Upper Pend Oreilles were returning leisurely from the hunt, intending to reach St. Ignatius at the Christmas season; the Kutenais camped for the winter with relatives on the Flatbow River in British territory; and the destitute Lower Pend Oreilles had separated into three groups, one huddled around the mission, a second struggling to reach it, and a third hunting buffalo with the Spokanes. Lansdale talked briefly with the chief of the Lower Pend Oreilles, Victor, who would not decide without a council if his people should move onto the reservation. The following March, Lansdale met the headmen of the tribe, who agreed to come onto the reservation but to cede no land. Many Lower Pend Oreilles wandered back to their older homes in the spring.[15]

Meanwhile, the peace held among the Indians. John Owen met some Upper Pend Oreilles at Medicine Rock divide, reporting "not a horse tied or one stolen during the hunt." Little Dog, the Piegan chief, paid a cordial visit to St. Ignatius. At the end of June, 1856, eight months after the Blackfoot council, Lansdale wrote the governor, "The Blackfeet and the Indians of this district now interchange friendly visits for trade, and for other purposes, freely and frequently."[16]

Forty families on the Jocko reservation, chiefly Pend Oreilles, started farming; they enclosed fifty-one fields and gardens that included 134 acres of wheat, 16 of oats, and plots of peas, potatoes, and vegetables, using tools, seeds, and instruction from the priests at St. Ignatius Mission. Because the 1855 treaty had not been ratified by the Senate, the government provided nothing, although Lansdale (through Stevens) submitted detailed lists of items needed and drawings of proposed mills, warehouses, and schools.

In the Bitterroot, the Flatheads' hunting and digging was impeded more and more by white cattlemen and settlers. As the result of shifts in population and new overland routes for immigration and trade, the Hudson's Bay Company closed out its business at Fort Hall, moving its wares to a log cabin called Fort Connah, built in 1846, six miles northeast of St. Ignatius, where trade continued under Michael Ogden while the company sought to replace Fort Colville with a new post on British soil.[17]

In view of Stevens' prohibition, Lansdale had sternly ordered the Bay in 1857 to stop trading with the Indians, but the company, referring to rights granted it in the 1846 boundary settlement, continued to sell and buy from whites and Indians.[18]

The center of intermontane commerce had moved and temporarily lay at Salt Lake City, from which place flowed bands of immigrants, some disillusioned by the desert, who came to pasture herds or take farm land in the Bitterroot Valley. In the fall of 1855 Neil McArthur, a Bay man, with Henry Brooks and L. R. Maillett, established a cattle- and horse-breeding station, using old Cantonment Stevens. Despite Stevens' ban, Indian traders entered the area in 1855–56, among them Mormon missioners who tried to convert the Flatheads from Catholicism. Among the arrivals were Marian and Henry G. Miller, she at sixteen the first white woman to live in Montana; they accompanied Lansdale from Fort Hall in 1856 to escape her Mormon parents' disapproval of their marriage. Many of the newcomers who intended merely to look over the valley built cabins and stayed. The Flatheads did not resist but were uniformly friendly in the manner of hosts.

No doubt the truce with the Blackfeet encouraged some of these migrants, but in the middle of 1856 the Crows, who had not been represented at the Blackfoot council, launched vigorous sorties against settlers' trains and other tribes in blind reprisal for their losses in war. Crow horse raiders ranged widely, and Fort Owen's proprietors again feared Indian attack. During the summer of that year, many Flatheads succumbed to smallpox. On a visit to the Bitterroot Flatheads early in 1857, Father Menetrey found:

> As regards morality, I can say that the Flatheads have gone to worse extremes than the wild nations who knew nothing of the Great Master who makes matrimony a holy and indissoluble partnership. But we must say to the praise of the Flathead chiefs, Victor, Ambrose, Moses, and Adolph, that these four men have never deviated from the path of honor and virtue.

The Jesuit observed that the Flatheads had never stopped regretting the loss of their missionaries; he prayed with them and the Flatheads stopped gambling and confessed "with a piety and sorrow of which I would not have believed Indians capable." After a second visit, finding the Flatheads sticking to their promise to stop gambling, Menetrey recommended that St. Mary's be reopened, but shortly after the Flatheads rode to buffalo and reverted to their native ways.[19]

To the west the Yakimas and their allies continued a furious campaign against white men. Father Ravalli went into the area to try to arrange peace. Stevens warned Lansdale in June:

> There cannot be much doubt that before the end of the summer many hostile Indians will find their way into the Bitterroot valley enroute for the buffalo country. In such an event I am decidedly of the opinion that no aid or comfort should be rendered them by the Indians of your agency but they should be expelled from the valley.

He would provide two thousand dollars, he added, "for preserving peaceable relations among the Indians."[20]

Lansdale's summation of the Flatheads' situation, written for Stevens, was that

> the position that this people occupy is critical and peculiarly trying. . . . They are placed between the now hostile Crows, and the traditionally

hostile but recently pacificated Blackfeet in the east, and their old neighbors and friends and relatives in the west, who are waging war upon their old friends the whites. Their country is traversed by the paths of western tribes leading to the large game of the eastern plains, and they at any time are liable to incursions of the hostile tribes of the west, who may seek to turn them from their old and steadfast friendship for the whites, or [commit] depredations upon their property as reprisals for their own losses sustained in the prosecution of their own insane and unjustifiable warfare.

Victor assured the agent that no enemy of the whites would be tolerated in the Bitterroot, and Lansdale closed his report, "Shall their friendship go unrewarded?"[21]

For his part, the governor sent the Indian office in Washington, D.C., a strong recommendation that it recognize the Flatheads' "good conduct since the war commenced and in all their previous history" by securing, if possible, fulfillment of the Hellgate treaty. From his supplies, Lansdale gave gifts to the Bitterroot Indians: a hundred fishhooks to the Flatheads, brass wire to Indians serving as guides, sinew thread to Father Ravalli, and to the friendly Piegan, Little Dog, cotton and sinew thread, pins, flints, brass tacks, needles, and a frying pan.

When spring came, most of Lansdale's restless employees left him, and he was himself recalled to Olympia late in the summer, leaving John Owen as special agent in charge of the Flathead nation. Owen continued his business as a trader. The departing doctor privately advised Owen that if the agency appeared in danger, he should flee to St. Ignatius, and left instructions that Owen should procure gunpowder and lead, if available, to issue "in safe portions to the needy of the Flathead nation" for hunting. Owen also should provide the Indians two beeves at Christmas and two at Easter for feasts and when possible allow half rations of beef to starving Indians, being cautious to slaughter first the unserviceable working oxen. He should be sure that the Indians recognized these provisions as evidences of good will.

Although Lansdale remained titular agent until mid-1857, intending to return, he spent the time away from the reservation investigating war claims against western tribes, while John Owen began his lonely struggle on behalf of the confederated Flatheads. Because there were no substantial buildings at the Jocko agency, Owen was authorized to conduct his business as agent from Fort Owen, fifty miles from the reservation.

Early in the spring of 1857 Owen sent a half-breed, Abram Finlay, to Olympia to learn the status of the Flathead treaty. Lansdale relayed Finlay's inquiry to Stevens, adding his own comments:

> No marvel the poor Indian is suspicious, and he becomes disaffected. Already they [the Flatheads] begin to object to the many whites settling in their rich grazing valleys. They also see the Great Father sends great annual presents of goods to his Blackfeet children, in fulfillment of the paper made at the mouth of the Judith in 1855. The Blackfeet are their old enemies.[22]

Owen informed the governor that the Jocko reservation had been

> in a state of excitement all winter. Some of the hostile and disaffected Indians from below have passed the winter in the jurisdiction of that agency, but what could be done with them? The Flatheads say we are dogs. They say that two years ago they made a treaty with their great friend, Governor Stevens, and have never heard anything from it since.[23]

Owen received no government funds; he resorted to buying necessities for the Indians from his own pocket. Victor, disgusted with the delay in ratification, vowed never to leave the Bitterroot.

The Flatheads scoffed to white men fencing land and planting seeds, "You are only tiring yourselves for nothing; you will sow the crops but we will reap them."

On June 2, 1857, Colonel James W. Nesmith assumed the superintendency of a combined Washington and Oregon territorial Indian service, formed over Stevens' objection that it was too large. Owen turned his pen on Nesmith, complaining of "unprincipled white men prowling through this country, and by their talk and conduct . . . well calculated to poison the Indian mind." The law-abiding whites, he wrote Doty, had considered "organizing a vigilance club."[24]

There was a continued drift of Mormon dissidents from Salt Lake. Owen declared that the Flatheads opposed Mormons among them, "growing out in all probability of the Indians here belonging to the Catholic Church." The agent, a Freemason, who visited Salt Lake regularly to buy trade goods and was known there as "pretty fond of his whiskey," became obsessed with fears for his personal safety from Mormons. He sent Nesmith a list of his property as a precaution against its loss to Mormons. Eventually Owen would confront Brigham Young in person to accuse Young of providing guns and ammunition to Snakes and Bannocks who raided the Bitterroot for horses.

The Flatheads saw their sanctuary, the Bitterroot Valley, breached as a haven for renegades, both red and white. The Nez Percés and Spokanes among them talked bitterly about Americans to the Flatheads. Kamiakin, the Yakima war chief, took refuge briefly among the Flatheads before surrendering personally to Owen on the Spokane River in May, 1859. General W. S. Harney said Kamiakin left the Bitterroot "on account of an officious interference with the Indians on the part of Mr. T, agent for the Flatheads." The Nez Percé buffalo band of some one hundred lodges wintered as usual thirty miles from the agency while Owen fretted, "I assure you they are the cause of great annoyance, killing cattle and stealing horses from neighboring tribes."[25]

As hunting intensified in the mountains near the reservation and the Bitterroot, game became scarcer, while, because of Indian hostilities, Stevens maintained in force his general prohibition against selling powder and ammunition to Indians regardless of their disposition or need. The Flatheads, as a result, approached their summer hunt for buffalo in 1858 "destitute of many things," Owen observed, but nonetheless Victor again sent Stevens word that he "need never fear the firmness and friendly feeling of the Flathead nation."[26]

The Flathead nation was merely a phrase, for the Flatheads proper held aloofly to their Bitterroot, the Pend Oreilles stayed near the mission, and the Kutenais lived at their village on Dayton Creek on the west shore of Flathead Lake—three disjoined peoples. Victor had neither the authority nor physical strength to unify them; ill, he was confined to his lodge for much of 1858.

Father De Smet, despite rheumatism that now limited his travels, returned to the Pacific Northwest in that year to try to extend the peace imposed by military force. Stevens finally was secure enough to repeal military law in the interior. The priest wintered in 1858–59 among the Coeur d'Alenes, the following spring visited his beloved St. Mary's—now in Owen's hands—and went to St. Ignatius, from where he took chiefs of various tribes to Fort Vancouver to confer May 18 with federal representatives. Alexander of the Pend Oreilles returned imbued with his impressions of the prison at Portland. He called his people together, ordered the wicked to step forward, whipped them forthwith, and then presided at a feast. De Smet moved on to Fort Benton and down river to St. Louis, his fears confirmed that Indian life was rapidly being destroyed by the whites.

The Indians realized what was happening to them. The Flatheads clung to their hope that the Stevens treaty would protect them. Owen again reported their concern "at the inroads made by the white man into their territory. They say we will all be swallowed up by the white tribe. . . . Roads are being cut through our country, game is growing scarce." The Flatheads believed "that they must depend on other means for their subsistence besides the buffalo which are yearly growing less. . . . They neither find them in such large herds or as close as in former years."[27]

The cession of Indian land under the Hellgate treaty created a widespread impression among whites that the Bitterroot would be opened for settlement immediately. As a result, new immigrant trains moved into the valley soon after the Senate at last ratified the treaty on March 8, 1859, "with but little opposition. . . . about three hours' debate," Stevens reported from the national capital. The president proclaimed the treaty on April 14. To the Indians, construction of the military road by Mullan from Fort Benton to Walla Walla confirmed that they would rapidly be overrun by settlers. Newcomers to the Bitterroot planned to remain, among them Captain Richard Grant, former trader at Fort Hall for the Hudson's Bay Company, with three hundred head of cattle, and D. E. Shaw of Champoeg, Oregon, with "bag and baggage," in Owen's words. Grant settled at Hellgate *ronde*.

The Indians threatened Michael Ogden and a Mormon trader on

Ogden's return from Salt Lake with supplies for his trading post. The reason for the Flatheads' distrust of Ogden is not clear but appears to have been anger over his methods of barter. The two white men alleged, however, that priests at St. Ignatius incited the Indians. With the Indians "in a most excited state," the Hudson's Bay Company withdrew Ogden, leaving Angus McDonald in charge with a staff of three laborers, a miller, and an Indian trader. Although the Flatheads and Kutenais rode as far as Fort Hope to obtain ammunition, the company lost its trade with the Spokanes, Coeur d'Alenes, and Pend Oreilles to American merchants—whom the Bay characterized as unfair, and Owen, a rogue. Changing its trading sites to conform to the boundary treaty, the Bay chose Fort Sheppard on the Columbia, located barely within British territory at forty-nine degrees, one minute, by Captain John Palliser. The new post's communication routes were inferior to those of old Fort Colville and, ironically, it would prove on resurvey to be on United States ground.[28]

The Flatheads were affected by their agent's strained relationship with the priests at St. Ignatius, the main source of supplies and farm implements for the Indians. One missionary charged that Owen was constantly intoxicated and unfit for his post. Doubtless Owen discouraged the Bitterroot Flatheads from patronizing the mission, and he seized the complaint by Ogden as an occasion to warn the missionaries against interfering with white immigrants. Owen first sent an employee, Henri M. Chase, to caution Father Menetrey, and then went in person to St. Ignatius, where he found Menetrey reading a copy of the 1855 treaty. Owen concluded that the priests advised the Indians to demand strict observance of the treaty—but, instead of delivering the warning he intended, Owen received a lecture from Menetrey, who pointed out that the priests attended "the bodily wants of the Indians; without us, they would starve. We plow for them; we sow for them." Owen went off grumbling that his Flatheads "raised ten bushels of wheat to one" for the Pend Oreilles.[29] The missionaries, with grudging charity, suggested that Owen's behavior resulted from a blow to his head by a windmill blade.

With ratification of the Hellgate treaty, the agent was directed to select a suitable site for a reservation agency, mills, and schools within the area recommended by Lansdale. Early in March, 1860, Owen reported finding "a natural mill-site at the mouth of the Jocko . . . canyon," and here he set about erecting a shelter. But the Flatheads' expectation that annuity goods, farm tools, seeds, and teachers would soon reach them glimmered with the news that the Assiniboins had penetrated the eastern slope of the Rockies to attack the main hunting camp of the Pend Oreilles, killing seventeen people, including one of Alexander's sons. The camp was saved by Piegans from a greater disaster.

John Owen then learned that of the $36,000 due the Flathead nation as a first payment under its treaty, $25,000 had been spent by federal agents. A bill of lading for goods consigned by the federal government to the "Flathead Indians of Oregon" and sent by steamer to Fort Benton listed 8,000 pounds of coffee, 12,000 pounds of rice, 16,000 pounds of brown sugar, and 10,000 pounds of Pilot [hard] bread, 1,761 blankets of various weights and colors, 6 plows, and a few axes, knives, pans, sickles, saws, augers, forks, and hoes. When the boat arrived, Owen also discovered fifty cloth frock coats and one ammunition case in the shipment.

He wrote a scathing letter to Washington:

> Hardbread is the last thing my Indians require, and it would have been much better, if flour was necessary, to have purchased the wheat in the Bitterroot valley and have it ground there. . . . I fear the Indians will not be satisfied in having so large an amount of property, a great deal of which is perfectly useless, forced upon them in payment for their lands.

The government should have bought useful items "such as guns, ammunition, kettles, tinware, etc., and etc., rather than so foolish a purchase."[30]

A few weeks later Owen learned that the coffee had been water-soaked. A vessel carrying it sank in the Missouri; it had been salvaged and sold to the Indian service. In anger Owen went to The Dalles, Portland, and Walla Walla, using the remaining $11,000 to buy wheat, farm equipment, seeds, and cattle for the reservation Indians. He also bought used equipment from John

Mullan, who was closing out his road project. It included a Page's patent sawmill, thirteen worn wagons (and one beyond use but "worth the money in iron and wood"), used harnesses, blacksmith tools, one plow, some nails, hand tools, cartridges, seventeen rifles that "may be required at any moment," bullet molds, tents, poles, stoves, one barrel of vinegar, rope, kettles, eight tin plates, and other castoffs. Mullan wrote the territorial Indian superintendent that the Flathead nation had "only one plow. . . . There are no more farms opened now than when I was in the valley before."[31]

The Flathead annuity goods, delayed at Fort Benton when the agent there refused to release them without specific authorization from the superintendent, reached the agency in November. Owen found the shipment short 205 yards of cloth, the blankets "far inferior to the Salem blankets," and the shawls and flannels flimsy. He advised the superintendent, "Since examining the goods with the invoice, I have no hesitation in saying that I could have purchased the same bill in Portland for one-third less money."[32]

Seven years had passed since Isaac Stevens paused to ask the Flathead Indians to make a treaty, and five since the council that negotiated it. The Flatheads' ground was rapidly being taken by white men and the game was disappearing. Enemies raided for horses. The Flatheads remained encircled and embattled. So they had been as far back as memory went.

CHAPTER 5

▲▲▲▲▲▲▲▲▲▲▲▲▲▲▲▲▲▲▲▲▲▲▲▲▲▲▲▲▲▲

THE JOCKO AGENCY:
"A PREPOSTEROUS ESTABLISHMENT"

▼▼▼▼▼▼▼▼▼▼▼▼▼▼▼▼▼▼▼▼▼▼▼▼▼▼▼▼▼▼

AT THE OPENING of the decade 1860–70, John Owen speculated that
"the united tribes of this Mount Jocko section could muster and
put in the field ten thousand warriors well mounted, well armed,
inured to the mountains, etc., and could with all ease subsist themselves upon game." The friendliness of the Flatheads, however,
belied Owen's dour view that a war was possible, while Owen's
encouragement induced an increasing number of white settlers to
locate in the Bitterroot Valley. Domineering Shoshonis passing
through the valley frightened the white farmers, cattlemen, and
merchants into considering a volunteer company for protection,
but none would be raised for seventeen years.

While the Flatheads remained in the Bitterroot, pursuing accustomed ways as well as they could, the Upper Pend Oreilles and a
mixture of Christian Indians from other tribes clustered around
St. Ignatius. Father Hoecken counted Creeks, Flatheads, Lower
Pend Oreilles, Spokanes, Nez Percés, Kutenais, Coeur d'Alenes,
and a few Blackfeet, who, "though of different nations, live together
like brethren and in perfect harmony."[1]

The mission continued to be the source of material assistance to
the confederated Flatheads. In answer to Hoecken's request, Father
De Smet in 1855 had sent agricultural tools and supplies to the
mission, including two dozen letterbooks. The following year,

Father Hoecken tried to start a day school for Indian boys, but it was abandoned as premature in 1857. In addition the mission spread its Christian influence. During the three months after relocation in 1854, the priests had baptized 79 Indians at St. Ignatius, 227 in 1855, and 47 in 1856. Between 1854 and 1860, they baptized 717 of various tribes, a number of them children whose parents were recorded as "pagan." Among the Indians baptized in 1855 were 150 Kutenais.

As the number of the faithful increased, Christian marriages displaced the native custom of marrying by living together and divorcing by living apart. In 1856 there were two Catholic weddings, the next year sixteen, in 1858 twenty-three, and the number continued to increase. Father Menetrey again visited the Bitterroot Flatheads.

Few Indians of the confederated tribes visited the Jocko Agency even in distress. Owen distrusted the Pend Oreilles and rarely saw the Kutenais, whom he reported living north of the Canadian border. After the Kutenais' annuity goods had lain unclaimed for one year, Owen sold them to pay some of the agency's debts. The agent and the priest who succeeded Father Hoecken, Father Menetrey, bickered over petty issues—the mission's price of fifty cents a head for cabbages, payment for lumber cut at the agency mill—and Owen did not encourage his Flatheads to visit St. Ignatius. Thus the Flatheads continued their nomadic lives while the Pend Oreilles, "by reason of the liberality of the missionaries in furnishing seeds, tools, teams, etc., went to work cultivating the soil, extending their old fields and forming new ones."[2] In 1856 the Pend Oreilles planted more than one hundred acres, a small tillage for their numbers but a beginning toward the agrarian future both their church and the United States government intended for them.

In their mountain-locked valley, white settlers circumscribed the Flatheads more each year—worn men wearing hard-used clothing, tieless shirts, broad-brimmed hats beaten by rain and sun, men accustomed to toil and men looking for a main chance. Gradually Indian men adopted the brimmed hats and pants, which they combined with moccasins and blankets. Owen quietly advised immigrants to improve the land and build homes while he maintained his official posture of resisting encroachment on Indian territory. As more whites came, many of them a rough breed, complaints increased of whiskey sales to Indians. Owen advised one settler, Samuel Martin, that by the intercourse act he would forfeit half his land to an informer and half to the government if convicted of supplying liquor to Indians, telling Martin that he could not over- look a second violation. To another, Owen sent a stern admonition: "Well do we know that an Indian when under the influence of liquor is no better than a cruel savage." The missionaries reported frequent bartering of whiskey to Indians. For compliance with regulations, the agent relied entirely on persuasion. "An agent's duty is unpleasant as things are, law is impotent, you are not sustained in things you want for the good of the Indians for want of troops," he complained to James Doty.[3]

Western Montana's immigration quickened with rediscovery of gold in the Deer Lodge Valley in 1860, on Willard Creek in 1861, on Grasshopper Creek one year later, in Alder Gulch in 1863, and in Last Chance Gulch in 1864. The last three discoveries brought rushes. With the influx of hundreds of white men and a growing commerce in goods and services, organization of local government became imperative. Montana was designated a territory in 1864 with Bannack its capital. Section 1 of the Organic Act excluded Indian reservations from the territory.

Although vegetables from white farms in the Bitterroot and Hell-gate districts sold in Virginia City, where potatoes brought seven cents a pound, the Bitterroot was not much farmed by the Flat-heads. The valley remained the gathering place for "western Indians" bound on their customary trails through Flathead country for the buffalo hunting grounds. Many of these were neither pro- tected nor obligated by treaties. These itinerants usually stopped to dig camas and bitterroot and, careless of any sufferance of the Flatheads and settlers, they accosted whites, stole their horses, knocked down fences, and trampled fields. In three years, 1,865 horses were reported stolen from Indians and whites in the valley.

For a few months in 1860–61 Owen was also agent to the Snakes and the Bannocks, persistent thieves of Flathead horses. These now invaded the Bitterroot, alternately bellicose and importunate, poor almost beyond belief, afoot leading bony horses, frail from starvation, naked or partly clothed in tattered castoffs. With those of the Salmon Falls and other remnant bands, they presented themselves to Owen for assistance. When he gave them food and blankets, he was "openly accused of trifling with them" by his white neighbors and fell out of favor with the Flatheads. On a visit to the Snakes, Owen found them living in fragile shelters of boughs and grass, "poor miserable naked starving wretches," hostile from their mistreatment by whites. The agent gave them some beef and canvas tents, but he was not allotted government funds to assist them, and he found no surplus in the consignments of shoddy blankets (often rifled en route) that reached the Flathead nation.

A few years later, an agent asked the confederated Flatheads what they wanted as annuities. They asked for work cattle, ox yokes and bows, chains, ticking, brown drill, blankets, axes and handles, files for saws, woolen and hickory shirts, powder, lead, waterproof percussion caps, and tobacco, indicating their desire to share the white man's technology as they saw it around them. That the Indian office failed to comply with requisitions for such goods rests partly on the fact that Washington, D.C., could not rely on reports from most of its agents and probably regarded the list from the Flatheads as goods the agent hoped to sell to settlers for his own profit.

Although Washington tried to learn the truth through field inspectors and special agents, it was victimized not only by conniving employees but by such fatuous ones as Dr. James A. Mullen, assigned in 1861 to brief service as physician to the Flatheads.

Since the kind and fostering hands of the government have been thrown around these children of the mountains, and they have, in great measure, fallen in with the habits and methods of thought peculiar to their white brethren, they of course have better notions of those general laws of health and disease, technically termed "hygiene," than they could have enjoyed in their former wild and nomadic life. My duties during the past year have developed the fact that whilst acute maladies are rare among them, chronic disorders prevail to an alarming extent, viz., consumption, scrofula, rheumatism, and inflammations of the . . . eye.[4]

At least this last remark was true, for lame, blind, and wheezing Indians were common.

As for peace, the physician mentioned that he had treated Pend Oreilles wounded by Assiniboins. Another observer reported that when Piegans attempted to steal Flathead horses, Moise (Moses) blew a horn, his son beat a drum to rouse the Flathead camp, and the thieves were captured but allowed to go after they were marked —their hair was cut short and their ears snipped.

In the middle of 1862, Owen resigned because of the failure of appropriations to reach his Indians. He had not been paid as agent for fourteen months and learned that the superintendent had received no report of the agency for the past two years. As agent, Owen bought many supplies from local merchants on credit. Upon resigning, he visited Portland in a vain attempt "to obtain funds to liquidate at least a portion of the indebtedness of my agency." He complained, "I have been compelled to contract a considerable amount of liabilities in order to carry on the current business of my agency," and thus had "exhausted my own private means."[5] The then territorial superintendent, Calvin H. Hale, assigned the Nez Percés' agent, Charles Hutchins, to replace Owen.

To reach the Flathead agency, Hutchins, unable to hire transportation at Lewiston, bought his own pack train. It was scattered by wolves his second night out (not an uncommon misfortune) and took two days to reassemble. After thirty-one days on the trail, Hutchins reached the Jocko. Owen had stripped the agency. In frustration, Hutchins wrote Hale that Owen

> discharged all hands, sacked the agency of every head of stock of all kinds, and most of the grain, sold and gave away the nails, lumber, agricultural implements, household utensils, and in short scraped the public property to the bed rock of that which was most indispensable in this country.

Owen had simply paid his employees in agency goods. A reputable Portland citizen appointed to investigate, Quincy A. Brooks, exonerated Owen, reporting to Hale:

I gather you have come to the conclusion that the major [Owen] has been guilty of a want of integrity. Whatever faults he may have, and he is not free from them, I think you will find that dishonesty is not among the number.[6]

From the resignation of John Owen until 1910, two factors affected the condition of the Flatheads: the skill of their agent, and the political climate in which he operated. It is evident from letters and reports that the Flatheads themselves were largely ignored in the conduct of the agency. They came and went, camped on the fringes of towns, complained, and starved. White men regarded the Indians as curiously invisible, except when the Flatheads got in the way. The change in agents in 1862 began a period in which the Flatheads, ostensibly subjects of much correspondence, were left largely to their own meager and diminishing resources. The political affairs of white men, in consequence, are germane to the history of the Flathead Indians.

With Owen's resignation the Flatheads lost a friend and confidant. Perhaps they sensed Owen's growing disorientation with white men and found in him a reflection of themselves, gradually losing ability to cope with the machinery of change. Hutchins did not live among the Bitterroot Flatheads, as Owen had, but moved into the shacks on the Jocko constructed for agency buildings. The Flatheads stayed near Owen's trading post, to which he added a commercial gristmill in 1863. Although the new agent considered the Flatheads his secondary concern because they were not on the reservation, Hutchins nevertheless asked George M. Pinney, the U.S. marshal for Montana, to proceed against whites who trespassed on Indian lands in the Bitterroot. Pinney held the letter in his desk for five months, then forwarded it to the commissioner of Indian affairs.

Early in 1863 Flatheads became involved in a confused accusation of depredations. Unimportant in itself, the incident suggests the desultory relationships between Indians and whites. Reliable witnesses said that, between Hellgate and Gold Creek, a wagon train led by Zeb B. Thibedeau encountered Flatheads returning from buffalo. Thibedeau sold the Indians whiskey. Intoxicated, they behaved badly, whereupon, with the counsel of white citizens, a Flathead chief exercised the Indian prerogative of destroying liquor found in Indian territory. The chief, Ambrose, and his band trailed Thibedeau's train, scattered its occupants by pretending an attack, dumped the remaining whiskey, but damaged no other goods. A second band of Flatheads looted the abandoned wagon train a few minutes later.

Eventually Thibedeau collected his men and the train limped into Cottonwood in the Deer Lodge Valley, where they met a third band of Flatheads. From these Thibedeau took horses to compensate for his losses, but this third band of Flatheads, reinforced by their hunting friends, reclaimed their horses at gunpoint. Agent Hutchins tried to identify the Flatheads involved, which was impractical, while whites told him Thibedeau exaggerated his losses, claiming eight thousand dollars. Hutchins sent a report to Oregon, only to discover that the Flathead Agency in 1863 had been transferred to the Idaho Superintendency.

Although the United States was now engaged in the Civil War, Hutchins went to Washington, D.C., to talk with the commissioner of Indian affairs, W. P. Dole, who advised the agent to divert funds to meet local conditions. Satisfied, Hutchins returned by ocean vessel to Portland and rode horseback to the Jocko. Rather than hire a doctor, he used the physician's salary to buy work and beef cattle at high prices, finding U.S. currency depreciated more than 30 per cent by war. For more than six months he received no communication from the Indian office, but finally heard that a letter awaited him at his old post, the Nez Percé agency. He sent a special messenger to get his letter, which proved to be a demand from Dole that Hutchins explain purchases not authorized by his quarterly requisition.

During 1863 Father De Smet once more visited the Rocky Mountain Indians. His presence allowed Fathers Joseph Giorda and Urban Grassi, stationed among the Blackfeet at St. Peter's, to renew appeals for Indian schools, and De Smet in turn petitioned the Sisters of Charity of Providence at Montreal. The next year, when eleven novice nuns were assigned to Vancouver, three were sent inland to the confederated Flatheads, joined on the way by a fourth from Sacred Heart Mission among the Coeur d'Alenes. The four reached St. Ignatius, where a building had been started for them, on horseback on October 17, 1864.

In December they opened a day school for Indian and white girls at a tuition of twenty-five dollars a month. Boys between the ages of five and twelve also attended, and in 1865 St. Ignatius became a boarding school. The nuns' pupils were mostly Indian orphans accepted as charity students; the nuns taught them household skills and English. The priests and brothers instructed the boys in manual and farming skills. "Plain common English education—spelling, reading, and writing, with the rudiments of arithmetic" was considered sufficient for Indians. "Anything beyond that, in our opinion, would be detrimental, not beneficial to him," remarked Father Lawrence Palladino a few years later. "It would but feed and encourage his natural indolence at the expense of what he needs most, industrial education."[7] Certain whites accused the priests of deliberately limiting the Indians' education in order to hold them captives to the mysteries of the Catholic church.

Agent Hutchins' main concern was to improve the agency headquarters, and to this end he contracted with a former sawyer at the agency to cut lumber for him. "This arrangement will not at all interfere with any privileges that the Indians might have for using the mill," Hutchins advised the Indian office, "as the mill . . . is located where it can never be of the slightest utility to the Indians." Taking Hutchins' word for it, the commissioner deleted funds for mill operation, whereupon Hutchins appealed for money to cut lumber for the Indian structures promised in the 1855 treaty. He persuaded the commissioner to restore funds and also to approve construction of a gristmill, completed in October, 1865, standing next to the sawmill and sharing its waterwheel. Unfortunately, the grain crops in 1865, 1866, and 1867 were badly damaged by crickets, and the Indians who farmed patronized the mission mill.

None of Hutchins' struggles improved the condition of the confederated Flatheads. The Flatheads proper continued to hunt and dig, relying on John Owen for counsel, while the Pend Oreilles and those Kutenais on the reservation depended on St. Ignatius Mission. Moreover, an overlay of bureaucracy now curtained Flathead affairs, a regimen in which the Flatheads participated only incidentally and which separated them politically from whites as the reservation was intended to separate them physically. With creation of Montana Territory, the Flathead agency was transferred to jurisdiction of its governor and acting Indian superintendent, Sidney Edgerton. Hutchins asked Edgerton for Indian funds, but the governor replied that "no such monies have come to hand." With Edgerton's approval, the agent sold eight plows belonging to the Flathead nation for thirty dollars apiece to pay debts. Then he received, as Indian funds, a draft on the United States depository in Oregon which could not be cashed in Montana. Hutchins went to Oregon City, cashed the draft at the wartime rate, and wrote the commissioner to ask that a Flathead reservation account be opened in New York, warning against sending a package of checkbooks by mail, however, in view of "the common belief that the contractors throw away all mail matter, other than letters, to save weight."[8]

Edgerton held an uncongenial view of Indians. He observed, in his message to the first territorial legislature, "I trust that the government will, at an early date, take steps for the extinguishment of the Indian titles in this territory, in order that our lands may be brought into market." In response to questions from Washington about the Flatheads, Edgerton was candid with Commissioner Dole, writing that he did not know much about Indian administration.

> The Indians in this territory have generally manifested a friendly disposition and I shall endeavor to cultivate friendly relations with them. I cannot answer all your interrogatories without holding further communication with Mr. Hutchins; as there is no mail route to the Jocko, I shall be compelled to wait until I can send through.[9]

A short time later, Edgerton pointed out that the duties of Indian superintendent had not been explained to him and that, because the agencies of his jurisdiction communicated directly with the commissioner, he believed he should be given a leave of absence as superintendent. For a period, 1865–66, the Flathead agency was returned to the Idaho Superintendency.[10]

With the inauguration of President Andrew Johnson, Hutchins

was replaced as Flathead agent by Augustus H. Chapman, a Republican wheelhorse from Charleston, Illinois, with no previous experience among Indians. In February, 1866, Chapman reached the Jocko agency, where he found Hutchins selling the stock and property to settlers and rebuying at depressed rates the vouchers with which he had paid his employees.

Chapman protested Hutchins' impoverishment of the agency as Hutchins had complained of Owen's. Until the act of March 3, 1875, Indian agents regarded their correspondence and ledgers as private possessions, hence the familiar plaint that the outgoing agent had taken all the records, sold the property, discharged the employees, and abused the Indians. In his turn each Flathead agent of this time requested funds to undo his predecessor's neglect of the Flatheads and subsequently wrote elaborate descriptions of his own progress toward civilizing the Indians. The federal Indian office regularly sent the Flatheads farm tools, but each incoming agent found no implements for Indian farms.

Unlike his predecessors, Chapman became friendly with Eneas, the sincere Christian chieftain of the reservation Kutenais, who had returned from Canada to Dayton Creek. Chapman called Eneas "the best chief of the confederated nation. He is younger and much poorer than either of the other head chiefs, . . . anxious to have a comfortable home, and insists the government provide the same for him. . . . Neither of the other chiefs want homes." The agent reported to Governor Caleb Lyon of Idaho Territory (ten days before Lyon left office) that the reservation Indians, returning from buffalo, were ill and hostile. "The Indians have great and just cause of complaint," he wrote. "Something must be done for this agency at once or all operations will come to a dead stop."[11]

The white settlers grumbled, in the meantime, about the breadth of open land reserved for a handful of indolent natives. A census of the confederated tribes in 1865 counted 239 Flatheads (only 55 men among them), 273 Kutenais, and 751 Pend Oreilles. The agency was so destitute that it could not afford to send wagons for annuity goods lying unclaimed in a warehouse at Fort Benton.

Buffalo hunting by Flatheads now involved greater perils: not only were settlers and prospectors rapidly filling the fertile Bitterroot, Hellgate, and Deer Lodge valleys, but the Blackfeet, assailed by Sioux on their eastern flank, renewed attacks on their old Indian enemies and on white intruders. Armed with repeating breech-loading rifles firing hollow-point expanding bullets, the Blackfeet killed nearly half a hundred men of the confederated tribes in 1865–66, according to Chapman's estimate. While natural deaths outran those from violence or starvation, the St. Ignatius Mission records showed ten deaths from warfare and fourteen from famine in 1867, seven and seven the following year, four and nine in 1869, and two from war and nineteen from famine in 1870.[12]

So virulent were the Blackfeet that the Piegan chieftain, Little Dog, and his son were slain by their own people for befriending whites. In April, 1866, the Jesuits closed St. Peter's among the Blackfeet for the safety of the mission staff. In that year, however, the Society of Jesus reopened St. Mary's in the Bitterroot, this time as a mission to serve white as well as Flathead Catholics. A new chapel designed by Father Ravalli rose a mile upriver from the St. Mary's of 1840–50. Fathers Ravalli and Giorda soon were joined at St. Mary's by a slight, red-haired French Jesuit, Father Jerome D'Aste. He had been studying mathematics in Paris when De Smet, recruiting for the Rocky Mountains, dressed him in Indian regalia, kindling in D'Aste a vocation for the missions.

This St. Mary's was far from isolated; around it, white civilization blossomed. Philip Ritz imported fruit trees for sale to settlers, and new land seekers, finding the bottom lands between Fort Owen and Corvallis taken, moved into the lower hills. Among the Flatheads, Victor, Ambrose, Moise (Moses), and Adolph had remained devout Catholics and promised to lead the tribe back to their Christian faith.

As acting governor of Montana, Thomas Francis Meagher raised a thousand civilian militiamen to meet an anticipated uprising of the Sioux, counting on financial support from the federal government. Until the federal authorities repudiated him, Meagher thus threatened all miscreant Indians with his armed volunteers. A literate, ebullient Irish patriot, Meagher swaggered about Montana in Edgerton's absence, visiting Indian reservations and declaiming in the villages. The Flathead Agency, he declared, was a preposterous establishment . . . very mischievously established and perverted. Two-thirds of this superb tract of country . . . ought, surely, to be thrown open to the whites by a modification of the treaty which makes it an exclusive estate for the Indians.[13]

During Meagher's tenure, and doubtless with advice from Edgerton, who was in the national capital, the commissioner of Indian affairs obtained concurrence of the secretary of the interior for removal of the Flatheads proper from the Bitterroot Valley, notwithstanding the unmet provision of the 1855 treaty requiring a survey. The secretary wrote the commissioner:

> It appears that . . . settlements have been made by the whites and the prospects are that the valley will soon be wholly occupied by them. In view of the circumstances, I concur . . . as to the propriety of obtaining the consent of the Indians to remove peacefully therefrom to the general reservation provided by the treaty, which you think practicable if they are paid for their improvements.[14]

Agent Chapman wrote numerous appeals for money for the Indians, advising the Indian office that, even though "there was not a single book or paper left in this office," his reconstruction of the records showed the government owed the confederated Flatheads $30,793. During the 1866 distribution of annuities, Chapman talked with the headmen—especially those of the Flatheads in the Bitterroot and the Kutenais—and found them unhappy and discouraged. "Unless the government assists them, they will all, or nearly all, starve," he reported the Indians had said. "You can form no idea of the poverty of a large portion of these two tribes and of their utter inability to get a proper start in the world, that is, in agricultural pursuits."[15] Yet the Indians would have no cause for complaint, declared Big Canoe, if the government would build them their homes and schools pledged in 1855.

While he demanded additional federal funds for the Flatheads, Chapman fraudulently sold lumber from the reservation mill to whites, falsified his ledgers to hide his profit, charged white men two and one-half dollars a head to graze cattle illegally on the reservation, and was alleged to have cached salt at various farmers' homes for future trading.

Whispers of these transactions reached Meagher, who sent the picturesque marshal, John X. Beidler, to investigate. Beidler, whom newspapers called "X," customarily wore a white slouch hat with immense brim, ample frock coat, loosely cut pants and shirt, and carried a bowie knife and brace of pistols conspicuously in his belt. He spent March 4 through April 5, 1867, on the Flathead reservation. As a consequence of his findings, Chapman was dismissed, his records impounded on Meagher's personal order, and the agent arrested as he hastily sold agency goods before attempting to leave.

The Flatheads' fifth agent was an odd, unctuous career Indian servant, John W. Wells, who had been a clerk in the Indian office fourteen years before he was sent into the field "to give his fellow clerks the benefit of his absence," an agency employee concluded. Without doubt the Indian office sent Wells to prepare the Flatheads proper for removal from the Bitterroot Valley. Southern by birth, a personal friend of President Johnson, Wells was authorized to inspect various Indian agencies in Oregon and Washington territories on the way to his post on the Jocko, spending six months en route. He reached Montana accompanied by his adolescent son and Major Levi L. Blake, hired in Oregon to be agency farmer.

"Tired, nearly starved, and frozen, and expecting welcome at the end of our protracted and painful journey, we arrived at the agency this evening," Wells wrote the commissioner on his first night among the Flatheads, "to find a state of things . . . which froze me with horror." Chapman left no food, nothing planted on the meager eighteen-acre agency farm, and only one broken plow.

Wells obtained funds for the agency through his long acquaintance in the Indian administration, but he soon exhibited the odd personal behavior that brought him to the remote Jocko. He imagined that wolves were about to attack his office and kept the entire agency staff on watch, guns at ready, throughout many nights to ward off phantom beasts. The Indians quickly recognized Wells as erratic and unreliable and stayed away from him. Blake resigned as farmer, succeeded by a huge bear of a former Hudson's Bay man, Captain Fitz Stubbs; Wells's boy, surprised in a liaison with the cook, fled to Portland. In his demented periods, Wells took to addressing a legless workman, Charles Schafft, as his son.

When lucid, Wells sympathized with the Flatheads but did nothing to remedy the government's neglect of them. Instead, he amused himself by concocting colorful nicknames for white men in the area—names that inevitably reached the men themselves. Shortly after arriving, Wells saw the painful return from buffalo of the Spokanes, "poor and destitute of horses, owing as well to the rigorous winter just passed as to the retaliation of the Blackfeet whose horses they stole." As they moved, the Spokanes purloined horses from Indians and whites, but Wells could not recover the animals. To stop depredations, the Indians must be persuaded to abandon buffalo hunting, he asserted, because the hunt "is only another name for a spree . . . a terror to peaceful citizens by its marauding concomitants."[16]

A month behind the Spokanes, the Bitterroot Flatheads returned, destitute and battered, so bruised that for the first time a band camped near the Jocko agency headquarters. Wells found the young men furious, ready to strike blindly at whites and other Indians in reprisal for their lost horses. He refused to issue them ammunition to hunt in the area until their anger cooled.

The Flatheads in the Bitterroot were called to council with Wells three months after he reached the Jocko. By now they could not have expected much to come of talking with white officials. Accompanied by several leading citizens—Angus McDonald, Stubbs, Judges Thomas Pomeroy and Jasper Rand, John Owen, and Father Giorda—Wells said the meeting would allow an exchange of views. The whites expected a first step toward removal to the reservation; the Indians doubtless saw this as another opportunity to appeal for relief. Victor, Ambrose, Isaac, Adolph, Arlee, Alexander, and a younger subchief, Stanislaus, met Wells in a tipi draped with a United States flag. They talked over a period of two days, but neither the Flatheads nor Wells mentioned two timely subjects: removal to the Jocko and damages claimed by whites in the Bitterroot for cattle butchered by Indians.

Wells seemed pleased with his "first business council with this interesting people," the Flatheads were puzzled, and the citizens of Montana derisive. A correspondent to the *Tri-Weekly Post* reported that Ambrose asked about annuities, Indian land titles,

John Owen, trader and Flathead agent. (Dr. A. A. Sallquist collection, Gonzaga University)

Ruins of Fort Owen, 1887. The adobe bastions originally were connected by an adobe wall. The compound was begun by Jesuit fathers and served as the second St. Mary's mission until sold to John Owen in 1850. (Montana Historical Society)

THE FLATHEAD AGENCY.

A sketch of the Flathead agency headquarters, from Thomas F. Meagher's "Rides through Montana," *Harper's New Monthly Magazine*, October, 1867.

MISSION OF ST. IGNATIUS.

A sketch of St. Ignatius mission from Thomas F. Meagher's "Rides through Montana," *Harper's New Monthly Magazine*, October, 1867.

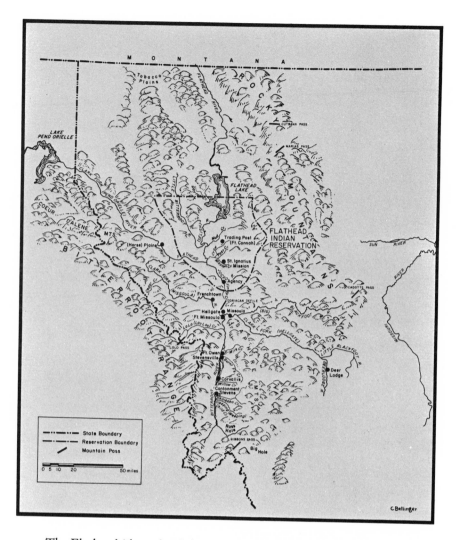

The Flatheads' homeland shortly after the beginning of white immigration, showing boundaries of the reservation and location of forts, missions, and settlements. Based on a map of Montana compiled for the General Land Office under direction of Captain William Ludlow, Corps of Engineers, and published in May, 1875. (National Archives)

St. Ignatius mission, 1866. (Montana Historical Society)

St. Mary's mission chapel in the Bitterroot, after restoration. This is the second chapel called St. Mary's. The log house at right was Father Ravalli's residence and workshop. (Gonzaga University)

Father Anthony Ravalli, S.J. (Dr. A. A. Sallquist collection, Gonzaga University)

Father Jerome D'Aste, S.J., 1890. (Gonzaga University)

Feast following the death of a Flathead chief's grandson. The long lodge, constructed by combining several tipis, is typical of ceremonial lodges used by the Flatheads near the end of the nineteenth century. The area is representative of the valleys of the reservation. (Montana Historical Society)

right to hunt and fish in any
Indian country where they are now
entitled to hunt and fish under
existing treaties Nor shall
anything in this agreement
be so construed as to deprive any
of said Indians, so removing to
the Jocko Reservation from
selling all their improvements
in the Bitter Root Valley

      James A. Garfield.
        Special Com. for the Removal of the
          Flatheads from the Bitter Root Valley

    Charlot. First Chief of the Flatheads.
        His   Mark
    Arlee Second Chief of the Flatheads
        His + Mark
    Adolphe Third Chief of the Flatheads
        His + Mark

Witness to Contract & Signatures
Wm. H. Clagett
D. G. Swaim J a u.s.a
W. F. Sanders
J. A. Viall
B. F. Potts Governor
     I certify that I interpreted fully
and carefully the foregoing contract to the
three Chiefs of the Flatheads named above —
Witness to Signature
           Baptiste Robear au
               Interpreter
B. F. Potts Governor
               His + Mark

Garfield treaty with Flatheads, showing that Charlot did not sign.

Indian girls at St. Ignatius, dressed for the Feast of the Nativity, 1886.
(Montana Historical Society)

The famous boys' band of St. Ignatius, pictured on the steps of Bishop Brondel's home in Helena. Brondel, near the top of the steps, wears the cross on his chest. (Montana Historical Society)

St. Ignatius mission, from the south, in 1891. The large building at right is the priests' home and boys' school. The mission church with steeple is at left, and the Mission Range in the background. (Gonzaga University)

Flathead children. (Frank Palmer, Eastern Washington State Historical Society)

Charlot, chief of the Flathead nation, from a stereopticon photograph by
N. A. Forsyth, Butte. (Montana Historical Society)

and the pledges of the Stevens treaty. Ambrose lamented that the Flatheads were worse off than their fathers, their land invaded, and their time-worn trails to buffalo intersected by immigration, whereupon Wells remarked that he was happy to see the Indians "looking well, strong, and fat, not sick," and adjourned the council.

Said the *Post*:

> Thus ended the farce—it can be called nothing else—no business of any kind being transacted. All are of the opinion that Mr. Wells is entirely unfit for the position he holds; he may do as a clerk in the department at Washington, but he has no tact to manage Indians . . . or get along with the employees of the agency.[17]

The correspondent commented that many residents believed Wells insane, especially under the influence of whiskey, "which is often." This remark reached a California senator. Wells was suspended for three months during an inquiry but reinstated. He occasionally visited Owen, whose journal observed that when they were together it was "Nip, nip."

Wells began a frenzied search for the identity of the *Post* writer, settling accurately on Judge Pomeroy, whom he challenged to a duel, and blaming tension between whites and Flatheads in the Bitterroot on "over-zealous newspaper correspondents." He asked permission to bring a delegation of Flatheads to Washington to discuss their removal, writing the commissioner, "The truth, sir, is that the Flatheads are intimidated. They are frightened, and I believe rather than risk an angry collision with the white settlers around them, they would be induced to do almost anything." Victor and Adolph both told Wells, he continued, "They would die rather than leave their homes on the authority of any man less than the Tyee at Washington, but if he said so, . . . it should be done."[18] He did not receive approval for a delegation to Washington.

Blackfoot raiders who had followed the Flathead hunters home in 1867 remained in the region through the summer, stealing Indians' and white men's horses. After they murdered two Indian women sleeping in a field, Wells asked for rifles and a howitzer to protect the agency. Montana's new governor, Green Clay Smith, disapproved the request. While the *Montana Post* called the Jocko reservation "a perfect Babel," Wells wrote Smith that his detective system was trying to catch whiskey smugglers. The agent also wrote Victor in the Bitterroot notes urging the old chief to stop liquor traffic there. Smith deputized the Missoula attorney, Washington J. McCormick, to discover whether Wells himself might be the smuggler.

When two drunken Indians attacked Judge Rand, Wells was ordered to the national capital to explain. McCormick was put in temporary charge of the agency, to be succeeded after eleven months by Michael M. McCauley, who had come to Montana to prospect. Unprepared to serve as agents, both were eminently acceptable to settlers. The agency had clearly become a device for protecting whites from Indians rather than a means of serving the confederated Flatheads. Despondent over the commissioner's refusal to return him to duty at Jocko, Wells shot himself in his rooms in Washington.

Near the end of his stewardship, McCormick reported that he had repaired the mill to grind grain for the Pend Oreilles, but the other agency buildings remained unfinished. Many Flatheads were too poor in horses to join the buffalo hunt, and those who went complained that the whites had driven the buffalo away from their familiar ranges on the headwaters of the Yellowstone.

During his time as agent, McCormick built himself a new home in Missoula with agency lumber, where he was to take his bride, Kate, the daughter of Christopher Higgins, Stevens' packmaster turned merchant. McCormick explained to the commissioner that gold had been discovered on Sibley Creek, one hundred and fifty miles north of Missoula, and that prospectors stole many horses as they rushed through the Jocko reservation. The Pend Oreille and Kutenai chiefs refused to help recover the horses until paid their salaries. McCormick said he bought the agency lumber for himself to raise money for the chiefs and "re-establish good feeling."[19]

At this mid-point in the decade of the 1860's, white farming and cattle raising was so general that the governor described the "230 miles between the Flathead agency and Virginia City" as "well settled for a greater part of the distance." The peripatetic promoter, Philip Ritz, wrote in the *Walla Walla Statesman*:

The valleys of the Bitterroot and Hellgate are much larger than I expected to find away up here in the Rocky Mountains, and are rapidly settling up with good, industrious, enterprising families. . . . This season they have raised in these valleys about 30,000 bushels of wheat and 15,000 bushels of oats and barley, besides great quantities of vegetables.

Below Hellgate, Frank Worden and Higgins had established a store in 1865, and in the next year added grist- and sawmill, calling the place Missoula Mills. (It would become Missoula.) Despite cricket ravages, they ground ten thousand bushels of grain in 1866 and in three years would double their output.

Unimpeded by the Flatheads or their agents, settlers since 1855 had established themselves not only on the Bitterroot River but along its tributary creeks: Ten Mile, Three Mile, Burnt Fork, Willow, Girds, Skalkaho, and Weeping Child. Their farms covered thirty miles up and down the valley. Whites in western Montana by 1865 numbered perhaps seven hundred; their farms totaled fifteen thousand acres; they operated two schools in the Bitterroot for their children; forty of their homes stood near Fort Owen in a hamlet called Stevensville. As no more than a dozen of the Flatheads farmed seriously, the whites wrote petitions demanding removal of the Indians, sending these documents to Washington, where the territorial delegation circulated them among influential men in the Indian service, the Congress, and the presidential retinue. At least one petition reached President Johnson.

Led by Higgins, a coterie of Bitterroot settlers petitioned the governor for arms to protect them from "impending attack" by the Flatheads. They alleged that the Indians burned haystacks and fields for two hundred miles around. Although this fiction appeared in New York newspapers, and consequently reached Congress, Governor Smith knew the Flatheads well enough to ignore this groundless alarm. He merely warned publicly against furnishing arms to Montana Indians. He could not well have bought guns from territorial Indian appropriations, for he had gambled away the funds of his superintendency.

In general the Flatheads enjoyed a good reputation. Known in the capital for their obdurate insistence on the terms of the Stevens treaty, the Flatheads had also received some national recognition as peaceful Indians through travel accounts and religious appeals. Adventure and historical portrayals (of varying credibility) of life among American Indians occasionally alluded to the Flatheads, usually in the vein of Ross Cox, who wrote, "Their bravery is pre-eminent . . . a love of truth they think necessary to a warrior's character. They are too proud to be dishonest, too candid to be cunning." Thomas James, who probably never saw a Flathead, described them as "a noble race . . . the Spartans of Oregon."[20]

A literary and religious outpouring at the time called the nation's attention to its treatment of Indians. Religious and social welfare spokesmen called for reform. Probably the white residents of the Bitterroot would not have consented to removing the Flatheads by military force, but the romantic notion of betrayed Indian innocence that served as public opinion also deterred the Indian office in Washington from seriously considering such a step.

The commissioner of Indian affairs therefore determined in 1868 to send an emissary to attempt amicable removal of the Flatheads, selecting for this person William J. Cullen, who had headed the Northern Superintendency from 1857 to 1861, during Buchanan's term. Cullen, an experienced Indian negotiator, expected soon to be appointed superintendent of Indian affairs for Idaho and Montana and was, consequently, eager to advance his candidacy by a personal triumph in Indian bargaining. He came west to meet many tribes and seek broad new concessions from them. Cullen believed that to extinguish Indian titles

> in a manner that will avoid further trouble, it will be necessary that I should meet, in addition to the different bands of Blackfeet Indians, the Snakes, Bannocks, Flatheads, Pend Oreilles and Kootenays. . . . I hold that disregard of the [Indian] claims, if not of Indians, in obtaining lands has been the primary cause of many of our Indian wars.

Designated a special agent, given twenty-seven thousand dollars for expenses and gifts to Indians, and directed to arrange a peaceful relinquishment of all Montana Indian lands occupied by whites, Cullen set out. Before the end of September, 1868, he implemented the Gad Upson treaties by which Bloods, Piegans, Blackfeet, Gros Ventres, River Crows, Bannocks, and Shoshonis were placed on reserves, were assigned agents, and ceded their unreserved lands. Accompanied by the acting governor and ex-officio Indian superintendent for Montana, James Tufts, Cullen reached the Jocko reservation on August 10. Upon learning that the agent, McCormick, had built himself a home with Indian lumber, Cullen promptly suspended him.

The agency itself consisted of several dilapidated structures, among them a two-room cabin that served as agent's quarters and office, and a log barracks with roof fallen in. Cullen found the barn also roofless and the mill dam washed out. The only animals on the place were two milch cows borrowed from St. Ignatius Mission. He reported:

> No improvements of any kind have been made for the Indians for whom this reservation and agency were designed, and the benefit of all that was done here . . . appears to have been reaped by the employees, of whom there are at present nine, with salaries ranging from $900 to $1,500 per annum. The agency is very much in debt. . . . I could find no record, letter, report, or data of any kind at the agency.

The physician, he added, practiced in Missoula.[21]

While Governor Tufts inventoried the agency, Cullen visited St. Ignatius, where he saw a large frame church, schoolhouse, dwellings, mills, shops, and cultivated fields. Some mission Indians were poor, "but others are comparatively comfortable and well off. They have raised this year about eight fields of wheat beside other grains and vegetables, all of which are in splendid condition." At religious services, about five hundred natives prayed in their own dialects. The nuns taught the girls in an unfinished schoolroom. (Cullen later sent the nuns five kegs of nails and each girl a new dress from Missoula.) Instructed by Jesuit brothers, said Cullen, "the Indians have made good progress in farming as well as the more necessary trades. The grist mill and saw mill have been run entirely for the benefit of the Indian and everything that has been done here seems to have but one common object."

At Fort Owen, Cullen and Tufts found the Flatheads, whose chiefs they summoned to a feast inside the adobe walls, "in destitute circumstances, . . . [but] remarkably peaceful and well disposed."

147

They listened to the usual complaints of neglect of the Stevens treaty, and then suggested that the Flatheads move to the Jocko. In response, old Ambrose said, "We hear a great road for the whites is to be built through the Jocko. If so, it would be no place for us. The Bitterroot is our old home. Here are the graves of our fathers, our own and our children's birthplace, and we wish to die and be buried here." The Flatheads agreed they would accept the Pend Oreilles and Kutenais in the Bitterroot, but they would not move. Wrinkled and bent, Adolph added:

> The grist mill and the saw mill are far away. We never see them. Young men are sometimes bad and we are afraid to live among the whites lest we have trouble with them. We want to know if our Great Father allows the whites to settle on our lands. Some of them threaten to shoot us.

Then Adolph gave a moving example of the deterioration of his people in the thirteen years since they had signed the treaty with Stevens. He held up his gnarled fingers and declared, "My hands—look at them. They are my tools and I scratch the ground with my nails." Touched, Cullen reported, "Upon inquiry we learned that the old man had planted a considerable crop this year, literally scratching it with his nails."

▲▲▲▲▲▲▲▲▲▲▲▲▲▲▲▲▲▲▲▲▲▲▲▲▲▲▲▲▲

CHAPTER 6

THE PEACE POLICY
AND THE GARFIELD CONTRACT

▼▼▼▼▼▼▼▼▼▼▼▼▼▼▼▼▼▼▼▼▼▼▼▼▼▼▼▼▼

WILLIAM CULLEN failed to relocate the Flatheads. He left them, indeed, believing they might yet negotiate for the southern half of the Bitterroot Valley as their own reservation. He promised they would hear some sure word of this possibility within two months, but he never wrote them. Cullen's congressional supporters, meanwhile, failed him, for on evidence that he betrayed Indians entrusted to his counsel he was twice rejected for appointment as the administrator of a proposed joint superintendency for Montana and Idaho. A few months after Cullen's council with the Flatheads, inauguration of Ulysses S. Grant as president introduced a profound change in Indian administration.

The nation's conduct of its Indian affairs had not altered significantly since passage of the Indian Intercourse Act of 1834 and transfer of the Indian bureau from War to the new Interior Department in 1849. Congress regarded the continuing Indian warfare as the consequence of inept handling of the savages. Grant openly considered the Indian service corrupt.

To repair its relations with Indians and to recommend means for harmonious expansion of westward settlement, Congress in 1867 voted an Indian Peace Commission. The commission in January, 1868, recommended that territorial governors no longer serve as ex-officio Indian superintendents, that the army evict trespassers on Indian lands, and that men in the Indian service be more carefully selected. One immediate result was designation of the army to supervise distribution of annuity goods, which also helped employ the surplus of officers following the Civil War.

The president started his own reforms. He permitted the Society of Friends to nominate agents for the Northern and Central superintendencies, and assigned surplus army officers to Indian administration. To Montana he sent Brevet General Alfred M. Sully as superintendent. Sully, who served on the Indian frontier during the Civil War and in eight years rose from captain to general, was said to have defeated the Sioux in 1863 at White Stone Hill, but his other encounters with Indians had been irresolute; he had lost to George Custer in regimental competition for rank; his punitive expedition against the Sioux impressed Father De Smet as glory seeking; and he was an advocate of mission societies as agencies for civilizing the savages. He assumed his duties as superintendent in Montana on July 27, 1869, and in military fashion ordered reservation agents to communicate with Washington through channels— his office.

Two days later, Major Alvan S. Galbreath, twice cited for gallantry as a Union captain, succeeded McCauley as Flathead agent. Galbreath had been at his post three days when an Indian boy cooking fish ignited a grass fire that destroyed the agency's grist- and sawmills. Many Indians and whites assumed the fire was set deliberately to protest "the late changes in the policy of the government in the assignment of army officers to duty in the Indian department," Galbreath reported.[1]

Sully's first reports made familiar reading at Washington: the Bannocks were starving, too poor in horses to hunt, eating gophers to survive; the western Indians going to buffalo stole horses and drank whiskey and "ought to be kept out of the territory, even by force if necessary"; the Flathead agency was "in a very bad condition, taking into consideration the length of time it has been established. . . . I have never seen any agency that shows so little done for it." The agency raised no crop of account, and the property McCauley left amounted to three worthless horses, six old oxen, forty swine, three broken wagons, four worn plows, and incomplete sets of tools. Unlike earlier visitors, Sully was not impressed with the progress of the Pend Oreilles as farmers.[2]

The Flatheads soon met the new superintendent, for the commissioner of Indian affairs directed General Sully to seek a new treaty with them that would put them out of the Bitterroot. In his council with the Flathead chiefs on October 7, 1869, Sully could not persuade the Indians to leave their homeland. They had concluded their only course lay in resistance. The general wrote an agreement with them which, instead, reserved the southern portion of the Bitterroot above Lolo Creek to the Flatheads, allowing the thirty or so white families already there to remain and others to enter the area with the tribe's consent. The Flatheads ceded the remainder of the valley.

In a curious eighth article, Sully's draft treaty provided that "nothing is to conflict with first rights of Major John Owen to his lands." This stipulation Sully credited to Owen's standing with the Flatheads. He reported:

> I offered them every inducement I could to give up all the valley except a sufficient portion for their use to farm, but they would not listen to my proposition. I am satisfied that there is some influence brought to bear to induce these Indians to act as they do. What my ideas are at this point, I cannot report officially for it is only what I think, not what I know.[3]

The influence doubtless was Owen, now virtually penniless and reduced to periods of alcoholic irrationality. (The Ohio congressman, James A. Garfield, would soon call him "a bankrupt and a sot." In 1871 Owen would sell Fort Owen to Washington McCormick to raise money and, a short time later, be judged insane.)

Owen recently had written the commissioner to plead for justice for the Flatheads. "At the instigation of Victor, head chief of the Flathead nation, I pen the following lines in behalf of these poor and justly deserving people," he said. "Scarcely a day passes without some of them visiting me to know what their great American Father has done regarding the lands of this valley." McCauley, "a blind, unsocial Irishman . . . [with] nothing in common with the Indians," had never spoken to Victor. Owen enclosed a letter from

Victor to President Grant, reviewing the Flatheads' amicable history, Stevens' promises, and closing:

> The country being filled up with white men have driven the buffalo off. They are not close or plenty as they were before the white man came among us to hunt for gold which they seem to love so much. We must farm or starve. May my words reach your heart. Simolson [Owen] tells us you are a great soldier. This makes our hearts feel good. Please hear us and help us.[4]

Superintendent Sully recommended that nothing be done to put his draft treaty into effect until he talked with the Pend Oreilles and Kutenais, then at buffalo, and he emphasized that Montana's leading men would not condone force against the Flatheads. "Persons holding high position in this territory express their opinion that every Indian should be allowed a farm for each family and then left to take care of themselves," he commented. "On account of this sentiment, and from other conflicting interests, I met with little or no success in my treaty operations." He did not commend his treaty, fearing "the Indians and whites living together on the [Bitterroot] reservation will be a constant source of difficulties, but it was the only treaty I could make, and the best terms I could get."[5]

Although the Sully treaty was never ratified, by consenting to locate the Flatheads permanently on reserved land in the Bitterroot Valley, Sully angered Montana's land-hungry immigrants. The *Helena Daily Herald* headlined an article, "Odious Treaty with the Flatheads," and called the Bitterroot Indians "vagabond relics of various northwestern tribes," declaring that Owen, "a certain patriotic (?) hermit," promoted the compact "in the hope of selling his fortified surroundings as suitable headquarters." The *Herald* asked citizens to "ask the Secretary of War and the Senate not to approve this treaty." The *New North-West* characterized the Bitterroot Indians as "a band of mongrels numbering bucks, squaws, papooses, and dogs only 300 or 400, not twenty of whom are Flatheads."[6]

Name calling introduced a new phase in the campaign for the Flatheads' land and soon was adopted by Montana's leading politicians. A petition signed at mass meetings to oppose the treaty was delivered by Montana's territorial delegate, James Cavanaugh, to President Grant requesting consideration.

Whites also vilified the Pend Oreilles and Kutenais. The grand jury at Helena asserted, "Their passage through our settled valleys should be prohibited," advancing the classic settlers' apology:

> Ours is a contest between civilization and barbarism, and we must risk our lives and sacrifice our hard earned property to defend them, unless the general government give us the means of defense. To this we are entitled, and we have left homes of comfort in the East to plant civilization in the wilderness.[7]

During the winter buffalo hunt of 1869–70, the Flatheads mingled with Gros Ventres, infected by smallpox. Fears of a new general epidemic spread. Flatheads and Pend Oreilles also joined Crows for the hunt, and advised the Crows sternly "not to receive anything from the whites," because the whites would then claim the Indians had sold their land. When Sully delivered the Crows their annuities, he found a few Flatheads among them, and had difficulty persuading the Crows to accept their goods.

The hunt failed. Reservation Indians took few buffalo and returned to the Jocko with little meat. Old women and children who stayed at home found little to snare or dig. Agent Galbreath loaned the men guns and ammunition to hunt on the reserve. "They come to me almost daily for assistance," Galbreath told Sully, adding that whites protested of Indians "who continually annoyed them by begging, and . . . if sent away without having their wants satisfied, they drive away stock and commit other depredations."[8] Faced with famine, the Flatheads and Pend Oreilles returned to the buffalo grounds with ammunition supplied by the agent.

The desperate hunt in early 1870 thrust the Flatheads again onto prairies befouled by smallpox and war. Gros Ventres continued to die; many committed suicide when they contracted the pox. War parties of Sioux stole horses. Two months earlier, the Flatheads had united with Crows; now they fought them. Flatheads and Pend Oreilles near the Judith killed the River Crow chieftain, Whitehead, captured five women, and frightened the Crows back to their

153

reservation, but, when Pend Oreilles tried to steal their horses, the Crows killed seven. Slowly convalescing, Gros Ventres attacked Crows while federal cavalry scattered marauding Blackfeet, who fled to the Belly River in Canada to regroup.

Withdrawing to the Jocko and the Bitterroot, some Pend Oreilles and Flatheads "planted their little crops" and, hearing rumors of buffalo in the Sweet Grass hills to their north, prepared to hunt there. Galbreath encouraged them:

> It is better they should go north to hunt than to the Musselshell, for although by so doing they run a chance of falling in with their enemies, the Piegans . . . yet they will avoid a greater danger in a possibility of a conflict with the whites on account of their love of whiskey and the cupidity of some of the settlers, for they cannot reach the buffalo country east of them without passing through settlements.[9]

As they moved north, Flatheads pillaged supplies in the goldfields on Cedar Creek, peopled in 1869 by prospectors who erected clapboard and tent towns. For a few months one of these was the largest settlement in western Montana. The Indians met a few discouraged prospectors squatting on reservation land.

Of the Flatheads, Galbreath said:

> It becomes more necessary every day that the Bitterroot question should be settled. . . . Much trouble is caused by the Indians getting whiskey. Many complaints were made by the whites that the Indians were throwing down their fences and turning Indian stock into the fields. Indians claim stock in possession of whites, and whites claim stock in possession of Indians. It is almost impossible for us to settle their questions when we go there, for the person in possession of stock claimed by others absents himself while I am in the valley.[10]

During the spring hunt, Victor, aging chief of the Flatheads, died in Crow country. His death encouraged some citizens to think that the strongest resistance to removal had passed. Putting whites out of the Bitterroot, as Sully remarked, was not "politic," for settlers now outnumbered Flatheads. New immigration, stimulated by dislocation from the Civil War, gold, and the promotional efforts of James M. Ashley, who succeeded Smith as governor, flowed into western Montana. Father De Smet wrote D'Aste from Washington that "it was the intent of the government to remove the Flathead Indians from the Bitterroot valley—*volens vel nolens.*"[11]

Probably western Montanans were willing to let the Flatheads stay in the Bitterroot as individual farmers if the Indians gave up their tribal lands. Although he earlier had discounted their work as farmers, Sully now commented that some Flathead farmers

are considered the best in the western slopes of Montana. The Pend Oreilles and Kutenais are by no means so far advanced. A large portion of these people, particularly of the latter tribe, prefer an idle, drunken life. But I think if the government would offer some inducement for them to settle, in a few years they would do as well as the Flathead farmers, and become useful citizens instead of beggars and vagabonds, almost in a starving condition half the time.[12]

To sustain the reservation Indians, the agent issued each head of a family two pecks of potatoes a week.

Galbreath augmented the funds available to his agency by reporting fictitious employees. When he was succeeded in mid-1870 by First Lieutenant George E. Ford, transferred from New Mexico, this fraud continued. The decision of Congress in 1870 to prohibit military officers from holding civil offices deposed Sully and Ford. They were replaced in the autumn by civilians.

The new territorial superintendent and Flathead agent were products of President Grant's "peace policy," his loosely contrived compromise with a handful of Protestant denominations allowing them a voice in Indian administration. A committee of Protestant philanthropists, the Board of Indian Commissioners, recommended policies to the Indian office and heard appeals from the field in matters of finance and supply. They also forwarded the churches' nominations for superintendents and agents to the president for his recommendations to the Senate.

When Indian reservations were parceled among denominations, Montana fell to the Methodists, save the Flathead reservation, given to the Catholics in view of the long tenure there of the Society of Jesus.[13] In these assignments, remarked Father De Smet, "the Indians have not been consulted as to the religion they desired to belong to." The new Montana superintendent, probably advanced

155

by Judge Hiram Knowles, was Jasper A. Viall, a native of Vermont who had recently been on the staff of the governor of Iowa. Viall quickly saw that, with a million dollars a year in Indian funds passing through his hands, he had stumbled into a fortune.

The Flathead agent, a Catholic from Washington, D.C., Charles S. Jones, called "a defaulting paymaster of the United States" by a territorial newspaper, installed G. D. C. Hibbs as clerk of the agency, replacing the Mason who had been Wells's nemesis, Judge Pomeroy.

Out of concern for Catholic Indians, a group of priests that included J. B. A. Brouillett, Toussaint Mesplie, and Leopold Van Gorp, persuaded the archbishop of Baltimore to appoint Charles Ewing as civil agent for the church in the capital in 1873, and the following year to name Ewing the Catholic commissioner for Indian affairs to deal directly with the Indian office and the Board of Indian Commissioners.

Viall imposed his direct administrative control on the reservation agents in Montana. Jones resisted and, within six weeks of his arrival on the Jocko, appealed to the commissioner of Indian affairs to resolve "a difference of opinion so wide and fundamental between myself and the superintendent of Indian affairs for this territory regarding our respective official rights, duties, and privileges" that the two could not agree on how to spend Flathead funds.[14]

Evidently neither Viall nor Jones knew at first that the federal government firmly intended to move the Flatheads from the Bitterroot, but Viall soon sensed the mood of settlers, observing to the commissioner, "It looks as if the white settlers have more interest in the removal of those Indians than the government has." He had not then (in December, 1870) seen the Bitterroot or the Jocko, "nor am I advised as to whether it is the policy of the department to influence the removal of the Flatheads."[15]

Viall also discovered the flourishing whiskey trade among Indians, employing a detective, Charles B. Hard, to identify traders who peddled whiskey for robes and furs in violation of their licenses. Jones and Viall, meanwhile, bickered over an agency physician, Viall forcing dismissal of a Catholic and appointment of Dr. J. H. McKee, an organizer and superintendent of Missoula's Union Sunday School and Bible Class, and a Republican. When the Catholic Flatheads learned the physician's religious affiliation, said Jones, they would not patronize him.

Indians long before had learned to discern the relative authority of white men. The Flatheads knew that their agent was being subverted by Viall's refusal to honor invoices, contravened in his directives, and attacked personally. Viall exploited the superintendency for himself and the agents who connived with him. When Jones appealed to Cavanaugh, the territorial delegate sent the commissioner a blistering protest: "Viall's integrity in the administration of his official duties does not stand unimpeached in the files of your department." He called the superintendent "a stranger appointed by the federal government through political influence to a lucrative office, who is seemingly responsible to nobody but favorites of the department." But Cavanaugh himself was at odds with the new governor, the ample Benjamin F. Potts, and Viall and Potts were overt supporters of William H. Clagett's campaign for Congress. Detective Hard and Indian agents F. D. Pease and A. J. Simmons contributed funds to Clagett's campaign.[16]

Cavanaugh attacked Viall in other letters to the commissioner, alleging, in one, the operation of an "Indian ring" centered around the superintendent to steal goods and money provided for Indians, while the *Montana Pioneer* portrayed Viall as manipulating his agents and post traders like puppets. No doubt the Indian office, subject to many pressures, regarded this as the angry airing of territorial politics—and stayed aloof. The federal agency's chief interest at the moment in Montana was to move the Flatheads.

Jones did not oppose removal. Once aware of the federal plan, he proposed that the Flatheads be moved from the Bitterroot to a new agency near St. Ignatius, offering the specious argument that the Flatheads resisted removal because the agency was too far from the mission. Near St. Ignatius, approximately eight hundred Pend Oreilles lived in log houses. On a personal inspection of the suggested new agency site, Governor Potts remarked that at the mission the nuns taught six white and nineteen Indian children in their school, and the Pend Oreilles now responded in Latin at mass.

At his first council with the Flatheads, Jones discovered that the late Victor's advisers had advanced themselves. The war chief, Arlee, acted as spokesman while Charlot (Little Claw of a Grizzly Bear), Victor's son and successor as head chief, said little. Jones's suggestion that the Flatheads move to the Jocko "caused quite an emotion . . . after a short silence," and the agent thereupon proposed instead that the Indians become United States citizens to acquire their present land under the Homestead Act, which "produced a very favorable impression."[17]

Not long after this meeting, Arlee and Joseph (Nine Pipes), two Flathead headmen, visited Jones at the agency, remaining three days, and discussing "the harrassments to which they were subject in their present homes" in the Bitterroot Valley. Arlee admitted that moving to the Jocko might be best, saying, "We would like to see the head chief in Washington [the commissioner] in order to talk over all the matters connected with our removal and to make arrangements for it."[18] Reporting this conversation, Jones predicted removal would be costly because, of ninety heads of families, forty-four were now prosperous farmers, some raising six hundred bushels of wheat annually.

Despite Arlee's consent to move, the Flatheads remained divided. Charlot, like his late father, resolved to stay in the Bitterroot. Jones misread the new chief's determination as weakness and failed to understand that Charlot's policy was to resist without forcing a confrontation. Jones advised Washington:

> They had selected Charlot to succeed Victor, but as he was weak and sickly, they had agreed among themselves on some young braves, ten in number, to act as police to aid Charlot in keeping law and order and making their people behave.[19]

When the Flatheads rode to buffalo on the Musselshell a few weeks after their council with Jones, Viall sent a detective, George Seaton, onto the plains to spy out whiskey traders and try to prevent collisions between tribes, although the two hundred lodges of

Blackfeet on the Sun River concluded a truce with the Flatheads, Pend Oreilles, and Kutenais allowing their unmolested passage. Settlers sometimes preferred Indian hostilities to truces because, as the *Missoula and Cedar Creek Pioneer* said, the peace

will result in opening a war-path for about 400 thieving [Canadian] Kootenays now infesting the valleys of the Jocko and Flathead [rivers]. The Blackfeet have hitherto shielded us from the ravages of renegade Indian thieves but this latest alliance increases the danger of losing stock all along the western slope.[20]

On one occasion during the hunt, Seaton arranged a council between Flatheads and Nez Percés to exchange horses stolen from each other. The Sioux mistakenly killed eighteen Flatheads in an ambush set for other horse thieves. The Flatheads killed three Sioux, then limped home to their valley (damaged by crickets and drought) to hold mourning feasts at St. Ignatius and at Burnt Fork Creek in the Bitterroot. Buffaloes and cows were barbecued. As in old times, the chiefs again gathered the property of the dead, paid the debts of each man, and led brief prayers. Wailing from the Flathead camp was "almost continual" for days, observed the *Pioneer*.

Circumscribed on the plains and in their homes, the Flatheads framed a petition to President Grant, translated for them by Father D'Aste, calling attention to "the importance and necessity of some final and definite action in regard to our future continuance and residence in the Bitterroot valley." Notwithstanding the guarantees of 1855, the valley was overrun with settlers "who impose on us in many ways. . . . We are, in violation of treaty obligations, as we conceive, encompassed on all sides by white settlers, even to the extent of villages in the midst of our settlement, and the result of the contact and association are drunkenness of our young men, to whom the whites will sell whiskey, as well as the demoralization of our women." The Flatheads asked to come to see the president, saying, "None of our tribe, living or dead, have ever been to see you but we hear of chiefs of other tribes who are always making war on you being allowed that privilege." Seven chieftains signed, including Charlot, Arlee, and Adolph.[21] No invitation came in answer to their appeal.

During May, 1871, Viall secured the first convictions of white men in Montana for selling liquor to Indians (near Missoula), one of them being found guilty by a white jury on the testimony of an Indian witness.[22] Above Fort Benton, whiskey traders retreated to Whoop-up, a settlement north of the British line, to continue operations.

Upon Clagett's election to Congress, he, Potts, and Viall visited the Jocko to choose locations for sawmill and gristmill to replace those burned in 1869. They awarded a construction contract to Horace Countryman, one of Clagett's cronies and father-in-law of Frank Woody, an influential Missoula attorney and politician, brushing aside Jones's protests. Next the three men went to the Bitterroot Valley, where they peremptorily ordered the Flatheads to move.

In Viall's letters to the commissioner, and in Clagett's, the Flatheads of the Bitterroot now became "remnants," while Potts wrote the commissioner that "the Flathead tribe proper is almost extinct; the number of the tribe, and those connected with it, heretofore reported to the department is largely in excess of the actual number." He estimated their total at no more than one hundred and fifty. Clagett privately assured residents that no part of the Bitterroot would be set aside as tribal lands. The surveyor general of Montana, John Blaine, joined Viall in declaring, "There are but three good Indian farms in the valley, and the settlers are willing to let these [Indians] remain, with such other Indians as could be persuaded to take possession of their farms."[23]

Calling the Flatheads remnants owning but three good farms were falsehoods intended to convince the Interior Department that it should act promptly to clear the way for settlers to patent their lands. Jones's census in 1871 counted 446 Bitterroot Indians, including 217 full-blooded Flatheads. St. Mary's records showed 522 Flatheads in the Bitterroot in 1866 and 548 in 1871.

Jones, as a Catholic and Democrat in a Methodist state ruled by Republicans, accomplished nothing for the confederated Flatheads, and early in 1871 Secretary of the Interior Delano let it be known that advancement of the Republican party outweighed religious affiliations in the Indian service. Father De Smet observed that agents nominated by denominations must favor re-election of the president if they hoped for Senate confirmation.

While Viall was out of the territory, Jones wrote a "painfull but imperative" accusation that the superintendent tried "to obtain unlimited control of the management and detailed control of this agency, to his own personal aggrandizement." Countryman's crews "commenced using the public stable for libidinous purposes" with Indian women, laughing that the contractor was a greater chief than the agent. Viall, said Jones, "endeavored to embarrass me in every way, . . . so as to obtain unqualified control over the agency as he has over those of the Crows, Blackfeet, and perhaps others."[24]

Meanwhile, Governor Potts asked the president to order a survey in compliance with the Stevens treaty and then remove the Flatheads from the Bitterroot. Grant issued his executive order on November 14, 1871, for relocation of the Flatheads on the Jocko reservation. The following May 16, Congress appropriated five thousand dollars to pay the costs of removal, and on June 5 voted fifty thousand dollars to compensate Indians for farms and improvements in the valley. The act of June also ordered a survey of the Bitterroot above the Lolo's mouth and provided that any Indian head of a family who renounced his tribal relations, so notifying the department before January 1, 1873, might select one hundred and sixty acres to be patented in his name. The *Weekly Missoulian* expressed editorial doubt that more than fifteen Indians were farming.

Ten days after passage of the June act, Secretary Delano appointed the Republican congressman from Ohio, James A. Garfield, a special commissioner to carry out its provisions. Garfield, established as one of the party's leaders in Congress, was thus absent from Washington during much of the inquiry into the promotion of Credit Mobilier stock which, despite his denials of cupidity, could have embarrassed him politically.

To comply with the act's stipulation that the Flatheads be notified of removal one month in advance, Viall advised the tribe formally on June 28 of the government's intent. No Indian commotion occurred. Arlee said that many of the Flatheads had decided to leave the valley before Grant's order was promulgated.

As commissioner to the Flatheads, Garfield represented the United States in a new capacity, empowered to negotiate a contract rather than a treaty. Washington had belatedly decided that Indians were not sovereign nations but, in fact, wards of the United States government. The congressman spent several weeks at his home in Hiram, Ohio, reading letters and documents that Delano sent him about the Flatheads, and perusing Lewis and Clark's published journals, and on the last day of July set out leisurely for Montana. H. L. Dawes, appointed by the department, could not go with him, and Garfield was pleased to have instead his old friend Major David G. Swaim.

Garfield and Swaim went by rail to Salt Lake City, savoring Republican hospitality en route, and by stagecoach to Montana. Garfield found the outdoors exhilarating; he rode beside the driver part of the way. At Gaffney's Station, where the road forked to Virginia City and Helena, Potts met Garfield to escort him to the capital, which had been located since 1865 at Virginia City. There Garfield was told that citizens of the Bitterroot feared an alliance of the Flatheads with the Nez Percés and Spokanes to resist removal.

A few days before Garfield's arrival, Potts had received a petition for one or two companies of federal cavalry to be stationed in Missoula, because "removal will result in an Indian outbreak unless prevented by the presence of U.S. troops." The petition also asked stringent measures to stop whiskey sales to Indians. It had been framed by one hundred and twenty men including F. L. Worden, Pomeroy, and McCormick.

The Flatheads had allied with the Nez Percés, as a matter of fact, but only to hunt during the winter of 1871–72, and together they lost approximately half their horses to severe weather and raiding parties. As the Nez Percés lingered unhappily in the Bitterroot after the hunt, the alarmed citizens of Missoula, Aetna, and Corvallis organized home guards and requested guns from Potts.

Of the whites' apprehensions, Garfield said:

It appears that some citizens of Missoula have for some time been selling whiskey to Indians in violation of the law, and that this has had much to do with the state of affairs among them. The same meeting of citizens at Missoula that asked for arms also asked for a force of three deputy marshals to aid in enforcing the laws against selling liquor to Indians.

Garfield saw "mercenary purposes" in the request for cavalry, and asked Potts to accompany him to Missoula.

"It soon became apparent that the chief anxiety of the settlers of the valley was to secure the establishment of a military post, and that the market which would thus be afforded for their home products, was really a matter of greater consideration than protection against hostile Indians," Garfield advised the commissioner.[25] The *Montana Post*, meanwhile, demanded editorially that the Flathead "menace" be driven from the Bitterroot.

On August 22, the Bitterroot Flathead chiefs met the Garfield party near St. Mary's Mission, where three elk- and buffalo-skin tents had been connected to protect conferees from the hot sun. Garfield's was the most prestigious delegation to the Flatheads since Stevens' visit, numbering such influential Montana men as Wilbur F. Sanders, Potts, Viall, and Clagett. Although intrigued by the "Indian mode of thought," Garfield found the council "somewhat tiresome," while the other white men were bored by hearing again the Flatheads' familiar protests and by their knowledge that, no matter what the Indians said, the decision for removal would stand.

After Garfield's opening statement, Charlot shook hands, said that Stevens promised the Flatheads they could stay in the Bitterroot, and as evidence showed Garfield the copy of the Stevens treaty his father had given him. Arlee, in his turn, declared that Stevens "promised that the Flatheads should be taught for twenty years how to read and write, and then they would be like the white men, and know how to do everything—but nothing had been done." Garfield felt this first day nearly aborted his mission, "for all the [Flathead] speakers concluded by the declaration that they claimed the Bitterroot valley as their home, and were wholly unwilling to leave it."[26]

He asked the chiefs flatly if they intended to disobey Grant's order for removal, and invited them to inspect the Jocko with him. He wrote in his diary that he almost failed, and wrote to the commissioner, of the survey promised, "that for seventeen years no steps have been taken in regard to it and they considered the silence of the government, on this subject, an admission that the valley was to be their permanent home." Doubtless Garfield had been encouraged by Potts, Viall, and the commissioner to believe the Flatheads ready for submissive removal.

During the evening, the Flathead chieftains conferred with Father Ravalli and the next morning agreed to look over the Jocko with the understanding that this would not imply their consent to move there. Garfield spent his evening in the Nez Percés' camp near Missoula watching a war dance and talking with Looking Glass and Eagle-against-the-Light, two chiefs. He found "no evidence that they had taken any part in the affairs of the Flatheads, except, that, being on their way to their annual buffalo hunt on the headwaters of the Missouri, they had invited the Flatheads to join them."[27]

The Flatheads and the Garfield party reached the Jocko on Saturday, August 24, witnessed a long victory dance, heard recitations of past conquests by reservation Indians, and on Sunday morning renewed their council. Garfield learned that the Bitterroot chiefs "had at last become divided in opinion among themselves on the question of the removal," and that Arlee and Adolph were willing, but Charlot was not.

Garfield, Viall, and Clagett drew a contract, had it translated for the Flatheads, and Arlee and Adolph signed with their marks. Charlot declined. Garfield concluded that Charlot wanted to talk further with his headmen at home. Arlee and Adolph mistakenly predicted, and the whites agreed, that "if preparations [were] made according to the contract, Charlot would finally consent to the arrangement, and go with the tribe." Therefore Garfield, putting his understanding in writing for the territorial superintendent, said, "In carrying out the terms of the contract made with the chiefs of the Flatheads . . . I have concluded after full consultation with you to proceed with the work in the same manner as though

Charlot, the first chief, had signed the contract."[28] When the contract was printed in the commissioner's annual report, Charlot's mark appeared as if he had signed the original document.

The Garfield contract permitted the Flatheads to claim any unoccupied lands on the reservation, where the government would fence fields and build them frame houses, twelve by sixteen feet, tightly battened, with eight-foot ceilings, dirt as insulation between inner and outer walls, and roofs of good pine shingles. Each would have a chimney, one window, and one door, excepting the chiefs' houses, which would consist of two connecting dwellings. Because the Flatheads would also be paid for their Bitterroot farms, Garfield advised the Flatheads to scatter and locate ranches in the valley that they could sell later.

With the contract concluded, Garfield retired to Missoula, where two hundred dollars' worth of gifts were distributed among the chiefs. (In honor of his accomplishment, Bitterroot citizens named a town Garfield, but the railroad later changed it to Victor.) In his report of his mission, Garfield described the deplorable state of the Jocko agency and urged the government to prosecute his contract with the Indians fully and promptly. He quoted a letter from William Welsh, the Philadelphian who served as first chairman of the Board of Indian Commissioners, who had written John Owen, "If the Indians cannot get their rights any other way, they are justified in combining for defense against coercion." Garfield believed this letter "had some effects in making the Indians again dissatisfied and unwilling to go to their reservation."[29]

Father Palladino wrote Garfield at his Ohio home, objecting that the land for the Flatheads "is the poorest location . . . that could be found within the limits of the Jocko reservation," rocky and barren, and quoted the Indians as feeling, "The Great Chief has no heart for the Indians, since he intends to make them settle down on rocks." Moreover, the Flathead site was so far from St. Ignatius that the priests, who did not oppose removal, "could not approve it, however, under those circumstances." Garfield replied politely that the Flatheads chose the place themselves, and appended the letter and his answer to his report.[30]

When Garfield's report appeared in print, Charlot believed his mark had been maliciously forged on the contract. This apparent fraud further embittered the Flathead chieftain against the white man who had taken his country and imposed an alien life upon him and his people.

CHAPTER 7

▲▲▲▲▲▲▲▲▲▲▲▲▲▲▲▲▲▲▲▲▲▲▲▲▲▲▲▲▲▲

THE LAST DAYS OF THE BUFFALO

▼▼▼▼▼▼▼▼▼▼▼▼▼▼▼▼▼▼▼▼▼▼▼▼▼▼▼▼

BY 1870 A TERRIFYING SUSPICION could be denied no longer: the buffalo were disappearing! With them went the base of Flathead ritual and economy. No doubt remained that the shaggy herds were going. News of a large herd now set off a heedless chase. The Indians and most whites failed to comprehend extermination as it occurred. Later, they felt that the buffalo had been wiped out suddenly; they blamed some single cataclysmic stroke, fixing on the massive slaughters for robes and sport that, in a few years between 1875 and 1882, would bring decimation of the herds of the Upper Missouri to its climax.

Nevertheless, the Flatheads continued to hunt buffalo throughout the period 1870–82. "They hear of buffalo *near*, i.e., 300 or 400 miles northeast, and are bound to go for meat," General William T. Sherman would say in 1878.[1] This period, culminating more than a century of systematic bison slaughter, also witnessed the last convulsive intertribal warfare on the Musselshell, the Judith, and the Yellowstone.

What killed the buffalo in large part was destruction of the range that supported it. William T. Hornaday, in 1887 investigating the extermination for the Smithsonian Institution, concluded, "The primary cause ... and the one which embraced all others, was the descent of civilization, with all its elements of destructiveness, upon the whole of the country inhabited by that animal."[2] But before whites came, Indians with horses had gradually expanded their destruction among the herds.

White men also relied on buffalo, as in 1862 when settlers joined Indian hunters to live through the winter on meat and in the spring to trade hides for seeds to resume farming, because crickets had ravaged the crops of western Montana. Until approximately 1875, however, Indians killed perhaps three times as many buffalo each year as white hunters. Robe sales averaging twenty-six thousand annually between 1815 and 1830 rose to seventy thousand a year between 1845 and 1853, mostly gathered by Indians. The principal Missouri River collection point, Fort Benton, shipped approximately twenty thousand robes each year from 1841 to 1861, and only a slightly diminished volume from the end of the Civil War through 1882.

Father De Smet estimated that Indians killed one hundred thousand bison each year for their own use. (Isaac Stevens guessed the Blackfeet alone used one hundred and fifty thousand.) The Indians favored the fattest cows. As early as 1844 De Smet wrote, "Buffalo and beaver are becoming more scarce every year and will soon fail them [the Flatheads] altogether. We hope the providence of God will come to their relief." By the outbreak of the Civil War, the Flatheads had to range a little farther each year to find bison.

The buffalo-robe trade and technological changes brought by whites altered the Flatheads' (and other Indians') utilization of buffalo. Flatheads now required less from each animal: the robe for use or trade, sinew, the tongue and other delectable meats, and perhaps ornaments or trophies. Less palatable and unsalable parts rotted on the prairies. The *Weekly Missoulian* remarked in 1875 on five Flatheads who killed one hundred and four fat cows and bulls and took only the hides, tongues, borses, sinews, and hump meat. Such a fortunate hunt as that of 1875, following a bountiful hunt in 1874, helped persuade the Indians temporarily that the buffalo really were not gone, while incessant warfare prevented an analysis that would have revealed the true shrinkage of the herds. As the Indians perceived no pattern to herd movement, they were easily convinced that the herds were simply somewhere else—for a time.

Two special investigators, Lieutenant Gustavus A. Doane and F. D. Pease, in 1873 described the Judith buffalo range in detail, estimating the northern herd now at not more than four million. They predicted, "In five years more, they [the buffalo] will probably cease to be the dependence of the Indians for food."[3] The Judith was a favorite Flathead hunting area. The Crows objected, meanwhile, that friendly tribes regularly violated their reservation boundaries to hunt, naming the Flatheads, Nez Percés, Bannocks, and Snakes, and complained that these Indians refused to join the common campaign against the Sioux.

Of the Judith, Doane and Pease reported, "It has not been the residing place for Indians for many years but has been held as a common hunting ground for all neighboring tribes, being frequented by parties of Sioux, Rees, Santees, Mandans, Assiniboins, Gros Ventres, Piegans, Pend Oreilles, Flatheads, Mountain and River Crows, Bannocks, Snakes, and Nez Perces for the purposes of hunting and war." On the upper Musselshell the two men saw "the bend of the river . . . alive with buffalo, and large parties of Indians . . . there among them making a great slaughter."

Doane and Pease argued that the Indian mode of hunting was exterminating the buffalo: "The truth of the matter is that the Indians kill off the cows only for robes," and the resulting disproportion of five bulls to each cow "at once tells the story of who kills the buffalo, it being well known that white hunters shoot cows, bulls, and calves indiscriminately." Doane said he believed the Indians shipped forty-five thousand dressed robes through Fort Benton in 1873. "Often the cows are killed, about one in three makes a robe, the others are rejected . . . and left to rot without being skinned. Thus 45,000 dressed robes represents 135,000 buffalo found dead." He added, "The Indians, finding great competition among the traders, conceive therefrom an exaggerated idea of their own importance. . . . They . . . actually believe that the buffalo robe is 'king' . . . and will grant them immunity from any depredations if they will only afterward consent to trade."

With Sioux and northern Crees pressing southward in pursuit of

buffalo, and the range constricting, bloody clashes changed intertribal relationships rapidly. When the Pend Oreilles returned from
their 1872–73 hunt with horses taken from their friends, the Crows,
Chief Michel declined to give them back: "We will not give up
any horses to the Crows. The Crows are sorry because we steal
their horses; we are sorry because they kill our people. . . . Last fall
a year ago the Crows stole thirty-one horses and a jackass from
my people while hunting on the Little Blackfoot."[4] The Crows also
accused the Bitterroot Flatheads of stealing their horses. The Flatheads' war chief, Arlee, complained that the Crows and Blackfeet
owned better guns than his people, and he refused to meet the
Crows again to make peace, saying he had tried too often. A camp
of Flatheads, Nez Percés, and Pend Oreilles near Missoula said
they intended to demand that the federal government give them
guns as good as those of Plains tribes.

The competition and danger on the hunting grounds convinced
the Flatheads to go in strength in 1873–74, in company with renegade Modocs, Yakimas, Utes, and others as well as the Nez Percés.
Nonetheless, when two Flatheads were killed by River Crows, the
Flatheads retreated from the Judith Basin to the Little Belt Mountains. The buffalo hunt was successful, but the Flatheads lost many
horses to Crow raiders. The Crow agent protested officially to the
Indian commissioner that Flatheads and other Indians roamed at
will through Montana, and demanded that they be kept at home.

Major N. W. Sweitzer, commanding Fort Ellis, reported the
Crows

at war with Sioux, Blackfeet, and Pend Oreilles, and at present with
the Flatheads. They hunt with the Snakes, Bannocks, and Nez Perces,
and until this summer with the Flatheads. These Indians only hunt
buffalo as a rule for the peltries. . . . Last year they sold 4,000 robes to
Crow traders; this is about the annual sale.[5]

Sweitzer also estimated Crow strength at seven hundred and
fifty warriors, well equipped with Spencer and Henry rifles. Appraisals of Indian fighting power reflected the settlers' abiding fear
of a united Indian uprising—apprehension with substance, for
during 1874 the Sioux convened a council of buffalo-hunting tribes

on the lower Yellowstone to advocate a consolidated front against the whites. Most of the tribes voted for war, but the Flatheads and Nez Percés demurred, saying the fighting was too far from their countries and they did not wish to join their enemies, the Sioux. Yet the Nez Percés, restless following the Modoc war in Oregon, refused to go to their reservation, and their agitation affected the Flatheads.

Tribal dislocation, crowding in the hunts, and frustration among the Indians—the psychological ravishing of Indian cultures—impressed white men as primarily opposition to migration. This notion seemed to be confirmed by Sioux attacks on wagon trains crossing the Bozeman and other Montana trails, killing of gold hunters in the Black Hills, and protests against violation of the Sioux treaty of 1868.

A gold rush to the Kootenay district of British Columbia in 1873–74 attracted throngs of prospectors through the Flatheads' territory and the mountains where they hunted smaller game, while a trade in farm produce and supplies grew between Missoula, the Bitterroot, and the mining camps, creating a constant traffic through Indian country.

New tribal alliances for the 1875–76 buffalo hunt aligned the Flatheads with their erstwhile foes. "All the Indians on this side—Crows, Bannocks, Nez Perces, Flatheads, and Snakes—are at war with the band under Sitting Bull," Sweitzer reported (referring in fact to Lame Bull, the Uncpapa war chief who, as Sitting Bull, directed some one hundred and seventy-five lodges of Uncpapas, Blackfeet, Sioux, Yanktonians, and Cheyennes clustered south of Fort Peck, while the medicine man, Sitting Bull, lodged near Canadian soil).[6]

For this 1875–76 hunt, one hundred and eighty-three lodges of Pend Oreilles, Coeur d'Alenes, Kutenais, Spokanes, Colvilles, and Flatheads, including six hundred warriors, crossed the mountains. "They were unusually well armed and ready for war if required. The Blood Indians . . . stampeded at their approach; but the Blackfeet proper had a friendly pipe and interchange of salutations with them," a correspondent from St. Ignatius advised the *Weekly Missoulian*.[7] Of this majestic party, one Indian was killed stealing

171

horses, two others shot by settlers for setting fire to prairies, and one slain by Kutenais who mistook him for an enemy.

To avert spread of Indian hostilities, Colonel John Gibbon reinstituted an order—first issued in August, 1871, but little observed—that friendly Indians off reservations travel with military escorts. Major Sweitzer, noting open preparations for warfare among buffalo hunters, recommended a military sally to disperse parties such as the large one that came from the Flathead camp. Governor Potts wrote the Flathead agent, asking that he keep his Indians on the reservation. The agent replied that Indian crops had failed, the government had provided nothing, and the Flatheads insisted on their right under the Stevens treaty to hunt without escort.

White citizens took no comfort in large, well-armed Indian movements, and were not reassured by the refusal of the Sioux to go onto reservations. On March 17, 1876, the army mounted a campaign to force the Sioux onto reserves, attacking Crazy Horse's band on the Little Powder River, continuing the assault throughout the summer, and finally compelling a Sioux surrender on October 27. The United States' losses included George Custer's entire column.

Many Sioux escaped to Canada, from where they launched raids against whites and other Indians. Fears multiplied that the Indians would unite. The *Missoulian* declared:

> The air is filled with rumors of Indian movements, which cannot be traced to any authentic sources. . . . If our troops operating in the Sioux country are again overtaken with disaster [as was Custer], the wild beasts of this country . . . may assume an attitude that shall invite destruction. While there is no cause for alarm, there is every reason why we should be prepared.[8]

White men scrutinized even the peaceful Flatheads for hostile gestures.

As the army moved against the Sioux, driving them northward, buffalo hunters of Canada pressed southward to find herds. Caught between the Sioux and pressure from the north, the Blackfeet complained to mounted police that northern Crees crowded them from their country. Without recognizing the true situation—that the bison were nearly wiped out—the Indians asserted that buffalo could not be found because retreating Sioux impeded the customary migration of herds.

Indian traders in buffalo country used whiskey freely in their operations. Doane advised:

As long as traders are allowed to penetrate the Indian country at random, far from the immediate supervision of the agents, so long the whiskey trade will be kept up. It is in full blast . . . all along the Missouri River, openly and publicly from Fort Benton to the mouth of the Musselshell.[9]

That the confederated Flatheads traded for guns and whiskey with these prairie merchants cannot be denied. Their agents often received complaints from various sections of Montana about drunken Flatheads. Other settlers appealed to the army. Finding a supply of whiskey, Flatheads on their way to buffalo stopped for two weeks on Beaver Creek, where they ritually fired the prairie grass, burning a settler's saw, a log house, and pastures. Intoxicated Flatheads set dogs on the same settlers' sheep four times in passing, while angry herders demanded help from the army. But suppression of the Indian liquor traffic became harder after Judge Hiram Knowles ruled in district court at Deer Lodge that whiskey could be carried legally through Indian country to a destination outside it.[10]

Governor Potts scolded the Flathead agent because his Indians were roaming without escort.

A band of them is reported to be engaged in firing the grass and timber on the Upper Big Hole River in Deer Lodge and Beaverhead counties and a band caused great fright in Meagher County a few days hence. As hostile Indians are causing depredations in several localities of the territory, the presence of your Indians in any of the settlements without escort will cause fright and may result in a collision between the settlers and Indians which we would all very much deplore.[11]

Some Flatheads, he added, had wandered through the capital a day or two earlier. In view of dwindling buffalo, and in the hope of dissuading the Indians from hunting, the federal government in 1876 contracted with Montana merchants to supply buffalo meat to Indian reservations.

Although the dread of an Indian alliance against the whites

173

centered on the Sioux, in July, 1876, the Flathead agent telegraphed the commissioner of Indian affairs his opinion that the Flatheads, Nez Percés, Blackfeet, Coeur d'Alenes, and Colvilles might unite. His report emanated from the activities of Dreamers, a cult of Indians who declared that the earth had been created complete, should not be disturbed by men, and a leader would arise among the Indians to raise the dead and expel white men. Blackfeet had already crossed the mountains, the agent said, "for the purpose of stealing and most probably to form an alliance with the Nez Percés and Flatheads." In December he sent a similar message to Fort Shaw, asking for troopers to protect settlers. The statement of a Canadian subinspector that the Sioux delivered tobacco as a peace offering to the Blackfeet, seeking their union with Crees and Crows in a general offensive against whites, heightened the foreboding.

Of the request for troops at the Flathead reservation, the secretary of war noted that in all of Montana the army had five hundred and twenty-six men of the Seventh Infantry and two hundred and fifty of the Second Cavalry, of whom five hundred were trying to contain the Sioux. "We have never had a garrison" in western Montana, he said, "and must risk the exposure now."[12] The Flat-heads were agitated, beyond doubt, and their young firebrands attracted to the Dreamers, but no evidence suggests they planned to attack settlers.

The agent, Charles Jones, had been dismissed July 5, 1872, a month before Garfield's council with the Flatheads, because Jones reported bogus employees on his payrolls. He admitted that

> John Richards was in fact myth, never having had an existence here, but coming down to me from my immediate predecessors, Captain Galbreath and Lieutenant Ford, hightoned army officers and supposed to be running the agency with all the rigidity of army rule.[13]

Contravened by Viall, Jones lamented,

> isolated and many hundreds of miles from the seat of government, I am now deprived for half of the last fiscal year, of the appropriations which legitimately belong to the agency; and at the same time that degree of credit with the surrounding community, which my personal and official conduct . . . had in some degree inspired.

Among the agency's debts he listed $1,097 worth of flour bought in 1871 from St. Ignatius Mission to prevent starvation among the Indians.

In Jones's cashiering, the *Weekly Missoulian* saw Viall's machinations as head of the "Indian ring," and published a bitter editorial alleging that fraud and religious conflicts existed throughout Montana's Indian service.[14] Jones returned to Washington, D.C., where he served as a director of the Bureau of Catholic Indian Missions.

Shortly after Jones's departure, Viall also left office as a result of a personal inquiry by Felix R. Brunot, chairman of the Board of Indian Commissioners, who gathered affidavits accusing the superintendent of fraud. The "Indian ring" indeed existed. Appointed a special assistant to the attorney general of Montana Territory, William Clagett investigated but somehow never could put his hands on incriminating records, and finally dropped his inquiry when the Indian office rejected his request for an annual retainer of thirty-five hundred dollars.[15]

Viall's successor, sanctimonious James Wright, soon after taking office proposed rules and moral standards for men appointed reservation agents. An Indian office clerk described Wright's letter as a "homily" on its file jacket. Wright urged that Indian and white children attend schools together on reservations, and proposed a mission at each agency as a Christian example. "I am sorry to say that at present, at no agency within this superintendency (with perhaps an exception in a degree at the Flathead agency) can these principles be carried out."[16]

The whiskey traffic increased when Viall left office, and, six months after Wright's appointment, the Grant administration discontinued territorial superintendencies. Wright became Crow agent, and Benjamin Potts remarked privately to the secretary of the interior, "I fear that the church policy when strictly adhered to places in the Indian service too many men like our late superintendent without business capacity or knowledge of men and things."[17] In ending superintendencies, Congress authorized the president to appoint instead five inspectors of Indian affairs.

In the fifty-one months after Charles Jones's dismissal, three Catholic agents came to the Flatheads: Daniel Shanahan, a Washington, D.C., publisher who served sixteen months; Peter Whaley, a Montana farmer who stayed almost twelve; and Charles S. Medary of New York, a former soldier, twenty-three months. This changing responsibility was too tenuous to help the Flatheads, but each agent in his way confronted the Flatheads' tribal warfare on the buffalo grounds, increasing demands for Indians to remain on their reservations, for public schooling for Indians, and for removal of the Bitterroot Flatheads under the Garfield contract.

Throughout the period of 1873 to 1877 the *Weekly Missoulian* published ominous predictions of Indian uprisings for the purpose of promoting a military post at Missoula. A number of these articles were written by Frank Woody and Washington McCormick, the latter now flourishing a billiard-cue cane fitted with a handle of the first silver mined in Deer Lodge County. Indians and whites recognized that the newspaper was misrepresenting the Flatheads to trump up a military post for commercial benefit, but continual intimations that the Flatheads might turn suddenly hostile did not improve their standing with whites.

Meanwhile the confederated Flatheads continued to ask for the improvements promised them in the Stevens treaty. They had told Garfield they wanted a government school at the agency, he had provided for one in his contract, and Clagett in 1876 wrote to remind Garfield that "the one great reason for their removal was that they wanted to get away from the secular control of the fathers at the mission in the Bitterroot valley, and have a school of their own at the agency."[18]

Schooling for Flatheads set off several controversies. Viall refused to award funds to St. Ignatius school because it was on private land. Founded in October, 1864, this school had operated in its early days with gifts the sisters begged from prospectors in territorial gold camps.[19] After an eighteen-month closure for lack of funds, the school, beginning in 1868, received federal support of twelve hundred dollars a year for one teacher and six hundred for an assistant. When the federal Indian office denied St. Ignatius' application to be paid per pupil, Commissioner Edward P. Smith suggested the priests increase their income by adding another teacher's name to the payrolls.

Several times the priests tried to obtain the funds appropriated for a Flathead reservation school. Once Father Palladino sent the government a bill for educational services, through the Board of Indian Commissioners. He wrote Brunot, "If the voucher cannot be paid, please return it. We shall keep it as a proof and record of the honesty of the past and present Montana Indian administration as well as its fair dealings toward Catholic Indian missions and missionaries." Brunot replied that schools lay outside the Board's purview.[20]

Schooling for Flatheads remained an issue when Shanahan, publisher of the *Irish Republican* in the national capital and a man of some means, was persuaded by former missionaries to accept the Flathead appointment, against his inclination. He set out for Montana expecting to play an important role in territorial development, but Montanans viewed him as "a strange kind of fish, a damn fine Irish Republican. He thinks he is going to revolutionize all the Irish of Montana, God help him."[21] As agent, Shanahan was soon too busy to advance himself or the Irish in territorial affairs.

Arlee cornered the new agent soon after his arrival to say:

> I did not want to move down to the Jocko reservation but Garfield promised that we should have a public school according to the old [Stevens] treaty. . . . There is a school at the mission seventeen miles away but it is of no benefit to the tribe. They educate girls there but no boys. We want our boys educated, not our girls. We want a school at the agency according to our treaty.[22]

Shanahan's cordial acceptance by St. Ignatius' priests and their defense of him in wrangles with Wright over agency funds put the agent in an awkward position to help the Flatheads by advocating a public school that would divert monies from the mission school. Perhaps to soften a blow to the school, Shanahan proposed that a hospital, promised to the confederated Flatheads in 1855, be opened at the mission under supervision of the Sisters of Charity who, with the Jesuit fathers, performed most of the medical services for Indians. Shanahan found pulmonary consumption, scrofula, and venereal diseases prevalent among the Flatheads.

Neither Flatheads of the Bitterroot nor those of the reservation actually saw much of Shanahan, who spent his first months as agent trying to carry out the Garfield contract, including construction of twenty houses, without federal funds. Nearly a year after his appointment no money had reached him. Personal business required his return to Washington, where he spent the period from November, 1873, through March, 1874, frequently visiting the Indian office to discuss the agency. Charles Schafft acted as agent in Shanahan's absence. The Indians of the reservation were starving while Shanahan talked, and rather than permit wholesale expirations from famine, Missoula merchants continued to provide foodstuffs on credit.

In the capital, Shanahan was counseled to offer additional inducements to the Bitterroot Flatheads to move, and was authorized to construct new agency buildings. On his return he promised Arlee possession of the old agency shacks and farms, and set about building new mills operated by steam, a barn, blacksmith shop, employees' quarters, office, dispensary, agent's house, and a school building.

When the Indian office sent no money for agency renovation, Shanahan diverted funds for it by firing employees and ordering the St. Ignatius school closed on April 1, 1874. He used these funds to continue building. The nuns defied him. "We managed, not however without considerable hardship to ourselves, to keep up the school in the customary manner," Sisters Remi and Paul Miki advised the commissioner.[23]

The mission priests charged that Shanahan closed the school "because we exposed some of his doings," and Charles Ewing demanded that the commissioner direct Shanahan "to revoke his order suspending the school and reappoint the agency blacksmith." Clagett viewed Shanahan's struggle with St. Ignatius as "a question whether the agent or the fathers will exercise control over the Indians," while an Indian inspector reported that the Jesuits in the Bitterroot were "exerting their utmost influence to keep the Flatheads away from the agency. But for them there would be no difficulty; there is no device or contrivance they will neglect to employ."[24] Ewing called this report distorted, alleging that Protestants connected with the Indian service advised the Flatheads to resist removal from the valley with force.

Apparently sobered by his service among the Flatheads, Shanahan had left his resignation with Ewing during his visit to Washington. Ewing now sent it to the commissioner, who named as agent Peter Whaley, a pioneer miner in Alder Gulch and farmer at Deep Creek valley, Meagher County. His appointment, approved by Catholic clergy in Montana, was protested by Governor Potts, who considered Whaley unsuited for the position.

Whaley restored federal support to the mission school and asked five hundred and twenty-five dollars in back pay for its teachers. As Ewing observed, Whaley "was selected because it was known he would act in harmony with the missionaries," and indeed the new agent recommended that the missionaries be granted greater authority over the confederated Flatheads because of their experience with Indians. The Flatheads thought otherwise. "Our new agent, Peter Whaley, is not fit to hold this office," one wrote to the president. "He is led by the Jesuit priests by the nose. . . . The priests and agent are a band of speculators. We believe in the Holy Catholic Church but not in this form."[25]

Whaley was pugnacious and inept. Once when the Pend Oreilles' chief, Michel, objected to threshing mission fields with agency employees, Whaley offered to fist-fight him. Although he requested more money, Whaley failed to use "a large portion of the money (from two thousand to four thousand dollars) appropriated for the Indians of the Jocko reservation," Ewing advised the commissioner. "Through the negligence of the agent in not applying it to the purposes indicated by the appropriation, [the money] has been conveyed into the Treasury; in consequence of which these Indians have suffered many hardships and great loss." Clagett said the Indians complained continually about Whaley.[26] The agent, suspended after eleven months, bought a farm near Missoula.

Charles S. Medary, a son of the noted Ohio publisher and Quaker, Samuel Medary, became Flathead agent on July 1, 1875. An officer in various army regiments between 1861 and 1870, Medary's posture was businesslike; he intended, said the *Missoulian*, "to inaugurate a new policy in the education of the Indians—to educate them to work and when he had graduated them in this branch of their education, their minds will be in a condition to receive further knowledge."[27] Although this statement implied change, Medary supported St. Ignatius until it became a contract school two years later.

Following Garfield's visit as they did, the agents Shanahan, Whaley, and Medary took part in moving Flatheads from the Bitterroot. The urgency for removal intensified when the Department of the Interior refused to issue patents for settlers' land in the valley as long as the Flatheads were there. Arlee wanted to amend the Garfield contract, writing the commissioner through Father Ravalli, "I will not consent to remove to the Jocko unless a good substantial house is built for me and the others, nor unless I have a written guarantee from the Great Father at Washington that I will never be disturbed there." At Charlot's request, the agent advised the president that Charlot "did not wish to remove from his present home in the Bitterroot valley . . . and hoped you would not attempt to force him from the home of his fathers after many years of kindness on their [the Flatheads'] part to the whites who have settled among, and finally seem about encompassing them."[28]

One of the first steps toward removal was to determine the land claims of the Indians in the valley. Superintendent Viall had delegated J. W. Winslett, an old resident who knew the Flatheads, to write down the names of those entitled to tracts. Winslett listed forty to sixty names but was such a poor speller—Charlot he called "Sherlock"—that Wright, on coming into office, declared that no more than twelve Indians on the list could be identified as land owners. Winslett appended thirty-three others claiming to be farmers, and the names of five Flatheads not farming who said they would not move. Eight of those claiming to be farmers were women, including Victor's widow, who used their sons and relatives as laborers.[29]

Viall lost the list, but Wright found it and visited the Flatheads. To the land commissioner he wrote:

They cannot be induced to peaceably remove at present, but ask that their chiefs be allowed to visit the President. I took pains to consult the prominent citizens of the valley, including the county surveyor of Missoula. From them I learn that there is not a conflicting claim between the Indians and the whites. The settlers have no objections to the Indians remaining among them providing they (the whites) can get title to their land.

Wright proposed to move the fifty farming Flatheads after their harvest. "They allege (and I fear with too good cause) that they have been cheated by their agents, and now want to talk with the Great Father face to face."[30]

Wright authorized the county surveyor to run boundaries for Indians' lands. When some of these claims crossed township lines, Secretary Delano counseled "a liberal interpretation" of regulations. "At the date of the passage of this act [June 5, 1872] the lands were unsurveyed, and it was impossible to determine how the lines run in surveys subdividing the territory under our system might affect the settlements and improvements made by Indians."[31] Charlot's was one of the claims crossing township lines.

Surveying Indian land was exasperating at best, for a number of claimants were absent at any given time, and

> those refusing to move to the Jocko reservation stated that the land was theirs by natural right and they would remain there as Indians, not as citizens, and we may survey their lands as much as we please but they would neither recognize survey boundaries nor pay taxes.

Shanahan attracted four hundred Flatheads to a feast where he urged them to move, but after eating Charlot declared, "Your promise of property and money make no impression on me. I once said *No* and I will not break my word now. I will obey force only; but (giving his hand to the major) never will raise my hands against the white man." Wright addressed a stern letter to Charlot, threatening to use the army, to which the chief replied, "You may use force to remove me from here, the lands of my fathers and people, but they [soldiers] will not make me afraid."[32]

Nevertheless, six Flathead families moved to the Jocko during the summer of 1873, and on October 11, after the harvest and root digging, Arlee led ten more families from the Bitterroot.

Shanahan advised the commissioner:

> I have the honor to report that Arlee (second chief) and ten other families have this day arrived at the Jocko, making sixteen families now removed here, thus practically settling the Flathead question. Arlee states that but a few of his people will become citizens; the greater portion of them having expressed a desire to settle here on their return from the hunting grounds. This chief having specially requested to live near me, in compliance with his wish I have given him possession of the old quarters heretofore occupied by agency employees.[33]

Shanahan provided the chief a wagon to move his household and the seventy-five-dollar cookstove stipulated in the Garfield contract. "In order to secure the active cooperation of Arlee, second chief of the Flathead Indians, in securing the removal of that tribe from the Bitterroot valley . . . I have promised to recommend him as head chief in place of Charlot who forfeited his right by refusing to move to the reservation, or in any way to comply with the laws of the government," Shanahan added, recommending that Arlee be recognized as chief of the confederated nation as of October 1.[34] This was done.

Arlee as chief was vain, stubborn, and surly among whites and Indians alike, but the confederated Flatheads understood that the United States preferred to deal with Indians through one spokesman and accorded Arlee the dignity of this position. If allowed to elect, Medary felt the Flatheads would have chosen Partee, and suggested at one time that Arlee be deposed in favor of Partee. Medary also told Charlot that he could be head chief again if he moved to the reservation, but Charlot turned him down. "He, Charlot, loves that [Bitterroot] valley and reveres the memory and words of his father who, it is stated, told him never to remove; that if he should ever be forced to remove, to go toward the rising and not the setting of the sun," said Medary. "He is not satisfied but that in a few years he may again be driven farther west if he should now remove to the reservation."[35]

As soon as Arlee's Flatheads reached the reservation, they clamored for shares of the fifty thousand dollars voted to compensate them. "These people are under the impression that payment would commence immediately after removal of any portion of the tribe and those now on the reservation say they will return to the Bitterroot valley if payment can't soon be made," Shanahan wrote the commissioner. He estimated the cost of carrying out the Garfield contract at $31,600 in the first year, including house construction, breaking and fencing land, introducing water for irrigation from Finlay Creek, subsistence, and the initial $5,000 payment of the $50,000.

Coincident with the Flatheads' demands for payment, the Indian office ordered able-bodied men between eighteen and forty-five to work for their agency, reservation, or tribe in order to earn the value of supplies or annuities distributed to them. The *Missoulian* predicted the plan would not succeed with the Flatheads. Indians with relatives in the Bitterroot exchanged frequent visits and fell into the habit of stopping at the agent's home en route for a meal.

By the end of the summer of 1873 the Missoula County surveyor completed his work for the Bitterroot Indians, assisted personally with his chain by Superintendent Wright after Shanahan refused to help. Although nine patentees remained at buffalo, and fifteen or twenty others also were absent, the surveyor reported, "There will be no impropriety in opening the land office [at Missoula] so that the whites can enter their lands as there is an abundance of unoccupied land in the valley where I can locate them [Indians] without interfering with anyone."[36]

Because he was paid one hundred dollars for each location, the surveyor was diligent, and, asserted a correspondent to the *Weekly Missoulian,* "claimed that the responsibility of selecting good locations rested on him; consequently every eligible vacant location within ten or twelve miles of Stevensville on both sides of the river has been surveyed for ... imaginary Indians."[37] The correspondent claimed that a census of Bitterroot Indians by Agent Jones, James Cowan, and W. E. Bass counted 34 Flathead men, 36 women, and 127 children—a total of 217 Flatheads—and 229 Indians of other tribes, and that only 31 of these families cultivated land.

Indian land claims in the Bitterroot, generally along roads and streams, clustered in the township of Stevensville. Charlot's place lay southeast of the village, adjacent to that of his father's widow.

A number of Flatheads who received patents, including Arlee and Adolph, moved to the reservation before the survey but did not thus forfeit their claims. When Indians returned to the valley from time to time, the surveyor obligingly located acreage for them. By the end of 1874 he filed sixty-six additional Indian claims, but the agent, then Whaley, declared that most of these Indians were hunting buffalo, and two or three seemed not to exist. "From the large number of claims (44 of the 66) which have been located for women," he observed, "I am inclined to the opinion that Mr. Hall [the surveyor] came near exhausting the tribe in order to find persons for whom to locate farms."[38] Most of the surveyor's vouchers for these locations were disallowed.

In December, 1873, the Bitterroot was opened for patenting by white persons who had occupied their land in the valley before June 5, 1872. Although the original period for making final proofs on these plots ended March 5, 1874, the slow sales of Indian acreage so delayed the patenting of settlers' claims that Montana's delegate, Martin Maginnis, abetted by a legislative memorial, secured a grace of twenty-four months. Congress simultaneously extended the Homestead Act to the Bitterroot. As time passed, other Flatheads moved to the Jocko. In the fall of 1875, Medary listed eighty-one adults and forty-two children, formerly Bitterroot residents, living on the reservation. Of the status of those who remained in the Bitterroot Valley, the agent declared, "They should in my opinion be treated and looked upon as citizens."

The Missoula County commissioners in the spring, 1875, ordered Bitterroot Indians taxed. In every case, the Indians refused to pay. When Potts appealed to the commissioner of Indian affairs to intercede for the county, the commissioner replied:

The property of these Indians is perhaps subject to local taxation, although if such a right is exercised by the territorial authority, in my judgment the persons thus taxed should be clothed with all the rights and bound to all the duties of citizens of Montana.[39]

The secretary of the interior suggested to Potts that Bitterroot Flatheads,

having abandoned their tribal relations and acquired property in severalty are subject to taxation with respect to that property equally with other property owners in the territory. I know of no law which exempts the property of Indians from taxation. It should be observed, however, that the lands patented to these Indians were made inalienable by law and therefore the land is not subject to sale for non-payment of taxes assessed thereon.

Taxing Indians, indicated the secretary, should be done "with a wise discretion."[40]

Missoula County, mired in debt, also attempted to tax the property of nine white men and two half-breeds living on the Jocko, or cause them to be driven off the reservation, but Medary refused to eject whites married to Indian women and, in several cases, adopted into tribes. The men paid no taxes.

Arlee demanded that the white men, chiefly cattle breeders, be put off the reserve; Michel agreed they could remain. "Arlee would have made no objections whatever had any one of his family been married to a white man," Medary said. "To show how unjust he is, I will state that he went so far as to commit a fraud upon the government and his own people, in order to draw Flathead pay for his favorites, that he gave the names of several Indians not entitled to pay to the former agent, Whaley, to be placed on the Flathead roll."[41] These names included Arlee's son-in-law, a pure-blood Pend Oreille who had never lived on the reservation. Arlee, added the agent, "is purely selfish in every particular and has neither the respect nor confidence of his people. The greatest drawback to removal of the Indians from the Bitterroot valley is the fact that Arlee is the chief."

Medary's defense of white cattlemen on the Jocko, his animosity toward Arlee, and an acrimonious exchange of words with T. J. (Jack) Demers, chairman of the county commissioners, charging that Demers ran his cattle illegally on the reservation, led to rumors that Medary would soon be replaced.

Commenting on Grant's peace policy, the *Missoulian* said, "At the Jocko agency . . . the rules and orders of the agent are set at defiance, by a portion of the Indians at least, and he has no force with which he can compel submission to them. This is the real condition on the frontier."[42] The editor urged transfer of Indian administration to the War Department—a national issue. The *New North-West* said the Flathead chiefs, dissatisfied with the agent, would use every means to remove him, and hinted at irregularities involving vouchers and property at the agency.

Medary was charged in county court by whites with grazing his own animals on Indian land, mismanaging the agency, and transporting liquor onto the reservation; he was convicted, largely on the testimony of reservation Indians, and fined six hundred dollars. "When it is known that cattle have been kept on the reservation for years by a number of persons, and that this is the only case that has ever been brought," opined the *Missoulian*, "it will appear something other than justice and the good of the Indians was sought. The whole matter . . . had its origin in an effort of our county commissioners to reach property of citizens on the reservation for taxation." Medary, the editor concluded, was a victim of "unmerited severity."[43] The U.S. district attorney, Merritt C. Page, was not as magnanimous. "Although it does not clearly appear from the evidence educed, I think it will be found on investigation that for the last two years the Indians have not received the $3,000 annuity provided for them," Page wrote the U.S. attorney general.[44] Medary had been dismissed before the judgment against him.

His departure in 1877 coincided with the closing of an era for the confederated Flatheads, for the year would inaugurate a new period in their acculturation. The buffalo were almost gone, and the old days were dying with their disappearance. Although fears of Indian retaliation had not been dispelled, the whites of Montana, in a patronizing spirit, soon would speak of "our Indians," and the *Missoulian* would say avuncularly that the Flatheads' "propensity for gambling ought to be suppressed, for the reason that the Nez Perces are better mounted, smarter, cleaner, and get away with our Indians all the time."

CHAPTER 8

▲▲▲▲▲▲▲▲▲▲▲▲▲▲▲▲▲▲▲▲▲▲▲▲▲▲▲▲▲▲▲▲

THE RONAN YEARS

▼▼▼▼▼▼▼▼▼▼▼▼▼▼▼▼▼▼▼▼▼▼▼▼▼▼▼▼▼▼▼▼

TOWARD THE MIDDLE OF 1877 a former newspaper proprietor, Peter Ronan, became agent to the confederated Flathead nation. The Indians and whites of Montana remember Ronan fondly, perhaps for different reasons, as an able and compassionate agent. Ronan had printed a newspaper in Virginia City and shared ownership of the *Rocky Mountain Gazette*, a Democratic journal in Helena. In 1873, while the *Gazette* rebuilt after a fire, he followed pretty Mollie Sheehan from Montana to California to persuade her to marry him. She was twenty-one and Ronan, thirty-six when they returned to Helena. The next year the *Gazette* expired after a second fire.

Ronan turned briefly to mining, served a term as undersheriff of Lewis and Clark County, and then on April 13, 1877, received the Flathead appointment as a political boon from Martin Maginnis, congressional delegate, fellow Democrat, and former partner in the *Gazette*. As agent, Ronan was paid fifteen hundred dollars a year and accorded the courtesy title of "major."

Ronan assumed direction of the Flathead Agency on June 1, finding Medary still on the premises negotiating a settlement of wages owed his interpreter, Baptiste Marengo. Ronan was the first agent to have access to his predecessor's accounts under the law enacted in 1875 making these public property.

Seventeen days after Ronan reached the agency, one hundred miles to the west two companies of United States soldiers of the command of General Oliver O. Howard fought nontreaty Nez Percés at Whitebird, Idaho, losing one-third of their force before retreating under an Indian counterattack. News of another Indian victory over troops, coming a year after the Custer disaster, renewed fears of spontaneous, united Indian uprisings in Idaho and Montana.

Lieutenant Colonel Wesley Merritt, who in 1876 had inspected the Bitterroot and Missoula areas to assess the desirability of a military post there, had concluded that "a large number of half-breeds and dissolute citizens who carry on contraband trade with the Indians reside in different parts of the valley. These people are, many of them, outlaws, and much to be feared as a cause of inciting the Indians by their trade and counsel." Merritt recommended, and the War Department approved, establishing a military post of one or two companies near Missoula, "all that is required to make everything safe."[1] In February, 1877, the president had authorized the post.

Now in mid-1877 reports of Nez Percés at war especially frightened residents in the Missoula region. "The Nez Perces fraternize with the Flatheads, Pend Oreilles, Coeur d'Alenes, Kalispells and Kootenays," cried the *Helena Daily Herald*, "and the dispatches indicate that a coalition has been formed by these Indians with the warlike Nez Perces, which may precipitate a destructive war upon western Montana."[2]

No coalition existed but, in the words of Father D'Aste of St. Mary's Mission:

As it happens on such occasions, timid people began to frighten the others by their conversation and suggestions of dangers. The idea that the Flatheads, who had been so much abused and were dissatisfied with the Sen. Garfield treaties might avail themselves of the chance to revenge themselves . . . excited greatly the minds of the settlers. They were watching closely these Flatheads; neither powder nor ammunition was sold to them although they needed them badly to kill some game, and what was worse, in the little village of Stevensville these suspicions were freely discussed in the presence of [a] halfbreed, who would report these conversations to the Indians. There were therefore bad feelings and mutual fears between the two races.[3]

Bitterroot residents petitioned Governor Potts for protection, saying that they were endangered "not only from Nez Perces, but from the large number of Flatheads living in the valley," and Potts advised the secretary of the interior that "great excitement prevails in Missoula and Deer Lodge counties. . . . The confederated tribes of Flatheads, etc., are restless and some of them have shown signs of being hostile for some time."[4] The Nez Percés visited Montana annually, knew the land well, and recognized the virtually defenseless position of its settlements, he added.

Earlier in the year, some members of Potts's own political party had accused him of maladministration, so now he moved quickly. On June 28, the governor sent Captain James H. Mills, editor of the *New North-West* and the territorial secretary and adjutant general, to investigate the concern at Missoula for "the Indian war in Idaho." Mills's objective was to justify stronger military protection, but without waiting for Mills's report Potts telegraphed President Hayes:

> Settlements in western Montana seriously threatened by Nez Perce Indians from Idaho. Settlers are fleeing their homes in Bitterroot valley to Missoula for safety. More troops are needed for Missoula. We are organizing and arming the people for defense. Flathead and other Indians are seriously disaffected.[5]

Potts also wrote Ronan, "In view of the anticipated Indian troubles in your locality, I request you, with some of your most influential fathers, seek the Flathead camp—Charlot's camp—and have a talk with the Indians and counsel peace and alliance with the whites."[6] Thus in his first month as agent, Peter Ronan faced an incipient Indian war of unpredictable ferocity and scope.

Late in June, forty-four men of Companies A and E, Seventh Infantry, reached the site chosen for Fort Missoula, where they erected a tool shed, lime house, and tents, working in constant rain. The fort's commandant, Captain Charles C. Rawn, visited Ronan to learn the Indians' intentions, and together the agent and commandant set out for the missions to talk with the Indians. At St.

Ignatius, with Fathers Leopold Van Gorp and Joseph Bandini present, "the Indians gave us unqualified assurance of their loyalty to the whites," Ronan wrote the governor. Rawn solicited Indian men to serve as his scouts, but they declined because he could not pay them. Rawn personally could not trust Indians, he acknowledged, but reassured himself that "their interest" required the tribes to remain peaceful to preserve their houses and horse herds.[7]

At St. Mary's Mission, Ronan and Rawn found Charlot and his family at Sunday mass, and arranged to talk to the chief through little Father D'Aste. Charlot admitted that many of his people were absent, but denied they had gone to war.

> This broad country [sweeping gesture] is our home. It is usual every year, after my people put in their crops, for them to go to the different camas prairies to dig roots for winter use, and while the women and children perform that duty, the young men hunt and fish. When the crops begin to ripen they return to their homes. They are on their way home now, I am informed, and twenty lodges are in camp near Missoula.[8]

In direct answer to Ronan, Charlot went on:

> It was my father's boast that the blood of a white man never reddened the hands of a single Indian of the Flathead tribe. My father died with that boast on his lips. I am my father's son and will leave that same boast to my children.

On the other hand, Charlot refused to align his people against the Nez Percés. According to Father D'Aste, "He was to remain with his people neutral, because he had a good many friends on either side, the whites in the valley and the Nez Perces. . . . But, he added, in case they would molest his people, he himself and his people would know how to defend themselves."[9] Adolph and Eneas visited Missoula from the reservation; both confirmed that the Flatheads would not fight settlers. Colonel Gibbon had given his party ammunition during the summer, Adolph declared, on assurance they would not attack whites. When Nez Percé runners visited Charlot, he urged them to tell their chiefs to avoid the Bitterroot if driven from Idaho.

After seeing Charlot, Ronan and Rawn encountered the deposed

Nez Percé chieftain, Eagle-against-the-Light, driving horses. He said he was trying to intercept his band with fresh mounts before they crossed the mountains westward into the war area and to bring them back in peace to the Bitterroot. When Ronan's and Rawn's reports were circulated, the panic in western Montana temporarily subsided.

Meanwhile, after the Whitebird engagement, the nontreaty Nez Percés in Idaho, including a small band under Looking Glass who had been digging bitterroot in the Lolo district, moved westward toward the Snake River and then turned abruptly eastward to evade the military column pursuing them. They fought skirmishes, and General Howard's main force came upon the Nez Percé camp on the Clearwater River on July 11, forcing a battle that resulted in a perilous siege of Howard's men, lifted when the Indians, weakened by dissent, broke before a general charge. Howard claimed a major victory.

Clearly unable to elude the army, on July 15 the Nez Percés counciled at Weippe, Idaho. Looking Glass, who had received information and advice from Angus McDonald's widow on the Flathead reservation, prevailed in advocating that the Nez Percés retreat through Montana, where they could hunt buffalo before going to asylum in Canada.[10] The chiefs discounted the warning sent by Charlot to go north through Kutenai country and avoid white settlements. The Nez Percés designated Joseph to organize and move the camp and Ollikot, his brother, to serve as one of a group of experienced warriors in a war council. Following this, the Nez Percé chieftains rode through their camp announcing the plan and telling their people not to shoot white civilians or steal cattle in Montana, because they would leave the war behind them when they left Idaho.

On the following morning approximately two hundred men, five hundred and fifty women and children, and two thousand horses (five hundred stolen from Chief Lawyer's treaty Nez Percés) set out in rain over the Lolo trail for the Bitterroot Valley. Howard's advance elements abandoned the chase temporarily when an Indian rear guard fired on them from ambush. The Nez Percés' decision to cross into Montana had not been unanimous: several families slipped out of the caravan to flee northward directly into Canada or to beg sanctuary among Colville, Coeur d'Alene, and Flathead reservation tribes.

The Nez Percés' subsequent retreat through Montana, since described poignantly many times, demonstrated that nomadic living on a broad scale was no longer feasible, that the military power of Indians had waned, that the Indians now relied on white technology, and that, as a result, new alliances seemed more expedient than traditional ones. The Nez Percés' movement, causing one of several alarms within a five-year period that hardened the whites' resolution to destroy all vestiges of Indian unity, signaled the true end of the old days for the tribes of Montana.

Despite fears that the Flatheads might join the Nez Percés, a tolerant voice rose from the white community in Montana. In an article headlined, "Justice to the Flatheads," the *Herald* commented:

It is Captain [Walter W.] DeLacy's opinion that there is no more danger from the Flatheads than from an insurrection of the whites in the valley. If the Indians have not taken kindly to paying taxes or working on the highways, we can afford to bear a little with them.[11]

Mills, however, reported that one of the frequent runners between Idaho and Montana warned the Flatheads that the Nez Percés would raid the valley. Flatheads prudently hid their horses. Of these ominous tidings, Father D'Aste said, "A government official sent a message to the governor ... announcing that Charlot (who was just cutting hay on his ranch) had gone with his warriors ... to join the Nez Perces."[12]

By July 1—before the Nez Percés' council to decide their course— the Bitterroot reacted to rumors of imminent war. Nineteen or twenty families fled from Stevensville to Fort Owen to repair the moldering breastworks; seven families decamped to Missoula; others built a sod fort north of Corvallis, and still others, a log barricade around a cabin on Skalkaho Creek; but the majority remained in their homes, armed and apprehensive. In one breath, Duncan McDonald, the reservation trader (son of Angus), said Arlee and Michel would remain peaceful (they warned the Nez Percés not to cross the reservation), but "preparations have long been progressing for an alliance of all Indians to fight the whites."[13] Rawn heard that four thousand rounds of ammunition had been shipped to McDonald; he admonished Ronan to see that the Indians got none of it.

Missoula residents raised a volunteer company, equipped with a Springfield muzzle-loading rifle of Civil War vintage, a bayonet, twenty rounds of fixed (paper-wrapped) ammunition, and a screw driver for each man at a rental of thirty dollars apiece.[14] Other volunteers drilled at Stevensville and Corvallis. Perhaps a few young Flathead men slipped away to join the Nez Percés. They were admittedly restive, and the chiefs directed the volunteer reservation police force of twenty-five men to jail anyone who attempted to join the hostiles. Ronan lured young Indians near Missoula back onto the reservation with gifts purchased from his own pocket. Generally, the chiefs controlled their people. Ronan found the Flatheads destitute rather than warlike; he asked the commissioner for authority to buy them food in the open market because requisitions took so long that many Indians might die before the papers were processed.

On July 14, Eagle-against-the-Light, accompanied by his friend Michel, the arthritic and hobbling Pend Oreille chieftain, asked Ronan to allow his eleven peaceable lodges to move from St. Mary's Mission to the reservation. The agent, knowing that another band of Nez Percés had been denied asylum by Coeur d'Alenes with the excuse that the tribe could not appear to harbor hostiles, refused Eagle-against-the-Light for the same reason. The Nez Percés, consequently, hovered uncertainly near Missoula, to the townsmen's consternation.

At this moment the son of the mountain chief of the Blackfeet visited the Jocko. Arlee assured Ronan that the Flatheads and Blackfeet had made peace during the winter—then remarked darkly that the Blackfeet complained bitterly of whites and talked of renewing war on the Flatheads unless they, too, joined a general Indian plot against the settlers. Ronan requested the governor to send him arms and ammunition to protect the agency. "Although I have no apprehension of any Indian trouble here, it is always well to be prepared for the worst." Potts refused Ronan's request. Mollie

Ronan noticed one day that the agency employees "had all stopped their work and were putting their firearms in readiness for use."[15]

Here matters stood—the Flatheads destitute, scattered, frightened, disunited; a wavering Nez Percé band near Missoula; and the Blackfeet conniving—when Montanans learned that the main camp of hostile Nez Percés was indeed bound over the Lolo trail toward the Bitterroot Valley.

Captain Rawn and a volunteer officer sent separate scouting parties to watch the trail. These scouts met several Indian informants whose reports, often conflicting, added to the valley's excitement. As the Nez Percés came on, Governor Potts called for volunteers from other towns to assist Missoula. Captain Rawn, ordered to obtain the Nez Percés' surrender or delay them until a force under Gibbon could arrive, erected a log-and-earth breastwork about a quarter of a mile long across the gravelly floor of Lolo Canyon and here stationed twenty regulars and fifty volunteers. Charlot and twenty Flathead men watched, saying they would not fight on either side, and the soldiers tied white armbands on the Flatheads to distinguish them from hostile Indians.

The Nez Percés sent word ahead they "did not intend to fight the citizens, only the soldiers," and approached confidently. Of the Indians at Rawn's barricade, Father D'Aste remarked, "Some halfbreeds had induced a few Indians, about fifteen, to join the whites . . . but they had neither arms nor ammunition; it was probably this that saved the settlement from a general massacre." Rawn estimated the Nez Percés' strength at three hundred and fifty warriors, well armed.[16]

The Nez Percés emerged quietly from the trail and camped two miles above Rawn's barricade. Bitterroot citizens urged the captain to avoid a battle, and a delegation visited Gibbon asking him not to engage the Nez Percés in their valley. Charlot warned Joseph to steal nothing and harm no one (in D'Aste's words) lest the Flatheads "strike you as his [Charlot's] fathers knifed the Blackfeet," and refused to shake hands with the Nez Percé chief.

Looking Glass, White Bird, and Joseph, Nez Percé chieftains, rode to Rawn's breastwork under a white flag, pronounced it a poor corral, and asked permission to pass in peace. Rawn replied that he could accept only their surrender. Father D'Aste described the Nez Percés as defiant of the army: "They had plenty of guns and ammunition but they were starving and wanted to go hunt buffalo. Some of the volunteers were willing to let them pass; some wanted to fight them." As the chiefs departed, Captain Rawn—to delay them in the valley as ordered—asked them to talk with him again the next day. The *Missoulian* published an extra edition with the headline, "Help! Help! White Bird Defiant. Come Running." Volunteers from Deer Lodge and other towns marched to rescue Missoula.

At the second meeting between Rawn and the Nez Percé chiefs, Governor Potts was present. He "felt it would be madness to attack the Nez Perces with an inadequate force," perhaps eying the seventy-five Nez Percé warriors astride their horses a short distance away, breech-loading rifles resting in their hands.[17] Rawn stationed armed volunteers above the council site before he met the Indians. The meeting achieved nothing, but the volunteers, realizing that the Nez Percés meant them no harm and fearful of provoking battle by a show of force, began leaving for their homes.

Near dawn the next morning (July 28), the Nez Percés moved their entire camp through a gully out of Rawn's sight, then emerged into view on higher ground above the barricade, with women and children driving horses and the men forming a picket line. Smiling and singing, the Nez Percés passed above the barrier out of range of the volunteers' needle guns, pursued by a straggling line of volunteers not eager to catch up. The Indians camped for the night upstream on the west bank of the Bitterroot River.

Realizing the fortification at Lolo had been futile, the volunteers now deserted Rawn in large numbers. His barricade became known as "Fort Fizzle," unfairly perhaps, for Rawn, a veteran of sixteen years in the regular army, hardly could have expected the Nez Percés to blunder into his position. His field reports notwithstanding, the captain prudently avoided confronting a superior force. The *Helena Daily Herald* reported:

> The Bitterroot volunteers, learning the character of the Indians and their peaceable disposition, declined to fight or oppose them and permitted them as heretofore to camp unmolested in the valley. Rawn,

with his little soldier squad, was powerless to object, had he . . . felt any disposition to do so.[18]

In a nighttime council the Nez Percés once more debated whether to proceed directly north into Canada or continue eastward, voting again to go to buffalo. When some volunteer soldiers wandered into the Indian camp, one who knew Looking Glass asked to shake hands, and, complying, the Indian chief sent them on their way, saying, "I am a good man. You can go." Father D'Aste hurried through an early Sunday mass in the morning so the Flatheads could observe the Nez Percés' progress through their country. The bishop of Omaha, John J. O'Connor, visiting St. Ignatius, avoided any mention of the Nez Percés when he preached on love and friendship.

At St. Mary's,

> Some prominent citizens of Stevensville came to the priests' house and had a talk with the [Flathead] Indians, considering what plan it would be prudent to follow. . . . During the meeting a Nez Perce, the old Piem'ch, who had a ranch by Corvallis, came in and on the part of the Nez Perce chiefs invited Charlot to visit them. But Charlot, true to his character, replied proudly that he had nothing to say to those chiefs, that he was sorry they had not minded him when he told them the way to go to buffalo by the Kootenays' country, which was almost unsettled by whites, and not to come to the Bitterroot . . . and now he wanted them to pass through the valley as fast as possible.[19]

When the Bitterroot volunteers showed no fighting spirit, and runners reported General Howard far behind waiting for axmen to clear the trail, the Nez Percés remained several days in the Bitterroot Valley.

Father D'Aste recalled:

> Immediately some of the prominent citizens, being aware of the near state of starvation in which the Indians were, drove in their camp wagons loaded with flour and got hard cash for it. The next day a good many of the Nez Perces rode well armed to Stevensville and there they bought, by the wholesale, provisions, calico, and other articles of clothing. Next day, in larger number, they came to the little village and in two days left more than $1,200 for articles they needed.[20]

Washington McCormick wrote Potts:

The Indians . . . have been paying exhorbitant prices for flour, coffee, sugar, and tobacco. They told the merchants of Stevensville . . . that they have money to pay for what supplies they wanted and if they did not sell they would take them by force. So far as I am advised they have killed no stock and molested no one, except to disarm two or three citizens, returning their guns, however, but keeping their ammunition. The people of the Bitterroot with their families are still in their fortifications and propose to remain there until the danger is past. . . . Their wheat crops are ready for the machine, and no one to harvest them while in many instances stock have broken into their fields and ruined their crops.[21]

Father Giorda noted in his diary that the Nez Percés traded all day, with "plenty of money, coin, dust, silver, and greenbacks." Captain Rawn observed that "some of the people at Stevensville and Corvallis traded with these Indians for everything they desired, whiskey included, and in one case ammunition." In his report of the war to Congress, the secretary of war wrote that the whites' fears "did not obliterate their sense of values to the extent of preventing them from selling the enemy substantial quantities of food and even ammunition." The *Weekly Missoulian*, replying to Colonel Gibbon's criticism that whites outfitted the hostiles, pointed out that the Nez Percés "declared their intention of having supplies, peaceably and for pay if they could, but forcibly if they must."[22]

On the second day, "the thirty-first, the valley ran a great risk," said Father D'Aste. "Unprincipled men sold the Indians whiskey, and there were about fifteen of them drunk. Had any shot been fired in a quarrel, a good many people had been killed. But fortunately one or two of their chiefs drove the drunken people to their own camp across the river and the peace was not broken."[23] One aged Flathead claimed that he flourished a revolver to protect a white woman from abuse by the Nez Percés.

Moving southward toward Gibbons Pass, the Nez Percés were amused by the fortifications at Corvallis and Skalkaho. When three young braves ransacked Myron Lockwood's farm, Looking Glass required them to leave three horses in payment. (Lockwood, a volunteer, would serve nine days against the Nez Percés in the Big

Hole, where his brother would be killed.) As the Nez Percés traveled, Potts called for three hundred volunteers in a proclamation:

> The Nez Perces were permitted to escape from Lolo Pass and encamp in the Bitterroot valley. These hostiles will soon attempt to pass through other portions of Montana. They are public enemies, who it is our duty as good citizens to meet and fight until they surrender.

The *Helena Daily Herald* printed a sarcastic letter, signed "Veteran," calling the Montana effort "a war of proclamations."[24]

Stevensville's residents, meanwhile, honored Charlot and his Flatheads at a community feast, where the chief pointed out how much better off his peaceable people were than the Nez Percés, now pursued by the army. Gibbon, coming up from Fort Shaw, rented mule wagons in the Bitterroot, reluctantly enlisted volunteers, whose capability he doubted, and on August 9 surprised the Nez Percés camped serenely without pickets in the Big Hole. Devastated by the dawn attack, the Nez Percés besieged Gibbon long enough to organize their retreat and then fled eastward across Montana. Like the Flatheads, the Crows refused them assistance and protected the settlers. The Nez Percés pushed on until, excepting fragmentary bands that escaped to British soil, they surrendered October 5 at Bear Paws, where they had stopped, believing themselves safely in Canada.

A short time later, General Sherman inspected the new Missoula military post, reporting:

> Had there been four companies here . . . the Nez Perces would not have dared to revolt. There remain of the same type and class the Flatheads, Pend Oreilles, Spokanes, and Coeur d'Alenes; all of whom claim the natural right to go where they please through Montana to the buffalo regions on the headwaters of the Missouri. The agent of the Flatheads came to see me . . . with a most intelligent priest who has charge of the mission of St. Ignatius, forty-two miles north of this [post] . . . . The agent has not a dollar, and no authority to promise them meat.[25]

Charlot complained, after the Stevensville feast, that the settlers and soldiers flattered and abandoned the Flatheads. Many Flatheads lost their grain, unharvested in the excitement; hail flattened most of the remainder. The reservation Indians, realizing the danger to any Indian caravan, conducted a small, discreet summer hunt—but with Charlot's people concluded they must undertake a major fall buffalo hunt to forestall famine.

During the Sioux campaigns of 1876, however, ammunition sales to all Indians had been prohibited, and, as the Nez Percés proceeded through Montana, the Indian office on August 3 reiterated its ban on sales of arms and ammunition to Indians. "For over thirty years these [confederated Flathead] Indians have procured their ammunition and guns without restraint," Ronan objected to the commissioner. "They have stood to protect the whites, and now instead of praise and encouragement they are to be prohibited from supporting their families." The agent warned, "Their young men will not be restrained if the Pend Oreilles and Kootenays make up their minds to have food or war." The *Missoulian* reported Pend Oreilles trying to buy two cases of Winchester cartridges for fifty dollars, saying they would starve without game.[26]

While the Flatheads prepared a massive hunt, Father Palladino, accompanying the army near Deer Lodge, wrote Ronan, "With the current excitement it is dangerous for any Indian to be at large," and Father D'Aste urged the agent to obtain permission for the Flatheads to use a northerly route, the Kutenai trail, to avoid settlements.

"Something must be done to call in all the roving bands of Indians to their reservations until after the present excitement and danger is over," declared the *Herald*. "It is a measure demanded for the security of whites and peaceful Indians alike. Not one person in a thousand can tell to what tribe an Indian belongs."[27] By the third week of September, Flatheads with other Indians began moving eastward in numbers to hunt.

Father D'Aste appealed to the governor:

I dare to write your excellency on behalf of the Flathead Indians of the Bitterroot valley. . . . They had this year very poor crops and some of them lost all by a heavy hailstorm. A good many of them have nothing to eat and therefore they are bound to go to buffalo. By the order forbidding to sell them ammunition, good many of them having bought, and paid dear, the new fashioned guns, they find themselves in the impossibility of procuring for themselves and family the only actual means of subsistence. They begin to believe and say that all the oaths of friendship from the whites were not sincere. Since the danger being past, they [whites] will force them to starve. Could you not have some arrangement made so that the Flatheads, starting now for buffalo, could get somewhere ammunition enough to procure the necessary meat for subsistence?

Charlot knew of the priest's letter, for his band stopped at the capital to ask Potts in person for ammunition. Potts turned them down.[28]

Too late to help, General Sherman recommended that the Flatheads, "who behaved so well in the recent Nez Perce war," be allowed to buy traders' powder and caps for muzzle-loading rifles, "good enough for hunting, but not metallic ammunition used only in war."[29]

A number of Flatheads eluded North West Mounted Police to purchase guns and ammunition in Canada; others obtained ammunition from Crows and perhaps Blackfeet who, with the Sioux, utilized a hand tool for reloading empty cartridge shells for which they searched battlegrounds. Remarkably, Charlot's hunters, crossing Montana before the Nez Percés' surrender, encountered no difficulty from whites.

Reservation Indians and "destitute Indians from other tribes" gathered near the agency for the annual Christmas distribution, but supplies were delayed, partly by the Nez Percé excitement and partly, as General Sheridan said, "by the unfortunate mismanagement which has generally characterized the transportation of Indian supplies—scheming contractors always manage to delay Indian supplies until winter, when the price of transportation is two or three times as much as in the summer."[30]

To "prevent hunger and want," Ronan again used his own money; he could "not resist the promptings of humanity and rather than see their sufferings continue, I took my own means . . . and purchased what was necessary," including two hundred bushels of wheat ground into flour.[31] The commissioner would not authorize assistance to the Bitterroot Flatheads, however, and, learning of this,

Charlot kept his people in buffalo country through the winter and first eight months of 1878.

While the Flatheads were hunting, new alarms terrorized whites in their home country. Eighteen Nez Percés attempted to return from Canada to Idaho, killing four white men one day's ride from Missoula and three others near Rock Creek, and starting rumors that Chief Moses planned to join them in western Montana with a fighting force. When soldiers from Fort Missoula killed six and wounded three, including Tabador, their chief, the Nez Percés retreated, but not before a number of Bitterroot settlers again fled their homes for safety in makeshift forts.

Meanwhile, a band of Bannocks deserted their Malheur reservation in May, 1878, and, joined by Paiutes and straggling Nez Percés from White Bird's group, swept across northeastern Oregon pillaging, killing cattle, and murdering isolated whites, pursued from May 30 until subdued September 4 by the army. In eastern Montana marauding Sioux struck across the border from Canada.

Settlers were further distraught over the recurrence of scarlet fever, which had first appeared mildly among white children in 1876, then among Indians, a number of whom died, and now in 1878 in virulent form claimed white children in the Bitterroot. Roving Indians threatened to spread the disease. "The Indians simply are homeless children, growing up in ignorance, idleness, and vice," declared the *Missoulian*. "In the interest of humanity it is a duty the government owes to the Indians to circumscribe their habits."[32]

Although authorized Indian hunting caravans were escorted two or three times a year by U.S. cavalry, Indians continually slipped away or disdained escorts. Settlers complained again that Flatheads fired prairies or roamed drunkenly through villages. Farmers in Smith's River valley in the Musselshell country petitioned the army to keep Indians at home, specifying Flatheads, Nez Percés, and Pend Oreilles, who "constitute a screen for the approach of hostile parties," and threatened to form a volunteer company for defense. The commandant at Fort Baker, forwarding this request, added that peaceful Indians amused themselves by frightening strangers, and the commandant at Fort Shaw, emphasizing the disappearance of buffalo, said the Indians compensated for poor hunts by butchering settlers' cattle.

Moreover, as migration brought sufficient white labor to many towns, the *Missoulian* wondered editorially "whether the continued presence of Indians about town is wholly beneficial," observing:

> The presence of Indians in town has not only been tolerated but encouraged, for the reason that they have made themselves useful in washing and scrubbing, in sawing wood, carrying water in the winter, and pulling weeds from gardens in the summer. . . . Their trade with business men, from the proceeds for their labors and sale of furs and skins, has been considerable.[33]

Responding to its citizens, the Montana legislature on February 5, 1879, memorialized the commissioner of Indian affairs to order Indians confined on reservations. "The Indians in Montana are nomads and as such are seldom on their reserve but roam at will through our agricultural and pastoral regions, frequently entailing losses upon our settlers," said the legislature, pointing out that, if Indians were restricted, immigration and industry would flourish.

When the commissioner did restrict Indians to reservations, Ronan protested that his Indians were "a harmless, industrious community," but that "every year renegade Spokanes, Umatillas, Colvilles, Lower Pend Oreilles and other Indians from the lower country infest the towns. . . . The drinking, gambling, and carouses of the lower country Indians would be reported in the local press and, as a matter of course, all excesses were laid at the door of the Indians of this reservation."[34] He ordered "all foreign Indians to their homes and was assisted in the enforcement of the order by the commanding officer at Fort Missoula," but believed that Indians of the Bitterroot and Jocko, who were related, should be allowed to visit one another. Moreover, he said, Indian farmers needed to leave the Jocko to sell produce and cattle in town, as well as conduct civilized business, citing as an example the widow Sabin who, after selling more than two hundred cattle, went to Missoula to bank her money for her children's education.

In the absence of manifest authority, settlers vexed by Indians called the nearest agent. Thus Ronan, at the request of whites, intervened (fruitlessly) in a dispute between six or eight families of white stockmen and thirty Indians detached from the Lower Pend Oreilles who hunted near Horse Plains, a district favored by Indians "from the Spokane and Columbia River country, gambling, drinking, and carousing around the white settlements."[35] The whites retaliated by poisoning Indian dogs, altering stallions, and working Indian horses in fields without payment.

For their part, Montana's Indians were apprehensive of a report, circulated by six nontreaty tribes that counciled at Spokane Bridge in 1877, to the effect that the whites intended to lock the Indians in corrals.

As the visible Indian administrator in the area, Ronan was for some years to deal with remnant bands wishing to locate permanently. Among these were ten lodges of refugee Nez Percés at Tobacco Plains, who asked Eneas, chief of the Kutenais, to allow them to settle on the reservation with his people. Among the Nez Percés was White Bird, himself, "now utterly broken in spirit and health and ... perfectly blind. White Bird and his family have not a horse left and the blind chief is being led thither on foot," Ronan advised the commissioner. But whites opposed harboring the once hostile nontreaty Nez Percés, and the commissioner directed Ronan to receive them only as prisoners of war. Ronan met the Nez Percé chiefs, Eagle-against-the-Light, Red Mountain, and Tukalikshimei (son of Looking Glass) at St. Ignatius Mission, with Father Joseph M. Cataldo as interpreter. They asked for "a home where our children can grow ... a place to stop for good." Despite Ronan's recommendation that these Nez Percés be settled on the Jocko, the federal government refused, and White Bird withdrew to Canada. "I am very poor now. I have lost all my children, all my brothers, all my women in the war, although I took no part in it," Eagle-against-the-Light sorrowed.[36] Individual Nez Percés, however, joined reservation families without authorization.

Notwithstanding restrictions on Indian movement off reservations and fears occasioned by roving bands, Charlot's Indians remained in the Bitterroot Valley. In accord with the Garfield contract, the Indian office issued them fifty-one patents for public lands.

Medary had passed these to Ronan, who was ordered to deliver them. The agent, talking with Charlot, found that the chief continued to cling to the Stevens treaty of 1855. "Charlot appreciates the government's strength and knows he can be forced," Ronan reported, "but he says if it comes to that, he will only ask the privilege to seek another home and another country of his choice."[37] Charlot refused a patent; he said he did not know the boundaries of his land because white men encroached on it.

"Myself nor my people never asked for such titles," he told Ronan of the Garfield contract. "We signed a paper which was carried around and gave our names. We did so under the impression we were asking the Great Father in Washington to give us the Bitterroot valley as a reservation." The chief regarded patents as a device to eradicate tribal unity and protested taxation on land the Indians considered their own by natural right. Ronan locked the patent documents in his iron safe. No Bitterroot Flathead would take what his chief rejected. The Flatheads, Ronan wrote, "are in a most deplorable and unsatisfactory condition," but they would not accept titles to their lands and they would not move to the reservation.

"It is clearly necessary, in my opinion, that some steps be taken to settle the question, either by sending a commission with power and instructions to act, or by inviting Charlot to a conference at Washington, when the intentions of the government for the welfare of his people might be thoroughly impressed upon him," Ronan wrote the commissioner. "An imperfect apprehension of the terms of the Stevens treaty . . . is the base of all the trouble. It takes time and patience to impress the exact terms of an agreement upon the Indian mind, but when once stamped there it is my experience they are the last to break their obligations, but the foremost to insist upon all the terms of the bond, as by them understood." To this Delegate Maginnis added his concern: "The Flatheads in the Bitterroot refused to receive their lands in severalty; they cannot go to buffalo without creating disturbances in the settlements; and they have done nothing. Their conduct has been good, especially in the Nez Perce war, but they are aggrieved and have been loud in their complaints." In contrast, on the Jocko, "more has been done in the last two years than during the whole time previous thereto since the treaty was made."[38]

In addition to their progress as farmers, reservation Indians sold four thousand dollars' worth of furs in 1879. They owned more than twenty-two hundred horses and three thousand cattle, and raised collectively twenty-three thousand bushels of wheat, four thousand of oats, and many vegetables. In its program to deliver starter cattle to Indians, the federal government gave them 706 head in 1879–80.

Ronan estimated that 70 per cent of the reservation Indians' subsistence came from civilized pursuits; 20 per cent from hunting, fishing, and digging; and the remainder from federal assistance. Ronan declared:

A few more years of encouragement by way of agricultural implements and in keeping their homes and mills running will make these people independent of government aid. Their reservation is one of the finest agricultural and stock ranges in Montana. No rations are issued here, and very few of the Indians leave the reservation for the chase, relying principally on their farms for support.[39]

With pride he mailed the commissioner a sample of wheat grown on the shore of Flathead Lake by Baptiste Ignace, using lake mists for irrigation.

The reservation farmers were mostly Pend Oreilles and mixed-bloods. Arlee's Flatheads seemed content with their shares of the Garfield payments for Bitterroot land and cared chiefly for horse herds. Three hundred and fifty Kutenais, remote from the agency, adopted farming slowly, although Eneas, their chief, bought equipment and seeds from his stipend to encourage them.

The young men of the confederated tribes were restless, for in earlier times the young depended on prowess in warfare and hunting for prestige and social advancement. Now hunting and warfare were largely closed to them. Chiefs promised Indian men they could hunt as rewards for tending crops, according to Ronan:

They say that one incentive for planting crops was their promise to their young people that some could hunt after the crops were in, if others stayed to take care of the herds and crops. They say that if they are not allowed to keep this promise, they will not be able to keep scattered bands from slipping away without authority. . . . Two of the chiefs will go along.[40]

Late in 1878 a large buffalo herd appeared again on the plains. The reservation chieftains—Arlee, Michel, and Eneas—petitioned the commissioner:

We cannot read words but from those we hear spoken from our agent and others, we feel that you have a good heart for the Indian. . . . For over thirty years we have had missionaries among us to teach us the Gospel and try to point out the trail which will lead to the white man's road. A great many of us have houses to live in—have good farms, fenced in—have good crops now planted—have families growing up around us, and our laws forbid that we have more than one wife. We have never had war or trouble with your people and during all our lives until last summer we could go to traders and buy guns and ammunition. While the Nez Perces were on the warpath we did not care to buy ammunition or guns, as it might look bad to the whites, since that tribe has always been our friends against the Blackfeet and Sioux, but when the war was over, our young men, after laboring in the fields and gathering their crops, thought it hard when the agent told them they could not buy ammunition with which to hunt. Our crops are now in, and the buffalo are only a short distance from us, across a northern trail which leads through no white settlements, and our young men desire to hunt them and procure meat while the old people stay at home to look after the crops until they ripen, when all return from the hunt and help to gather them. . . . We cannot throw away our good guns as they cost us very much and we have forgotten the use of the bow and arrow.[41]

Permitted to hunt with military escort, the Flatheads failed. Not only did they obtain little meat, but a party under Andre, the reservation police chief, ventured into Canada, where Blackfeet and Assiniboin scouts ordered them to go home or fight. Wisely, the Flatheads turned back.

When the hunters reached Missoula, "some fifteen or twenty Flathead warriors rode down Main Street and up Front Street with a Sioux scalp carried aloft on a scalp-stick. They were provided with blank cartridges which they fired off at intervals, and yipped as they

Ka-Ka-She (Gonzaga University)

Louison, Flathead nation judge and head man, taken by E. H. Boos, Missoula. (Montana Historical Society)

Kutenais raising a sun dance lodge near Camas, 1908. The shaman who called the dance also selected the sacred pine which was used in building the lodge and stood atop it to supervise a construction. (Montana Historical Society)

General Henry Beebe Carrington, who removed Charlot's band from the Bitterroot valley. (Dr. A. A. Sallquist collection, Gonzaga University)

Left to right: Charlot, General Carrington, Michel Revais, and Peter Ronan. Although not identified, the picture doubtless was taken on or about the time Charlot moved from the Bitterroot to the reservation. (Gonzaga University)

Charlot and his band leaving the Bitterroot valley, October 17, 1891. Stevensville is in the background. (Montana Historical Society)

Charlot, chief of the Flathead nation, in 1903. (Montana Historical Society)

Bishop Brondel lays the cornerstone at St. Ignatius for the brick church, in 1891. (Gonzaga University)

St. Ignatius mission, November 16, 1895, photographed by the Montana Department of Agriculture. The brick mission church replaced the original wooden chapel which burned. (Montana Historical Society)

Indian men at St. Ignatius, wearing clothing that ranges from the western dandy at left to the fullblood in blanket, second from left. Taken in 1909 by the U.S. Reclamation Service. (Federal Records Center, Seattle)

Two unidentified Indian men on the porch of the priests' house, St. Ignatius. After dressing in their finery for the photographer, according to a note on the back of the picture, they were indignant that the colors did not show and the priest painted a picture of them to mollify them. The hairstyles and skin clothing are authentic but the cotton shirts under these date from a later time. (Gonzaga University)

An Indian cabin on the reservation. This is not Charlot's, but fits the description by Carrington of Charlot's surroundings. Indians usually moved into tipis during the summer and left the poles pitched year round. (Federal Records Center, Seattle)

An Indian sod-roofed cabin at St. Ignatius mission, 1909. The high building in the rear is the mission water tower. U.S. Reclamation Service photograph. (Federal Records Center, Seattle)

Gentle Bird, a Flathead photographed in Omaha during the exposition of 1898. (Dr. A. A. Sallquist collection, Gonzaga University)

Burning infected Indian tipis on the Flathead reservation during the
smallpox epidemic of 1901 at the direction of Dr. George S. Lesher,
agency physician. (Rebecca Lesher collection, Gonzaga University)

Indian men gambling, Flathead Reservation, 1910, according to caption by the U.S. Reclamation Service. (Federal Records Center, Seattle)

went along," relishing the gapes of whites who watched, said the *Missoulian*.[42] They held a scalp dance at night.

In the fall of 1879, when sizable buffalo herds again appeared, the blind, seventy-year-old Big Canoe commanded his last Flathead chase (he died the following May), but the universal hunt was dampened early by the murder of a white man twenty miles from the Blackfoot agency and by clashes with the Sioux. The Flathead hunt succeeded, although settlers again declared that the Indians indiscriminately butchered cattle with buffalo, and General Terry reported numerous white hunters slaughtering buffalo at the same time. Under such conditions, buffalo hunting was precarious without glory. The hunter risked everything; the farmer prospered at home.

"Never in the history of this reservation have the Indians enjoyed a more prosperous season," Ronan told the Indian office in 1880, describing "snug houses, well-fenced fields of waving grain, vegetable gardens, and thriving stock and permanent appearance of the homes of the industrious portion of the tribes." The exemplar of the farmer "has a tendency each year of inducing the more careless and improvident to follow the example of husbandry and thrift . . . to give up their wandering and hunting."[43]

When Archbishop John Charles Seghers, the tall, spare coadjutor to the archbishop of Oregon City, laid the cornerstone of a new St. Ignatius church on August 7, 1879 (although the church would not be dedicated until 1889) and confirmed one hundred and four Indian children into the Catholic faith, visiting chieftains from the treaty Nez Percés, Umatillas, and Coeur d'Alenes discoursed on the advantages of tilling the land, adopting white men's ways, and educating Indian children to be industrious and self-reliant. Yet the archbishop's arrival at St. Ignatius was celebrated Indian fashion by one hundred mounted Flatheads, directed by Father D'Aste, firing rifles and riding furiously around the prelate's vehicle, the reservation ambulance.

"The faith and fervor of these Indians is really wonderful," the archbishop observed, "but their singing is bad, fearful, horrible; loud yells without audible pronunciation." Arlee's reservation Flatheads took the occasion to petition Seghers for a chapel near the agency headquarters. At St. Mary's the archbishop endured a similar noisy reception. In an interview, Seghers counseled Charlot to move to the reservation. The chief respectfully declined. Of this talk, the archbishop wrote, the Flatheads "occupy the ground that has been theirs for time immemorial, and . . . now the government, with one stroke of the pen, declares it to be theirs no longer. The next thing will be some expressions of astonishment on the part of the government that there is another Indian war."[44]

During 1879 the mission printed a Salish language dictionary, the culmination of Father Mengarini's early labors to record the language, and of Fathers Diomedi's and Giorda's continuation of his studies. It was intended primarily to instruct missionaries in the Flathead dialect and consequently related pronunciation and grammatical structure, as far as possible, to Latin; it defined terms as missionaries perceived them in the minds of Flatheads, and such words as "seduction" were defined in Latin rather than in English, although the dictionary was fundamentally to translate Salish to English and English to Salish. The most remarkable of sixty-six items produced by the St. Ignatius press between the years 1879 and 1899, it was hand set over a period of four years by Indian boys directed by W. J. Harber, a white compositor employed by the mission, using a five-hundred-dollar press imported from St. Louis.[45]

The mission boys' school in 1879 was converted to a boarding school under a contract between the Indian office and the Bureau of Catholic Indian Missions. By 1880 the girls' and boys' boarding schools operated together, with thirty-five to forty girls and fifty-five to sixty boys enrolled, usually more pupils than federal allotments supported. About half the pupils stayed at school twelve months of the year, although in summer the classes were curtailed and manual skills emphasized. The boys learned carpentry, blacksmithing, painting, and cutting and sawing wood, and the girls, housekeeping (including quilting and fancy work) and gardening. Taught to read and write English, the children also used the *Young Catholic Reader*, common in eastern parochial schools, as their religious textbook. The Indians were taught as if white. By 1880 perhaps fifty-five reservation Flatheads could read and write English.[46]

In reservation trading stores the Flatheads bought items like those in Missoula's shops: earrings at 14 cents a set, finger rings, carpet slippers, boots, axes, pans, silk, buttons, pocket knives, clothing, gunpowder, padlocks, ladies' shoes for $1.72 a pair, sombreros (very popular), and Canadian blankets at $3.02.

Ronan reported:

All are cash transactions or trades of merchandise for articles the Indians may have to barter. Traders (at least the licensed traders) have kept regular book accounts with the Indians and I see no reason why an Indian should be deprived of credit at the post trader's store when he can go into neighboring towns and procure credit, where the merchants are only too glad to cultivate the Indian trade, as the Indians of this reservation are regarded as honest and punctual in their payments.

Moreover, the Indians understood values.

As a general thing the reservation Indians are fully capable of protecting themselves in trade and if prices do not suit them at the licensed trading post (being well informed as to prices) they have an intelligent and independent way (like white people) of hitching up their teams and carting their produce to where they can make the best terms.[47]

Among all ages, white clothing was adopted when it suited better than traditional dress—sombreros and cloth pants for the men, bandannas and bright shawls for women—leading to the curious combinations that delighted frontier photographers. Yet Flathead women who made calico dresses cut them to the ankle-length patterns of skin clothing memorized in childhood, and a good many older Indians continued to wear long hair and wrap in skin robes.

In the climactic two years following the Nez Percés' war, the old days truly faded except in memory and occasional celebrations. Michel, who adopted Ronan's first son into the Pend Oreille tribe, gave the boy his own name, Plenty Grizzly Bear, then mourned, "Now, I have no name," and put aside his fringed leggings, his guns, and his horses as a nameless one, until the Lower Pend Oreilles, given some ponies, agreed that he might assume the name of a dead chief.

Charlot's Indians, poorest of the confederated Flatheads, clung more than their reservation relatives to traditional Indian dress.

Ronan doubtless set the confederated Flatheads' acculturation in its proper light when he observed a few years later that "this is rather an enforced condition among many of them, caused by the disappearance of game and the necessity of gaining a living by cultivating the soil."

▲▲▲▲▲▲▲▲▲▲▲▲▲▲▲▲▲▲▲▲▲▲▲▲▲▲▲▲

CHAPTER 9

CHARLOT'S STAND IN THE BITTERROOT

▼▼▼▼▼▼▼▼▼▼▼▼▼▼▼▼▼▼▼▼▼▼▼▼▼▼▼▼

In 1879 the retiring commissioner of Indian affairs, Ezra A. Hayt, enunciated a national policy of allotting lands in severalty to Indians, "thus to foster the pride of individual ownership of property, instead of their former dependence on the tribe." Succeeding commissioners advanced this view. Commissioner Hiram Price in 1882 declared:

> The allotment system tends to break up tribal relations. It has the effect of creating individuality, responsibility, and a desire to accumulate property. It teaches the Indians habits of industry and frugality, and . . . in the end it will relieve the government of large annual appropriations.

Until 1887 Congress enacted none of the bills introduced to allot reservation lands, but allotments in severalty and the dismantling of tribal unity remained at the base of federal Indian policy. Many whites sincerely believed no other course practical.

The Flatheads felt the effects of this national plan. The years 1882 to 1895 finally brought the Flatheads together on their reservation, and then began dismemberment of the reservation as a tribal preserve. The instrument of federal policy on the Jocko was allotment; it followed extension of the Northern Pacific Railroad through the reservation and mixing of dislocated Indian bands into the reservation's population.

At the same time, the confederated Flatheads struggled among themselves to accommodate a judicial system imposed by the federal government, while economic competition alienated full-blooded Flatheads from mixed-bloods residing on the reservation. No Flathead mistook these signs of change—he saw them everywhere, affirming the repression of old ways.

"Numerous Indian parties have shuffled into town during the past week. They have been hunting buffalo, and either their animals are too poor to pack provisions or they did not get any," reported an 1880 *Missoulian*. Agent Ronan, hearing drum beats, dispersed the dancers, for the government banned war ceremonials and the agent explained that the Flatheads, dancing themselves to exhaustion, were susceptible to pneumonia and other ailments.

Now that whites outnumbered the Indians, the whites showed their impatience with native ways openly. Said the *Missoulian*:

> It is certain that there is not an Indian on the face of the earth that belongs to the town of Missoula, and it does not seem the correct thing that citizens should be liable to be stoned on the public highways or be subjected to intimidation or search as has too frequently happened during the past year. A decent regard for the welfare of the settlements in this county teaches us that the Indians must go.[1]

Asked by citizens to drive Indians from Missoula and camps near town, the commandant at Fort Missoula deferred to civil authorities, and the Indians lingered. A reporter asked one Flathead where he got whiskey.

> He said it was no trouble to get all he wanted; much of it was supplied by a Chinaman who worked at Fort Missoula; much of it came from soldiers who were anxious to cultivate friendly relations with Indian women, and there were several white men around town who would buy the whiskey and receive pay for their trouble.[2]

In compliance with the federal order to keep Indians on reservations, Ronan occasionally sent chiefs to round up strays, but few nomads belonged to the reservation tribes. They hung around to irritate white citizens by cadging food and liquor.

In 1882 the Northern Pacific petitioned for right of way for its main line across the Jocko reservation, having chosen—after twelve years of depression and indecision—a route north of Lake Pend Oreille. Although most of the confederated Flatheads opposed the line, "regarding the road as fatal to their interests, and the sure precursor of abandonment of their homes and lands to the whites," the assistant attorney general who negotiated with them, Joseph Kay McCammon, concluded an agreement on September 2, 1882, by which the Flatheads ceded a strip two hundred feet wide and fifty-three miles long.[3]

The railroad route ran north from Missoula through the narrow Coriacan defile, westward along the valleys of Finlay Creek and the Jocko to the Clark Fork, and emerged from the reservation near the mouth of the Missoula (Flathead) River in the vicinity of Paradise, Montana. It is sharp, rock-bound country with no alternative routes. In their three-day council with McCammon, Arlee—in an essay at sharp bargaining—asked one million dollars for the right of way, which McCammon rejected out of hand.

"You [white men] told us that after awhile we would be intelligent and rich like white men," Eneas grumbled. "We are poor now. We try to have whites assist us, and they won't because we are Indians." Arlee said:

We are not dissatisfied or hostile toward you or the government. We only want a fair bargain. . . . My forefathers, our chiefs . . . were like men with veils over their heads; they could not see. . . . When Governor Stevens arrived and he began talking about this part of the country, they had no idea of their country; they were stupid. They signed the treaty. This reservation was offered by the man who made the treaty and we are holding onto it.[4]

For 1,430 acres of right of way and stations, sidings, and depots, the Northern Pacific paid the Flatheads $16,000, and to individual Indians whose farms it crossed, $7,625.

McCammon obtained the Flathead chiefs' consent by promising that he would represent very strongly to the federal government the Indians' desire to move the reservation's northern boundary to the Canadian border, annexing to the reserve a mountainous, timbered region suitable for hunting and fishing, where only eight white families squatted in a cluster at the head of Flathead Lake. Nothing was done to adjust the northern borderline, and Ronan subsequently wrote McCammon, at the chiefs' insistence, that "the young men and malcontents have been sowing the seeds of dissension by claiming that you made a distinct promise that the country would be given the Indians."[5] In anticipation of annexation, the chiefs warned the settlers by the lake to leave. The annexed territory, argued the chiefs, would provide room for western Indians "who would be welcomed to a home on their reservation."

One cannot overstate the enthusiasm of settlers for railroads, for the tracks at last embraced the frontier in national fraternity and commerce. The railroad itself forecast that its completion would result in the "prompt, thorough, economical, and humane settlement of the Indian problem in the Northwest." The Flatheads viewed the road differently. It would be one more incursion, one more push backward from their lands.

As the rail line approached, Flatheads ejected Northern Pacific surveyors from the reservation until Ronan explained the surveys were to determine damage to farmlands. Soon he advised the commissioner:

> An immense crew of railroad constructors is now at work west of the reservation, consisting of 7,400 with camp followers, gamblers, ex-convicts, and lewd women. They are rapidly advancing to the borders of the reservation, accompanied by portable saloons, gambling houses, etc. Merchants and traders of all descriptions also advance with the construction party.[6]

Although saloons could not stand on Indian land, there was no abatement of diversions as the railroad builders crossed the preserve.

Many Indians furnished piles, ties, and cordwood for the railroad; Flathead cattlemen sold its agents beef at high prices. Under its contract with the Indians, the railroad gave them free transportation, "thus enabling the loafers, drunkards, and gamblers of the lower country to come up here," Father Van Gorp scolded, adding, "Many Nez Perces, who escaped at the time of Joseph's surrender ... have of late invaded the reservation, defying all authority and generally trying to demoralize these Indians."[7] Seventy railroad workers protested as a group the sale of whiskey to "renegade Indians." Ronan disbanded the volunteer Indian police as unequal to the furor surrounding construction.

An epidemic of smallpox progressed along the railroad line in 1882, reaching Missoula, and quickened in 1883 after Indians broke into the Weeksville pesthouse to steal patients' blankets; then it waned in mid-year. Shortly after, when whites skirmished at Evaro with a handful of drunken Indians, a frightened telegraph operator tapped the message, "We are all surrounded. . . . Send help for God's sake." But the encounter subsided within minutes.

In his annual report for 1883, Ronan wrote:

> As a proof that the Indians of this reservation, while undoubtedly brave, are also law-abiding, I refer with pride to the fact of the completion of the Northern Pacific Railroad through their lands, and against their strongest wishes, without any annoyance or opposition being offered to the railroad company that for a moment could be termed serious.[8]

With construction of the railway, another observer said, "Sawmills along the entire route were rapidly clearing off the best pine timber, and ruining the trout streams by the clogging sawdust." A local recession set in when the construction crews moved eastward. Not far behind them came immigrants seeking homesteads along the tracks, knowing nothing of the Flatheads' history and earlier dignity, seeing around them rootless, beggar Indians who should be removed as obstacles to settlement.

The confederated Flatheads' dress revealed the divisions that civilization worked among them. When Archbishop Seghers visited St. Ignatius a second time,

> The procession presented a fantastic appearance, from the well-clad and thrifty looking cultivators . . . in their suits of black, to the wild followers of the chase, some in scarlet blankets, with broad beaded belts, others in gala-trimmed buckskins and head dresses of eagle feathers, but civilized costumes largely prevailed.[9]

The Indians beat on anvils and fired guns to greet the archbishop at the agency.

The older, full-blooded Flatheads who had not become thrifty-looking cultivators found themselves poor and hemmed in. "Many consider their changed mode of living, from lodges to houses, and from their hitherto simple food to the more complicated cookery of the white man, has had an injurious effect on their health," Ronan observed. Mollie explained, "When the tribes on the Flathead reservation followed their own nomadic way of living . . . they were a clean, healthy, picturesque people; most of them could not learn clean and hygienic ways of living year in and year out in the same house."[10]

While the railroad was being built through the reservation, Charlot's hope of holding the Bitterroot as his home weakened. The Northern Pacific had claimed odd sections of land in the valley under its land grant, but the secretary of the interior ruled against the railroad in January, 1883, partly due to the work of John Mullan, the road builder, now a Washington attorney who represented Bitterroot settlers. With this ruling, the unoccupied land in the valley was open for taking. The congressional act of February 11, 1874, had extended the Homestead Act to the Bitterroot, the secretary explained, and his decision left Charlot's Flatheads with only the land described in the fifty-one patents in the agency safe.

Because, as the *Missoulian* said, "the coming of the railroads to Montana has placed the two races in close contact, and many misunderstandings and difficulties have arisen," Congress appointed a commission to report on the condition of Montana Indians.[11] A subcommittee, comprised of stumpy, florid Senator George G. Vest of Missouri and Montana's Delegate Maginnis, visited St. Ignatius on September 6, 1883. When they stepped off the train at Arlee, Vest was amused by the consternation of some five hundred Chinese railroad laborers "as the Indians extended us a welcome in one of their characteristic dances, accompanied by a good deal of noise and much reckless riding of their ponies around the Chinese camp."

Michel, speaking for the reservation chiefs, told the investigators "emphatically that they wished their reservation to remain as it is, and that they desired to hold their lands in common and not in severalty," Vest reported. The reservation Indians recited their familiar plaints: their land was invaded, their people corrupted, and pledges to them unfilled.

Arlee frequently interrupted Michel when the talk turned to the mission schools, Vest noted, "and we subsequently ascertained that the Jesuits had put Arlee's son to work in the harvest, and that the old chief had indignantly removed him, declaring he sent the boy there to learn how to read and write, not to work like a squaw." Vest was so favorably impressed by the conduct of the St. Ignatius Mission schools that he championed them for some years afterward.

On Sunday, September 9, the delegation moved to Stevensville, accompanied by Hugh McQuaid of the *Helena Independent*, who, like many newspapermen from smaller towns, filed stories to the metropolitan newspapers. They saw Father Ravalli, now partially paralyzed, "lying in his little room with its crucifix and books, [where] he prescribes for the sick and even performs difficult surgical operations."[12]

Charlot came to St. Mary's Mission with five head men to meet Vest and Maginnis, telling them, "Your great father, Garfield, put my name to a paper I never signed, and Arlee is drawing money to which he has no right." According to newspaper accounts, the stocky chief went on: "We are only a few. We are poor and weak. You want to place your foot upon our neck, and grind our face in the dust, but I will not go. I will go to the plains." After Vest reminded him that Joseph had tried to go to the plains, Charlot threw down his hat and stomped on it, crying, "You may take Charlot to the reservation—but Charlot will have no breath in his nostrils. Charlot will be dead!"

McQuaid's report, doubtless impregnated by the speech of Indians in popular fiction, appeared widely in newspapers. The Butte *Inter-Mountain* editorialized, "The old chief talks like King Philip, or one of Cooper's lords of the forest." Charlot, as a matter of fact, did not speak English, and although the eloquence in McQuaid's stories escaped Vest's stenographer, its circulation in newspaper accounts brought Charlot modest and fleeting recognition in great cities as a prince of the mountains.

Vest summarized the council:

The publication of the [Garfield] agreement with Charlot's signature or mark affixed to it created the impression that all trouble with the Indians had terminated, and a large white immigration poured into the Bitterroot valley. The result is that the Indians who adhered to Charlot are yet in the valley, miserably poor, with one or two exceptions, surrounded by whites who are anxious for their removal, and the young men, with no restraint upon them, lounging around the saloons in

Stevensville and utterly worthless. As the case now stands these Indians have no title to any portion of the Bitterroot valley, as they refuse to take the patents, and are defying the order of the President for their removal.

Vest and Maginnis could not induce Charlot to move to the reservation; they finally agreed that he should visit Washington to talk over the matter. With this concession and McQuaid's portrayal of him, Charlot emerged as a sympathetic figure; he never yielded the noble posture that issued from the 1883 dispatches. Yet, if the Indians "be asked their opinions individually (not making the chief their mouth-piece), a large majority will be willing to move to the Jocko reservation," Ronan told the congressional investigators.[13]

In the middle of January, 1884, Charlot left for Washington by railroad, accompanied by his interpreter, Michel Revais, four head-men, and Agent Ronan. As they departed, rumors of gold in the Coeur d'Alene Mountains started a winter rush into Idaho, and renewed prospecting in western Montana uncovered lead quartz near Frenchtown and gold on Lightning Creek near Horse Plains. Between local prospecting and promotion of Thompson Falls as a supply camp for the Coeur d'Alene rush, the country was soon flooded with more white men.

On the journey, Charlot was unusually talkative. He questioned Ronan closely about feeding the crowded population of Chicago. In the capital, the Flathead delegation attended dinners given for them by John Mullan, McCammon, and Senator Vest; they called on Gustav Sohon, the onetime soldier artist, and spent a moment with President Arthur. Mullan, Vest, and Maginnis joined the business conferences in Secretary H. M. Teller's office, where Charlot was intrigued by the secretary's swivel chair.

The chief remarked that everyone in Washington seemed to be in a hurry and talked much. Confronted by the city's buildings and traffic, with evidence of wealth on all sides, Charlot told Ronan that in his Bitterroot cabin he was freer to do as he pleased than the nation's important men.

Teller offered Charlot an annual pension of five hundred dollars, a house, restoration of his chieftainship of the Flathead nation, and homes and cattle for his people if they moved to the reservation.

"The old chief maintained a stubborn silence, and when the secretary offered him a paper to sign he refused it with an angry gesture," the *Missoulian* said in a report probably written by Ronan.[14]

The Flathead delegation remained in Washington for nearly a month, during which Charlot and Revais were hospitalized at the secretary's direction for operations to forestall blindness from iritis. Charlot's failing sight was improved, but nothing could be done for Revais.

Although Charlot refused to leave the Bitterroot, he told the secretary (and later confided to Father Van Gorp) that he would allow his people to accept their patents. Charlot was told he could live in the valley as long as he remained peaceful and friendly to settlers. In a side conversation with Ronan, Teller instructed the agent to offer inducements to the Bitterroot Flatheads to move without their chief, and authorized him to supply Charlot's people with food and implements as a gesture of the government's good intentions toward them.

To any Bitterroot family that moved, Ronan subsequently promised one hundred and sixty acres of unoccupied reservation land, a house, a wagon, two cows, and implements. Seventeen families left the Bitterroot to settle on a plateau on the north side of the Jocko River near the agency, where Ronan built their houses and turned the ground in their fields, setting one hundred Indians to work on irrigation ditches for the new arrivals. "I have no hesitation in saying that if the same policy is carried out in the future . . . it will be only a brief matter of time until Charlot's band, with the exception of that chief and a few of his relatives, will be settled on the reservation," Ronan predicted, but when more Bitterroot families moved, the government gave them nothing. Five years later Ronan would say, "They live upon this reservation and are yet unprovided for, except by their own exertions and the small assistance I can give them."[15]

Those who stayed in the Bitterroot existed in poverty. "Poor people, they behaved well during the holy days," Father D'Aste wrote from St. Mary's Mission shortly after Christmas, 1884.

We have had since the fifteenth of this month over eighteen inches

235

of snow . . . and very cold weather. And yet the Indians came to camp around the mission. . . . It was a pitiful sight to see the poor women going, during the coldest weather . . . trying to keep up their supply of firewood . . . in order to prevent their families, living in cotton lodges, from freezing at night. . . . They all, with the exception of a few halfbreeds, came to confession. And seeing them, you would think they had plenty of everything, for they looked content and happy. . . . What will be the future of the Flatheads? I am afraid that plenty of suffering is in it for them. They are now very poor, and if the government fails to come to their help . . . I am afraid that starvation will get the lot of them."[16]

Acting on his instructions from Washington, Ronan issued farm tools to Charlot's band. "The chief returns from the agency with a long line of wagons, handsomely painted . . . and laden with agricultural implements of every description, also bacon, coffee, tea, sugar, oatmeal, soap, etc.," said the *Missoulian*. Ronan believed the gifts "encouraged and [have] given these poor people faith in the promises and fostering care of the government should they leave their homes and remove to the reserve."[17]

Although Charlot would not go to the Jocko, nomadic bands of other tribes were eager for land on reservations. Congress in 1886 authorized a Northwest Indian Commission to negotiate with Indians in Minnesota, Dakota, Idaho, Washington, Oregon, and Montana to modify contracts, relocate bands, and obtain further land cessions. In the spring of 1887, when the commission (comprised then of Congressman John V. Wright of Pennsylvania, Jared W. Daniels, a veteran of twenty-seven years of Indian arbitration, and H. W. Andrews of the Department of the Interior) talked with Father Van Gorp at Gonzaga College in Spokane Falls, he urged them to see Charlot, saying, "I believe that now he would be very willing to treat with this commission for removal to the Jocko. In fact, he expects to—his people are anxious to move over to the Jocko, but Charlot's not moving detains them."[18] The commission was not empowered to confer with Charlot, however, and did not discuss removal with him.

At Sandpoint, Idaho, the commission contracted with Lower Pend Oreille (Kalispel) bands to relinquish claims to Washington and Idaho lands, and then obtained consent from the confederated Flatheads to move the Pend Oreilles onto the Jocko reservation, promising a new gristmill and sawmill and a blacksmith shop as inducements. While most Spokanes settled among the Coeur d'Alenes, a few of them also moved to the Jocko under an agreement with the commission.[19] Pend Oreilles began arriving at the Flathead Agency the following August, some transporting goods by horse-drawn travois, and others riding the Northern Pacific (which charged the Indian office $8.10 for each adult). A group remained in Idaho, saying they would not move, then changed their minds and pestered Ronan for railroad tickets.

A band that demanded homes on the Jocko consisted of approximately one hundred Canadian Prairie Crees and Santeux, refugees from Louis Riel's 1885 rebellion in the North West Territory. A representative of this group, Pierre Boucher (Ronan called him "Busha") in August, 1887, requested asylum for sixty families living on Sun Creek. These ill-fated revolutionaries barely had survived their two years in the United States, for they fled Canada with nothing. The Assiniboins of Fort Belknap reservation divided rations secretly for a few months with the Crees. When a Canadian police sergeant entered the United States in September, 1885, to arrest the refugees, they moved constantly to evade him while a coterie of American sympathizers clamored for their amnesty.

Riel's lieutenant, Gabriel Dumont, a beefy former trapper, met President Arthur, made platform addresses in the United States, and toured briefly with a Wild West show, rallying public reaction in support of the Crees, which finally led the federal government to say that it would "not connive at their being kidnapped," whereupon Canada withdrew its sergeant.

The Crees, driven from the Judith Basin by U.S. troopers, wintered near Fort Assiniboine, where the garrison fed them rather than watch them starve. A miniscule political tempest arose over the use of the Indian office's "starving fund" for the Crees, while the Indians traded horses, guns, clothing, and everything else of value for food for their women and children. Some starved nevertheless.

The band walked to Fort Belknap, were fed, and sent away. They scavenged throughout 1886, many sickening and some dying from eating dead cattle loaded with strychnine thrown on the range to poison wolves. In the winter of 1886–87 the Montana legislature voted five hundred dollars to avert famine, but many Crees existed by eating frozen cattle.

Charles A. Larrabee, an Indian office employee, circulated a memorandum: "Whatever their crimes in Canada, they have done us no wrong.... We cannot allow them to starve on our territory!"[20] He recommended that the Crees be located permanently on the Flathead reservation. Thus Boucher approached Ronan. Learning of his mission, one Montana newspaper said:

> It is stated that the band of British Cree Indians who have been for two years a constant source of annoyance, trouble, and expense to Montana want to settle on the Flathead reservation. . . . They have been in a chronic state of poverty, beside their natural condition of laziness. . . . Send these Crees back to their own country. Give them no asylum here. The whole Cree nation will be down here in a few years if this detachment is allowed to settle.[21]

Although the commissioner of Indian affairs favored "as a simple act of humanity . . . [giving them] a chance to earn their bread when that is all they ask," the confederated Flatheads denied the Crees a place on their reservation. Despite this, Boucher brought fifty to the Jocko shortly before Christmas, 1888, declaring, "The Crees have resolved to settle on this reserve with or without the consent of the Indians who belong here." The Flatheads demanded to be rid of the Crees, and Ronan wrote the commissioner, "The Cree young men are not desirable. . . . Most of them are gamblers. Many are dissolute in their habits and none have sympathy with the Indians of this reserve either in blood or religion." The Crees remained. Ronan admitted they "had nothing upon which to live, and depend for food upon the generosity of the Indians of this reservation."[22]

By refusing to go, the Crees became landless residents of the Jocko reservation, working as cattlemen and laborers. By July, 1890, more than eighty Cree families would be living on the Jocko, and others would come. When Ronan called new Cree arrivals together to order them to leave, he said:

It was a pitiful sight to see strong men with tearful eyes listen to the order, which involved a wearisome march back across the Rocky Mountains . . . without provisions to support their almost naked and famished wives and children. They appealed for time to earn something and I granted them permission to remain until after harvest, providing no drinking, dancing, or gambling should be indulged in.

Ronan could not bring himself to drive the Crees away.

Finally in November, 1892, the confederated Flathead council again demanded the Crees' expulsion, declaring that they had "enough of renegades and gamblers of their own tribes . . . without being troubled and annoyed by foreign Indians." Ronan warned of famine if the Crees were turned out in winter, and again they stayed.

Cannily choosing Washington's birthday anniversary in 1894, the Crees of the Flathead reservation petitioned the U.S. secretary of state to give them a portion of the Blackfoot reservation in Montana.[23] The agent, describing them as "almost the serfs" of the Flatheads, reported two hundred and fifty on the reservation, subsisting by selling railroad tourists trinkets of polished cow horns as buffalo souvenirs. Among the petitioners for Blackfoot land were Boucher, Peter Dumont, and others whose names appeared in testimony of the trial of Louis Riel.

When the Blackfeet refused the Crees, they remained among the confederated Flatheads. In 1895 Congress appropriated five thousand dollars to eject them from Montana under military guard. (First Lieutenant John J. Pershing was among the officers detailed to round up Riel refugees.) Some two hundred from the Flathead reservation, with military escort, trudged through Missoula where a reporter found among them Chippewas, French, and half-breeds complaining they were being deported unjustly. Routed through Great Falls, many "hurried back to Montana as soon as the soldiers were gone."

In 1901 the then Flathead agent evicted forty-seven Crees infected with smallpox, occasioning a protest from residents of western Montana towns, and a year later an enrollment agent counted more than one hundred Canadian Crees among the residents of the Flathead reservation. In 1909 the agent would write, "There

239

are a number of Cree Indians on this reservation, they are not enrolled, and little attention is paid them."[24]

The government added no land to the Flathead reservation's estimated 1,433,600 acres to make room for bands newly admitted and did not relocate the northern boundary. The territorial surveyor, indeed, placed the northern boundary four or five miles south of its proper line, marked by a range of low hills. The chiefs mentioned this error to Senator Vest in 1883, but nothing happened, and the commissioner ordered a new survey in 1887 without notifying the Indians, probably because Ronan warned they would resist it.

White settlers encroached on reservation lands even where boundaries were distinct; some of them married Indian women and brought sons onto the reservation on the pretext of cutting rails or cultivating fields for Indian relatives. Ronan reported:

> I can see that if a peremptory stop is not put to this, that the choicest locations on the reserve will be located by such people. The Indians generally are opposed to their young women marrying white men, and claim with a good deal of truth that their women are only sought after by worthless fellows merely to obtain a foothold on the reserve, and when a young woman marries one of them she must sever her reservation rights.[25]

Interracial marriages were to cause legal complications in land titles, but they were of little consequence to half-breeds, emerging as the influential cattlemen and ranchers of the reservation, who abetted whites in their trespasses. To the full-bloods, the white incursion by marriage was galling. The Flathead headman, Louison, asserted:

> Garfield told us to put out all whites from our reserve, even if they were married to Indian women. If an Indian woman marries a white man, she must follow her husband. . . . We do not know what to do about the white men having cattle on the reservation. A white man will buy cattle and put them in the hands of a halfbreed and say he has sold them to him. We know it is not so, but we can't help it.[26]

With immigration, the railroad hamlets of Arlee and Ravalli (the reservation distribution point), Demersville at the head of Flathead (Missoula) River navigation, and Ashley and Selish at the head of

Flathead Lake became focal points of racial friction. Settlement north of the lake warranted a stagecoach line by 1885, and in the next year more than two hundred residents subscribed labor to improve the road. A steamboat line opened on the lake in 1885; a second, in 1887.

The reservation Indians, who regarded the country as theirs, "have an ugly habit of pulling down fences . . . to cut off a few hundred yards of travel," complained one farmer, while another, calling them "Uncle Sam's pets," accused Flatheads of stealing his traps and told Ronan, "I will shoot an Indian as soon as I would a wolf or coyote if they don't keep out of here."[27] Indians trapping fish were fined by the Selish justice of the peace.

Particularly troublesome to settlers were Kutenais from Dayton Creek, their camp on the west shore of Flathead Lake, who by preference wandered, lived off the country, and visited relatives in British Columbia and at Tobacco Plains, a rolling plain of bunch grass extending southward across the international border eleven miles into northwestern Montana. Although most Indians there were nomads, the *Missoulian* found "at the south end of Tobacco Plains . . . an Indian village consisting of some twenty houses—good, substantial cabins . . . a very different class from the roaming vagabonds they are generally supposed to be."[28]

During 1885 disease killed a number of Dayton Creek Kutenais, and whites protested that their wandering spread the ailment. Then rumors of a "war council" on Tobacco Plains—in reality a trading rendezvous—raised the old fears of an Indian union against whites. For a time the United States and Canada corresponded about the sale of liquor to Tobacco Plains Indians by Ramsdell Brothers and other traders there, and the Canadian deputy minister for Indian affairs wrote the American commissioner confidentially, urging closer supervision of these natives.

On occasion the settlers' uneasiness became vigilantism. When a white man was murdered near Horse Plains in June, 1887, a mob from Ashley lynched two Dayton Creek Kutenais, ignoring Chief Eneas' suggestion that a trial might have a "salutary effect" on Indian vagrants.[29] Not long after, ten Indians murdered three white men camped beside a trail, and other Kutenais attacked supply trains. Whites retaliated by murdering a hunting party of the Pend Oreille chief's family. Thereafter, Negro troopers from Fort Missoula periodically maneuvered in the Demersville area to daunt the Indians.

By contrast to many settlers' distrust of Indians, Mollie Ronan recalled:

> As the years passed, we came never to shut a window or a door in our house except against the weather, and no door or window was ever locked. The Indians might stalk into the house at any time of day; they never came with sinister intent, nor took anything, nor did any harm; they either stated their business . . . or they squatted down idly in silence until the spirit moved them to depart.

Nevertheless, Agent Ronan reported, "The building of the Northern Pacific through the reservation . . . caused so much lawlessness along the line that I deemed it best to disband the old [volunteer police] force and organize a paid force under immediate control of the agent."[30]

To take law enforcement away from agents, however, Secretary of the Interior Teller in 1882 directed that reservations establish courts of Indian offenses with three Indian judges, remarking:

> There is no special law authorizing the establishment of such a court, but . . . the policy of the government for many years past has been to destroy the tribal relations as fast as possible, and to use every endeavor to bring the Indian under the influence of the law.

If one defines the law as a systematic and formal application of force by the state in support of explicit rules of conduct, establishing Indian courts imposed a political regimen as well as a judicial system on the Flatheads. The Indian court overnight diminished the chiefs' judicial function, for in the old days, explained Arlee, "When an Indian killed another, the chiefs called together all the Indians, gave the killer's horses and property to the family of the victim, then told the killer not to do it again." For crimes less serious than murder, the chiefs in historic times customarily imposed sentences of cutting hair, whipping, or public scorn. Teller's circular instituted fines and imprisonment as punishments.

The Flathead reservation court, organized in July, 1885, with

Joseph (Grizzly Bear Stand Up), Baptiste Ka-Ka-She (Spotted Foot), and Louison (Red Owl) as judges at seven dollars a month, issued rules for conduct that prohibited the sun, war, and scalp dances; "the practices of so-called medicine men, who operate as a hindrance to the civilization of any tribe"; preventing children from attending school; buying wives; plural marriage; theft; and "outrages against the Northern Pacific Railroad such as displacing switches, placing obstructions on the track, shooting at telegraph insulators, cutting wires, and camping on the right of way." The regulations further provided, "It shall also be the duty of the court to suppress gambling, burning of grass, catching horses of travelers . . . with a view to extorting money, [and] killing stock in revenge for stock breaking into fields." Ten paid reservation policemen were appointed.[31]

With organization of the reservation court, the Indians resisted prosecution in territorial courts. The 1885 Indian appropriation act provided that

all Indians . . . [committing a crime] either within or without an Indian reservation, shall be subject therefor to the laws of the territory, . . . and shall be tried therefor in the same courts and in the same manner, and shall be subject to the same penalties as are all other persons.[32]

This provision, challenged, was upheld by the United States Supreme Court several years after its passage. But the legal status of Flathead Indians was far from clear, and such rulings as those of Hiram Knowles, the district court judge, confused the issue further, for he held that Indians involved in crimes on the reservation could not be tried in civil courts.

Arlee, as first chief of the confederated Flatheads, who had become "a fat and pompous old monarch of the forest," now asserted his authority out of jealousy of the judges. As befitted a chief, Arlee dressed in a fringed buckskin shirt and leggings, beaded vest, belt, pouch, moccasins, and a brightly colored blanket, and "always wore, with the air of its being a crown, a brass dog collar around the crown of his hat," carrying the eagle's wing as his badge of office.[33]

Arlee told a *Missoulian* reporter that judges and police cruelly mistreated prisoners, citing one hundred and twenty lashes meted a woman, and a man hung forty-eight hours by his hands for attempting to escape. The judges felt the lashing "a proper punishment for the women who deserted their husbands and took up with other men, especially as this crime is becoming prevelant" among the confederated tribes. Of Arlee, Judge Louison said, "Arlee tries to break the law, but we try not to pay any attention to him as we know he does not make the law."

On the complaint of Indian Inspector Henry M. Marchant, the commissioner ordered whipping by judges stopped, as the chiefs earlier had been directed to abandon it. Louison commented:

When we had no liquor our people were good. I was a boy when the first white man brought us liquor and many have been killed on account of this liquor and now they drink whiskey every day. They get it from every direction. Now, what can we do to stop this? I whip every one of my children [members of the tribe] for this drinking but now this whipping is stopped I think my children will be glad so they can get drunk without being whipped. It is not the priest who taught us to whip. Two young Indians years before I was born were taken to school among the whites and when they came back home among our people they taught us to whip our bad children.[34]

Despite the influence of the judges, the chiefs held the respect of older Indians—but they were often ignored by the younger. At a council in 1889 to discuss the liquor traffic among Pend Oreilles and Kutenais, Ronan declared the debauchery and drunkenness the worst in his memory, and said to Eneas, "It is my opinion that the beginning of all Indian trouble is whiskey." The chief responded:

Michel [Revais], tell the agent when the Great Father first sent him to us, he was a much younger man than he is today. His children have grown up around him on our reservation and I see one of his boys with him who was born in our country.

I was also young and strong—I looked like a chief—I felt like a chief. In my youth our nation was at war with a great many tribes, and the last of our enemies that we made peace with was the Blackfeet. I was the war chief of my tribe and was called Big Knife. Today we are at peace with all of our enemies. The Blackfeet are our friends, and some of their children are at school with our children at the mission.

Until within a few years, there were few white people near our reservation. Now they surround us on all sides, thick almost as the leaves of the forest. When you came here there was only one white family living at Horse Plains. No white people at all at Thompson Falls; no miners in the Coeur d'Alenes; and where the big city of Spokane Falls now stands I remember of but two white families living there. . . . In the days I speak of, my young men could get but very little whiskey—none knew the taste of it but those who hung around your settlements. It is different today! They have acquired the habit and love the influence of whiskey, and in spite of your laws can procure all they can pay for.

In the old times I would take my whip in my hand and chastise any of my Indians that broke the law either by getting drunk or committing adultery, or any other crime, and they feared me and my authority. . . . I could control my children then—I call my tribe my children. Take the whip from my hand, I have no control. We have no good jails like the white people—no other mode of punishment in our camp, and the wild and dissolute young men laugh at talk when it is not followed by punishment. The heart of a white man must be very small if he cannot see the necessity of authority by a chief in an Indian camp; and when I lose the use of the whip I lose all power to control my people.[35]

Yet Arlee enjoyed influence. He played a central role in harboring two Indian murderers on the reservation; once he led an armed squadron of Flatheads that headed off a posse sent to capture the fugitives. Snarled the *Missoulian*:

The people of this country have been troubled considerably in the past year with Indian outrages of more or less violence. North of the Flathead reservation the settlers dare not leave their houses unguarded and they must be more or less armed to even protect their persons. . . . The fact that no Indian gets punishment for his crimes adds to the unpleasant features. In fact, the people are beginning to ask if they had better not take the law into their own hands and give notice to any Indian found off the reservation that he will be regarded as a bad Indian.[36]

Despite the allegation that no Indians were punished, civil authorities convicted and hanged four confederated Flathead youths as murderers—while a number of "bad" Indians traveled in parties with chiefs who bore Ronan's letters certifying them as trustworthy.

In Washington, Congress—after years of consideration—passed the General Allotment Act on February, 1887, by no means unanimously. The legislation, usually called the Dawes Act, provided for giving patents to Indians for their reservation land and conferring citizenship on those who forswore their tribal affiliations. The Indian office considered the act so significant a turning point in Indian relations that in 1890 Commissioner Morgan would urge reservation Indians to observe February 8 as Franchise Day—although its function of making citizens of Indians was deferred.

But the Flatheads did not want patents to their land, as Ronan advised the commissioner shortly after passage of the Dawes act.

Owing to the prejudices of the several chiefs and of the headmen of the tribes, a large majority of the Indians of the Flathead reservation are yet averse to the taking of land in severalty. The older members of the tribes, and also the young men who have not received any of the advantages of education, go to swell the majority against land in severalty, because they are loath to give up their savage customs. They say at councils and at their fireside talks that the residue of the land will be sold by the government to white settlers, thus breaking up their reservation and mixing the Indians up promiscuously with the whites.

Again Ronan reported, "The Indians are averse to allotments of land in severalty, owing partly to their deep prejudice against the word 'survey.' The Indians of the Flathead reservation claim they have been robbed already by a survey," that is, the location of the northern boundary.[37]

In addition to the confederated Flatheads' opposition to taking reservation lands as individual farmers, the Flatheads proper remained in the Bitterroot. They had never taken patents to their land, although Charlot said they might. When in 1889 Congress authorized the Bitterroot Flatheads to sell their patented land, and Arlee died on August 8, the time seemed right for another attempt to move Charlot and his remaining band to the Jocko. Thirty-two reservation families had already migrated to the reservation, and Ronan said that "Indians of Charlot's band . . . often come to the agency to inquire what the government will do for them if they give up their lands in the Bitterroot."[38]

For the task of appraising Bitterroot lands for sale and removing the last of Charlot's people from the valley, the secretary of the interior chose an aging soldier, author, lecturer, lawyer, and politician, General Henry Beebe Carrington, who was emerging from two decades of unjust national censure as commander of the men involved in the Fetterman massacre, the loss of eighty troopers under Brevet-Colonel William J. Fetterman in a trap sprung by combined forces of Sioux, Cheyennes, and Arapahoes at Peno Creek, Wyoming, on December 21, 1866. Now sixty-five, Carrington was a proud little man (Indian adversaries called him "Little White Chief") with a zeal for civilizing Indians. He limped from a thigh wound suffered when his revolver fired accidentally while he was galloping his horse. Carrington was to prove diligent in his assignment, a prolific report writer, and an incessant petitioner for more money. In his first correspondence with the Indian office from his home in Hyde Park, Massachusetts, Carrington remarked that the compensation offered seemed small but he might not be out of pocket if he could complete the Bitterroot task in five or six months.[39]

The graying general prepared himself by reading reports of the Flathead agent, perusing the Lewis and Clark journals, and filling a notebook with land-title maps sketched from federal records. His strategy must be to move Charlot voluntarily or shatter the chief's remaining influence. To this end, acting on the advice of Michel Revais and Eneas François (Fronsway), shortly after reaching Montana Carrington invited all the tribal leaders to meet in Ronan's parlor, promising Charlot that he would not talk business. On the Sunday appointed, the agent's home filled with Flatheads eager to sign "consents" to sell their Bitterroot land. Charlot lounged in "a large rocking chair near the table, but a little back, where he would . . . not appear to have come, except from curiosity, or to meet his friends."[40]

Seven leading men signed to sell, while Charlot "sat in silence, sullen in manner, pulling at his pipe." Carrington questioned Charlot politely about his history, and after two hours the chief departed. Several days later, moving to Stevensville, Carrington found many citizens and Indians assembled in the streets "in the vain expectation that a few hours, or possibly a few days, would

247

complete the work" of appraising more than two hundred quarter sections.

Sensitive to Charlot's comment that "white men order Charlot to come to them, but never visit Charlot," Carrington rode a rented buggy over the rough road to the chief's farm two miles from town, finding Charlot fixing a plow in front of his cabin. The chief owned small wheat and corn fields, and in disorder around his cabin Carrington saw broken farm equipment, a tipi, a few lean horses, some hogs, chickens, dogs, and a cow. Piles of robes and blankets—the cabin's only furnishings—served as beds.

Noting Charlot's poverty, the general promised him bacon, sugar, tea, and tobacco, and Charlot immediately dispatched two sons to fetch these. (The next day, Carrington received numerous Indians "flocking into town for similar manifestations of the white man's . . . regard.") After talking with Charlot, Carrington avoided a council of headmen where the chief might sway his people. Instead, finding the Indian titles vague and garbled, Carrington resolved to see each landowner individually to comply with the congressional requirements for appraisal and sale.

Taking the patent documents from the agency safe, Carrington set out to verify each tract, persuade its owner to sell, and attach a "consent" for sale. Flathead land claims lay in nine different townships, and, although only fifty-one patents had been issued, fifty-six Indians appeared to hold valid titles. Many patents in the Bitterroot belonged to Flatheads living on the reservation. Errors and curiosities came to light: both Charlot and Louis Vanderburg, a headman, lived on lands other than those described in their patents; Mary Mouchelle owned half the land on which the Pine Orchard Farm of fifty thousand fruit trees stood, living contentedly in a canvas lodge near the orchard; an old, ignorant Indian, Stephen James, had consummated a "confused trade" with Thomas M. Slocum whereby Slocum leased Chief Adolph's land for ninety-nine years for three hundred and sixty-five dollars; G. A. Bennett had appropriated the tract allotted to Esuck Red Wolf and used as pasture the acreage belonging to the widow Susteen; Edward (French Ed) Caron held a lien on the late Arlee's land for twenty spools of wire and fencing worth two hundred and eighty dollars; and so on.

Determined to do his work well, Carrington obtained separate certifications of family lineage and land rights from Revais, Father D'Aste, and old Eneas François for each Indian claimant. He explained in his report to the commissioner:

> This precaution was taken because the misnomer of patentees, repeated marriages and widowhoods, and different sets of children with the same baptismal names, as well as the protracted absence of men, women, and children on their fall hunt, had caused decided differences, even among the interpreters themselves.[41]

To validate "consents" of minor heirs and one insane allottee, Carrington sued in the district court. With no funds to hire an attorney, the general—a member of the U.S. Supreme Court bar—served as his own counselor.

Carrington rented a ground-floor room in the Stevensville hotel, where he talked with the Indians, expressing the hope that the Flatheads would agree to move as a group. Whites peered in at the windows, Charlot was a constant visitor as interviews continued for days, and finally when Vanderburg, Charlot's "chief companion in the visit to Washington, with his son, stepped to the table and signed, [and] the immediate approval by the much beloved Father D'Aste followed, Charlot seemed impressed by the loneliness of his position," Carrington recorded. He also mentioned that "the personal cleanliness [of the Flatheads] which the early writers noticed ... had ceased to be noteworthy."

At last only the Bitterroot Indians most faithful to their chief, and Charlot himself, remained to sign "consents." Carrington talked to the chief for nearly six hours on a Saturday; he learned that Charlot's reluctance to move arose from the chief's refusal to admit a change of mind after so many years of clinging to the Bitterroot. The discussion ended abruptly when Charlot was called to separate two drunken Indians fighting in a street. He whipped them apart.

The following morning (November 3, 1889), as Vanderburg and others watched from across the street, Charlot came with his grandson, Victor, sat awhile on Carrington's stoop, finally knocked and went in, followed by others who had hung back. He verified their names as they signed to sell. Then Charlot sat on the floor for nearly half an hour, smoking his pipe, and at last said, "I will go with Big Heart to the Jocko. I will sign." Carrington placed the chief's hand over his own heart as a pledge. (Reporting his success to the commissioner, the little general alluded to the meager appropriation for his work.)[42]

In an old, badly focused photograph, a row of indistinguishable white men wearing black suits and shapeless hats stands facing the camera. From this blurred rank two men of small stature somehow emerge: the old general, ramrod erect, kepi set squarely on his head, and a few figures to his left the scowling, dark face of the chief, wearing a stovepipe hat. It is clearly not a victorious moment for either man, but one of high duty.

Charlot dictated his demands: preservation of a two-acre Indian burial ground within the so-called Owen tract in the Bitterroot, award to himself of Arlee's reservation farm (Carrington demurred, "If just arrangements could be made with Arlee's widow"), a two-seated covered spring wagon to visit his people, food for his people until they moved from the Bitterroot, and on the reservation cows for families with children. Carrington advised the chief to be ready to move the following spring, remarking in his account to the commissioner that drought had damaged the harvest and the Flatheads were "in comparative want. The young men are demoralized and lazy."

After Charlot signed, the citizens of Stevensville gave the Indians a banquet and ball in the high school building. Charlot took the seat of honor—Carrington noticed the chief winced when white speakers referred to the Flatheads as "savages"—and after the public dinner ended at midnight, the chief and twenty-seven others enjoyed a private meal arranged by the banquet committee.

CHAPTER 10

▲▲▲▲▲▲▲▲▲▲▲▲▲▲▲▲▲▲▲▲▲▲▲▲▲▲▲▲▲▲

THE CONSTRICTING RESERVATION

▼▼▼▼▼▼▼▼▼▼▼▼▼▼▼▼▼▼▼▼▼▼▼▼▼▼▼▼▼▼

WITH THE FLATHEADS' CONSENT to sell their Bitterroot land, General Carrington announced his appraisals of individual tracts, trying to set his prices low enough that white men who occupied the land could buy it, and recommended that his appraisements and maps be published as a guide for prospective settlers. The valuations ranged from $200 for small, unimproved patents to $3,000 for the best tracts. Combined, the fifty-six appraisements totaled $97,931.33.

Charlot's 160.81 acres, of which 20 were cultivated, were appraised at ten and eleven dollars an acre; his father's land, fronting on the river, at eight to twenty dollars; and Vanderburg's, containing the best timber of Indian patents, at twelve dollars. Terms for purchase were to be one-third down, one-third in one year, and the final one-third in two years.[1]

Unfortunately, only the best patents sold. A national depression, first evident in 1890 and grinding to full force in 1893 to 1895, deterred expected sales to new settlers. The 1887 act authorizing the Indians to sell their Bitterroot land stipulated that all the ground must be sold before the Flatheads moved to the reservation. When the lands did not sell readily, Ronan fed the Flatheads. By April, 1890, the commissioner—and eventually the secretary of the interior —made personal visits to congressmen, urging that Charlot's people be allowed to go to the Jocko immediately. Carrington, who had returned to Massachusetts, wrote the commissioner to suggest that he be sent again to Montana, saying, "I feel that I could do much toward preparing the way for their dropping of the tribal relations and settling down to individual family responsibility and self-support." He mentioned that he had borrowed money to finish his appraisements in the Bitterroot and now lived on an annual income of three hundred and twenty dollars.[2]

Carrington was certain the Flatheads were on the threshold of adopting white civilization, citing as evidence Michel Revais's humming of such tunes as "Sweet Bye and Bye," "Marching through Georgia," and "John Brown's Body" rather than native refrains.

As summer, 1890, approached, the Butte Butchering Company, among other merchants, complained to Ronan that Bitterroot Flatheads were creating a nuisance, hanging around begging and eating entrails and discarded meat scraps. Ronan appealed to the commissioner: the Flatheads could not hunt without violating game laws, and could not be stopped from hunting and begging because the War Department classified them as domesticated Indians free to come and go as they wished.

Ronan wrote in midsummer:

> The last arrangement with this unfortunate band, and the delay in its consummation, has entirely discouraged the Indians. They are now helpless and poverty stricken on their land. . . . The hope was given them when their consent was obtained for an appraisal and sale of their lands and improvements that the arrangements would be made to remove them to the Jocko reservation before the first of March, 1890, in order to give them an opportunity to select lands on the reservation and to put in crops to harvest this year at their new houses. With that in view they could not be induced to plow or sow their lands in the Bitterroot valley. They are now destitute of means.[3]

By December Ronan reported the Flatheads selling their wagons, harnesses, and farm implements for provisions, saying, "They are now entirely without anything upon which to live." Charlot sent a messenger to the agency begging relief. Carrington declared, "One hundred years of Indian history presents no sadder instance of indifference and neglect than to have left them for a year, to live mainly on roots."[4]

Just before adjournment in March, 1891, Congress heeded Secretary John Noble's repeated appeals to provide funds and allow the Flatheads to leave the valley, and Carrington returned to the Bitterroot to supervise Charlot's exile to the reservation. Everything had been thrown off schedule by Congress' neglect, the general fretted.

The whole would have been completed in sixty days, including removal, if my carefully considered suggestions had been carried out. There has been so much of congressional indifference to the disposal of this small, peaceful, friendly, poor, and unarmed band that I propose, for once, that a contract made with them shall inure as fully to their benefit as if they were strong, rich, and powerful, like the Sioux. . . . The Indians view it as a test of good faith, after years of deferred hope, and two years of financial distress on account of unfulfilled expectations.[5]

When he arrived at Stevensville, Carrington recalled:

Chief Charlot soon appeared with other Flatheads, accompanied by their women and children. His first act was to produce his "Almack," which he began at parting in 1889. It consisted of two pine sticks carefully squared to the half inch and joined at two ends by a buckskin tie. A notch had been cut in 1889. . . . From that date, without omission, a notch had been cut daily with crossmarks, like X, for each Sunday, for Christmas, and other feast days.[6]

Charlot refused to discuss removal until his people were fed. Carrington consequently persuaded Amos Buck, Henry Buck, and other Stevensville merchants to furnish food and supplies as gifts, piled on the board sidewalks, and the village filled with Indians. Charlot wore his red vest, felt hat with eagle feather in front, his hair long and braided. Some Flatheads waited in Stevensville ten days for Father D'Aste to come from St. Ignatius as their adviser, and weeks passed while others went off hunting. A few acres of their land sold while they waited.

Finally, on October 10, Charlot declared that the time had come; he called his people to council, they prayed, and announced they would go to the reservation, asking that no soldiers accompany them. Carrington had deliberately kept

most of the adult, able-bodied Indians out of town, and hunting their

winter supply of meat. . . . They prove tractable, obedient, and willing.
. . . Michief-makers endeavor to make the Indians dissatisfied, and
others, to take advantage of the delay, to drive away purchasers who
came and remained at expense, to purchase [land].⁷

Seven days later, following an all-night feast, the Flatheads assembled at dawn, loaded horses and wagons, and at seven o'clock
started for the reservation. They passed through a Bitterroot Valley
no longer Indian, but crossed by telegraph wires, dotted with brick
buildings, its streams bridged by steel and timber, and its lands
closed by wire fencing. A *Missoulian* writer estimated the caravan
at two hundred and fifty Indians, four hundred ponies, a few cows,
and "household effects," as the Flatheads passed through Missoula
about noon. Carrington described it:

> The trailing lodge poles . . . with ample space between for pack horses,
> loose cattle and ponies, and the great variety of dogs, all in bunches,
> were under such quick control as only skillful Indian herders could
> accomplish. Gay blankets, feathers, necklaces, ornamental leggings
> and moccasins, with faces freshly painted in the morning, had full
> share in the display.

Young Indian men policed each street intersection to prevent stray-
ing.

At dusk in driving rain, the column stopped to camp. In the St.
Ignatius baptismal record book Father D'Aste wrote in spidery
French:

> On the seventeenth day of October, 1891, Chief Charlot and 157 of his
> tribesmen left their native land, the Bitterroot valley, and migrated to
> Jocko prairie. The U.S.A. promised them that the Jocko prairie would
> be their home forever.

Two days later, as the Bitterroot Flatheads neared the reservation,
they paused to dress their finest and repaint faces in brilliant ver-
million and ochre; then, as the agency buildings came in sight, the
men hoisted the United States flag and advanced at a gallop, whoop-
ing and firing their guns. A delegation of reservation tribes awaited
them, and a five-day feast began, although the travelers were so
tired that the camp fell silent by midnight of the first day. Carring-

ton reported, "Every family, and over 400 head of stock of Charlot's band, none missing, were placed in camp near the agency buildings Saturday afternoon at four o'clock." Joseph Laumphrey's wife had fallen from her horse and broken her hip, the only incident of the march. Carrington remarked, "Agent Ronan did not anticipate this successful removal."[8] In the testy little general's mind, he at last had triumphed over aboriginal suspicion, bureaucratic bungling, and congressional apathy.

When Ronan and Charlot together considered locations for Bitterroot families, Charlot selected for his own the fertile acreage of a wealthy half-breed, expecting the agent to evict its occupant. Ronan refused, explaining that many half-breeds had come as employees of the Hudson's Bay Company before the reservation was established, whereupon Charlot accused him of favoring half-breeds. By the end of November, most new homes for Bitterroot Flatheads were built (a number of Indians took their own contracts at one hundred dollars), all but two with cooking stoves, and before Christmas occupied.

The reservation Indians muttered that the newcomers got everything, while Charlot again requested Arlee's farm. "I have no complaint to make against Chief Charlot," Ronan wrote the commissioner. "He is a just and agreeable man, but is a believer in the fulfillment of promises. He has always kept his word and expects the word of others to be kept." Meanwhile, the Charlot band lounged "without energy enough to commence the cultivation of the soil; unless fields are plowed and fenced for them, [they] will always require the issuance of rations, as most of them refuse to help themselves, relying totally on promises given."[9]

With arrival of Charlot's people, the Ursuline nuns opened a branch school near the agency in a two-story building erected by the Jesuits at a cost of forty-five hundred dollars. Poorly attended, the school would be discontinued in 1898. Charlot complained of schooling that, when Indians learned English, they got whisky easier.

The Charlot Flatheads often called at Ronan's house to remind him their Bitterroot lands had not been sold. By November, 1897, only eighteen full tracts and parts of eight others would be sold. The

Missoulian would note the Indians' complaints of further encroachments and add, "Failure to sell the 4,520 acres [remaining] was doubtless owing to the high appraisement and the depreciation of all value in Montana during the panic."[10]

Despite Carrington's meticulous identification of patent owners, Ronan found

> many complications, claims and counter claims caused by the fact that few lived (at the time of their removal) upon the lands as originally allotted, but had swapped or traded about a great deal. These people are very much alive to their interests, and their greed and jealousy have made it exceedingly difficult to give a complete list of the rightful heirs.[11]

The Bitterroot lands would be reappraised in 1899, and Cyrus Beede, the U.S. Indian inspector assigned the task, would find that in the decade since Carrington appraised them the lands had attracted many trespassers, while others who had purchased patents had sold them. Forty-one would remain unsold in 1899 but, when prices were lowered, new immigrants would buy them for fifty-five hundred dollars in aggregate.[12]

Even after Charlot's people were put on the reservation, the citizens of western Montana believed that the confederated Flatheads occupied far more land than they would ever use. In his legislative message of 1883, Governor J. Schuyler Crosby had expressed the general feeling:

> The Indian problem is complicated by the duty on the one hand of being just, and even generous, to a people who once owned the whole territory, and on the other hand, by that irresistible law of nature under which a lower yields to a higher civilization. The vast acreage per capita now surrendered to tribes who neither mine, plow, or pasture it, excites some discontent among the white population.

Immigrants reaching Montana on the Northern Pacific entered a region dominated by white rather than aboriginal culture. They saw no reason to brook eccentric savages. Between 1880 and 1890 Missoula County's population grew from 2,537 to 14,427, not counting persons on the reservation. The town of Missoula, a divisional railroad headquarters, numbered 3,426 by 1890. A network of subsidiary railways, stagecoach routes, and steamers on rivers and lakes connected the railway with settlements north and south of its main line.

In addition to Missoula, the county had twenty-two post offices, half a dozen of them in the districts above Flathead Lake which had been little occupied by whites before the railroad came, and others such as Como, Corvallis, Skalkaho, Stevensville, and Victor in the Bitterroot Valley. During 1888 Congress granted the proposed Montana & Northern Railway a right of way across the Flathead reservation and, although that road was never built, in 1889 James J. Hill's Manitoba line disclosed its plans to extend westward from Great Falls, spurring new immigration into northwestern Montana, where the line was expected to run.

The native life these newcomers saw had been fractionated by internal and external stresses. (Soon some tribes—but not the confederated Flatheads—would ghost dance to wipe away white civilization and return the old times.) Before the Christmas holidays of 1890, when reservation Indians looked forward to their usual feasts at the agency, Peter Ronan closed his warehouses to Flatheads until they stopped dancing, drinking, and gambling.

Strong elements among the confederated Flatheads defied Ronan during the turmoil of a political campaign to succeed Arlee, conducted between Big Sam, the tallest man on the reservation, and Judge Louison, a "self-important individual" (as Mollie Ronan saw him), who wore a beaded Indian vest and tall beaver evening hat as symbols of authority. Sometimes on judicial errands he donned a blue military jacket. Freed from toil by marriage to a wealthy woman, Louison each Sunday harangued outside the mission church, bewailing the times and erosion of old customs.

Each candidate sought "the support of reckless Indians to silence the more responsible," and denounced the agent and federal policy. They and their supporters rode through the reservation with faces painted, wrapped in blankets, asserting the superiority of Salish tradition and blood, jeering to half-breeds working in fields that the full-bloods would run them off the reserve. "They attract young men, and the element has grown so strong in Jocko Valley that they defy Indian police," Ronan lamented. "The unruly element is most-

257

ly Bitterroot Indians, young men, abetted by the two old men."[13] These Indians declared that Garfield promised them freedom from restraints on the reservation.

Charlot's arrival on the reservation and restoration as head chief ended the campaign but did not repair the divisions among the confederated Flatheads. An Indian inspector remarked sometime later:

> There are many breeds among them and many vexatious questions are constantly arising as to their rights, both judicial and property. Many of them have so small an amount of Indian blood that to all appearances they are white and when off the reservation enjoy all the rights and privileges of citizens.[14]

Materials for construction of the Great Northern, as the Manitoba railroad generally was called by 1891, were shipped by Northern Pacific to Ravalli, hauled by wagon across the reservation to Flathead Lake, and sent by steamer to Ashley. Hundreds of workmen and settlers entered the region. In the construction towns, ran a contemporary account, "fifteen saloons gaily lit were filled to the door with wild men and wild women, yelling, singing, dancing, and cursing, with glasses lifted high." Some camps were so lawless that the railroad locked its cars passing through them.

The steamer *Tom Carter* debarked five hundred and eighty-six passengers at the head of the lake in five days of April, 1891. By spring of that year the Northern Pacific temporarily refused additional consignments to Ravalli because the station was full and freight piled along the tracks for miles. As soon as roads dried, fifty thousand pounds of goods moved daily by wagon across the reservation between the Northern Pacific and the construction crews of the Great Northern.

Near Ashley a new town called Kalispell rose in the hayfields; it claimed one thousand inhabitants and four hundred structures (four of brick) by November, 1891, and became the county seat in 1893 when Flathead County was sliced from Missoula. The Great Northern tracks reached Kalispell before Christmas, 1891, running through the country north of the Flathead reservation, the country the Indians had wanted to annex.

Signs of civilization rose everywhere. Granville Stuart, the state land commissioner, in 1892 saw many sawmills in the upper Flathead valley "which have culled the most valuable trees to the base of the mountains," and from Frenchtown to Iron Mountain station (on the Coeur d'Alene branch of the Northern Pacific) the land filled with squatters. To these new arrivals, Indians on reserved lands were obstacles to opening the country. In the rear door of a Kalispell tailor shop a four-inch porthole allowed patrons to shoot at passing Indians for amusement. One white man who thus murdered an aged Indian woman was convicted of discharging a firearm within the city for lack of witnesses to support a more serious charge.[15]

Moreover, settlers resented competing with Indians for game, complaining that the Flatheads ignored state regulations that prohibited hunting large animals between February 1 and August 10 or killing at any time for hides only. Ronan wrote the editor of the *Missoulian*, "I am not prepared to say if it is a crime for any Indians to kill game for food at any season of the year." The commissioner of Indian affairs two years later said,

> The privilege of hunting in open and unclaimed land was granted to the Indians by the treaty of July 16, 1855 ... and unless the conditions existing at that time have changed as to render the guaranties inoperative, I do not see how they can be denied the privileges which they still claim.[16]

The chiefs refused to punish full-blooded Indians for violating tribal custom or state regulation, because, they said, half-breeds flaunted custom with impunity. Ronan told of an Indian wife who ran off with another man,

> knowing that they could not return and live together on this reservation ... resorted to the state court, and through an advertisement in one of the county papers, as service of process, divorce was procured, and the couple returned to the reservation to live together after marriage by a justice of the peace. The chiefs and headmen claim that such a class should be ordered to leave the reservation.

However, standing on their rights under state law, the couple remained.[17]

The chiefs declared that liquor caused most of their troubles—yet it gave young men a sense of power and invincibility like victory in the hunt or war. An inspector, assigned to investigate after a Missoula woman complained directly to the president of the United States, reported that Arlee traders sold whiskey to Indians, a resident at the foot of the lake had delivered whiskey to reservation Flatheads for years via Demersville, and whiskey was sold without restrictions on lake steamers. Violations of the half-century-old intercourse act, reported to the U.S. marshal, were never prosecuted because the marshal forbade his deputies to act without his consent and never gave it.[18] On the station grounds at Ravalli, interlopers living in shacks, "rough, drinking, gambling . . . undesirable neighbors for Indians," were removed by personal order of the commissioner.

Meanwhile, settlers and adventurers, attracted first by the Kootenay mines and next by construction of the Great Northern, appeared in the fertile valley of the Kootenai River in northern Idaho, squatting on land near Bonners Ferry. Because the Northwest Indian Commission's contract with the Kutenais provided them places on the Flathead reservation, whites demanded that the Indians along the river be moved to Montana.

J. I. Anthony wrote Ronan:

> There is quite a number of settlers that now would take up land, but wherever they go they find an Indian's notice claiming 160 acres . . . with a white man's name as witness on the notice. So the white man gets the benefit of the land, either for hay or range, and to cover it up the Indian will put in a few potatoes. Now, if this land is given to them, they will use it just the same as now.[19]

The Indian office ordered Ronan to recommend disposition of the Kutenais.

After talking with Isaac, the Kutenai chief, Ronan reported the band's unanimous wish to remain in Idaho:

> But a short time will elapse ere the country will be settled, and the Indians are forced and driven from their hunting and camping grounds. Therefore no time should be lost in giving them titles to their lands. . . . These Indians are like children. They must have a guardian over them—a farmer in charge or some other authority—otherwise, they will not do anything for themselves.[20]

The commissioner preferred to relocate the Kutenais; he directed Ronan to convince them to move, reminding the agent that "it is the policy of the department to persuade this class of Indians to remove and to take allotments upon some reservation." Richard Fry of Bonners Ferry wrote Ronan that Indians "drink, gamble, and come away robbed and filled with fire water" at a saloon for Great Northern construction workers.

Pressed to depart, the Kutenais asked to be settled with the Dayton Creek band, Ronan reported shortly after. "Seeing that it was hopeless for them . . . as they were already run over by white settlers, or land grabbers who in some cases located on Indian claims by force of arms, or at least the exhibition of that persuasion." Chief Isaac now lay ill in his lodge, and Moses, a subchief, tried to lead some families to Canada but was turned back at the border. The Indians sought advice from David McLoughlin, "a mixed blood and the father of a large Kootenay family—an educated man and the son of Dr. McLaughlin who in the early history of Oregon managed the Hudson Bay Fur Company. David McLaughlin . . . considered a member of the Kootenay tribe, is an old man, born in 1821." Ronan fed the Kutenais as they counciled.

Half-breeds and traders exploiting the Kutenais wanted them to stay in Idaho, but finally all save eight families, who chose allotments in the valley, agreed to move to the Flathead reservation. As late as 1904 settlers and Indians in the Kootenai valley would be asking for resurveys to clarify land ownership. (With the Kutenais' consent to move, the secretary of the interior suggested that General Carrington might be useful in removal. Ronan ignored the proposal.) Counting the Bonners Ferry Kutenais as two hundred and twenty-seven people "living in thin cotton lodges," Ronan prepared to move them by horse and by rail in April, 1892.

When aggressive violations of the Indian boundary near Dayton Creek eventually discouraged many Idaho Kutenais from settling there, however, more than half of the Bonners Ferry people migrated to Canada. In 1897 an Indian inspector would report that the Idaho Kutenais on the Flathead reservation numbered ninety-seven, observing that the United States had failed to keep its agreements with them.

Disputes over Indian boundaries arose in part from an incomplete survey in 1887 by a U.S. deputy surveyor, Edmund P. H. Harrison, who placed Dayton Creek partly outside the reservation and located the northern boundary south of the natural features intended to mark it. Ronan, using the Stevens treaty, survey field notes, and the Northern Pacific contract with the confederated Flatheads, established the Dayton Creek Kutenais' title sufficiently to obtain allotments for nineteen heads of families, but white men trespassed Indian fields to cut hay, saying "they intended to cut the hay and hold the ground unless arrested by lawful authority." Even an opinion by Elbert D. Weed, U.S. attorney for Montana, that "under the law, the title of these Indians to the land was absolute from the time the selections were made and officially certified," failed to deter intruders. An uneasy truce and alternating possession of the disputed fields resulted, to be settled in 1904 when another agent persuaded thirteen Indian allottees to sell for approximately one dollar an acre. This returned the Kutenais from thirty to one hundred and sixty dollars for their allotted lands. Another surveyor, Samuel Bundock, declared himself unable to find where Harrison's survey ended.

As he tried to solve the Kutenais' boundary dispute, Ronan received letters from Horse Plains citizens asking permission to take contested ground there, because "the Indians cannot claim all the land."

Ronan for some years had resisted encroachments on the reservation by cattle herds of white men, resorting as early as 1885 to impounding animals as strays. When he appealed for aid from the U.S. Department of Justice, the *Missoulian* warned, "It would be well for persons who know their cattle are grazing upon the Flathead reservation illegally . . . to drive them away, as the agent is fully determined to carry out the regulations of the Indian department," against intrusions.[21] But by 1890 the agent, hampered by rheumatism, could no longer oversee the reservation in person, and the grazing controversy remained unsolved when he took his daughter Mary to the World's Columbian Exposition in 1893.

In Chicago Ronan underwent a complete physical examination. The physician found Ronan's heart enlarged, recommended a lower elevation, and the agent went briefly to Puget Sound, then—oppressed by a premonition of death—returned to the reservation. Mollie was ill. Ronan rode horseback to Arlee to telegraph Missoula for a physician, returned to his home, lay down on the bed, and with a deep sigh died.

Two days later, on August 22, 1893, a sorrowing escort of Indians carried his casket to the Missoula Catholic cemetery. The *Missoulian* eulogized:

> Seventeen years ago Major Ronan was appointed agent to the Flatheads, Pend Oreilles, and Kootenays, and they developed under his watchful eye from warlike tribes of savages into educated, thrifty, industrious, law-abiding men. No Indian agency in the United States has a better record than the Flathead.[22]

A review of the reservation seemed to confirm the material progress of the confederated Flatheads under Ronan. "Everything hereabouts presents a very satisfactory appearance toward the desired good—Civilization and Christianity," wrote an Indian inspector, noting that, although older Flatheads continued to wrap in blankets, most of them owned houses and fenced fields. St. Ignatius School was thriving, and a brick Gothic church costing twenty-seven thousand dollars had been dedicated at the mission in July, 1893. A clerk in the Indian office summarized the inspector's report:

> This is a good contrast to other agencies in respect to rations, many are self-supporting, due in great part to the indefatigable efforts of Jesuit missionaries, the results being plainly seen. Thinks too much praise cannot be given to the conduct of this agency.[23]

Reporting her husband's death to the commissioner, Mollie Ronan recommended his clerk (a distant cousin), Joseph T. Carter, as successor, and the special agent who closed out Ronan's affairs, Thomas P. Smith, concurred. Smith also selected ten Flathead boys from the mission school to attend Carlisle. Carter's appointment, confirmed in September, "meets the approval of the people of this city, and is looked upon as a graceful tribute to the family" of Peter Ronan, said the *Missoulian*. In 1895 Carter would marry Mary Ronan.

The new agent reported in October, 1894, a reservation population of 1,654 members of confederated tribes, 65 Lower Pend Ore-illes, 173 Flatheads of Charlot's band, 67 Kutenais from Idaho, and 106 Spokanes. Of these, an estimated seven hundred had adopted white men's clothing entirely. Reservation Indians occupied 620 houses of an average value of forty dollars—although they often pitched canvas tipis in the yards for summer living—and Carter said 90 per cent earned their subsistence in civilized pursuits (chiefly farming and stock raising), 2 per cent by hunting, and 8 per cent (Charlot's people) by government rations. During his first year as agent, Carter recorded no divorces, no polygamous marriages, and no whiskey sellers on the reservation.[24]

Ronan's passing stilled a strong voice against allotting Flathead reservation land in severalty. The federal Indian office had heeded his warnings that the Flatheads unalterably opposed allotments, but with a new agent and the passage of time the questions of land use and ownership were revived, complicated by uncertain northern and western boundaries for the preserve. Moreover, many whites concluded that the Flatheads opposed allotment on the advice of the mission priests; they advocated a government school and looked for other ways to diminish the influence of St. Ignatius, and in this were abetted by some members of confederated tribes.

Lacking Ronan's diplomacy and forcefulness, Carter soon fell to bickering with Indians and whites. He blamed his difficulties with the confederated Flatheads on half-breeds, naming Duncan Mc-Donald, "a meddlesome halfbreed, an ex-trader, who desires to shine as a man of influence and who properly belongs on the Nez Perce reservation." By contrast, Mollie Ronan thought McDonald "not then aware of the advantage to him of making capital of his Indian ancestry. . . . He was anxious to appear to be a pure-blooded Scotchman like his father."[25]

The 1895 Montana legislature memorialized Congress to open the Flathead reservation for general settlement, a measure intro-duced by State Senator William H. Smead of Missoula County. The bill was unanimously supported by western Montana. The *Mis-soulian* editors believed that opening the reservation "will certainly add a great deal to our taxable wealth as well as assist very materially in building up the town." The *Inter-Mountain* estimated that surplus Indian land would support twelve thousand five hundred white families. A citizen's typical opinion appeared in the *Missoulian*, "Why should this fine tract of land be reserved for a few dozen half casts . . . to the detriment of thousands of willing and anxious homeseekers?"

Field agents of the Indian office, on the other hand, consistently urged that the Flatheads hold onto their land. One of these, John Lane, recommended fencing the northern boundary to stop trespassing. "I think the Indians should never consent to the disposal of the surplus land, but in addition to their allotments, should hold the grazing land in common," he advised the commissioner.[26]

This same agent reported Carter energetic and honest, but the agency itself decaying except for a new office. He mentioned that "the non-progressive portion of Charlot's band . . . are located immediately above the agency, polluting and fouling the water which at present runs in open ditches. The health of all the agency employees is menaced by the present system of water supply." But the Indians' health was generally good, barring prevalent consumption.

Carter welcomed temporary reinforcement from one F. M. Cory, carrying credentials of a secret agent of the U.S. Treasury Department, who enforced agency regulations with vigor. Arriving late in 1895, Cory rapidly took the reservation's problems in hand; by November, said the St. Ignatius house diary, "Mr. Cory has already done away with the idle Crees, and with the cattle belonging to unauthorized white people." When Cory decreed that tribal leaders could adjudicate matrimonial disputes and punish malefactors, he "restored to the Indian chieftains the authority which the agent, Mr. Carter, had considerably weakened."[27]

Cory collected $1.60 a head for whites' cattle discovered on the reservation, impounding animals until fines were paid, and in a few days turned over $586.50 to Carter. He organized a roundup of stray horses, evicted Nez Percés illegally on the reservation, and identified whiskey peddlers.

Finally stock raisers of Horse Plains protested Cory's activities to U.S. Representative Charles S. Hartman of Montana, who forwarded their petition to the commissioner with a personal note:

"I sincerely hope that you may be able to issue an order which will relieve the citizens from the requirements fixed by the agent, and will have returned to them their stock which have strayed upon the reservation." The federal government responded to Hartman that Cory was an impostor, his credentials forged.

Cory, convicted of defrauding cattlemen by collecting fines, was sentenced to nine months in the state penitentiary. "His work on the reservation had been most beneficial," one of the priests wrote in the mission house diary. "He got the place rid of all the roaming Crees, secured the land from all foreign cattle, and made a good many wise regulations concerning marriages. . . . He had acquired an influence over here which no U.S. agent ever had."

Carter, authoritarian by instinct, tried to continue Cory's stringent policing, angering many white men. He refused to return impounded cattle or rebate fines; he charged that six hundred animals tended by a squaw man, Wilkes Markle, belonged really to J. A. McGowan, founder and leading merchant of Horse Plains; he removed one cattleman, Eugene Humbert, from the reservation in irons and with Indian police repulsed the sheriff who answered Humbert's complaint.

The confederated Flatheads murmured against Carter, telling an inspector, Marcus D. Shelby, that the agent employed Indians without paying them, was slow to respond to their requests, sent one Indian to work in a mine owned by the Ronan family, and refused transportation for the agency physician to attend ailing Indians.

When a fifteen-year-old boy, Benjamin F. Murray, burned the boys' dormitory at St. Ignatius on November 16, 1896, his ninth day in school, Carter allowed him to be jailed in Missoula until his trial and conviction. (The priests drew a circle in red around Murray's name in the school enrollment record.) The agent championed a quarter-blood Chippewa living on the reservation who refused to allow sale of his property to satisfy a debt of six years. The Montana Supreme Court in March, 1897, ruled against the Indian, whereupon the *Missoulian* remarked, "Indian reservations are no longer asylums for dishonest debtors."[28]

A few weeks after the 1895 Montana legislature had memorialized Congress to open the Flathead reservation, Congress unexpectedly appropriated funds for another commission to negotiate with the Flatheads and other tribes to cede surplus lands. The commission, authorized by an act of July 13, 1892, had not previously been funded, perhaps because negotiation seemed useless when Ronan described the Flathead reservation chiefs and full-bloods "bitterly opposed" to allotments and to surveys, adding that some younger Indians favored allotment but said nothing because their view was unpopular.

Now, three years after authorization, Congress responded to agitation from the West by funding the Crow, Flathead, Northern Cheyenne, Uintah, and Yakima Commission, fated to be known as the Crow, Flathead, Etc., Commission even in federal documents, an inept body that would spend seven years in the field, conclude but three contracts with Indians, and persuade Congress to ratify only one.

News of another negotiation for land made the Flatheads more restless, while the whites, anticipating a further reduction in Indian land holdings, demanded that the Indians observe game laws and pay personal property taxes. The justice of the peace at Kalispell fined vagrant British Crees $222.15 for shooting game, despite a protest of the disproportion between crime and penalty by the British Columbia superintendent of Indian affairs. But when Montana Game Warden Joseph Booth arrested fifteen confederated Flatheads near Horse Plains with pack horses loaded with deer, Carter refused to allow their prosecution on the ground that treaties permitted the Indians to hunt where they pleased.

Some months later, as thirty or forty lodges camped to hunt near Horse Plains (now generally called Plains), citizens complained of depletion "by the redman and butcher." A *Missoulian* correspondent wrote in familiar vein, "Something ought to be done and done quickly to prevent the Indians from destroying this valuable game country or it is more than likely that the settlers will take the law into their own hands."[29]

The Crow, Flathead, Etc., Commission reached Missoula in March, 1897, from the Yakima reservation, where they had failed to secure land cessions. One of the three members, Colonel J. B. Goodwin of Atlanta, Georgia, accompanied by his wife and two sons, acknowledged that he "was not familiar with the conditions or the lands of the Flathead Indians." The other two members, Benjamin F. Barge of Ellensburg, Washington, and Charles G. Hoyt of Beatrice, Nebraska, proved similarly uninformed.

In two councils the commission was contravened by Charlot. No sooner had the three commissioners recessed negotiations than the Flatheads wrote Senator Thomas H. Carter requesting permission to visit Washington to protest attempts to take more land from them.

An Indian field agent, William J. McConnell, said one of the commissioners told him they hoped to obtain cession of the western half of the Flathead reservation for one and one-half million dollars. McConnell advised the commissioner of Indian affairs, "The spirit of justice and fairness to the Indians should impel the department to interpose and prevent the consummation of the proposed treaty," for the Flatheads were not farmers but cattlemen who needed the rangeland they were being asked to sell. McConnell continued:

> The people adjacent to the reservation are, of course, anxious for the commissioners to succeed, ... as they anticipate a great benefit will be derived from distribution of such a large sum of money, and the few men who are large stock owners know that they will practically own the land thus ceded, as it is not susceptible to settlement by those proposing to carry on farm operations and it is only valuable to those who have means to stock it. The Indians have been driven to the wall and it seems that a large number of people through selfish motives would, if possible drive them over the wall.[30]

When reservation headmen gathered on Easter Monday to talk again with the commission, Michel failed to appear. The St. Ignatius priests found the ninety-two-year-old Pend Oreille chieftain, now blind, dying in his lodge on Mud Creek. The commission, busy on other reservations, did not keep its appointment with the Flatheads. McConnell suggested that it be given the additional task of concluding contracts to supersede those of the Northwest Commission, which Congress had failed to ratify. Under one of these unratified compacts the Kutenais and other bands had moved into the Flathead reservation expecting lands and houses, he said, and were now clustered in shacks near the agency with "no lands to cultivate or other means of support. The promises made these people should be carried out."[31] He recommended that Jocko irrigation be extended to water farmland for the Lower Pend Oreilles.

Petitions from settlers, the Cory affair, and Indian grumbling convinced Washington that a more politic agent should be named. Consequently, in December, 1897, the state senator who drafted the memorial to open the reservation, W. H. Smead, was appointed to succeed Carter. Republican, a former army lieutenant, and state senator for four years, Smead was eminently suitable to whites; he was "one of the best federal appointments in the state," said the *Missoulian*. He took charge of the Flathead reservation at a time when the Northern Pacific declared the demand for land the greatest in fifteen years.

Smead was businesslike toward Indians, not inclined to smile on old customs; he soon lost the reassuring presence of troops when the Twenty-Fifth Infantry left Missoula for the war with Spain. Said the *Missoulian*:

As soon as they knew that the troops had been withdrawn from Fort Missoula, [the Indians] became restless and in many ways began to show their savage nature. They leave the reservation in bands without permission and the Indian police are kept busy rounding them up. They appear in and around Missoula in larger numbers than ever before. They are insolent, and in many ways exhibit their contempt of the whites.[32]

But Montana seemed proud of its Flatheads when fourteen of them under Louison participated in the U.S. Indian Congress at Omaha in October, 1898, living on the exposition grounds with representatives of other tribes in native costumes and lodges for the edification of visitors. About this same time, an intertribal trade in Indian goods was revived when many families attended the renewal of the Piegan sun dance. Flatheads going to the Piegan camp took pouches of corn husks and yarn and dressed hides to barter for beaded clothing.

Smead learned that alcohol, boxed and labeled as freight, was bootlegged to the reservation by lake steamer and messenger. Believing himself too widely known to obtain evidence, Smead requested a special agent to spy on the liquor traffic. "These Indians are becoming quite prosperous and a class of saloon keeper in the adjoining towns are supplying them with a great amount of whiskey and alcohol," he advised the commissioner.[33]

Complaints of hunting by Flatheads continued. Residents of Missoula and environs formed a chapter of the League of American Sportsmen, claiming one hundred and seventeen members, to offer a ten-dollar reward for each person convicted of violating game laws. "The state ought to offer a bounty on these worthless Indians that infest this part of the country," fumed the *Libby News*. "They destroy more game and stock than the lions and coyotes." The superintendent of the Lewis and Clark Forest Preserve charged that Flatheads not only slaughtered game but set fires, prompting the pugnacious land commissioner, Binger Herman, to write the secretary of the interior, "It is an infernal shame that these red devils are allowed to roam all over this country, killing game out of season, setting fire to the country, and doing about as they please." Flatheads had been known, declared Herman, "to start fires in order to drive game to certain points."[34]

The commissioner of Indian affairs informed Montana agents of his wish that "Indians refrain altogether from entering forest reserves for the purposes of hunting at any season of the year." Smead posted notices to this effect and told the local forest supervisor that he would issue passes to Flathead families leaving the reservation:

> This pass will name or enumerate any women or children entitled to be with the person with the permit. . . . In the past a good many of the full bloods have, in order to keep their children from school, left the reservation before the beginning of the school year and have remained away until late in the fall simply to keep their children out of school.[35]

The Montana legislature prohibited Indians from bearing arms off the reservation, but the state game warden agreed with the agent that he would not prosecute violators.

About this time, full-blooded Flatheads adopted a midwinter ceremony, a shamanistic ritual of coastal origin introduced to the reservation by nontreaty Lower Pend Oreilles and Spokanes. For five or six years the Flatheads had been attending similar rites near

Perma. Known as the Blue Jay ceremony, the dance was held in a medicine lodge constructed around a ritual fir tree and connected in mythology with legends of Coyote. The participants, usually numbering sixty or seventy men and women, wore blankets and moccasins. After four days of ceremonial sweating, the lodge was erected and dancing started on the fourth night.

The dancing lasted two days, while shamans interpreted the gibberish of men dressed to represent the powerful Blue Jays; it ended with ceremonial "killing" of the Blue Jays. The midwinter rite was believed to ensure health and prosperity for its participants and occasionally was intended as an attack on enemies through the power of the shamans. Its adoption was part of a pattern of shutting out the white world by withdrawal into old ways—an attitude many full-blooded Flatheads tried to pass on to their children.[36]

Despite their grievances, many whites found Flatheads colorful. The *Missoulian* reported:

A party of Indians going on their annual hunt passed through the city today and attracted considerable attention by their splendor. The horses were good ones and the saddles ... were covered with miniature bells which tinkled as the party passed. The bucks were all fixed up in new blankets, etc., but it was the squaws that attracted attention. They were fixed up in the height of Indian fashion, too, but a feature of their toilets were parasols . . . carried with as much grace as possible.[37]

Quite different was the evident prosperity among reservation cattlemen, particularly Michel Pablo, Alexander Matt, and Charles Allard. It renewed the Missoula County commissioners' determination to levy taxes on mixed-bloods and whites on the preserve. Pablo was assessed at the rate of $153,650, but protested that he was a ward of the government, not liable to taxation, and the assessment excessive. "I beg to state that Mr. Pablo is a resident of this reservation, an Indian, and a ward of the government," Smead wrote the commissioners. "I respectfully request ... that his name be erased from the assessment roll."[38] Several paid assessments under protest, Smead ejected a deputy assessor from the reservation, and a number of tax cases were brought in the courts. The reservation cattlemen who qualified as Indians were exempted from taxation by the county. Pablo and Allard visited the commissioner in Washington to protest, but he would not intervene, and in 1899 the confederated Flatheads began allowing white men to graze cattle on their reservation under leases.

Smead was the first non-Catholic agent to the Flatheads since Grant's peace policy had begun, and in his term the relationship changed between agent and priests. Ronan and Carter had patronized the mission school, ignored requests for a government school, and done nothing about the commissioner's invitations to send Flathead boys to the Fort Shaw government school opened in 1892. A Mason, Smead did not defer to the Jesuit fathers, and said openly he believed the reservation needed several schools. He angered the priests by requiring Indians to obtain marriage licenses from his office.

Bitterroot Indians had expected a government school since 1855, and in 1876 had appealed to Garfield to advocate one for them. By the time the government had opened Carlisle Industrial School in Pennsylvania in 1879, Chemawa in Oregon in 1880, and three others in 1884, the peace policy was in wholesale reversal, but from Shanahan's peremptory order to close in 1874 to the appointment of Smead, the mission school had had no formidable opposition. Visitors uniformly praised St. Ignatius, among them Senator Vest, who declared the Jesuits provided "the only practical system for the education of the Indian." Vest assisted St. Ignatius in obtaining federal appropriations.

The Catholic Indian Bureau in 1873 undertook distribution of funds from the federal government and the churches to Catholic mission schools, and lobbied for higher federal appropriations. In 1878, renamed the Bureau of Catholic Indian Missions, it obtained a federal contract for a manual labor school at St. Ignatius, under which the government would pay four thousand dollars annually for the education of forty Indian boys. The contract was increased to sixty in 1880, and one hundred pupils in 1883, despite the sedulous opposition of Commissioner Hiram Price (1881–85), whom Vest called "a bigot. He thinks any man a criminal who takes a drink of anything but water or tea, and he hates the Roman Catholic church."[39]

Price ordered agents to keep Indian schools filled by withholding rations or annuities from parents if necessary, and directed the adoption of uniform textbooks. During his time as commissioner, reservation schools were transferred from special to general Indian appropriations and in the process St. Ignatius was omitted from the budget in 1885. Vest restored the Flathead school funds through a special appropriation.

In 1886, St. Ignatius again was funded by a special appropriation of $22,500, secured when Vest (after Montana's congressman, J. K. Toole, declined to act) struggled from his sickbed to steer the bill. The new commissioner, John D. C. Atkins (1885–88), "a rigid public economist and a still more rigid member of the Presbyterian church . . . when he heard of our success in getting the appropriation for St. Ignatius . . . expressed . . . great indignation and blamed Congress sharply for having made a special appropriation for any other than a government school," Charles Jones, now a director of the BCIM, wrote Father Palladino.[40]

Despite requests by the Flatheads for a government school and attempts in Washington to cut off the mission school, St. Ignatius enjoyed its most prosperous years from 1886 to 1899, with annual federal contracts to educate as many as three hundred boys and girls at one hundred and fifty dollars each—fortunate years, for as early as 1885 the Bureau of Catholic Indian Missions began reducing its contributions because of faltering patronage and smaller collections in parish churches for Negro and Indian missions.

In its fourteen prosperous years, St. Ignatius averaged thirty-one thousand five hundred dollars annually in federal support. In those years, St. Ignatius enrolled children from the Flathead, Kutenai, Nez Percé, Cheyenne, Lower Pend Oreille, Piegan, Upper Pend Oreille, Cree, Blackfoot (twenty-five boys and twenty-five girls carried free by the Northern Pacific), Colville, and Spokane tribes, providing each with civilized clothing and instructing them as white children in city schools were taught.

The school music consisted of popular ballads, Civil War ditties, and Italian operatic airs, although at the Washington's birthday anniversary program in 1896, the priests admitted that the boys "sing altogether too high; it is actually painful to hear them. Their acting as a rule is poor, monotonous, unnatural." Reading, writing, ciphering, catechism, and the household and manual arts provided the curriculum. Grades ranged from E for "excellent" to D for "detestable."[41]

Among the mission school pupils with historic names were six Boucher boys and four Boucher girls, and Charlot Victor, who at age twelve, attended St. Ignatius in 1892. The school regularly accepted more children than federal funds supported, and gradually expanded its numbers and its facilities, including the short-lived school at the agency. In 1890 the Jesuits contracted with Ursuline nuns to conduct a kindergarten for Indians and half-breeds at St. Ignatius—and also "to wash and mend for priests and boys of the boarding school."

Significant changes in Indian school administration occurred in 1891, however, when Commissioner Thomas Morgan (1889–93) announced he would henceforth contract directly with schools rather than with the Bureau of Catholic Indian Missions, stating his opinion that support of sectarian Indian schools violated the federal constitution. "While friends were in the Indian Office we did not suffer much; but with the present head running mad on his system and avowedly opposed to contract schools, we could only hope to get what was left," a director of the bureau wrote Father Van Gorp. The Indian office also appointed four supervisors of Indian education, combining into one district Montana, Oregon, Washington, Wyoming, Idaho, northern California, and Nevada, and in the following year opened its Fort Shaw school.

Morgan directed that Indian schools teach courses "such as are ordinarily pursued in similar white schools," promote toil and patriotism, and omit mention of "the wrongs of the Indians and . . . the injustice of the white race."[42] While Morgan protested that his detractors "maliciously misinterpreted" his views as anti-Catholic, the commissioner thus took the jurisdiction of mission schools away from religious agencies.

The district supervisor of Indian education, William M. Moss, was no less enthusiastic about St. Ignatius than earlier visitors, however, describing it as "the largest and best of any contract school I have visited." In the kindergarten, he reported, "Very few . . . can speak Indian and have to talk to their parents through an interpreter. . . . It is the purpose of the sisters to keep all here until ten years old regardless of advancement." Moss's one suggestion for improvement was to teach Indians to use two sheets on their beds.[43]

After his appointment as agent, Smead expressed frequent concern for the large number of Indian children not in school. A school supervisor and disbursing agent, R. C. Bauer, estimated that of five hundred Indian children on the Flathead reservation, no more than one hundred and sixty attended St. Ignatius. (The mission school reported an average daily attendance of 240 until 1899.) He suggested opening a government school near the agency in the former Catholic school building there:

> My recommendations in this matter are based upon the idea that an educated Indian is the best Indian that ever lived, and that only through education and Christianization can the Indians of this country, Flathead or otherwise, be utilized as citizens."

Bauer inquired whether the priests would sell St. Ignatius, remarking that, if not, the government would build a large school to "freeze out" the mission.[44] Smead sketched the floor plans for a proposed government school at the agency.

With Bauer's concurrence, the St. Ignatius contract fell to one hundred and sixty pupils in 1899, to eighty in 1900, and was discontinued at the close of that school year.

The agent's encouragement of a government school occasioned a public breach between him and little Father D'Aste, who noted in the St. Ignatius house diary, "Two wagon loads of children from the upper valley were gathered by the Indian agent and sent to Fort Shaw. The agent is at open war with me, and tries his best to crush the mission." He sent Smead angry protests, to which Smead replied that "the schools ought to be able to get along," while reporting to the commissioner that the Jesuits "do not look with favor upon the establishment of government schools on this reservation."[45]

A government day school opened in the agency schoolhouse,

rented from St. Ignatius, on September 1, 1899, its first teacher Miss Louisa McDermott, and its preference full-bloods. Smead said he would send children to school without their parents' consent, if he must.

A handful of Indian pupils also enrolled in the public school at Arlee, established for settlers' children in a restaurant in 1897. This was to be the future pattern; public schools would be opened at Jocko (Dixon) in 1903 and St. Ignatius in 1910. By 1913, nine public schools enrolling whites and Indians were to be operating on or near the reservation. The Flathead Agency school, begun as a day school, would become a boarding school in 1901, revert to a day school in 1909, and close in 1914. Throughout these years, agents and superintendents complained often of inadequate quarters, and said that many boys and girls ran away each year. Smead wrote a prospective teacher:

> We have a small school in old rented buildings greatly crowded. The former superintendent and his wife (matron) occupied two small rooms . . . and I see no way in which arrangements can be made for any more room for you. One of these rooms is now in use for a girls' dining room, temporarily, pending the arrival of the new superintendent.

Similar government schools were opened in 1906 at Ronan and Polson and in 1909 at Camas, but closed in 1914 as Indian pupils transferred to public schools.[46]

In 1899, when few Flathead children enrolled in the government school at the agency, Smead blamed Charlot, "an ignorant, stubborn old Indian. He has great influence over his people and has used his influence to prevent the people from sending their children to the government school."[47]

Charlot perhaps did deter school attendance, for he opposed Smead, and with a delegation of headmen retained a Missoula attorney, Charles H. Hall, who sent a polite, factual statement to the commissioner that "these intelligent Indians" strongly resisted Smead's administration. They alleged now that the agent permitted unauthorized cattle on the reservation and overcharged Indians at the agency mill. Other allegations against Smead, prepared by William Parsons (an attorney from Pendleton, Oregon, who had come to the Flathead reservation to represent Umatillas in a purchase of horses), were disregarded when the inspector, Cyrus Beede, said the Indians complained because Charlot told them to.[48]

In the midst of furor over schools and agent, the Crow, Flathead, Etc., Commission reappeared on the Flathead reservation with different membership for sporadic negotiations between October, 1900, and April, 1901. Montanans were critical of this "carpet-bag commission . . . appointed from different sections of the United States at handsome salaries," in the words of the *Missoulian*. During a recess, a federal Indian inspector reported, "The Indians do not want the commission back."[49]

State Senator Tyler Worden of Missoula introduced a joint memorial in the legislature asserting:

> If proper persons, who are citizens of Montana and familiar with said Indians . . . were appointed as a special commission . . . such portions of said reservation as are deemed advisable would be speedily opened for settlement.

If the reservation were opened to whites, added the *Missoulian*, they would pay taxes and breed cattle instead of "worthless cayuses."

The commissioners eventually asked the confederated Flatheads to sell 450,000 acres of their preserve, "everything north of the line between Missoula and Flathead counties." Smead estimated the sale would bring a million dollars, or seven hundred for each Indian, and one commissioner brushed aside Indian objections with the remark that this was "simply a business proposition." Half-breed cattle owners and Charlot were again decisive. "You all know that I won't sell a foot of land," Charlot declared. Isaac, speaking for the Kutenais, said, "Before we make a new treaty, we want to know about the boundary lines of this reservation. . . . That is all I have to say, and you had better hunt some people who want money more than we do." Referring to a recent payment for Bitterroot lands, Louison chimed in, "We intend to go to Washington, as we now have plenty of money to go with."[50]

Charlot forbade his people to discuss a sale further when the commissioners failed to produce credentials at his request. The commissioners gave up their attempts to negotiate with the Flatheads; they recommended instead that the reservation be allotted in severalty, and on May 4, 1901, the secretary of the interior, after reading their report, assigned the three members to other duties.

CHAPTER 11

▲▲▲▲▲▲▲▲▲▲▲▲▲▲▲▲▲▲▲▲▲▲▲▲▲▲▲▲▲▲

CONCLUSION—ENROLLMENT AND
ALLOTMENT

▼▼▼▼▼▼▼▼▼▼▼▼▼▼▼▼▼▼▼▼▼▼▼▼▼▼▼▼▼▼

SHORTLY AFTER the Crow, Flathead, Etc., Commission closed its bargaining with the confederated Flatheads, Congress directed the secretary of the interior to report on the degree of civilization among the nation's Indians and the advisability of reducing the size of reservations. The resulting report on the Flathead reservation—it was rarely called Jocko anymore—was submitted by veteran inspector Frank C. Armstrong.

Armstrong counted a reservation population of 1,734, approximately half of them of mixed blood, largely of French extraction. The French descendants of fur trappers and other white men who had married Indian wives owned the largest cattle herds and occupied the choicest reservation land, south and southeast of Flathead Lake.

No more than one-fourth of the full-bloods farmed or owned cattle; most of these lived in the valley between the mission and Flathead Lake. Because the mixed-bloods "get all the benefits of the reservation," they sided with Charlot in opposing allotment, but paid him no heed otherwise.

Half the fullblood element, which includes the Kootenay band . . . near Dayton Creek, and a majority of the Bitterroot band, under old Chief Charlot, located near the agency, are the most non-progressive and backward Indians on the reservation. Much of this is due to

279

Charlot's bad influence, who . . . is opposed to everything which tends to civilization or advancement of the Indians.[1]

Armstrong recommended surveys to verify Indian claims, expanded irrigation, and eventual allotment of the reservation, "to put these Indians in a condition to support themselves and to abolish the ration and annuity system, which is a curse to every reservation where it is allowed to continue," and "in great measure [to] weaken his [Charlot's] influence by drawing off his following and getting the younger and better element of his gang on irrigated lands."

Thus the pattern for opening the Flathead reservation to settlement by whites was set out as Armstrong proposed: after the completion

of a proper and complete roll . . . the land of this reservation should be surveyed, the land should be regularly allotted, sufficient reserve retained for a common cattle range, and the surplus land disposed of, and those portions [remaining] of the reservation opened.

This was the course pursued by Joseph M. Dixon of Missoula. Soon after he was elected United States representative to Congress in 1902, the *Daily Missoulian* called on him "to abolish the Montana Indian reservations or reduce them to sensible limits," declaring that reservations constituted "barriers to progress." As Missoula County attorney from 1892 to 1896, Dixon understood the white attitude toward the Flathead preserve. Dixon said later that he studied the treaty of March 17, 1854, between the United States and the Omahas, in which article 6 authorized allotment of land to Indians, and concluded that allotment was also intended in article 6 of the 1855 treaty with the confederated Flatheads. Charlot, shown this meaning of the Stevens treaty, admitted, "That makes sweat."

Therefore Dixon introduced a bill in 1903 to allot lands in severalty to the Flatheads and open their remaining lands for settlement. In support of Dixon's proposal, the *Missoulian* argued:

No one denies that they [Flatheads] are the rightful owners, but as they are unable to control society, society must control them. The individual Indian must make sacrifices for the good of society in general, as well as the individual white. . . . There is a demand for throwing open parts of the Crow and Flathead reservations for settlement. For years commissions have endeavored to induce the Indians to relinquish their land under treaty rights, and commissions have failed, principally because a few men on these reservations who have large stock interests have succeeded in inducing the Indians to withhold their signatures from treaties.[2]

After lengthy hearings by its Committee on Indian Affairs, the House passed the first version of Dixon's bill on April 2, 1903, with one challenge, that of Representative Charles D. Burke of South Dakota, who objected to "the new policy that we now seem to be adopting . . . of getting as much as possible for the Indians without any consideration whatever of those who may assume the responsibility of developing and building up homes on the frontier." Burke read into the record a letter from the acting commissioner of Indian affairs estimating that the Flathead reservation population numbered approximately 1,270, that from 1860 to 1880 Congress had expended $431,001.08 on these Indians, and from 1880 to 1902, a total of $198,917.48.[3] Without other opposition, Dixon's bill became law on April 23, 1904; it was to be amended several times in the next six years, before the Flathead reservation was opened.

Agent Smead doubted that some mixed-bloods were entitled to allotments and recommended enrollment promptly to afford these an "early determination of their standing," adding:

Some of the mixed bloods and some of the fullbloods are becoming very prosperous. Some of their farms and improvements compare favorably with the well regulated farms of the whites in old settled communities. How necessary it is, therefore, that these lands should be surveyed so that these people may know where their lines are.[4]

In addition, a variety of court opinions placed mixed-bloods in doubtful legal possession of reservation lands. Generally, the courts held that those whose fathers were United States citizens could not qualify as members of Indian tribes.

In advocating enrollment, Smead also urged (as had other whites) that reservation Flatheads be required to rid themselves of "worthless ponies." In 1903 he began a levy on horses and cattle amounting to one dollar a head for each animal above the number of one hundred grazed on the reservation by a single owner, defending his tax as providing funds for poor and infirm Indians. The agent wrote white cattle owners:

> It is my desire to make a five-dollar per capita payment to the Indians on or about October 1, 1903. This payment is to be made from the proceeds of the collection of the grazing tax. I am of the opinion that if I can do this there will be a much better feeling among the Indians and it will entirely take the wind from the sails of that class of breeds who are crying "job" and "robbery," etc. It will *show* the Indians the money is being collected in their behalf. . . . Now, I am a little short of funds to make this payment, and . . . I am writing you to ask that you send me the second payment on your first quarter. Of course I understand that it is not due.[5]

Because the tax had been approved by the secretary of the interior, and the confederated Flatheads asserted they received none of the money, Charlot and nine headmen visited the secretary in person, attracting attention on the way to Washington by wearing blankets and, when they met the secretary, carrying tomahawks. The group included the three Indian judges, Auguste, new chief of the Kutenais, and Charlie, chief of the Pend Oreilles. Duncan McDonald served as interpreter. Charlot argued that the levy penalized Indians who demonstrated wealth in the old way by owning a great number of horses; he estimated that approximately fifteen hundred reservation Indians owned forty-five thousand cayuses among them. The secretary refused to rescind the tax.

For a few years in the first decade of the twentieth century, the Flatheads sold as many as nine thousand ponies a season to brokers, who retailed them to stylish Atlantic seaboard families as children's mounts. Elimination of the horse herds, as Smead recommended, would apply new pressure for full-bloods to farm or breed cattle rather than pass their days tending horses. But the Flatheads took neither his views nor his tax kindly. Smead wrote the district attorney to ask if the law would punish Indians who interfere "by threats and menaces" with tax collection.

> Recently during the cattle roundup a band of Indians headed by a couple of Camas Prairie Indians (a band that don't recognize the authority of the United States or agency officials) undertook to

prevent me from collecting trespass tax from a number of white men, saying they themselves proposed to collect the tax. They even went so far as to take cattle from the owners and hold them for several days.

Although the Camas Prairie band gave up the horses without taxing their owners, Smead declared, "Now this is a bad lot of Indians and have been defying the government long enough."[6]

Looking back, it is evident that under Smead the confederated Flatheads were herded involuntarily toward opening their reservation, while the agent improved his personal circumstances. Often he acted precipitously, as he did in 1901 when he banished infected Crees from the reservation during a smallpox epidemic so severe that even older Indians co-operated instead of concealing the disease from their agent. Smead deterred the spread of smallpox to white communities by setting up two tent isolation camps, quarantining the Bonners Ferry Kutenais during the winter of 1901–02, and burning the lodges of infected Flatheads.

Meanwhile, the federal government continued to place stray Indians on established reservations. In 1902 the commissioner ordered Smead to negotiate with the Rocky Boy Chippewa band to settle them on Flathead lands. The chief, Rocky Boy, contended that his people had lost their lands in Wisconsin when the Chippewa Commission allotted acreage while the band was hunting in Montana. When they learned their lands had been taken, the Rocky Boy Indians stayed in Montana.

Smead visited Rocky Boy in his camp at Anaconda, recognizing a few Crees ejected from the Flathead reservation among the group. The Anaconda chief of police knew Rocky Boy well; he explained that most of the chief's people, descended from Indians residing near Chippewa Falls, Wisconsin, had come to Montana five years earlier. Nevertheless, Smead recommended, and the commissioner agreed, that no action ought to be taken, because half the band were Canadian Crees illegally on United States soil. Rocky Boy was not so easily dismissed; he had written the president of the United States on January 14, 1902, on behalf of his "band of Chippewa Indians that for years have been wandering through different parts of the United States without a home," and his letter was referred for solution.[7]

A special agent assigned to investigate the Rocky Boy band, Thomas Downs, found them near Garrison in 1903, apparently in good health, eking out an existence by selling beads and polished cow horns to tourists on the Northern Pacific. "It does seem like some provision ought to be made to care for all of those who are American born, and especially to educate their children," Downs observed, estimating the band at one hundred and three and recommending that they be placed on the Flathead reservation.[8]

The confederated Flatheads emphatically rejected Rocky Boy, but the wily Chippewa chieftain turned for counsel to John W. James, an Anaconda attorney. "It certainly would be a good thing from a sanitary viewpoint for the State of Montana" if the federal government could settle the band, James wrote U.S. Senator Paris Gibson of Great Falls. Rocky Boy saw Gibson in person to explain that he wanted a place only for members of his band born in the United States.[9] Gibson appealed to the Indian office without avail and then tried to buy, with contributed funds, a portion of the Flathead reservation for Rocky Boy, but the confederated tribes refused to sell.

The next year Rocky Boy walked to Missoula to ask Congressman Dixon to secure him a reservation through congressional benevolence, but nothing came of this. In October, 1905, the chief and his band walked from Anaconda to Missoula to see Dixon again, pitching their camp near the slaughterhouses to scavenge food. Although Dixon wrote several letters for Rocky Boy, the Flatheads steadfastly refused to accept him, and the possibility of settling Rocky Boy on the Flathead reservation finally was abandoned in July, 1908, when Dixon advised Senator Carter, "The Flatheads do not seem to be kindly disposed toward cultivating a closer relationship" with the Chippewas.[10] During 1909 the citizens of Helena fed and clothed Rocky Boy's people, the Great Falls *Tribune* campaigned editorially for their permanent relief, and land was set aside for them—but settled by whites before they reached it. The band would hover near Havre until 1916, when Congress finally allocated 56,063 acres of former Fort Assiniboine as their reservation. Rocky Boy, their chief, died in 1917.

To prepare the confederated Flatheads for allotments in severalty, the Indian office sent a special agent, Charles S. McNichols, onto the reservation in the fall of 1902 to enroll tribal members—that is, to verify their membership in a confederated tribe and their right to lands. In some cases, McNichols gave Indians new names, for the commissioner had decreed (twelve years earlier) that Indians must adopt family names like the whites, suggesting that each take an English Christian name and use his Indian as his surname, shortened if too long. By November, McNichols had enrolled approximately five hundred and compiled a list of one hundred and twelve other Indians whose claims to allotments were questioned by the tribal chiefs and judges.

A number of persons located on desirable land—some holding up to two thousand acres—seemed to lack tribal affiliations necessary for enrollment. McNichols confirmed Smead's view, "All . . . the wealthy Indians are inclined to oppose enrollment on the ground that it is a step toward allotment. For this reason, progress is very slow."[11] Approximately one-fourth of the confederated tribe members could not be enrolled because they were absent hunting.

The enrollment further aggravated full-blooded Flatheads, many of whom re-emphasized the old ways. Others simply moved so the agent could not find them. Some went to an Indian gambling tournament near Anaconda, reported humorously by the newspapers, which claimed that a Cree lost his wife in betting with a Flathead. When Smead left the agency to visit the state legislature, a number of reservation Indians "went on a continuous toot," until their liquor supply was traced to Smead's Chinese cook. On an inspection of the Flathead reservation, a federal investigator noted:

> It cannot be said that they are easily governed, as a large number of them do not want to obey their agent in any particular. They do their business in their own way and never consult him unless they get into trouble; most of them drink intoxicating liquor to excess.[12]

The investigator saw that most male Indians now wore civilized clothing but wrapped in blankets in colder weather. The women wore costumes cut to traditional patterns and continued to speak Salish.

Children educated in English, remarked another observer, en-

285

dured bitter conflicts in homes where adults spoke Salish. (Nearly three decades later, a Catholic missionary would observe that only twenty-seven of ninety old Indians on Camas Prairie understood English, and therefore these old people could not be served by priests with no command of Salish, who succeeded Jesuits at Polson and Ronan parishes.) Intermixtures of new and old ways abounded; many older Indians continued to dig camas and bitterroot annually, living as nomads on the country until distribution day at the agency, while intense rivalry with wagers of blankets, saddles, and bead-work marked baseball games between St. Ignatius and agency teams.

With the concurrence of tribal judges, Smead prohibited Indians from carrying firearms on the reservation. He required Indians who owned wagons to contribute labor to maintain the roads. The reservation Indians, meanwhile, increasingly regarded the Fourth of July as a display for white spectators, organizing an Indian circus, dances, and feast for visitors. Here the divisions among confederated Flatheads were evident; the old Indians submerged themselves deeper in the past while many younger and mixed-blood Indians promoted the colorful aspects of a synthetic native life to achieve status among white men. Between the two worlds, a great many lost Indians wandered.

After twelve months on the Flathead reservation, McNichols submitted his final enrollment roster of 1,656 persons. For a year afterward, individual Indians not enrolled appealed to the Indian office for inclusion. Neither Flatheads nor whites accepted McNichols' roll, and in March, 1904, a Missoula attorney, acting for Indians and Missoula citizens, filed forty-two charges with the secretary of the interior against Smead, alleging that the agent, among other malefactions, enticed Indians to enroll by telling them they would receive three thousand dollars cash and one hundred and sixty acres each.[13]

The agent so zealously aided one Missoula attorney in canvassing for patronage that the Flatheads generally believed that only this lawyer could enroll them, and a number already enrolled paid him four hundred dollars to enroll again. Frank Woody declared to the Indian office that Smead conspired with the attorney to mulct Flat-

ABOVE: Flathead family on the reservation, c. 1910. Probably photographed during a celebration staged for white spectators. The older man, left, holds the equipment of a medicine man; the woman wears a beaded bag typical of later-day Flathead artistry, and her ankle-length dress is traditional; the younger man, right, is dressed in a costume for a dance with bells and warrior's headdress. (Frank Palmer, Eastern Washington State Historical Society)

BELOW: Flathead men show finery, probably for a ceremonial dance for white spectators, c. 1910. (Frank Palmer, Eastern Washington State Historical Society)

Beaded cradle board, Flathead reservation, July, 1906. Beadwork was one of the few Flathead artistic skills remaining by this date. (Montana Historical Society)

Gregory Stuyochin, Lower Pend Oreille (Kalispel), photographed in 1906 by T. W. Tolman. The pipe-tomahawk, beaded vest, and pouch, were typical of fine Flathead dress of the time. (Montana Historical Society)

Family group, Flathead reservation, 1908, according to the caption on this stereopticon photo. (Montana Historical Society)

Wealthy men of the Flathead reservation, 1908, photographed for stereopticon viewing. Second from the right is Ka-Ka-She. The headdresses were not traditional but were acquired by trading with Plains tribes. (Montana Historical Society)

Ka-Ka-She, center, with supporters. Although other Indians are not
identified, two are believed to be men who accompanied him to Washington to protest opening the reservation: next to Ka-Ka-She, on the left
(wearing the peace medal on a chain) is Charles Moolman, and on the
right, wrapped in a blanket and seated, Sam Resurrection. (Gonzaga
University)

Flathead Indians, c. 1910 (Frank Palmer, Eastern Washington State Historical Society)

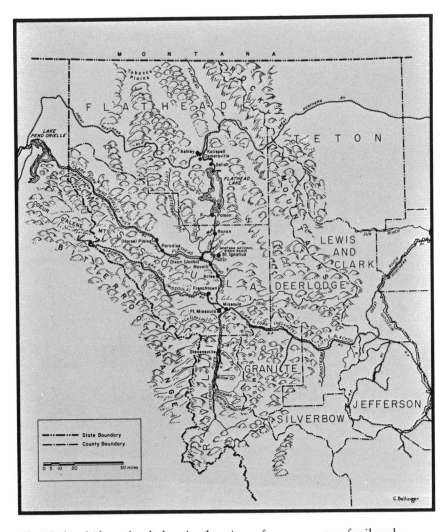

The Flatheads' homeland, showing locations of towns, routes of railroads, and boundaries of states and counties. Based on a map of Montana compiled from records of the General Land Office and published in 1897 by the Department of the Interior. (National Archives)

heads of twenty thousand dollars in fees. The Indians, for their part, alleged that Smead peddled liquor through his cook, sold reservation cattle to the merchant who held the agency meat contract, refused to pay his gambling losses to Indians, delivered Indians inferior flour in underweight sacks from the agency mill, and cited other derelictions.[14]

Following an inquiry, Smead was succeeded as agent by an undistinguished fellow Missoulian, Republican, and Mason, Samuel Bellew. Smead formed a real estate company with Elmer E. Hershey, former receiver of the Missoula land office, to exploit growing interest in reservation land. Using Smead's handsome book, *Land of the Flatheads*, as promotional literature, their Flathead Reservation Homestead Agency sold memberships all over the United States at five dollars each, guaranteeing to assist clients in locating choice land when the reservation was opened. Smead claimed to have precise maps developed during his seven years as agent.

In his first year, Bellew distributed fifteen thousand dollars in grazing taxes among confederated Flatheads, which doubtless helped many whose crops were damaged by an unusually dry summer. The funds came mainly from levies on the larger herds, among these the animals of Allen Sloan, a quarter-blood Chippewa married to a Flathead woman and adopted by her tribe. Missoula County tried again to tax reservation cattlemen. The commissioners assessed Sloan's property at $8,260 and asked taxes of $159, and assessed the property of Michel Pablo, of Mexican parentage, at $65,307, based on his ownership of 200 buffaloes, 1,339 cattle, and 54 horses, putting the tax at $1,248. The county hired attorney Parsons to carry Pablo through the courts as a test of its authority to tax non-Indian residents of the Flathead reservation. Judge Knowles barred state proceedings against persons living on the reservation.[15]

With challenges to McNichols' roll, Bellew suspended the agent's grazing tax, because he could not be sure which Flatheads were entitled to share its proceeds. In 1906 the reservation cattle industry would begin a decline in the face of lower national beef prices and high costs of production and transportation. Herds depleted during the earlier years were not rebuilt, and several thousand animals were driven to Canada for sale. The range shrank as Indians fenced allotments. When in 1909 the agent would raise the grazing tax from one to two dollars a head, a stockman would write:

> It happens that this country has conditions different from the east side of the Rockies. Here cattlemen breed and raise our own cattle, and two dollars will be almost prohibitive. It requires about five years to mature an animal. They have to put up hay to winter the stock, so the tax really only covers summer grazing.

The tax would remain at one dollar.[16]

Thomas Downs, reviewing McNichols' enrollment lists, reported that McNichols virtually ignored the Lower Pend Oreilles, and in certain other bands enrolled "only those who have been able to employ an attorney." He indicated that one legal firm in Missoula had verified all enrollments. The Camas Prairie band of one hundred and eleven Pend Oreilles refused to enroll, but McNichols learned their names. The commissioner ruled, however, that enrollment must represent information obtained from the Indians themselves.[17]

On the basis of Downs's report, the commissioner directed him to make a new roll of the confederated Flatheads. Completed in May, 1905, this enrollment named 2,133 persons entitled to allotments. Downs listed 640 Pend Oreilles, of whom 242 were full-bloods, 387 mixed, 7 adopted Indians, and 4 adopted whites. He enrolled 557 Flatheads: 233 full-bloods, 305 mixed, 16 adopted Indians, and 3 adopted whites. The Kutenais numbered 556: 210 full-bloods, 342 mixed, 2 adopted Indians, and 2 adopted whites. Of 197 Lower Pend Oreilles, 161 were full-bloods, 35 mixed, and 1 adopted white. The Spokanes numbered 135: 55 full-bloods, 80 mixed. Other tribes: 14 full-bloods and 34 mixed.

Apparently no Indian contested inclusion of the ten white men enrolled as tribal members. On the other hand, for many years afterward individual Indians, many in distant sections of the United States, appealed for recognition of their claims to membership in one of the reservation tribes. A council of headmen decided these appeals. Of these applicants, three hundred and five would be added to the roll before original allotments were completed.[18]

With enrollment, the older Flatheads determined to keep some of the reservation for collective lands, enlisting William Q. Ranft, a Missoula attorney, as their advisor. Ranft soon advertised in the *Missoulian* that he represented "practically all of the claimants for enrollment upon the Rolls of the Flathead Indian Reservation, makes a specialty of this practice," and encouraged any persons believing themselves entitled to enrollment to consult him. Letters reached him from many sections of the United States.

Not long after, Ranft organized a company which, like that of Smead and Hershey, promised to assist settlers in locating desirable land when the reservation opened. Ranft claimed his firm, the Flathead Reservation & Information Agency, owned forty-five thousand cards describing forty-acre tracts. Later he expanded this company as the Flathead Reservation Agency of Kansas City, charged ten dollars as a subscription fee, issued detailed maps made "in his two years on the reservation as enrollment agent," and published the monthly *Western Homeseeker*.

Charlot led the efforts to hold some of the reservation as tribal land. In defiance of the commissioner's order to him to stay home, Charlot traveled to Washington to ask President Theodore Roosevelt to create a forest preserve for Indians as a source of firewood and logs for cabins, to guarantee Indian water rights for irrigation, and to provide relief for poor, crippled, blind, and infirm Indians. An aged, unsmiling chieftain, Charlot set off on the Northern Pacific, wrapped in a blanket, black hair hanging in braids, chin in hand, staring moodily from the railcar window.

Commented the *Missoulian*:

> Chief Charlot of the Flatheads is irreconcilable. He is a grand and pathetic figure in Montana. He has no use for the whites. . . . [He] is a crownless monarch on a seatless throne. There was a time, it is said, when the old chief was without guile, but he has developed into a diplomat. . . . Putting all sentiment to one side, the Indian is no more entitled to a special timber reserve than the white man nor should the government provide for him in any way after tribal relations are severed. . . . Charlot is too old to adapt himself to conditions. He has not been treated fairly, and, consequently, feels bitter toward the whites who have taken his lands and who are pushing his people farther back. Though we may feel sorry for the old man, a grand old man, we also feel that he must bow to the inevitable.[19]

Dixon amended the act to provide a five-thousand-acre timber preserve for the Flatheads before Charlot's train left Missoula.

In Washington the chief watched the inaugural parade, chatted briefly with the president to complain that the government was unfair in forcing Indians to become white men, but received little assurance. It could not have been a satisfactory conversation. Charlot returned to Montana, "thinking, thinking all the time," according to his interpreter, Antoine Paschell, educated at St. Ignatius School. The land promoter, Smead, declared, "It is safe to say that within five years from the opening of the reservation, that 25,000 people will live upon it, and within ten years it will support a population of 50,000 people."[20]

In the middle of 1906 a veteran servant of the Indian office, John K. Rankin of Lawrence, Kansas, began surveys and allotments on the Flathead reservation. "So far [he] has met with no opposition on the part of any, but instead there seems to be a desire by all to have their homes definitely located and the lines established," the commissioner announced in August.[21] Suspicious old Charlot asked to see Rankin's credentials and was shown his letter of appointment. The chief then dispatched Antoine Moise (Moses) and Alicot with interpreters to ask President Roosevelt to halt allotments. Bellew learned these Indians were in Washington when they telegraphed him for money to get home, having failed to sway Roosevelt.

When Secretary of the Interior James R. Garfield consented to be Missoula's guest on July 4, 1907, he also agreed to confer with the reservation chiefs. Nearly five hundred mounted Flatheads met his train, and, after the Indian dance that featured Garfield's entertainment had been cut short, several Indian leaders told the secretary that they opposed opening their reservation.

Both Charlot and Moise reminded Garfield of these conversations in September when they wrote him to protest again. "All my people sorrow," Charlot said.[22] Garfield had judiciously left the reservation before the annual Fourth of July celebration started. About twenty-five hundred Indians attended it for ten days, including Chippewas, Crees, Nez Percés, Coeur d'Alenes, and Blackfeet, to gamble, race horses, and stage a sham battle for white spectators.

The Flathead agent, Bellew, called together the chiefs in September, 1907, to choose two Indian members of a board of appraisement that would set values on reservation land to be sold. With Charlot's approval, the confederated Flatheads selected mixed-bloods, Duncan McDonald from the north and John Matt from the south end of the reservation, passing over the demand of full-bloods for their own men. Rankin considered the choices "as good as any. No very good material among them." On Dixon's recommendation, W. F. Hubbart of Kalispell and Andrew Logan of Missoula were appointed citizen members, and F. X. Salzman, a U.S. Forestry Service employee who had served on the Yakima board of appraisement, was named distributing agent and secretary. In Indian office jargon, the five became "the Salzman commission."[23]

With Charlot's public acquiescence to appraisement, a rump group of full-bloods began their own persistent opposition to opening the reservation. It is difficult to know, after the passage of years, whether this minority dissent consisted of malcontents or whether, for their opposition, these full-bloods were labeled pariahs. For one of them, Sam Resurrection, a Flathead subchief of many years, the campaign seemed mainly a way to travel and buy whiskey at the expense of his Indian supporters.

The newspapers treated these protesters with amusement. When Resurrection, Charles Moolman, and Judge Ka-Ka-She wrote President Roosevelt in August, 1908, the *Missoulian* printed their letter with its struggling grammar and misspellings. The letter, a rambling historical account of good relations between Flatheads and whites, asked Roosevelt to keep the reservation intact and direct the Northern Pacific to restore free rides for Indians between Billings and Umatilla.[24]

Resurrection again wrote Roosevelt, "When they made the treaty, Stevens told the three chiefs this would be a reservation as long as there was an Indian here," and complained the appraisers were "giving the land away." He ended, "Well, I will close as a friend, hoping to hear from you soon."[25]

Late in 1908 Resurrection, Moolman, and Ka-Ka-She went to Washington, taking Jackson Sundown as interpreter. Usually Indians in the capital city without permission were ignored, but the commissioner made an exception in deference to Ka-Ka-She's seventy-three years, although he scolded the delegation for bringing Sundown, who was not considered legally married, saying, "The authorities cannot recognize you as representing your tribe."[26]

Despite a second trip to the national capital by the same three headmen, the force of the Flatheads' protests withered as allotment progressed. Of Resurrection, a Flathead agent asserted:

> This Indian is one of the most dissolute, shiftless, worthless that we have. . . . He keeps himself from starving by living off Indians who pay no attention to his advice or teachings. . . . His pet delusion seems to be that if he can get to Washington he can prevent the opening of the reservation, or failing . . . can at least have adopted a plan of separating the mixed and fullblood Indians, that part of the reservation given to the mixed bloods to be opened, but no white men at all to be allowed on that part given to the fullblooded. By playing upon the feelings of the old-time fullblood Indians . . . Sam Reselection [*sic*] has not only turned their passive resistance in many cases to open antagonism, but has retarded, or prevented, their adoption of progressive methods.[27]

Allotment of the Flathead reservation closed September 25, 1909. Rankin had allotted 2,390 Indians 80 acres of farmland or 160 of grazing land apiece, as they chose, and reported 13 Indians refused to make selections. A series of amendments to Dixon's act to open the reservation reserved 2,524.7 acres for tribal uses, 6,774.92 acres for the agency, 43.62 acres for townsites, 4,977 for power installations, and 18,521.25 acres for a national bison range. Later, additional confederated Flatheads received allotments, and 45,714 more acres were reserved as electric generating and reservoir sites.

The land for a bison range recognized the agitation by the American Bison Society for a national or state herd to preserve the buffalo heritage. In 1908 the society reported 1,722 surviving buffalo in private herds owned by sixty-four persons and estimated no more than 325 wild buffalo remained. Many of those in private herds had been bought from Pablo's, begun when Peter Ronan persuaded Indian hunters to drive two young buffalo cows and a bull from a wild herd through the mountains to the reservation. These mingled with cattle owned by Charles Allard and Pablo. Ronan noted "tempting offers . . . to sell the herd," but urged that the federal government "take steps to secure the buffalo, which are among the last remnants of the millions that roamed the great American plain in former days."[28]

Shortly after completion of Rankin's field work in 1908, Bellew resigned. He was succeeded on November 30, 1908, by an erect man with military bearing, Fred C. Morgan of Missoula, a faithful Republican previously employed as reservation bookkeeper. One of Morgan's first steps was to organize a business committee of influential men of the reservation.[29] (In December the title of agent was discontinued, and Morgan was designated superintendent of the reservation.)

The Flathead, Coeur d'Alene, and Spokane reservations were to be opened for settlement simultaneously under the supervision of James W. Witten, chief law clerk of the General Land Office. Homeseekers were to register for a drawing that would determine the order in which lands would be selected. Eleven offices in Missoula and Kalispell were named registration places for the Flathead reservation and as the moment to begin registering for the drawing approached—midnight between July 14 and 15, 1909—hotels in both towns filled. The *Missoulian* estimated at least one thousand persons had come to register in person from various parts of the United States, although mail entries were accepted. Some eager land seekers slept in registry office hallways, and promptly at midnight signing began. Although no more than six thousand useful locations existed, 104,896 persons registered for the Flathead drawing.

In the meantime, the appraisers had worked since early 1908 to price the surplus lands. To John Matt the commissioner wrote, "The appraised values should not be beyond the reasonable value of the lands in their virgin state, for it is clearly to the benefit of the Indians to have their land settled by progressive white people."[30] Appraisements continued for more than four years. At first they were secret, but in 1911 Flathead prices would be published in advance of sales as the result of experimentation with selling methods on the Rosebud and Pine Ridge reservations. The board generally valued Flathead land at $1.25 an acre for grazing, $2.50 for second-class agricultural, and $5.00 for first-class agricultural tracts. As the appraisers worked, Sam Resurrection, Ka-Ka-She, and Moolman sent the commissioner a petition bearing one hundred and thirty-four names protesting opening of the reservation.

Drawings to determine the order of selection of Indian lands began at Coeur d'Alene, Idaho, on August 10, 1910. Montana State Senator Edward Donlan of Missoula arranged that his twelve-year-old daughter, Christina, would draw for the Flathead. A wooden platform enclosed in chicken wire and draped with United States flags was piled with envelopes mixed by pitchfork, and, as five hundred spectators watched, Christina drew the first name, Joseph Furoy, a young married farmer recently become father of a daughter, who lived near Warsaw, Indiana. After three days, when four thousand names had been taken from the pile, Witten closed the drawing. John Matt now formed a company with a Northern Pacific engineer, S. E. Cutler, to help successful registrants locate on the Flathead reservation, the third such enterprise.

First sales took place in seven townsites: Dayton, Polson, Arlee, Ravalli, Dixon, St. Ignatius, and Ronan. Of these Ravalli was the largest, the starting point of the stageline to Flathead Lake, and Arlee, once busy as railroad shipping center, stood nearly deserted. "Since the sale of the townsites, there has been considerable whiskey brought on the reservation," Morgan wrote a special Indian service officer. Many persons inquired about leasing reservation land. To them, Morgan replied that no person or firm could lease more than six hundred and forty acres, explaining, "The idea in leasing the land is to teach the Indian how to farm on a small scale, not the bonanza farming that has characterized the West for so long." Lessees for one to three years would be required to fence the land; those for five years would have to build houses and pay cash for their leases.[31]

During 1909 many confederated Flatheads worked their allotments and fenced their land. As he saw the final parceling of the land, Charlot wrote the commissioner asking him to dismiss Morgan, but warned against letting Morgan know of his protest. But a mission priest said the Indians simply resented Morgan's stern attention to duty.

At Christmas, 1909, Morgan learned that Charlot lay near death. The old chief had been troubled with a liver ailment, feeling so poorly the preceding September that he declined an invitation to meet Dixon on the Crow reservation. For several weeks after Christmas, the agent took Charlot a bowl of soup daily. Confined to his bed of robes, Charlot failed rapidly and on Sunday, January 9, the withered chief turned his face from the wall to bid Morgan good-by. At two o'clock the following morning, Charlot died, stanch in his Catholic faith. In the St. Ignatius house diary, one of the priests wrote, "January 10, 1910—Chief Charlot died this morning. He made a nice death."

Scores of whites paid their respects to Charlot's widow, Isabel, among them the Missoula painter, Edward S. Paxson, to whom she gave her late husband's photographs.[32] During the second week of February, the confederated Flatheads elected Martin, Charlot's son, as their chief.

Fifteen days after Charlot died, the federal government announced that Flathead agricultural lands would be opened for entry by settlers on April 1. Approximately eighteen hundred homesteads of 40 to 120 acres under irrigation would be available, and twelve hundred homesteads of 160 acres without irrigation might be settled, totaling 1,126,587.72 acres. Witten notified the registrants whose names had been drawn.

Soon after selection began, President Taft signed a Dixon bill authorizing Indians to sell sixty of their eighty allotted acres. The *Missoulian* editorialized:

The permission granted the Indians to sell their lands down to 20 acres will place much of the most desirable land in the reserve upon the open market and add materially to the available land for the homeseekers who are coming this spring. The sale of the Indian lands is so safeguarded by the law that speculation will be practically barred and it will be impossible for shyster speculators to victimize the Indians.[33]

In addition to the irrigated homesteads offered for selection, much of the Indian land was irrigated, and the government proposed to water more than one hundred thousand acres. Recommending systems of irrigation had been customary for nearly seventy-five years, as various agents and inspectors filed their reports. Small ditches scratched in the ground watered St. Mary's fields in

Father De Smet's time; other makeshift canals irrigated Indian land and mission fields near St. Ingatius.

Although Ronan boasted in his 1880 report that "the necessity of irrigation is seldom known" in the Jocko Valley, in 1892 he requested and was given permission to enlarge one canal and dig a new one for $5,870, using Indian labor, to divert irrigation water from Finlay Creek and the Jocko River. In 1895 an Indian inspector, despite "the fact that the thermometer registered 30 degrees below zero the three days I was driving over the reserve," estimated the cost of various potential irrigation sites, and the following year, Joseph Carter reported "twenty or twenty-five families have settled and made for themselves comfortable homes and secured abundant crops" on the Jocko because "during the year . . . I laid out two ditches for Indians . . . and individual Indians dug them without further aid from any source."[34]

Smead enlarged the Jocko system in 1899, employing Indian workmen at a dollar and fifty cents a day, and in 1903, citing a recent survey by a civil engineer he had been authorized to hire, estimated a canal to water the Mission Valley would cost no more than ten thousand dollars. The allotting agent, Rankin, in his turn called attention to irrigation possibilities on the Flathead reservation, and in 1907 Dixon persuaded Secretary Garfield, Frederick Newell, director of the Reclamation Service, and Indian Commissioner Francis Leupp to tour the reservation for an informal survey of its irrigation potential.

During 1907 the commissioner and Newell agreed to divide responsibilities for the Blackfoot irrigation project in Montana, and this compact, ratified May 29, 1907, by the secretary of the interior, became the basis for cooperative development of Flathead irrigation. Under it the commissioner chose localities and the director recommended the design of the system, located its structures, and supervised construction.[35]

Service engineer R. S. Stockton, during the summer of 1907, surveyed the Flathead reservation, concluding that at least 153,000 acres could be irrigated, roughly half by gravity and the remainder by pumping, using water from the Jocko, Flathead, and Little Bitterroot rivers and Mud, Crow, Post, Mission, and Dry creeks.

Dixon amended the Indian appropriation bill of 1908 to authorize fifty thousand dollars to begin irrigation on the Flathead and in 1909 secured two hundred and fifty thousand for construction, to be reimbursed by the sale of lands and timber to settlers. The first of these appropriations permitted a start of construction in the Jocko and Mission valleys and near Polson; the second, boring the 1,700-foot Newell tunnel to divert the Flathead River where a power plant was to be built. (The tunnel, completed in 1911, was not used until 1928, when the Montana Power Company secured a federal license for the site.)

The Jocko and Mission valley systems covered a potential of thirty-three thousand acres at an estimated cost of fifteen dollars an acre, but early development consisted of six thousand acres in the Jocko, forty-five hundred in the Mission, and three thousand in the Polson districts. A number of persons whose names had been drawn for land selections came to look over the construction in person.

By the beginning of the 1910 crop season, each district received water. In its work the Reclamation Service hired as many Indians as practical,

> largely and successfully employed on clearing brush, trimming and burning and sawing of logs, while nearly all the team work was done with government or hired white men's stock.... It was found necessary at all times to keep enough white men to handle all the mules owned by the service.

Irrigation on the Flathead failed during its first season because, as the Reclamation Service reported, many Indians and settlers

> were new to land and irrigation methods and they started the season wrong by waiting until the crops were suffering before they considered using water. In the Jocko valley, there was said to have been a general understanding among farmers that they would show that water was not needed ... for growing grain.

By the end of 1911, the Flathead project was 15 per cent completed.

Compared to the interest in registering for Flathead lands, selections by those whose names had been drawn were trifling. Clerks in the land offices at Missoula and Kalispell called the names of eligible selectors in the order drawn; those present answered and were given ten days to choose and file on reservation acreage. But the land offices were almost empty. The names echoed in nearly vacant hallways as the clerks called one hundred a day and then one hundred and fifty.

For a few weeks in May, 1910, prospectors rushed onto the reservation in response to ancient tales that the Indians knew of secret lodes. "There is good reason to believe that there are valuable mines on the reservation," Smead maintained in his promotional book. "Many specimens of high grade ore have been found there and with the opening . . . it is believed that mines of great value will be located." No claims of significant worth were staked.

As the monotonous calls for absent selectors continued, the *Daily Missoulian* remarked, "Interest in Flathead land is small, and most names are called to empty hallways." The land offices completed their calls on September 30: at Missoula, 119 selections had been recorded; at Kalispell, 99. Less than one-fourth of the reservation land appraised had been sold.

Half a century later, only a few more than two thousand producing farms would lie within the bounds of the Flathead reservation. A total of eighty-six thousand acres would be irrigated. Persons affiliated with the confederated Flatheads would be operating approximately one in seven of the farms, with the remainder belonging to non-Indians. Ranchers and skilled laborers would live well and hold high positions in the community. Many older Flatheads would still live by digging and hunting, be poor, and cluster in their own camps. There would be 321 Indians on the reservation who were landless, among them Cree and Chippewa families whose children attended St. Ignatius.

When original allottees died, their land was divided among their heirs. By 1920 individual shares of one-ninth of eighty acres would be common and in one case a grandson would inherit six eighteen-hundredths of his grandfather's allotment. Usually these scraps of allotments were sold as quickly as petitions could be approved allowing their sale.

After selections were made by those whose names had been drawn, the remaining unclaimed land was declared open for settlement under the general homestead laws of the United States as of November 1, 1910. By early October the cabins of squatters appeared, but only a handful of homesteads were taken. The passing of Indian title to the land was notable now for disinterest and apathy.

Nevertheless, the Flatheads were at last dispossessed of their communal lands and thus launched on lives of toil and piety.

APPENDIX

THESE SIXTEEN NUMBERED SECTIONS, to which the reader is directed in the notes, are meant to extend his understanding of the story. They include biographical summaries of four persons apparently not published elsewhere, additional contemporary correspondence and comment, and historical highlights that impart the flavor of the times and circumstances.

1. Allegations that the British depleted beaver reserves deliberately were leveled by Smith, Jackson, and Sublette in "Memoir to the War Department," Executive Document 39, U.S. Executive Documents 1830–31, and the *North American Review*, January, 1840, 135. The latter says in part, "This territory being trapped by both parties is nearly exhausted of beavers; and unless the British can be stopped it soon will be entirely exhausted, and no place left within the United States where beaver fur in any quantity can be obtained." The charge should be viewed in the light of commercial and political rivalry, although John McLoughlin remarked on exhaustion of the Snake country in a letter to George Simpson, March 20, 1831, published in Barker, *Letters of Dr. John McLoughlin, Written at Fort Vancouver, 1829–1832*, 182–88.

2. Stevens' notice to the Hudson's Bay Company to cease trading on United States soil is in a letter to P. S. Ogden, December 20, 1853 (HBC A11/71/365–66). According to Bay files (especially

A6/27/80), the company temporarily assigned titles to its lands and posts south of 49° to individuals in its service and discontinued hunting and trapping in the United States. In the Stevens Papers at the University of Washington (microfilm reel 3), a letter from Stevens to William F. Tolmie, chief trader, Hudson's Bay Company, January 9, 1854, argues that the treaty guarantees the company its possessory rights only, saying, "It surely will not be claimed that the right to trade is a possessory right." Ogden and Dugald Mactavish of Hudson's Bay replied January 16, 1854 (also University of Washington), that they had sent Stevens' notice to London and in the meantime were not authorized to suspend trading. Shortly after, Stevens was buying militia supplies from the company.

3. John Owen apparently thought Ben Kiser a competent interpreter, and reported Kiser's death in the Bitterroot Valley on April 23, 1856, in a letter to Stevens dated May 11, 1856. Stevens wrote the commissioner of Indian affairs on September 2, 1856 (Washington Superintendency, 1853–74, National Archives), "Everything which Major Owens says in relation to my Flathead interpreter at the council I concur in. Ben Kiser's mother was stolen in Kentucky when a small child by the Shawnees and became the wife of a Shawnee chief. Kiser was one of the boldest, truest, and most intelligent of the mountain men—he spoke English well—had by his industry secured a competency to his family and was relied on by the Indian Service of this territory for good counsel and good offices in the affairs of the Flatheads."

4. Washington J. McCormick wrote from Fort Owen, May 6, 1887 (published in the *Weekly Missoulian*, May 20, 1887) that he had been looking over the poll record of apparently the first vote in Montana at Council Grove, eight miles below Missoula. The poll book was dated July 9, 1855, a date on which Stevens was there to council with the Flatheads. Stevens cast the first ballot of fifteen for territorial delegate. They elected John Owen a justice of the peace and defeated a prohibition on liquor 14 to 1. Captain C. P. Higgins and Thomas Adams were election judges, and James Doty, election clerk. Those who voted were: Stevens, William H. Pearson, R. H. Lansdale, Henry Palmer, Joseph Lamare, William Simpson,

Charles Hughes, Martin Prudhomme, Doty, Henry R. Crosbie [*sic*], Higgins, S. S. Ford, Jr., Adams, F. H. Burr, and John Canning, in the order their names appeared.

5. Fort Connah, a new Flathead post, was built in 1846 six miles northeast of St. Ignatius, where the Hudson's Bay Company continued to trade with Indians while it sought a location on British soil to replace Fort Colville. Neil M. McArthur established Fort Connah, was succeeded in 1847 by Angus McDonald, transferred to Fort Hall, and then returned to the Bitterroot to go into business buying worn horses and cattle from migrant trains to freshen for sale to the next year's migrants. McDonald remained in charge until 1852, was transferred to Colville, but returned in 1858 and took up permanent residence. Connah itself was a frame cabin sixteen by twenty-four feet, roofed with bark, and surrounded by a wooden pallisade of upright logs. The Bay refers to it as Flathead post in its correspondence. When the commission appointed to place values on British possessory rights in the United States completed its work, the United States paid the company $450,000 in gold coin in 1871 for Fort Connah.

Duncan McDonald, the son of Angus, in a letter to C. N. Kessler written in 1918 (a copy is in the Montana Historical Society), said he was born at this Flathead post in 1849, calling Fort Connah a shack about one-quarter of a mile from Flathead Post. The Pend Oreille chief, Silipstoo, warned Angus McDonald not to build a cabin too near the creek, because heavy brush made good cover for Blackfoot raiders. See Albert Partoll, "Fort Connah," *Pacific Northwest Quarterly*, Vol. XXX (1939), 399–415.

6. Edgerton was irritated to discover a special Indian agent, Oliver D. Barrett, roaming through Montana and reporting directly to Washington, D.C. He considered Barrett a political spy. In contradiction of Edgerton's assurance to Washington that Montana Indians were friendly, Barrett reported the military "miserably armed and poorly mounted" and the Indian difficulties by no means ended. Directed by his superiors to talk with Edgerton, Barrett delayed nearly twelve months en route to the territorial capital at Bannack, arriving finally with "one broken down mule and two

blankets ... the wreck of the outfit with which he started one year ago," the outraged Edgerton advised the commissioner. Edgerton sold the mule for ninety-five dollars and gave the blankets to Indians, but he could not rid himself of Barrett as easily. When, during Edgerton's absence, the acting governor, Meagher, dismissed Barrett, the special agent sold forty or fifty annuity blankets to support his continued investigations and appealed to the federal Indian office, which reinstated him. Letters relating to these episodes include: Barrett to CIA, October 27, 1864; Edgerton to CIA, August 16, 1865; D. H. Hopkins, Meagher's secretary, to CIA, October 26, 1865 (all M234, Roll 488, National Archives). Seven letters from Barrett to Edgerton are among the manuscripts of the Montana Historical Society.

7. William Cullen is mentioned in *Contributions*, Historical Society of Montana, Vol. II, 291, and in Owen, *Journals and Letters of Major John Owen*, II, 121 and 122. He had been superintendent of the Northern Superintendency from May 13, 1857, to March 27, 1861; in 1862–63 raised and commanded the Cullen Guard, which served under Colonel H. H. Sibley against the Sioux in Minnesota; was a peace commissioner, 1867; was nominated as superintendent of the Idaho and Montana Indian services July 25 and December 11, 1868, but not confirmed on either occasion. For letters supporting and petitions opposing his appointment as superintendent, see the records of the secretary of the interior, Records Group 48, "Papers relating to the recommendation of W. J. Cullen as superintendent, etc.," in the National Archives. Cullen was defeated by accusations of incompetence, collusion with fur merchants at Fort Benton, and misrepresenting his political affiliation.

8. An article in the *Rocky Mountain Gazette*, Helena, December 16, 1872, says in part, "Mr. A. J. Viall ... who went on to Washington to save his head, found upon reaching there that his wisest policy was to resign, and accordingly did so. The Herald of this city takes occasion thereon to indulge in a magnificent puff of his administration. ... We hold it to have been most disastrous to Montana, though, in this connection, it is but fair to say the fault was not wholly in Colonel Viall as he was in many cases but the instrument

to carry out the orders of his superiors. The fault is in the Indian policy of the government . . . which is in the estimation of nine-tenths of our people, a fraud from top to bottom."

In an obituary for Viall published September 29, 1910, the *Butte Miner* reports that after his service as superintendent, Viall became a rancher near Judith Gap, and about 1895, through his friendship with Judge Knowles, was appointed crier of the United States court in Butte, where he was serving at the time of his death from a heart attack on September 27.

9. Doane and Pease wrote an appendix F to their report, entitled, "Indian Traders, Whiskey, and the Robe Traffic," which says in part: "The larger dealers do not trade whiskey, but they sell it to emissaries of the vilest class on credit without asking questions, and afterwards buy robes and skins of these people at the previously stipulated price." The two investigators identified a traditional Indian rendezvous, on the north bank of the Yellowstone where the road from the Crow agency to Bozeman crossed the river, as a favored point for whisky distribution.

Colonel Gibbon wrote the assistant adjutant general, Department of the Dakota, March 6, 1875 (M234, Roll 503, National Archives): "The practical operation of this traffic is as follows: The licensed trader establishes himself or his agent on or near the line of the [Crow] reservation, on the north bank of the Marias River. Directly in the vicinity of this licensed trader and on the south bank (that is, off the reservation) the illicit trafficker establishes himself and exposes his vile poison for sale or exchange for robes. The licensed trader receives, entertains, and harbors the illicit trader and his wares and receives from the latter the robes, etc., which he gathers in from the Indians in trade for whiskey and ammunition. . . . The whole country along the Teton River and north to the Marias is reported to be occupied by Indian camps and whiskey traders." At higher headquarters, General Philip H. Sheridan indorsed the report with the comment, "I presume the Indian Bureau looks upon it in the light that some people look upon social evils, as a thing that must be tolerated."

10. One of the reasons federal surveying was delayed in Montana was President Johnson's veto in 1866 of a surveying district for the

territory because the bill to establish it granted twenty-one sections to the New York & Iron Mountain Mining & Manufacturing Co. When a district was authorized in 1867 (14 Stats. 542), the appropriations for it were small. Helena served as the territory's only land office until 1874. The grand jury for the territory, according to the *Weekly Missoulian*, November 4, 1874, declared: "A majority of the surveys in the counties of Missoula and Deer Lodge have been made with a reckless disregard for law, that leaves the condition of the settlers upon the public domain . . . truly deplorable. We find that . . . monuments have not been established at all, or in so light or unsubstantial a manner as to have become obliterated. . . . The monuments not being discoverable, the settlers are compelled to have recourse to the field notes and plats . . . so imperfect that it is impossible to find the points thereon designated; while in some instances . . . there are reasons to believe that the surveys were never actually made at all and that the field notes were manufactured."

11. General Sheridan wrote the general of the army, April 7, 1877 (M234, Roll 507, National Archives), "The Indians save every shell they fire, and pick up every one white men or soldiers throw away, and refill them as perfectly as is done by machinery, using a cut down percussion cap for the fulminator. In Col. McKenzie's last fight many shells of this kind were found, as well as one of the little instruments used in filling the shells. The Indians even use our cast off boxes for packing ammunition thus made."

12. The Dawes Act (24 Stats. 388) was amended in 1891 to answer Indian protests of the legal concept of head of the family, and provided thereafter equal shares of land to all Indians: 80 acres of farm land or 160 acres of grazing. In 1906 the act was further amended to delay citizenship for Indians until expiration of a twenty-five-year trust period. Many congressmen believed the objective of the act was, as a minority report to the allotment bill of 1880 said, "to get Indian lands and open them up to settlement."

13. A widely circulated story of the conversation between Carrington and Charlot was told first by Rev. M. L. Rickman, but much of his version cannot be confirmed by Carrington's letters or reports. The version appeared in the *Daily Missoulian*, January 7, 1906, and was reprinted January 23, 1910. In it, Carrington says to

Charlot: "There is a train coming down the track and a little calf is in its way. The big chief in Washington is the train, Charlot is the calf, and I am the whistle, come to warn you—you must get out of the way.... Indians must move to the Jocko."

14. There are several versions of the origin of the Pablo buffalo herd. The herd first belonged to Pablo and Charles Allard, but when Allard died in 1896 his heirs sold their half to various buyers. Pablo rebuilt his herd by purchases, including some animals from a Kansas herd that were driven overland to Montana. He sent animals to the Pan-American Exposition at Buffalo, New York, provided some for a Wild West show that operated briefly in 1902, and customarily exhibited animals at the Missoula County Fair, but for some reason would not sell buffalo to augment the Yellowstone National Park herd. In May, 1907, foreseeing the end of the range with opening of the reservation, Pablo sold five hundred animals to the Canadian government for $150,000, setting off the outcry by the American Bison Society that the United States should preserve the bison in a federal herd. Ronan's version of the origin of the herd appears in the text. Another story, told by Charles Aubrey, a veteran Indian trader, in the *Weekly Missoulian* of October 18, 1907, and in similar detail by Ernest Harold Haynes in a manuscript, "Our National Animal, the Buffalo," Vol. LIX, 57, in the Johns Collection, Carnegie Public Library, Kalispell, says that Walking Coyote, a Pend Oreille, brought the buffalo to the Flathead reservation as an act of penance for breaking his marriage vows (or shooting his wife, as Haynes says) about 1878. The mission priests turned the animals over to Allard, who persuaded Pablo to join him in maintaining the herd. By 1888, William Hornaday reported thirty-five purebred buffalo in the herd.

15. Among the Flathead reservation holdings of the Federal Records Center, Seattle, are Thomas Downs's roll of the confederated Flatheads, a volume of notices of hearings to determine heirs, which is interesting for the addresses in each case, three ledger books reporting heirship records up to 1915, and a ledger book of fee patents that includes property descriptions (all box 56481). Not only do these records indicate intermarriages between families, as between the Charlots and Vanderburgs, but they offer opportunities

for intriguing speculation on the origin of certain family names that are similar to those of men known to have been with the Lewis and Clark party, Ogden's expeditions, and other exploring and trading patrols. Some of these names can be traced, of course, through Phillips and Malouf's, "Flathead, Kutenai and Upper Pend Oreille Genealogies," a mimeographed study found, among other places, in Claims Case 61 (National Archives). The heirship records indicate what happened to Indian allotments on the reservation. Shares of one-ninth were common among first-generation heirs; in an extreme case, when Delino F. Cahleemos died in 1915, his daughter, Louise Ashley, received 360 eighteen-hundredths of his land, as did two other heirs; ten persons received 36 eighteen-hundredths each; and a great grandson, who got the smallest part, received 6 eighteen-hundredths. Many Indians who appear in the narrative are named; for example, Jackson Sundown, whose property went to Charles Allard by purchase, and Benjamin Murray, who received an allotment despite burning the mission school in 1896.

16. The staff of the National Archives provided biographical information of Fred C. Morgan from the records of the Bureau of Indian Affairs. Morgan was born in New York about 1871 and moved to Montana about 1884. He worked for the *Missoulian*, served on the city council of Missoula, and at one time was acting mayor. He served one term in the state legislature. On July 1, 1907, he became bookkeeper and scaler at the Flathead reservation, and then agent. In 1917 he was appointed agent at the Colville Agency, in 1920 a special supervisor with the Bureau of Indian Affairs, and in 1922 superintendent of the Mescalero Agency.

NOTES

Abbreviations

AFC   American Fur Company

BCIM   Bureau of Catholic Indian Missions

CIA   Commissioner of Indian Affairs

CR   Hiram Martin Chittenden and Alfred Talbot Richardson, *Life, Letters and Travels of Father Pierre-Jean De Smet, S.J., 1801–1873.* 4 vols.

FRC   Federal Records Center, Seattle

GU   Gonzaga University: Archives of the Oregon Province, Society of Jesus

HBC   Hudson's Bay Company Archives, London

NA   National Archives and Records Service of the United States

RCIA   Annual *Report of the Commissioner of Indian Affairs*, cited with year of publication.

WSU   Washington State University

Key to Citations of Files in the National Archives

M5   Microcopy 5, followed by a roll number, designates the microfilmed records of the Washington Superintendency, 1853–74. Correspondence not on film is designated Washington Superintendency.

M234   Microcopy 234, followed by a roll number, designates the microfilmed letters received 1824–80 by the Bureau of Indian Affairs and predecessor offices.

0000–00   A register number followed by a hyphen and the last two digits of the year designates correspondence logged by the Bureau of Indian Affairs 1881–1907. Thus, 1234–96 designates letter 1234 in the year 1896. During this period, letters received were registered chronologically as received without regard for subject matter or originating office.

decimal   From 1907 to 1930 Indian office correspondence was filed by decimal-subject classification. Some correspondence was simply filed by subject category.

CHAPTER 1:

1. Gregory Mengarini, "Memoirs," manuscript, 1848, microfilm (GU), translation from G. R. Lothrop doctoral dissertation, University of Southern California, 1970.

2. A. J. Partoll, "Flathead-Salish Name in Montana Nomenclature," *Montana Magazine*, Vol. I (January, 1951), 37–47.

3. Mengarini, "Memoirs"; HBC 208/e/1.

4. C. I. Malouf, "Cultural Connections between the Prehistoric Inhabitants of the Upper Missouri and Columbia River Systems," doctoral dissertation, Columbia University, 1956, 172–73.

5. HBC B69/e/1.

6. John Owen to CIA, May 3, 1869 (NA).

7. C. E. Schaeffer, "Moulded Pottery among the Kutenai Indians," *Anthropology and Sociology Papers* of the University of Montana.

8. C. Medary to CIA, February 19, 1876 (M234, Roll 505, NA). It is possible that Victor alluded to the Flathead concept of the east as a region of life, and the west as one of darkness.

9. R. D. Stubbs, "An Investigation of the Edible and Medicinal Plants Used by the Flathead Indians," master's thesis, University of Montana, 1966, 34: "Plant ceremonial practices have been largely forgotten."

10. Mengarini, "Memoirs"; C. E. Schaeffer, "An Acculturation Study of the Indians of the Flathead Reservation of Western Montana," manuscript, American Museum of Natural History.

11. Gillett Griswold (ed.), "Archeological Sites in the Flathead Lake Region, Montana," *Anthropology and Sociology Papers* of Montana State University; Schaeffer, "Acculturation Study," 12.

12. Hazard Stevens to J. U. Sanders, secretary, Society of Montana Pioneers, August 29, 1913. Supplied to the author by Hazel E. Mills, Washington State Library.

13. E. D. Branch, *Hunting of the Buffalo*, 49–51.

14. J. C. Ewers, *Horse in Blackfoot Culture*, 33.

15. Mengarini, in "Memoirs," observes that as soon as a boy is five or six,

he prays, eats, and leaves his parents' lodge with bow and arrows. He hunts in the meadow until dusk, and no one asks where he has been. At fourteen, his parents no longer direct him. If they condemn his insolence, he and companions may mount horses and move two or three hundred miles away.

16. Mengarini, "Memoirs."

17. Homosexuals of either sex, called *berdaches* by whites delicately using a corrupted French term, found recognized places in Flathead society. Investigators do not agree on whether Bundosh was man or woman.

18. Mengarini, "Memoirs"; Schaeffer, "Acculturation Study."

19. N. J. Wyeth, *Correspondence and Journals*, 54.

20. Ewers, *Gustav Sohon's Portraits of Flathead and Pend O'Reille Indians*, 15; A. B. Smith to David D. Greene, February 6, 1840, quoted in C. M. Drury (ed.), *Diaries and Letters of Henry H. Spalding and Asa Bowen Smith Relating to the Nez Perce Mission 1838-1842*, 137-38.

21. Clark is said to have fathered a son among the Flatheads, introduced ceremoniously to whites later as Peter Clark and mentioned in a letter, Flathead agent to CIA, May 3, 1896 (M234, Roll 489, NA).

CHAPTER 2:

1. P. C. Phillips, *The Fur Trade*, II, 308.

2. David Thompson, *David Thompson's Narrative, 1784-1812* (R. Glover, ed.), 296.

3. *Ibid.*, 303.

4. *Ibid.*, 305-306. Hudson's Bay Company maps place the original Flathead post at 48° 11' 10" N.

5. Reuben to M. Lewis, April 21, 1810, quoted in L. O. Saum, *Fur Trader and the Indian*, 58.

6. Ross Cox, *The Columbia River* (E. I. and J. R. Stewart, eds.), 122.

7. Mengarini, "Memoirs."

8. Ross, report March 10, 1825 (HBC B69/e/1).

9. Cox, *The Columbia River*, 134-36.

10. *Ibid.*

11. J. Palliser, *Papers of the Palliser Expedition, 1857-60* (I. M. Spry, ed.), 575.

12. Governor and council to Simpson, May 19, 1823 (HBC A6/20/108d); F. Merk, *Fur Trade and Empire*, 242-46; list of stations, 1823 (HBC A6/20/90d).

13. Ross, report March 10, 1825 (HBC B69/e/1).

14. Spokane House report, HBC B208/e/1; R. H. Ruby and J. A. Brown, in *Spokane Indians*, temper this view of the Spokanes, especially 50-51.

15. Merk, *Fur Trade and Empire*, 44-45. Simpson's decision to outfit Snake brigades at Fort Nez Percés was partly based on his erroneous belief that the Umpqua River rose in Utah and would provide a water route.

16. J. McLoughlin to J. W. Dease, November 18, 1826 (HBC B223/b/2, fo. 37). Dease died at the post in 1830.

17. Ross, report March 10, 1825 (HBC B69/e/1); Ross, "Journal, 1824" (T. C. Elliott, ed.), *Oregon Historical Quarterly*, Vol. XIV (1913), 386–88.

18. Mengarini, in "Memoirs," says, "Flatheads, like other tribes, have their tribal and martial music. It distinguishes them from other tribes when all gather. No words, but the sounds of chromes, accompanied by a drum."

19. G. J. Garraghan, *Catholic Beginnings in Kansas City*, 93. (Hereafter cited as *Kansas City*.)

20. McLoughlin to Francis Heron, June 28, 1831 (HBC B223/b/7, fo. 2d).

21. Pilcher's report January 24, 1831, appended to the message of the president, 21 Cong., 2 sess., *Sen. Doc. 39*.

22. McLoughlin to Work, September 7, 1829 (HBC 223/b/5, fo. 20).

23. There are many versions of the "battle of Pierre's Hole." This follows N. J. Wyeth, *Correspondence and Journals*, 159–60. Josephy, in *Nez Perce Indians and the Opening of the Northwest*, 77, identified the defenders as Gros Ventres.

24. Wyeth, *Correspondence and Journals*, 188–89.

25. Wyeth to Henry Hall and Messrs. Tucker and Williams, November 8, 1833, in *Correspondence and Journals*, 73–78.

26. Wyeth to Messrs. Tucker and Williams, July 1, 1834, in *Correspondence and Journals*, 138–39.

27. W. H. Gray, *History of Oregon*, 170–72.

28. Mengarini, "Memoirs"; American Fur Company letters 2885, 4848, 4108, and 6127, in the library of the New York Historical Society. See appendix, item 1.

29. Ross, report March 10, 1825 (HBC 69/e/1).

30. Ogden to Simpson, March 10, 1849 (HBC D5/24, fo. 364d); Douglas to John Black, January 26, 1852 (HBC A11/71/34-7).

CHAPTER 3:

1. Joseph Rosati, December 31, 1831, in L. Palladino, *Indian and White in the Northwest*, 11.

2. F. Haines, "Nez Perce Delegation to St. Louis in 1831," *Pacific Historical Review*, Vol. VI (1937), 71–78. The story has enlarged with repetition, illustrated in C. T. Johnson, "Evolution of a Lament," *Washington Historical Quarterly*, Vol. II (1908), 195–208. In a partial memoir written late in life, Father Anthony Ravalli dates the first Flathead delegation as 1836 (GU).

3. Baptiste's story appears in two separate letters: Father Paul Muset to Palladino, March 30, 1897, and Father J. Bandini to Father J. D'Aste, September 12, 1888 (GU). Although they differ in some details, both recount interviews with Baptiste and both say he attended school before De Smet's ordination in 1827.

4. G. J. Garraghan, *Kansas City*, 93.

5. Mengarini, "Memoirs." Ravalli's incomplete memoir (GU) gives the same version but dates the delegation of seven as 1837. Bishop Rosati told Ravalli his version personally when they talked in Rome in 1843, so that Ravalli, in writing his memoirs, would have known of the 1831 delegation to St. Louis.

6. A. Ross, *Fur Hunters of the Far West* (K. A. Spaulding, ed.), 211.

7. Thompson, *Narrative*, 82.

8. Mengarini, "Memoirs." Illim-Spokanee, in this version, assumes an unusual role. He was respected but regarded at the time as a harmless old man. Ruby and Brown, in *Spokane Indians*, 59, say Illim-Spokanee died about 1829.

9. Jason Lee, "Diary, April 20–July 16, 1834," *Oregon Historical Quarterly*, Vol. XVII (1916), entries of June 20 and 21 and July 4, 1834. Before setting out, Jason conferred in New York with George Simpson of the Hudson's Bay Company, and Simpson, as a consequence, forecast a migration that would injure the fur trade.

10. J. McLoughlin, "Document among the Private Papers of Dr. John McLoughlin," *Transactions*, Oregon Pioneer Association, 1880, 50.

11. S. Parker, *Journal of an Exploring Tour Beyond the Rocky Mountains ... with a Map of the Oregon Territory* (1842 ed.), 80–82. Father J. D'Aste, in a manuscript, "St. Mary's History" (GU), also reports the visit of an unidentified Protestant missionary to the Bitterroot sometime between 1834 and 1836.

12. Memoirs of Ferdinand Helias, S. J., in G. J. Garraghan, *Jesuits of the Middle United States*, II, 246–47.

13. E. Laveille, *Life of Father De Smet, S.J.*, 102, quoting a De Smet letter of October 29, 1839.

14. Garraghan, *Jesuits*, II, 252–53.

15. CR, I, 221–34; W. L. Davis, "Peter John De Smet: the Journey of 1840," *Pacific Northwest Quarterly*, Vol. XXXV (1944), 40–41.

16. CR, I, 293 and 305.

17. *Transactions*, Oregon Pioneer Association, 1890, 131.

18. Mengarini, "Memoirs"; J. Joset, "Loyola, an Indian Chief," a manuscript of which page one is missing (GU).

19. Mengarini, "Memoirs."

20. CR, I, 338–39.

21. Joset, "Chronology of the Rocky Mountain Missions," manuscript (GU); CR, I, 319 and 327–28.

22. Mengarini, "Memoirs."

23. CR, I, 362.

24. Palladino, *Indian and White*, 52. J. C. Ewers to William Laney, S. J., August 10, 1944, says Ewers cannot find Nicolas' name among the list of

those baptized, although Nicolas and his family of five, supposedly baptized Christmas Day, 1841, at St. Mary's, were apparently the first Piegans baptized (GU).

25. De Smet wrote Blanchet on August 10, 1840, "The Shoshones and Snakes are anxious to have a mission established in their country; the Flatheads and Pend Oreilles have nothing more at heart. The Nez Perces seem to me to be tired of their so-called ministers with wives and manifest a strong prediliction for Catholic priests. Hence, without advancing any farther into this country, we shall find enough work in these mountains to keep us busy for some years." Quoted in Davis, "Journey of 1840," *Pacific Northwest Quarterly*, Vol. XXXV (1944), 126.

26. Garraghan, *Jesuits*, II, 288–89.

27. Mengarini, "Memoirs."

28. Mengarini to Roothaan, September 26, 1844, in G. R. Lothrop, "Father Gregory Mengarini, an Italian Jesuit Missionary in the Transmontane West," doctoral dissertation, University of Southern California, 1970, 108; Mengarini, "Narrative," manuscript (GU).

29. Ravalli to Palladino, December 8, 1879 (GU).

30. St. Ignatius baptismal record compiled by Hoecken (GU); Joset, "Loyola, an Indian Chief," manuscript (GU); Hoecken to De Smet, n.d. (c. 1855), Hoecken letterbook (GU).

31. Ravalli to Palladino, December 8, 1879 (GU).

32. CR, II, 570–71.

33. Garraghan, *Jesuits*, II, 420.

34. Mengarini, "Narrative" (GU). This episode was deleted from the version printed as "The Rocky Mountains" in *Woodstock Letters*, Vol. XVII, 293–309, and Vol. XVIII, 25–43.

35. Mengarini, "Memoirs"; Mengarini to father general, February 21, 1838 (GU) in which he identifies the Indian only as "the scandal monger." In his memoirs, Mengarini names him as Little Faro, who lost a son to the pox.

36. Joset to Father Joseph Simmen, October 29, 1849, in Garraghan, *Jesuits*, II, 354–55.

37. Roothaan to president, Society for Propagation of the Faith, April 19, 1848 (Davis Notes, GU).

38. Mengarini to Roothaan, September 30, 1847 (GU).

39. Garraghan, in *Jesuits*, II, 66–107, discusses St. Mary's.

40. Ravalli to Palladino, December 8, 1879 (GU).

41. Mengarini, "Memoirs."

42. Ravalli to Palladino, December 8, 1879 (GU); Ravalli to Martin Maginnis, n.d. (c. 1871) in St. Mary's records (GU).

43. Accolti to Roothaan, November 20, 1852, in Lothrop dissertation, "Father Gregory Mengarini," 129.

44. Grant to Sir George, January 31, 1851 (HBC D5/30, fo. 184).

CHAPTER 4:

1. Mengarini, "Memoirs."

2. Stevens' instructions to Doty are in four letters, three dated October 3, 1853, and one October 7, 1853, in the Stevens Papers, University of Washington (microfilm reel 1).

3. Stevens to CIA, December 29, 1853 (Washington Superintendency, 1853–74, NA). In the Stevens letterbook, Washington State Archives, a letter to CIA, September 8, 1853, says Mullan has gone to the Musselshell to learn Flatheads' views.

4. C. M. Gates (ed.), *Messages of the Governors of the Territory of Washington to the Legislative Assembly, 1854–1889*, 4. See appendix, item 2.

5. Stevens to CIA, January 31, 1854 (Washington Superintendency, 1853–74, NA).

6. Hoecken to De Smet, n.d. (c. 1855), and Joset, "Loyola, an Indian Chief," manuscript (both GU). Menetrey first urged the Pend Oreilles to move to Flathead Lake but was overruled by Chief Alexander.

7. Population from Stevens to CIA, May 5, 1856 (Washington Superintendency, 1853–74, NA).

8. Hoecken's diary is at Gonzaga University. The account is based on Doty's record, "Stevens Journal, 1855" (M5, Roll 26, NA), and Hazard Stevens, *Life of Isaac Ingalls Stevens*, unless otherwise noted. For Kiser (Kyser), see appendix, item 3.

9. Stevens, *Life*, II, 82.

10. *Ibid.*, II, 90. Nevertheless, as Hazard Stevens says in his letter to J. U. Sanders, August 29, 1913, "At the campfire for several nights after the treaty was made the gentlemen of the party agreed that the point made by Big Canoe was a hard one to answer and that these Indians showed a friendly and philanthropic spirit far excelling the whites."

11. 12 Stats. 975. See appendix, item 4.

12. Stevens to CIA, July 16, 1855 (Washington Superintendency, 1853–74, NA).

13. Lansdale to Stevens, October 2, 1855 (M5, Roll 22, NA).

14. H. Stevens letter, 1913; copy provided by Hazel E. Mills of the Washington State Library in Olympia. See A. J. Partoll, "Blackfeet Indian Peace Council," *Frontier and Midland*, Vol. XVII, No. 3 (1937), 199–207.

15. Lansdale to Stevens, December 1, 1855, and January 1, 1856 (both M5, Roll 22, NA).

16. Owen to Stevens, May 11, 1856; Lansdale to Stevens, April 1 and June 30, 1856 (all M5, Roll 22, NA).

17. See appendix, item 5.

18. HBC A6/206, November 30, 1856; HBC A11/71/649, A11/71/671, and A11/71/669.

19. Menetrey to De Smet, August 15, 1857, in Garraghan, *Jesuits*, II, 388–89.

20. Stevens to Lansdale, June 1 and 4, 1856 (M5, Roll 22, NA).

21. Lansdale to Stevens, November 1, 1856; Stevens to CIA, November 1, 1856 (both M5, Roll 22, NA).

22. Lansdale to Stevens, March 31, 1857 (M5, Roll 22, NA).

23. Owen to Doty, April 25, 1857 (M5, Roll 22, NA).

24. Owen to Nesmith, January 9, 1858 (M5, Roll 22, NA).

25. Owen to E. R. Geary, May 31, 1859 (M5, Roll 22, NA). Geary succeeded Nesmith.

26. Owen to Nesmith, February 2, 1859 (M5, Roll 22, NA), and September 18, 1858, in J. Owen, *Journals and Letters of Major John Owen* (S. Dunbar and P. C. Phillips, eds.), II, 183–86.

27. Owen to Geary, August 16, 1859 (M5, Roll 22, NA).

28. Fort Sheppard (originally Shepherd), Blankenship to Sir George, February 25, 1859 (HBC A11/71/1032–33); Grant to Fraser, November 3, 1859 (HBC A11/71/1047–48).

29. Owen to Geary, October 10, 12, 16, and 18, 1859 (M5, Roll 22, NA).

30. Owen to Geary, May 25, 1860 (M5, Roll 22, NA). Owen apparently first saw the bill of goods in Geary's office. Geary had approved it.

31. Mullan to Geary, April 5, 1860 (M5, Roll 23, NA).

32. Owen to Geary, December 3, 1860 (M5, Roll 22, NA).

CHAPTER 5:

1. Hoecken to De Smet, April 15, 1857, in CR, IV, 1247. Hoecken credited John Mullan with helping to build the mission buildings.

2. Lansdale to Stevens, June 30, 1856 (M5, Roll 22, NA).

3. Owen to Doty, April 25, 1857 (M5, Roll 22, NA).

4. Mullan to Owen, May 27, 1861 (M5, Roll 22, NA).

5. Owen to Kendall, July 17, 1862, in Owen, *Journals and Letters*, II, 276–77.

6. Brooks to Hale, October 31, 1862, and January 30, 1863 (M5, Roll 22, NA).

7. L. Palladino, *Education for the Indian*, 10.

8. Hutchins to CIA, October 3, 1865 (M234, Roll 488, NA).

9. Edgerton to CIA, December 24, 1864 (M234, Roll 488, NA).

10. See appendix, item 6.

11. Chapman to CIA, April 20, 1866; Chapman to Lyon, forwarded to CIA, April 2, 1866 (both M234, Roll 488, NA).

12. *Liber Mortuorum*, St. Ignatius (GU).

13. T. F. Meagher, "Rides through Montana," *Harper's New Monthly Magazine*, No. 209 (October, 1867), 583.

14. Secretary to CIA, May 14, 1866 (M234, Roll 488, NA).

15. Chapman to CIA, October 5, 18, and 28, 1866 (M234, Roll 488, NA).

16. Wells to CIA, May 7 and 12, 1867 (M234, Roll 488, NA).

17. *Ibid.,* June 14, 1867 (M234, Roll 488, NA); *Tri-Weekly Post* (Virginia City and Helena), July 2, 1867.

18. Wells to CIA, September 9 and August 4, 1867 (both M234, Roll 488, NA). Schafft said Wells challenged Pomeroy to a duel.

19. McCormick to CIA, February 20, 1869 (M234, Roll 489, NA); McCormick to James Tufts, August 31, 1868, Congressional documents, serial 1366, 668–75.

20. The general impression of the Flatheads as portrayed in contemporary literature is considered in Saum, *Fur Trader and the Indian*, 99, from which this discussion borrows.

21. Cullen's report to CIA, August 22, 1868, and minutes of his council with the Flatheads (both M234, Roll 489, NA), from which the narrative is taken. See appendix, item 7.

CHAPTER 6:

1. Galbreath to Sully, August 26, 1869 (M234, Roll 489, NA).

2. Sully to CIA, August 31, October 6 and 11, 1869 (M234, Roll 489, NA), and May 4, 1870 (M234, Roll 490, NA).

3. Sully to CIA, October 20, 1869 (M234, Roll 489, NA). Sully acted in lieu of a civilian negotiator. His treaty included a house valued at not less than four hundred dollars for each family, a plow, yoke of oxen, and fencing of two acres, and a sawmill and gristmill to be operated by the government for twelve years.

4. Owen to CIA, May 3, 1869 (M234, Roll 489, NA), enclosing a letter in his hand signed with Victor's X.

5. Sully to CIA, October 20, 1869 (M234, Roll 489, NA).

6. *Helena* (Montana) *Daily Herald*, October 27, 1869; *New North-West* (Deer Lodge, Montana), October 27, 1869.

7. Jury report, October 9, forwarded by Sully to CIA, October 21, 1869 (M234, Roll 489, NA). An Indian office circular of June 12, 1869, placed under military control those Indians not on reservations and authorized the army to consider them hostiles, if necessary.

8. Galbreath to Sully, November 14, 1869 (M234, Roll 489, NA).

9. *Ibid.,* May 4, 1870 (M234, Roll 489, NA).

10. *Ibid.,* May 18, 1870 (M234, Roll 489, NA).

11. *Ibid.,* July 26, 1870 (M234, Roll 490, NA), estimating Victor's age as eighty-five. St. Mary's *Liber Mortuorum* 1866–94 (GU), under date of July 4, 1870, records Victor's death; the priests thought him about eighty. Sully to CIA, May 4, 1870 (M234, Roll 489, NA); De Smet to D'Aste, February 11, 1871, in CR, IV, 1336.

12. Sully to CIA, May 4, 1870 (M234, Roll 489, NA).

13. Methodists were fully as strong in Montana as Catholics. The 1870 census listed five structures for each in the territory, but Methodist churches were in towns and at least three Catholic churches were on Indian reservations. At Stevensville there were a northern and a southern Methodist church. The Methodists were given the Blackfeet, Crows, and Milk River Indians, and the Catholics, the Flatheads.

14. Jones to CIA, November 3, 1870 (M234, Roll 490, NA). Viall biography in appendix, item 8.

15. Viall to CIA, December 9, 1870, and to Jones, November 12, 1870 (both M234, Roll 490, NA).

16. Cavanaugh to CIA, April 7, 1871 (M234, Roll 491, NA); Stanley R. Davidson, "1871: Montana's Year of Political Fusion," *Montana Magazine*, Vol. XXI, No. 2 (Spring, 1971), 44–55.

17. Jones (marked "personal") to CIA, December 8, 1870 (M234, Roll 490, NA). According to P. C. Phillips and C. I. Malouf in "Flathead, Kutenai and Upper Pend Oreille Genealogies," 4–5, Charlot and Arlee were grandsons of brothers, Charlot of Three Eagles and Arlee of Cumpecht (Tipi Painted Red).

18. Jones to CIA, January 23, 1871 (M234, Roll 490, NA).

19. *Ibid.*, December 8, 1870 (M234, Roll 490, NA).

20. *Missoula and Cedar Creek Pioneer*, July 27, 1871.

21. May 7, 1871 (M234, Roll 491, NA). The signers were Charlot, Henry (Arlee), Adolph, Francis, Laurence, Henry, and Joseph Nganta (Nine Pipes).

22. Viall to CIA, May 17, 1871 (M234, Roll 491, NA). The convicted were Joseph Grooms and John Davidson, according to the minutebook, Second Judicial District of Montana Territory, May 13 and 17, 1871.

23. Potts to CIA, September 8, 1871; Blaine to commissioner, General Land Office, October 24, 1871 (M234, Roll 491, NA).

24. Jones to CIA, May 17, 1872 (both M234, Roll 493, NA). 42 Cong., 3 sess., *House Res.*, March 14, 1871, directs the secretary of the interior to furnish a copy of charges against Viall.

25. Garfield to CIA, November 15, 1872 (M234, Roll 492, NA). The general account of negotiations is taken from Garfield's "Diary," in J. Hakola (ed.), *Frontier Omnibus*, 347–58, and Garfield report, *RCIA 1872*, 109–18. The manuscript report is frames 200–32, M234, Roll 492 (NA).

26. Garfield's "Diary," *loc. cit.*, August 22, 1872; Garfield to CIA, November 15, 1872 (M234, Roll 492, NA).

27. Garfield to CIA, November 15, 1872 (M234, Roll 492, NA).

28. The dates here follow Garfield's "Diary," *loc. cit.*, which says the contract was signed Monday, August 26, although his report indicates the Indians passed that day looking for homesites and signed on August 27. The printed contract appears with the Garfield report, *RCIA 1872*, 109–18.

29. The letters appear with the Garfield report, *RCIA 1872*, 115–17, and

also on M234, Roll 500 (NA). Garfield indignantly remarks that the board "would go so far as to resist by force the execution of the laws," perhaps here recognizing the Indian office's willingness to embarrass the board. Garfield's advice to the Indians appears in Hall to Bevier, July 17, 1874 (M234, Roll 500, NA).

30. *RCIA 1872*, 115–17, and also M234, Roll 492 (NA).

CHAPTER 7:

1. P. H. Sheridan and W. T. Sherman, *Reports of Inspection Made in the Summer of 1877*, 44. G. F.Weisel (ed.), in *Men and Trade on the Northwest Frontier as Shown by the Fort Owen Ledger*, 95, says the Flatheads realized the buffalo were disappearing as early as 1861.

2. W. T. Hornaday, in *Extermination of the American Bison*, 464–65, also lists secondary causes: man's reckless greed and destructiveness, absence of government protection, preference of hunters for cows, stupidity of buffalo, and perfection of repeating rifles.

3. Doane and Pease report to CIA, February 19, 1873 (M234, Roll 498, NA). Apparently the bulk of the report and its appendices was Doane's work, and, although it contained information on the buffalo published elsewhere, the report offered considerable personal observation.

4. Charles Schafft to Daniel Shanahan, December 29, 1873 (M234, Roll 500, NA); *Weekly Missoulian*, March 5, 1874.

5. Sweitzer to assistant adjutant general (hereafter, AAG), Department of the Dakota, January 5, 1874 (M234, Roll 500, NA).

6. *Ibid.*, March 7, 1875 (M234, Roll 500, NA).

7. *Weekly Missoulian*, January 13, 1875.

8. *Ibid.*, July 26, 1876.

9. Doane and Pease to CIA, February 19, 1873 (M234, Roll 498, NA). See appendix, item 9.

10. Knowles to R. F. May, May 5, 1874 (M234, Roll 499, NA).

11. C. Medary to CIA, enclosing Potts's letter, August 6, 1875 (M234, Roll 502, NA).

12. Secretary of war to secretary of the interior, August 5, 1876 (M234, Roll 505, NA).

13. Jones to CIA, June 27, 1872 (M234, Roll 493, NA), and July 6, 1872 (M234, Roll 492, NA); Viall to CIA, August 5, 1872 (M234, Roll 493, NA).

14. *Weekly Missoulian*, December 19, 1873. Palladino to Felix Brunot, November 20, 1872 (GU), blamed Viall for delaying payment of $1,097. Clagett to CIA, December 15, 1871 (M234, Roll 492, NA), alleged that Jones not only falsified vouchers but appointed his thirteen-year-old son, William, as head miller.

15. Secretary of the interior to CIA, December 7, 1872, forwarding Brunot documents (M234, Roll 492, NA); Clagett to CIA, May 25 and July 21, 1873

(M234, Roll 494, NA); secretary of the interior to CIA, July 15, 1873 (M234, Roll 495, NA). When Jones refused to return to Montana for trial in 1874, the U.S. attorney general instructed that suits against him be dropped.

16. Wright to CIA, March 11, 1873 (M234, Roll 494, NA).

17. Potts (private letter) to secretary of the interior, July 17, 1873 (M234, Roll 495, NA).

18. Clagett to Garfield, December 24, 1876 (M234, Roll 507, NA).

19. *New North-West*, April 15, 1874, says the school opened August 26, 1863, but L. Taelman, in *Diamond Jubilee*, gives the date used here.

20. Palladino to Brunot, May 4, 1873, and reply, May 29, 1873 (both M234, Roll 494, NA).

21. C. C. O'Keeffe (known locally as Baron O'Keeffe) to J. Cavanaugh, April 21, 1874 (M234, Roll 498, NA).

22. Shanahan to CIA, July 18, 23, 26, and August 1, 1873 (all M234, Roll 495, NA).

23. *New North-West*, April 25, 1874; sisters to CIA, October 31, 1875 (M234, Roll 502, NA).

24. Van Gorp to Maginnis, November 29, 1874 (M234, Roll 502, NA); Ewing to CIA, May 4 and October 29, 1874 (M234, Roll 498, NA); Clagett to Garfield, December 24, 1876 (M234, Roll 507, NA).

25. Ally-quil-quil-squaw, written by Duncan McDonald, to the president, November 1, 1874 (M234, Roll 500, NA).

26. Ewing to CIA, December 11, 1876 (M234, Roll 504, NA); Clagett to Garfield, December 24, 1876 (M234, Roll 507, NA).

27. *Weekly Missoulian*, June 2 and July 29, 1875.

28. Arlee to CIA, October 10, 1872 (M234, Roll 492, NA); Jones to the president, March 11, 1873 (M234, Roll 495, NA).

29. Winslett's list is frames 360-63, M234, Roll 496 (NA). On April 25, 1872 (M234, Roll 496, NA), Louis Matte submitted an invoice for blacksmith work on farm implements, naming twenty-two Indians including Charlot and four women, indicating these, at least, were farming in the Bitterroot.

30. Wright to CIA, March 11 and 15, 1873 (M234, Roll 496, NA).

31. Secretary of the interior to General Land Office, May 14, 1873 (M234, Roll 495, NA).

32. Shanahan to CIA, July 12, August 4, and November 28, 1873 (M234, Roll 496, NA); Shanahan to Wright, April 21, 1873 (M234, Roll 496, NA).

33. Shanahan to CIA, September 16 and October 11, 1873 (M234, Roll 496, NA), and May 14, 1875 (M234, Roll 503, NA).

34. *Ibid.*, December 12, 1873 (M234, Roll 490, NA).

35. Medary to CIA, February 19, 1876 (M234, Roll 505, NA).

36. Hall to CIA, July 26, 1873; Wright to CIA, August 2, 1872 (both M234, Roll 497, NA). A list of those for whom Hall located land: frames 379-94, M234, Roll 497 (NA); maps of Indian locations, frames 395-404,

same roll. Three claims were suspended as conflicting with that of John Owen.

37. *Weekly Missoulian*, August 26, 1874.

38. Whaley to CIA, December 5, 1874 (M234, Roll 500, NA); secretary of the interior to CIA, January 12, 1875 (M234, Roll 502, NA). Hall received a compromise payment of one thousand dollars. See appendix item 10.

39. Secretary of the interior to Potts, May 31, 1876 (M234, Roll 504, NA).

40. CIA to secretary of the interior, May 25, 1876, quoted in *Weekly Missoulian*, June 21, 1876.

41. Medary to CIA, January 28, 1876 (M234, Roll 505, NA).

42. *Weekly Missoulian*, January 17, 1877.

43. *Ibid.*, May 4, 1877.

44. Page to attorney general, December 28, 1876 (M234, Roll 508, NA).

CHAPTER 8:

1. Merritt to AAG, Division of the Missouri, February 8, 1876, quoted in *Weekly Missoulian*, March 29, 1876.

2. *Helena Daily Herald*, June 20, 1877.

3. D'Aste, "Nez Perce War," manuscript (GU).

4. Potts to secretary of the interior, June 21, 1877 (M234, Roll 508, NA).

5. Telegram, June 29, 1877 (Record Group 94, No. 3721–77, NA). Mills assisted the governor during June and July in organizing volunteer companies.

6. Potts to Ronan, June 29, 1877 (M234, Roll 507, NA). *Weekly Missoulian*, June 22, 1877, notes the arrival June 19 of Captain Charles C. Rawn to establish Fort Missoula.

7. Ronan to Potts, July 10, 1877 (M234, Roll 507, NA); Rawn to AAG, Fort Shaw, July 16, 1877, quoted in A. E. Rothermich (ed.), "Early Days at Fort Missoula," in Hakola, *Frontier Omnibus*, 387.

8. Ronan to Potts, July 10, 1877 (M234, Roll 507, NA).

9. D'Aste, "Nez Perce War," manuscript (GU).

10. The account of the Nez Percé invasion relies on D'Aste's manuscript and Ronan's correspondence, and will not agree in particulars with other published accounts. Duncan McDonald, in "Old Nez Perce Woman," manuscript, c.1887, Montana Historical Society, says his mother sent a message to her grandnephew, Looking Glass, recommending a Nez Percé retreat through the Bitterroot Valley rather than through the Jocko, as Looking Glass first intended.

11. *Helena Daily Herald*, June 28 and 30, 1877.

12. D'Aste, "Nez Perce War," manuscript (GU); Mills's report, July 1, 1877, enclosed with Potts to secretary of the interior, July 3, 1877 (M234, Roll 508, NA).

13. McDonald quoted in M. Ronan, "Memoirs," master's thesis, University of Montana, 1932, 267.

14. Rolf Y. H. Olson, "Nez Perce, the Montana Press and the War of

1877," master's thesis, University of Montana, 1956, 172, citing a bond, C. P. Higgins to Potts, July 12, 1877.

15. Ronan to Potts, July 17, 1877 (M234, Roll 508, NA); M. Ronan, "Memoirs," 263 and 266.

16. Rawn quoted in *Helena Daily Herald*, July 26, 1877; D'Aste, "Nez Perce War," manuscript (GU).

17. *Weekly Missoulian*, August 3, 1877.

18. *Helena Daily Herald*, August 1, 1877; *New North-West*, August 10, 1877. The latter portrays Potts leaving Fort Fizzle to rally Higgins' Missoula volunteers to prevent a Nez Percé circumvention of the barricade, a version not found elsewhere.

19. D'Aste, "Nez Perce War," manuscript (GU).

20. *Ibid.*

21. McCormick quoted by C. E. S. Wood, "Chief Joseph, the Nez Perce," *Century Magazine*, May, 1884, 138.

22. Giorda memorandum, July 30, 1877 (GU); Rawn to AAG, Department of the Dakota, September 30, 1877, in Rothermich, "Early Days at Fort Missoula," 391; Report of the secretary of war, 45 Cong., 2 sess., *House Exec. Doc. 1*; *Weekly Missoulian*, August 31 and November 30, 1877.

23. D'Aste, "Nez Perce War," manuscript (GU).

24. Proclamation appeared in the *Helena Daily Herald*, July 31, 1877, and the letter, August 6, 1877.

25. W. T. Sherman in Sheridan and Sherman, *Reports of Inspection, 1877*, 43–44.

26. Ronan to CIA, August 20, 1877 (M234, Roll 507, NA); *Weekly Missoulian*, August 24, 1877.

27. *Helena Daily Herald*, July 24, 1878.

28. Potts to secretary of the interior, October 1, 1877, transmitting D'Aste's letter, September 25, 1877 (M234, Roll 517, NA).

29. Secretary of war to secretary of the interior, October 3, 1877 (M234, Roll 511, NA), quoting Sherman. See appendix 11.

30. Sheridan to U.S. adjutant general, November 1, 1877 (M234, Roll 508, NA).

31. Ronan to CIA, December 24, 1877, and January 15, 1878 (both M234, Roll 511, NA).

32. *Weekly Missoulian*, January 18, 1878.

33. *Ibid.*, February 8, 1878.

34. Ronan to CIA, May 7, 1879 (M234, Roll 515, NA).

35. Ronan to AAG, Department of the Dakota, July 16, 1878 (M234, Roll 512, NA).

36. Ronan to CIA, July 24 and November 10, 1879 (M234, Roll 515, NA), and July 28, 1880 (M234, Roll 517, NA).

37. *Ibid.*, August 20, 1878 (M234, Roll 514, NA).

38. Maginnis to CIA, September 25, 1879 (M234, Roll 514, NA).

39. Ronan to CIA, July 2, 1877 (M234, Roll 507, NA).

40. *Ibid.*, May 6, 1879 (M234, Roll 515, NA).

41. Apparently translated by Michel Revais and forwarded by Ronan to CIA, May 1, 1878 (M234, Roll 511, NA).

42. *Weekly Missoulian*, September 27, 1878.

43. *RCIA 1880*, 105–109.

44. *Weekly Missoulian*, October 17, 1879, quoting Seghers' letter to Rev. J. J. Jonckan, Victoria, V.I., September 1, 1879.

45. W. P. Schoenberg, *Jesuit Mission Presses in the Pacific Northwest, passim*; *Weekly Missoulian*, August 26, 1881. Mengarini published a grammar of the Salish language in New York in 1861.

46. J. B. A. Brouillett to CIA, May 12, 1877 (GU).

47. There were four licensed traders on the reservation: McDonald, T. J. Demers, Antoine Revais, and Joseph Loyola. Ronan wrote the CIA November 5, 1879 (M234, Roll 515, NA), and December 29, 1879 (M234, Roll 517, NA), protesting Indian office circular 35 (1879) requiring traders to deal for cash, because many traders on other reservations used redeemable tokens or tickets.

CHAPTER 9:

1. *Weekly Missoulian*, April 18, 1879.

2. *Ibid.*, September 3, 1880.

3. *Report in Relation to an Agreement*, 47 Cong., 2 sess., *Sen. Exec. Doc. 44.*

4. *Ibid.*

5. *Report of a Select Subcommittee of the Senate Concerning the Condition of the Indian Tribes in the Territories of Montana and Dakota*, 48 Cong., 1 sess., *Sen. Rep. 283*, 241–42, (Hereafter cited as *Condition of the Indians*.)

6. M. Ronan, "Memoirs," 341.

7. Van Gorp to Vest, September 12, 1883, in *Condition of the Indians*, 248–49.

8. *RCIA 1883*, 101.

9. *Weekly Missoulian*, August 11, 1882.

10. *RCIA 1882*, 103–104; M. Ronan, "Memoirs," 303.

11. *Condition of the Indians*, especially 225–32. Quotations in the narrative not otherwise cited are from this source.

12. *Ibid.*, 231.

13. Ronan to CIA, July 19, 1883, in *Condition of the Indians*, 239–41.

14. H. B. Carrington, "Exodus of the Flatheads," typescript, n.d., Carrington Family Papers, Yale University Library, chap. 8, 9; Ronan to CIA, February 12, 1885 (3554–85, NA), and December 23, 1889 (37146–89, NA); *Weekly Missoulian*, February 15 and 22 and March 18, 1884.

15. Ronan to CIA, December 23, 1889 (37146–89, NA).

16. D'Aste to Father Dewey, December 29, 1884 (GU).

17. *Weekly Missoulian*, August 15, 1884; *RCIA 1885*, 128.

18. 54 Cong., 1 sess., *S. 166*, introduced December 3, 1895, to ratify contracts made by the Northwest Indian Commission; Van Gorp to Father Stephan, director, BCIM, March 5, 1887, and Stephan to Van Gorp, March 22, 1887, quoting CIA to Stephan, March 21, 1887 (GU).

19. Contract with the confederated Flatheads, April 27, 1887 (NA).

20. Indian office memo signed [Charles A.] Larrabee, October 21, 1887; Ronan to CIA, October 19, 1887 (28329-87, NA), and August 7, 1888 (20220-88, NA); *RCIA 1888*, 157.

21. *Weekly Missoulian* clipping, undated, in Ronan to CIA, December 18, 1888 (31742-88, NA).

22. Ronan to CIA, December 18, 1888 (31742-88, NA), July 21, 1890 (23021-90, NA), and November 30, 1892 (43537-92, NA).

23. J. T. Carter to CIA, March 6, 1894 (11314-94, NA), enclosing the Cree petition.

24. V. Dusenberry, in *Rocky Boy Indians*, mistakenly combines these Crees with the Rocky Boy band of Chippewas but supplies details of the Cree removal, especially 4 and 6–9. *Daily Missoulian*, April 9, July 23, and August 8, 1896; June 27, 1901; and November 6, 1902; F. C. Morgan to C. L. Davis, Haskell Institute, December 13, 1909 (FRC).

25. Ronan to CIA, April 13, 1886 (10775-86, NA).

26. Report of Henry M. Marchant, May 23, 1889 (16830-89, NA).

27. *Weekly Missoulian*, June 16, 1882; June 26 and November 6, 1885; Thomas C. Smith to Ronan, n.d., 1885 (24767-85, NA).

28. *Weekly Missoulian*, July 23, 1880.

29. Ronan to CIA, September 9, 1889 (26690-89, NA). A vivid personal recollection of these events appears in F. B. Linderman, *Montana Adventure*, 20–58.

30. M. Ronan, "Memoirs," 288.

31. *Weekly Missoulian*, July 10, 1885.

32. 23 Stats. 385, upheld by U.S. Supreme Court, 118 USR 375; *RCIA 1889*, 24–25.

33. M. Ronan, "Memoirs," 314–15.

34. Marchant to U.S. attorney general, May 23, 1889 (16830-89, NA), quotes Louison.

35. Ronan to CIA, June 12, 1889 (16035-89, NA).

36. Report of Captain D. B. Wilson to post adjutant, Fort Missoula, November 20, 1889 (36888-89, NA). Alexander G. Swaney, in "Murder at Wolf Prairie, 1887," typescript, 1971 Montana Historical Society, says sixty-four painted Kutenais intimidated Demersville by "promiscuous" shooting, but correspondence files of the Indian office do not sustain this.

37. *RCIA 1889*, 230; Ronan to CIA, June 3, 1887 (14895-87, NA). See appendix, item 12.

38. Ronan to CIA, January 23, 1888 (2877–88, NA), in which Ronan gives the population of Charlot's band as 278.

39. H. B. Carrington to CIA, September 14, 1889 (26002–89, NA).

40. Much of the account is based on Carrington, "Exodus of the Flatheads." Uncited quotations are from this source. The pages of the typescript are numbered separately by chapter; hence, the meeting at Ronan's office is chap. 6, 2–5, and Stevensville, chap. 7, 1–3. Carrington's letters written during his service among the Flatheads do not always agree with "Exodus," written sometime later. The other major sources for this discussion are: Carrington to CIA, November 1, 1889 (31955–89, NA); and Carrington report, 51 Cong., 1 sess., *Sen. Exec. Doc. 70.*

41. 51 Cong., 1 sess., *Sen. Exec. Doc. 70.*

42. Carrington, "Exodus of the Flatheads," chap. 7, 6, and chap. 8, 2–9; Carrington to CIA, November 1, 1889 (31955–89, NA), and November —, 1889 (31202–89, NA). See appendix 13.

CHAPTER 10:

1. 51 Cong., 1 sess., *Sen. Exec. Doc. 70.*

2. Carrington to CIA, April 7, 1890 (11613–90, NA); Carrington, "Exodus of the Flatheads," chap. 10, 2–13. Uncited quotations in this chapter are from this latter source.

3. Ronan to CIA, June 2, 1890 (17468–90, NA), July 21, 1890 (23021–90, NA).

4. *Ibid.*, December 6, 1890 (38638–90, NA); "Report of Special Agent H. B. Carrington to the Secretary of the Interior," typescript, n.d., Carrington Family Papers, Yale University Library, 5.

5. Carrington to CIA, August 25, 1891, two letters (31713–91 and 31715–91, NA).

6. Carrington, "Exodus of the Flatheads," chap. 10, 5–6.

7. *Ibid.*, 2–13; Carrington to CIA, August 25, 1891 (37294–91, NA).

8. Carrington to CIA, October 19, 1891 (38181–91, NA); *Weekly Missoulian*, October 21, 1891; D'Aste note in Byrne collection, box 12 (GU).

9. Ronan to CIA, October 24, 1891 (39445–91, NA), November 27, 1891 (42825–91, NA), and December 14, 1891 (45331–91, NA). Charlot made various demands on Carrington and Ronan. An undated Indian office memo with Ronan's correspondence reads, "See if you can find anything of record showing that Arlee's property was promised Charlot when at Washington."

10. *Daily Missoulian*, November 11, 1897.

11. Ronan to CIA, January 11, 1893 (2127–93, NA).

12. 30 Stats. 597 authorized reappraisal of Bitterroot land. Cyrus Beede to secretary of the interior, July 25, 1899 (37418–99, NA), and July 31, 1899 (37390–99, NA).

13. Ronan to CIA, January 2, 1891, quoted in Ronan to CIA, April 20, 1891 (15179–91, NA).

14. C. F. Nesler to CIA, January 28, 1899 (6138–99, NA).

15. Carter to CIA, April 10, 1896 (14317–96, NA).

16. A. B. Upshaw, acting CIA, to Ronan, November 11, 1885 (NA).

17. Ronan to CIA, July 6, 1891 (24873–91, NA). Newspaper items and Indian office correspondence indicate this was not an isolated incident.

18. J. W. Crawford, special agent, to U.S. attorney general, July 12, 1891 (4545–91, NA).

19. Anthony and others to Ronan, July 24, 1889, enclosed with Ronan to CIA, August 6, 1889 (22436–89, NA).

20. Ronan to CIA, October 16, 1889 (29817–89, NA).

21. *Weekly Missoulian*, May 24, 1893.

22. *Ibid.*, August 23, 1893.

23. P. McCormick to CIA, December 2, 1893 (46270–93, NA).

24. Carter, annual statistical report, October 20, 1894 (42614–94, NA).

25. Carter to CIA, February 6, 1894 (6591–94, NA); M. Ronan, "Memoirs," 318.

26. Lane to CIA, February 7, 1896 (6433–96, NA).

27. Discussion from house diary, St. Ignatius Mission, November 8 and 13, 1895, and January 31, 1896 (GU); C. S. Hartman to CIA, March 10, 1896 (14139–96, NA).

28. Marcus D. Shelby to CIA, August 12, 1897 (34201–97, NA); *Daily Missoulian*, March 19 and 26, 1897; St. Ignatius attendance records, 1888–99 (GU).

29. *Daily Missoulian*, October 1, 1897.

30. McConnell to secretary of the interior, August 27, 1897 (37112–97, NA).

31. McConnell to CIA, December 6, 1897 (51930–97, NA).

32. *Daily Missoulian*, June 18, 1898.

33. Smead to CIA, August 24, 1901 (47166–01, NA), November 2, 1901 (62538–01, NA).

34. *Libby* (Montana) *News*, January 20, 1899; Herman to secretary of the interior, August 1, 1900 (37818–00, NA).

35. Smead to J. B. Weber, August 27, 1903 (FRC).

36. C. E. Schaeffer notes, "Flathead (Selish) Medicine Ceremony," typescript, 1935, Department of Anthropology, American Museum of Natural History.

37. *Daily Missoulian*, August 4, 1898.

38. Smead to CIA, April 3, 1899 (15965–99, NA), and April 6, 1899 (16086–99, NA). Pablo and Allard represented the Council of Nine formed among mixed-blood cattlemen to represent reservation Indians in their protests on fees and taxation.

39. Vest to Van Gorp, November 5, 1883 (GU).

40. Jones to Palladino, March 21, 1886 (GU).

41. Based on St. Ignatius school records, box 6 (GU).

42. Morgan to Rebmann, July 6, 1891 (GU); R. V. Belt, acting CIA, to agents and school superintendents, August 10, 1891 (GU); Morgan, *Indian Grammar, Primary and Day Schools.*

43. Moss's report, August 6, 1896 (33647–96, NA), to which is appended a description of courses of study, books, and schedules, showing the children attended school from 9:00 to 11:30 A.M. and 2:00 to 4:30 P.M.

44. Thomas Hefling to Father George de la Motte, June 21, 1899, quoting Bauer (GU).

45. St. Ignatius house diary, September 10, 1901 (GU).

46. Smead to W. J. Root, April 1, 1904 (FRC); I. M. A. Berven, "History of Indian Education on the Flathead Reservation," master's thesis, University of Montana, 1959, *passim.*

47. Smead to CIA, October 26, 1900 (53861–00, NA).

48. Beede to CIA, August 25, 1900 (45670–00, NA), with Hall and Parsons letters.

49. F. C. Armstrong report, 57 Cong., 1 sess., *House Doc. 406*, 35.

50. There were actually several councils, and quotations were taken from the reports of the commission dated January 3, 1901, January 12, 1901, and May 4, 1901 (24033–01, NA). At one point, the commissioners asked the Flatheads to name their price. The file copy of their report bears a marginal notation, "This plan was emphatically condemned in I.O. [Indian Office]."

CHAPTER 11:

1. 57 Cong., 1 sess., *House Doc. 406*. Armstrong's portion is dated June 30, 1901.

2. *Daily Missoulian,* March 13, 1903, and October 2, 1910. The Dixon Papers were given to the University of Montana and reserved for a biography of Dixon by Jules Alexander Karlin.

3. *Congressional Record,* XXXVIII, part 6, appendix, 102–103.

4. Smead to CIA, June 21, 1902 (37104–02, NA).

5. Smead to Hubbart Cattle Company, September 3, 1903 (FRC).

6. Smead to Rasch, June 16, 1903 (FRC).

7. CIA to secretary of the interior, April 26, 1902 (31617–02, NA).

8. Downs to CIA, October 3, 1903 (64536–03, NA).

9. James to Gibson, March 25, 1903, and Gibson to "My Dear Miles," March 28, 1903 (31617–03, NA).

10. Dixon to Carter, July 8 and 11, 1908, quoted in J. A. Karlin, "Senator Joseph M. Dixon and Rocky Boy," addendum to V. Dusenberry, *Rocky Boy Indians,* 10–12. The band is consistently identified as Chippewa in Indian office correspondence, although some Crees attached themselves to it, notably Little Bear, a leading participant in the Riel rebellion.

11. McNichols to CIA, November 3, 1902 (66432–02, NA); CIA Morgan to Indian agents, March 19, 1890 (GU).

12. Tinker to CIA, September 20, 1903 (63796–03, NA).

13. *Daily Missoulian*, March 28 and April 10, 1903; Smead to W. F. Hubbart, May 3, 1903 (FRC).

14. *Daily Missoulian*, July 4, 1903; June 28, August 11, December 11, and December 21, 1904.

15. 48 Fed. 670; 73 Fed. 60.

16. John Herman to F. C. Morgan, December 1, 1909 (FRC).

17. McNichols' roll was dated September 19, 1903; CIA to secretary of the interior, March 10 and September 25, 1905 (1175–05, NA), and Flathead file 053, n.d. (NA).

18. Downs's roll, dated May 25, 1905, in Flathead file 053 (NA) and box 56481 (FRC). See appendix, item 15. In 1921, allotments were made to 920 confederated Flatheads born after the first allotment. The Indian Reorganization Act of June 18, 1934 (48 Stats. 984), prohibited further allotments.

19. *Daily Missoulian*, March 18, 1905.

20. *Ibid.*

21. *RCIA 1906*, 75 and 256.

22. Charlot to Garfield, and Moise to Garfield, both September 7, 1907, in Flathead file 308.1 (NA).

23. Rankin to CIA, October 14, 1907, and CIA to secretary of the interior, October 14, 1907, both Flathead file 054 (NA).

24. *Weekly Missoulian*, August 21, 1908.

25. Resurrection to Roosevelt, February 27, 1908 (NA).

26. CIA to Ka-Ka-She, February 22, 1909, and to Senator T. H. Carter, February 20, 1909 (NA). In correspondence, the names of the Indians are spelled in several different ways.

27. F. C. Morgan to CIA, August 17, 1911 (NA).

28. *RCIA 1888*, 157; Ronan to CIA, March 25, 1892 (11802–92, NA). See appendix, item 14.

29. See appendix, item 16. Members of the business council were Mose Delaware, Joe Peon, Angus McDonald, Charlot, Duncan McDonald, Charles Allard, Pierre Magpie, and John Matt, according to a notice of meeting from Morgan, September 11, 1909 (FRC).

30. Acting CIA to Matt, March 4, 1908, Flathead file 304 (NA).

31. Morgan to William E. Johnson, chief of special officers, December 17, 1909; Morgan to John M. Stevens, Rushville, Indiana, October 7, 1909; and Morgan to P. L. Colman, Carson, Washington, December 24, 1909 (all FRC).

32. *Daily Missoulian*, January 11 and 13, 1910. Paxson's photographs, a number of his paintings, and twenty-seven diaries from his time in Montana are in possession of his grandson, who proposes to publish them. Heirship record (FRC) gives Charlot's age as 80; his widow, Isabel, 79; son, Martin, 55; and daughter, Ann Felix, 47.

33. *Daily Missoulian*, March 13, 1910.

34. P. McCormick to CIA, February 18, 1895 (8492–95, NA); *RCIA 1896*, 185.

35. The discussion and quotations are from U.S. Bureau of Reclamation, *Project History of the Flathead, Montana, 1909–23*, I.

BIBLIOGRAPHY

IN ADDITION to the National Archives of the United States, this study relies in substantial measure on two collections: the archives of the Oregon Province of the Society of Jesus at Gonzaga University, and the materials amassed by the late Father William Lyle Davis, S.J., for his projected study of Father De Smet.

The holdings of the Oregon Province consist of approximately nine hundred archival boxes of mission records and papers of individual Jesuits from Washington, Oregon, Idaho, Montana, and Alaska, and of thousands of manuscripts and photographs. The collection also contains an estimated five thousand volumes published on Indian subjects, about one-third of them rare or scarce, and selected documents on microfilm from European and Canadian Catholic archives.

The De Smet and related materials gathered by Father Davis are also at Gonzaga. They include excerpted documents from Catholic archives in Rome, Brussels, Lyon, Paris, Quebec, Montreal, Ottawa, and St. Louis, and perhaps four hundred published books on Indian subjects. Family papers purchased from the De Smet heirs in Chile have been acquired by Washington State University and are described in Father Davis' article, "Papers of Father Peter John De Smet, S.J., in the Washington State University Library," *The Record*, Friends of the Library, Vol. XXX (1969), 7–40.

Among the Davis papers remaining at Gonzaga are extensive handwritten notes from the files of the Hudson's Bay Company, a microfilm copy of Father Nicholas Point's three-volume memoirs, and a microfilm of the 1848 manuscript by Father Gregory Mengarini called "Memoirs" in the notes. The Mengarini manuscript, in Italian, is translated in the doctoral dissertation of Gloria Ricci Lothrop.

In addition to these, I used the I. I. Stevens papers of the University of Washington covering the period 1835–62 and the papers of Carl P. Russell at Washington State University. The Russell papers are noteworthy for their classification of extracts from many sources relating to the trading, trapping, and transportation of fur. Earle Connette, librarian and chief, manuscripts-archives division of the Library at Washington State University, in 1970 published an indexed register to the Russell papers.

In 1971 the Federal Records Center, Seattle, received the records of the Flathead Agency for 1875–1952. These deserve a more careful investigation than I have been able to give them. The shelf list produced by the Center's staff is a useful guide to these holdings, and the staff is very helpful.

The Montana Historical Society holds manuscripts and photographs relating to the Flatheads, as well as selections of agency and superintendency correspondence on microfilm from the National Archives and the National Park Service files. Two local collections with materials on the Flatheads are the Sam E. Johns collection in the Carnegie Public Library, Kalispell, consisting of ten volumes of clippings and articles (of which the Montana Historical Society has typescripts), and the historical research files of Neil Fullerton, Thompson Falls, now in the Montana Historical Society. The Society also holds fifteen volumes of John Owen's journals and correspondence, 1851–71. University of Montana students have written a series of theses on aspects of Flathead and related history.

My constant reference was the valuable preliminary inventory compiled by Edward E. Hill, *Records of the Bureau of Indian Affairs*, 2 vols., Washington: National Archives, 1965. Also useful is Laura E. Kelsay, comp., *Special List No. 13, List of Cartographic Records of the Bureau of Indian Affairs*, Washington: National

Archives, 1954. These allowed me to raise all kinds of niggling questions that the staff of the National Archives answered with courtesy and accuracy.

The following list is categorized by manuscripts, other unpublished materials, books and pamphlets, articles, government publications, and newspapers, and represents those consulted for this study. Some provided the basis for portions of the narrative. Not all support my conclusions, and their listing here should not be so interpreted.

Edited journals, books, and correspondence are listed by author and cross-referred when confusion seems likely because of the general success of an edited edition. Although this is not intended as a critical bibliography, I remark on occasion on the location or contents of an item.

MANUSCRIPTS

Biggerstaff, Lee. "Brief History of Homesteading on the Flathead Indian Reservation," typescript, 1964, Montana Historical Society, presented by the Big Flat Pioneers with a scrapbook.

Blanchet, Archbishop Frances Norbert. "Catholic Missionaries of Oregon," Portland, 1878, Bancroft Library, University of California, Berkeley.

Burr, F. H. "Diary," 1857, W. H. Coe Collection, Yale University; microfilm at Montana Historical Society.

Carrington, Henry Beebe. "Report on the Flatheads," typescript with autograph corrections, Carrington Family Papers, Yale University Library.

———. "Report of Service among the Flathead Indians, 1889–1890," typescript, Carrington Family Papers, Yale University Library; original of 51 Cong., 1 sess., *Sen. Exec. Doc. 70.*

———. "Report of Special Agent H. B. Carrington to the Secretary of the Interior," typescript, n.d., Carrington Family Papers, Yale University Library.

———. "Exodus of the Flatheads," typescript, n.d., Carrington Family Papers, Yale University Library.

Chalfant, Stuart A. "Aboriginal Territories of the Flathead, Pend Oreille and Kutenai Indians of Western Montana," Defense Exhibit 24, Indian Claims Case 61, in the National Archives.

D'Aste, Father Jerome, S.J. "Historical Notes on the Flathead Mission," n.d., 19 pages of various sizes with emendations by Father Lawrence Palladino (?), Gonzaga University.

———. "Nez Perce War of 1877," n.d., eight pages on legal tablet, Gonzaga University.

Doty, James. "Journal of Operations: Governor Stevens, 1855," among Records Relating to Treaties, December 7, 1854, to June 9, 1863, in the National Archives; also available on Microcopy 5, Roll 26, in the National Archives, and in typescript made in 1919 by William S. Lewis, Spokane Public Library.

Frusch, Charles W. "Bitterroot Valley in the Spring of 1858," typescript, n.d., Montana Historical Society, of a manuscript at the University of Montana. Frusch was employed by John Owen.

Indian Claims Commission of the United States. "Docket 61: *Confederated Salish and Kootenai Tribes of the Flathead Reservation, Montana, v. the United States of America*. Decided August 3, 1959," Record Group 279, in the National Archives. This group consists of ten boxes, 174-A through 174-J, containing published and unpublished materials.

McDonald, Angus. "Nez Perces Campaign," n.d., Montana Historical Society.

McDonald, Duncan. "Old Nez Perce Woman," c.1887, Montana Historical Society.

Malouf, Carling I. "Economy and Land Use by the Indians of Western Montana, U.S.A.," claimant's exhibit 5, Indian Claims Case 61, in the National Archives. A typescript, 1952, at the University of Montana.

Mengarini, Father Gregory, S.J. "Memorie delle Missioni delle Teste Piatte contenenti brevi nozioni cosi antiche che moderne di tutto cio che riguarda questa nazione in particulare," 1848, General Archives of the Society of Jesus, Rome; microfilm, Gonzaga University; translation in Gloria Ricci Lothrop dissertation.

———. "The Rocky Mountains: Memoirs of Father Gregory Mengarini," n.d., 59 pp., in Oregon Province Archives, Gonzaga University, differing in minor elements from version published in *Woodstock Letters*.

Mumbrue, Daniel P. "Memoirs: 1867–1947," typescript, Montana Historical Society.

Noyes, A. J. "Major J. B. Catlin's Story of the Arrival of the Lewis and Clark Expedition at Ross's Hole: Told by the Indian Woman, Victio," typescript, n.d., Montana Historical Society.

O'Malley, Father Michael, S.J. "Northwest Blackrobe: The Story of the

Life and Work of Father Joseph Cataldo, S.J., 1837–1928," October, 1905, based on Cataldo's dictation to O'Malley, at Gonzaga University.

O'Sullivan, Father John, S.J. "History of the Rocky Mountain Missions," typescript, n.d., Oregon Province Archives, Gonzaga University.

Pambrun, Andrew D. "Story of His Life as He Tells It." Edited by Ceylon S. Kingston, typescript, n.d., Eastern Washington State College.

Phillips, Paul C. "1855 Land Values," typescript, September 30, 1953, in Indian Claims Case 61, National Archives.

———. "History of the Confederated Salish and Kootenai Tribes of the Flathead Reservation, Montana," petitioner's exhibit 1, Indian Claims Case 61, National Archives.

Point, Father Nicholas, S.J. "Memoirs," 3 vols., 1860, St. Mary's College, Montreal; microfilm in Davis collection, Gonzaga University.

Ross, Alexander. "Report of Flathead Post, Winter, 1824–25," March 10, 1825, Hudson's Bay Company Archives, B69/e/1.

Sanders, Wilbur F. "Notes on Montana History," 1885 (?), Bancroft Collection, Bancroft Library, University of California, Berkeley.

Schaeffer, Claude E. "An Acculturation Study of the Indians of the Flathead Reservation of Western Montana," 2 vols., typescript, 1935, Department of Anthropology, American Museum of Natural History.

———. "Flathead (Selish) Medicine Ceremony: Notes Secured, Winter of 1935, at Flathead Reservation, Montana," typescript, 1935, Department of Anthropology, American Museum of Natural History.

Swaney, Alexander Grant. "Murder at Wolf Prairie, 1887," typescript, 1971, Montana Historical Society.

Two-good, Phyllis. "Historical Anecdotes of Western Montana," typescript, n.d., Montana Historical Society.

Walker, Joel P. "Narrative of Adventures," 1878, Bancroft Collection, Bancroft Library, University of California, Berkeley.

Wheeler, W. F. "Angus McDonald and the First Discovery of Gold in Montana," typescript, n.d., Montana Historical Society.

Wright, Superintendent C. C. "General Information about the Flathead Indian Reservation in Western Montana," typescript, May 16, 1945, Oregon Province Archives, Gonzaga University.

Other Unpublished Materials

Albright, Robert Edwin. "Relations of Montana with the Federal Government." Doctoral dissertation, Stanford University, 1933.

Anastasio, Angelo. "Intergroup Relations in the Southern Plateau." Doctoral dissertation, University of Chicago, 1955.

Berven, Irene M. Alvstad. "History of Indian Education on the Flathead Reservation." Master's thesis, University of Montana, 1959.

Biggar, Hugh J. "Development of the Lower Flathead Valley." Master's thesis, University of Montana, 1951.

Brockmann, C. Thomas. "Modern Social and Economic Organization of the Flathead Reservation." Doctoral dissertation, University of Oregon, 1958.

Buntin, Arthur Roy. "Battleground: A Narrative and Evaluation of Intertribal Warfare on the Buffalo Plains of Eastern Montana and Adjacent Areas Prior to 1880." Master's thesis, University of Montana, 1952.

Cappious, Samuel Lloyd. "History of the Bitterroot Valley to 1914." Master's thesis, University of Washington, 1939.

Davis, Leslie B. "Remnant Forms of the Traditional Folk Narrative Salvaged among the Upper Pend Oreille Indians of Montana." Master's thesis, University of Montana, 1963.

Fee, Dexter S. "Government Policy toward the Principal Indian Nations of Montana, 1851–1873." Master's thesis, University of Montana, 1934.

"Fullblood Flathead Indian Montana Study Group." Mimeographed. University of Montana, 1947.

Hakola, John W. "Development of a Policy towards Irrigation in Montana to 1908." Master's thesis, University of Montana, 1951.

Kelly, Gerald L. "History of St. Ignatius Mission, Montana." Master's thesis, University of Montana, 1954.

Lang, Samuel V., Jr. "Children of the Flathead: A Study of Culture-and-Personality in a Changing Society." Master's thesis, University of Montana, 1965.

Lothrop, Gloria Ricci. "Father Gregory Mengarini, an Italian Jesuit Missionary in the Transmontane West: His Life and Memoirs." Doctoral dissertation, University of Southern California, 1970.

McElroy, Harold Lewis. "Army Frontier in Montana." Master's thesis, University of Montana, 1949.

Malan, Vernon D. "Language and Social Change among the Flathead Indians." Master's thesis, University of Montana, 1948.

Malouf, Carling Isaac. "Cultural Connections between the Prehistoric Inhabitants of the Upper Missouri and Columbia River Systems." Doctoral dissertation, Columbia University, 1956.

Olson, Rolf Y. H. "Nez Perce, the Montana Press and the War of 1877." Master's thesis, University of Montana, 1964.

O'Neal, Jerome S. "Flathead Law, Past and Present." Master's thesis, University of Montana, 1968.

Partoll, Albert J. "The Selish: Spartans of the West." Master's thesis, University of Montana, 1930.

Ronan, Margaret. "Memoirs of a Frontier's Woman." Master's thesis, University of Montana, 1932. Margaret Ronan's transcription of her mother's story with added comment.

Sampson, William R. "Doing the Needful: John McLoughlin's Business Correspondence, 1847–1848." Doctoral dissertation, University of Alberta, 1968.

Seifried, Richard Dwight. "Early Administration of the Flathead Indian Reservation, 1855 to 1893." Master's thesis, University of Montana, 1968.

Smurr, J. W. "Struggle of the Flathead Indians to Save Their Ancestral Home from Invasion by White Men." Script for a pageant-masque presented at Missoula, August 26–28, 1941, at the University of Montana.

Sprague, Roderick. "Aboriginal Burial Practices in the Plateau Region of North America." Doctoral dissertation, University of Arizona, 1967.

Steckler, Gerard George. "Charles John Seghers, Missionary Bishop in the American Northwest, 1839–1886." Doctoral dissertation, University of Washington, 1963.

Stubbs, Ron D. "An Investigation of the Edible and Medicinal Plants Used by the Flathead Indians." Master's thesis, University of Montana, 1966.

Trepp, John Merlin. "Music at St. Ignatius Mission, 1854–1900." Master's thesis, University of Montana, 1966.

Wilkerson, Michael L. "Fort Owen: An Artifact Analysis." Master's thesis, University of Montana, 1968.

Books and Pamphlets

Arrington, Leonard J. *Great Basin Kingdom*. Cambridge, Harvard University Press, 1958.

Athearn, Robert G. *Thomas Francis Meagher: An Irish Revolutionary in America*. Boulder, Colo., University of Colorado Press, 1949.

Bagley, Clarence B. *Early Catholic Missions in Old Oregon*. 2 vols. Seattle, Loman & Hanford, 1932.

Baker, Paul E. *Forgotten Kutenai.* Boise, Idaho, Mountain States Press, Inc., 1955.

Barclay, Wade Crawford. *Early American Methodism 1769–1844.* 2 vols. New York, Board of Missions and Church Extension of the Methodist Church, 1950.

Barker, Burt Brown. *Letters of Dr. John McLoughlin, Written at Fort Vancouver, 1829–1832.* Portland, Oregon Historical Society, 1948.

Beal, Merrill D. *"I Will Fight No More Forever": Chief Joseph and the Nez Perce War.* Seattle, University of Washington Press, 1963.

Berthrong, Donald J. *Southern Cheyennes.* Norman, University of Oklahoma Press, 1963.

Bischoff, Rev. William N., S.J. *Jesuits in Old Oregon.* Caldwell, Idaho, Caxton Printers, Ltd., 1945.

Branch, E. Douglas. *Hunting of the Buffalo.* New York and London, D. Appleton and Company, 1929.

Brosnan, Rev. Cornelius J. *Jason Lee, Prophet of the New Oregon.* New York, Macmillan Company, 1932.

Brown, Dee. *Fort Phil Kearney.* New York, G. P. Putnam's Sons, 1962.

Brown, Mark H. *Flight of the Nez Perce.* New York, G. P. Putnam's Sons, 1967.

Brown, William Compton. *Indian Side of the Story.* Spokane, C. W. Hill Printing Co., 1961.

Burns, Rev. Robert Ignatius, S.J. *Jesuits and the Indian Wars of the Northwest.* New Haven, Yale University Press, 1966.

Catlin, George. *North American Indians.* 2 vols. Philadelphia, Leary, Stuart & Co., 1913.

Chaffin, Glenn. *Last Horizon.* Somerset, Calif., Pine Trail Press, 1971. A history of a family residing in the Bitterroot Valley since 1864.

Chittenden, Hiram Martin. *American Fur Trade of the Far West.* 2 vols. New York, Press of the Pioneers, Inc., 1935. Reissue of 1902 publication.

——, and Alfred Talbot Richardson. *Life, Letters and Travels of Father Pierre-Jean De Smet, S.J., 1801–1873.* 4 vols. New York, Francis P. Harper, 1905.

Clark, Ella E. *Indian Legends from the Northern Rockies.* Norman, University of Oklahoma Press, 1966.

Clarke, Charles G. *Men of the Lewis and Clark Expedition.* Vol. XIV in Western Frontiersmen Series. Glendale, Arthur H. Clark Co., 1970.

Collier, Donald, Alfred E. Hudson, and Arlo Ford. *Archeology of the*

Upper Columbia Region. Seattle, University of Washington Press, 1962.

Corley, Patricia. *Story of St. Mary's Mission*. Oakland, Tribune Press, 1941.

Coues, Elliott. See Meriwether Lewis, *History of the Expedition*, and Alexander Henry, *New Light on the Early History of the Great Northwest*.

Cox, Ross. *Adventures on the Columbia River, including the Narrative of a Residence of Six Years on the Western Side of the Rocky Mountains*. 2 vols. London, Henry Colburn and Richard Bentley, 1831.

———. *The Columbia River*. Edited by Edgar I. Stewart and Jane R. Stewart. Norman, University of Oklahoma Press, 1957.

Cutright, Paul Russell. *Lewis and Clark: Pioneering Naturalists*. Urbana, University of Illinois Press, 1969.

Davis, Rev. William Lyle, S.J. *History of St. Ignatius Mission*. Spokane, C. W. Hill Printing Co., 1954.

De Smet, Rev. Peter John S.J. *New Indian Sketches*. New York, D. & J. Sadlier & Co., 1863.

———. *Western Missions and Missionaries: A Series of Letters*. New York, P. J. Kenedy, 1859.

———. *Life, Letters, and Travels*. See Chittenden and Richardson.

Drury, Rev. Clifford Merrill, ed. *Diaries and Letters of Henry H. Spalding and Asa Bowen Smith Relating to the Nez Perce Mission 1838–1842*. Glendale, Arthur H. Clark Co., 1958.

———. *Elkanah and Mary Walker, Pioneers among the Spokanes*. Caldwell, Idaho, Caxton Printers, Ltd., 1940.

Dusenberry, Verne. *Rocky Boy Indians: Montana's Displaced Persons*. No. 3, Montana Heritage Series. Helena, Historical Society Press, 1954.

Ewers, John C. *Blackfeet: Raiders on the Northwestern Plains*. Norman, University of Oklahoma Press, 1958.

———. *Gustav Sohon's Portraits of Flathead and Pend O'Reille Indians, 1854*. Washington, Smithsonian Institution, 1948. Smithsonian miscellaneous collections, Vol. 110, No. 7.

———. *Indian Life on the Upper Missouri*. Norman, University of Oklahoma Press, 1968.

Ferris, Warren A. *Life in the Rocky Mountains*. Edited by Paul C. Phillips. Denver, Old West Publishing Co., 1940.

Florian, Rev. Martin, S.J. *Story of St. Mary's Mission*. N.p., April, 1959.

Fritz, Henry E. *Movement for Indian Assimilation, 1860–1890*. Philadelphia, University of Pennsylvania Press, 1963.

Garcia, Andrew. *Tough Trip through Paradise.* Edited by Bennett H. Stein. Boston, Houghton Mifflin Co., 1967.

Garraghan, Rev. Gilbert Joseph, S.J. *Catholic Beginnings in Kansas City, Missouri.* Chicago, Loyola Press, 1920.

———. *Chapters in Frontier History.* Milwaukee, Bruce Publishing Co., 1934. Chapters on Father Point and Father De Smet.

———. *Jesuits of the Middle United States.* 3 vols. New York, America Press, 1938.

Gass, Patrick. *Journal of the Voyages and Travels of the Corps of Discovery under the Command of Capt. Lewis and Capt. Clarke . . . 1804, 1805, and 1806.* Pittsburgh, David McKeehan, 1807.

Gates, Charles M., ed. *Messages of the Governors of the Territory of Washington to the Legislative Assembly, 1854–1889.* Seattle, University of Washington Press, 1940.

Giorda, Rev. Joseph, S.J., Rev. Joseph Bandini, S.J., and Rev. Gregory Mengarini, S.J. *Dictionary of the Kalispel or Flat-head Indian Language.* St. Ignatius, Mont., St. Ignatius Press, 1877–79.

Gray, William H. *History of Oregon.* Portland, Harris & Holman, 1870.

Griffin, Rev. J. S. *Historic Sketch, Descriptive of Jesuit Warfare, together with a Defensive Appeal Addressed to the Younger Ministers and Intelligent Laymen of the Congregational Churches of Oregon and Washington.* Hillsboro, Ore., J. S. Griffin, 1881.

Griswold, Gillett, and David Larom. *Hellgate Survey.* Mimeographed. *Anthropology and Sociology Papers* of Montana State University, No. 16, 1954.

———, ed. *Archeological Sites in the Flathead Lake Region, Montana.* Mimeographed. *Anthropology and Sociology Papers* of Montana State University, No. 15, 1953.

Hafen, LeRoy R., ed. *The Mountain Men and the Fur Trade of the Far West.* 10 vols. Glendale, Arthur H. Clark Co., 1965–1972.

Haines, Francis. *The Buffalo.* New York, Thomas Y. Crowell Co., 1970.

Hakola, John W., ed. *Frontier Omnibus.* Missoula, Montana State University Press, 1962. Collection of articles previously published in *Frontier and Midland.*

Hendry, Anthony. *York Factory to the Blackfeet Country: Journal of Anthony Hendry 1754–55.* Edited by L. J. Burpee. Royal Society of Canada, *Transactions,* Series 3, Vol. I (1907).

Henry, Alexander. *New Light on the Early History of the Great Northwest: Manuscript Journals of Alexander Henry and David Thompson.* Edited by Elliott Coues. 3 vols. New York, F. P. Harper, 1897.

Hoopes, Alban W. *Indian Affairs and their Administration, with Special Reference to the Far West, 1849–1860.* Philadelphia, University of Pennsylvania Press, 1932.

Hornaday, William T. *Extermination of the American Bison.* Washington, Smithsonian Institution Reports, 1888, Part 2.

Howard, Helen Addison, and Dan L. McGrath. *War Chief Joseph.* Caldwell, Idaho, Caxton Printers, Ltd., 1958.

Hutchens, John K. *One Man's Montana.* Philadelphia and New York, J. B. Lippincott Co., 1964.

Hyde, George E. *Indians of the High Plains from the Prehistoric Period to the Coming of Europeans.* Norman, University of Oklahoma Press, 1959.

Jablow, Joseph. *Cheyenne in Plains Indian Trade Relations, 1795–1840.* American Ethnological Society Monographs, No. 19, 1950.

Jackson, Donald, ed. *Letters of the Lewis and Clark Expedition, with Related Documents, 1783–1854.* Urbana, University of Illinois Press, 1962.

James, Thomas. *Three Years among the Indians and Mexicans.* Edited by Walter B. Douglas. St. Louis, Missouri Historical Society, 1916.

Johnson, Olga Weydemeyer. *Flathead and Kootenay.* Glendale, Arthur H. Clark Co., 1969.

——. *Story of the Tobacco Plains Country.* Caldwell, Idaho, Caxton Printers, Ltd., for the Pioneers of Tobacco Plains Country, 1950.

Josephy, Alvin M., Jr. *Nez Perce Indians and the Opening of the Northwest.* New Haven and London, Yale University Press, 1965.

Jung, Aloysius M., S.J. *Jesuit Missions among the American Tribes of the Rocky Mountain Indians.* Spokane, Gonzaga University, 1925.

Kappler, Charles J., comp. *Indian Affairs.* See government publications.

Kennedy, John E. *Story of St. Mary's Mission.* Hamilton, Mont., Kennedy, 1941.

Kittson, William. *Journal of Snake Country Expedition, 1824–25.* Published as appendix A to Ogden's *Snake Country Journals 1824–1826.* See Ogden.

Last of the Buffalo: Comprising a History of the Buffalo Herd of the Flathead Reservation and an Account of the Great Roundup. Cincinnati, Tom Jones, 1909. Mostly photographs.

Laveille, Eugene, S.J. *Life of Father De Smet, S.J.* New York, P. J. Kenedy and Sons, 1915.

Leeson, Michael A. *History of Montana.* Chicago, Warner, Beers & Co., 1885.

Lewis, Meriwether, and William Clark. *Original Journals of the Lewis and Clark Expedition, 1804–1806*. Edited by Reuben Gold Thwaites. 8 vols. New York, Dodd, 1904–1905.

———. *History of the Expedition under the Command of Lewis and Clark*. Edited by Elliott Coues. 3 vols. New York, Dover Publications, Inc., 1964.

———. *Letters of the Lewis and Clark Expedition*. See Donald Jackson.

Lewis, Oscar. *Effects of White Contact upon Blackfoot Culture*. American Ethnological Society Monographs, No. 4, 1942.

Lewis, William S., and Paul C. Phillips, eds. *Journal of John Work*. Cleveland, Arthur H. Clark Co., 1923.

Linderman, Frank B. *Montana Adventure*. Edited by H. G. Merriam. Lincoln, University of Nebraska Press, 1968.

McLoughlin, John L. *Letters of John McLoughlin from Fort Vancouver to the Governor and Committee*. Edited by E. E. Rich. 3 vols. (First series, 1825–38; second series, 1839–44; and third, 1844–46.) Toronto, The Champlain Society, 1941–43.

———. *Letters, 1829–1832*. See Burt B. Barker.

McWhorter, Lucullus V. *Hear Me, My Chiefs!* Edited by Ruth Bordin. Caldwell, Idaho, Caxton Printers, Ltd., 1952.

Malouf, Carling I. *Archeology of the Canyon Ferry Region, Montana*. Mimeographed. *Anthropology and Sociology Papers* of the University of Montana, No. 11, 1950.

———. *Notes on the Archeology of the Big Hole Region, Montana*. Mimeographed. *Anthropology and Sociology Papers* of the University of Montana, No. 4, 1950.

———, and Thain White. *Recollections of Lasso Stasso*. Mimeographed. *Anthropology and Sociology Papers* of the University of Montana, No. 12, 1952.

Mathias, Baptiste, as told to Thain White. *Firsts among the Flathead Lake Kutenai*. Mimeographed. *Anthropology and Sociology Papers* of the University of Montana, No. 8, 1952.

Memorial Souvenir: Jason Lee: Memorial Services at Re-interment of Remains. Salem, Ore., June 15, 1906.

Merk, Frederick, ed. *Fur Trade and Empire: George Simpson's Journal . . . 1824–25*. Cambridge, Harvard University Press, 1931.

Merriam, Alan P. *Ethnomusicology of the Flathead Indians*. Chicago, Aldine Publishing Co., 1967. Viking Fund Publications in Anthropology, No. 44.

Mishkin, Bernard. *Rank and Warfare among the Plains Indians*. American Ethnological Society Monographs, No. 3, 1940.

Montana and Her Metropolis. Helena, *Herald*, 1868.

Morgan, Thomas. *Indian Grammar, Primary and Day Schools*. Carlisle Industrial School, c.1891.

Morse, Rev. Jedidiah. *Narrative of a Tour Performed in the Summer of 1820, under a Commission from the President of the United States, for the Purpose of Ascertaining, for the Use of the Government, the Actual State of Various Indians of Our Country*. New Haven, S. Converse, 1822.

Nelson, Ruth Ashton. *Handbook of Rocky Mountain Plants*. Tucson, Ariz., Dale Stuart King, 1969.

Ogden, Peter Skene. *Snake Country Journals, 1824–26*. Edited by E. E. Rich. London, Hudson's Bay Record Society, 1950.

———. *Snake Country Journals, 1827–28 and 1828–29*. Edited by Glyndwr Williams. London, Hudson's Bay Record Society, 1971.

Oglesby, Richard Edward. *Manuel Lisa and the Opening of the Missouri Fur Trade*. Norman, University of Oklahoma Press, 1963.

Ordway, John. *Journals of Captain Meriwether Lewis and Sergeant John Ordway Kept on the Expedition of Western Exploration 1803–06*. Edited by Milo M. Quaife. Wisconsin Historical Society Collections, Vol. XII (1916), 31–402.

Osgood, Ernest Staples, ed. *Field Notes of Captain William Clark, 1803–05*. New Haven and London, Yale University Press, 1964.

Owen, John. *Journals and Letters of Major John Owen*. Edited by Seymour Dunbar and Paul C. Phillips. 2 vols. New York, Edward Eberstadt, 1927.

Pace, Ralph S. *Lolo Trail*. Lewiston, Idaho, Printcraft Printing, Inc., 1970.

Palladino, Rev. Lawrence, S.J. *Anthony Ravalli, S.J.: Forty Years a Missionary in the Rocky Mountains: Memoir*. Helena, George E. Boos & Co., 1884.

———. *Education for the Indian*. New York, Benziger Brothers, 1892.

———. *Indian and White in the Northwest*. 2nd rev. ed. Lancaster, Pa., Wickersham Publishing Co., 1922.

Palliser, John. *Papers of the Palliser Expedition, 1857–60*. Edited by Irene M. Spry. Toronto, The Champlain Society, 1968.

Parker, Samuel. *Journal of an Exploring Tour Beyond the Rocky Mountains . . . with a Map of Oregon Territory*. 3rd ed. Ithaca, N.Y., Mack, Andrus & Woodruff, 1842.

Partoll, Albert J. *Grass Dance of the Salish*. Missoula, Historical Society of Western Montana, April 9-11, 1959. A pamphlet printed for a demonstration.

Phillips, Paul C. *The Fur Trade*. Concluding chapters by J. W. Smurr. 2 vols. Norman, University of Oklahoma Press, 1961.

——, and Carling I. Malouf. *Flathead, Kutenai and Upper Pend Oreille Genealogies*. Mimeographed. Missoula, 1952.

Point, Rev. Nicholas, S.J. *Wilderness Kingdom: Indian Life in the Rocky Mountains, 1840-1847*. Translated and introduced by Rev. Joseph P. Donnelly, S.J. New York, Holt, Rinehart and Winston, 1967.

Porter, Mae Reed, and Odessa Davenport. *Scotsman in Buckskin: Sir William Drummond Stewart and the Rocky Mountain Fur Trade*. New York, Hastings House, 1963.

Priest, Loring Benson. *Uncle Sam's Stepchildren: Reformation of United States Indian Policy, 1865-1887*. New Brunswick, Rutgers University Press, 1942.

Prucha, Rev. Francis Paul, S.J. *American Indian Policy in the Formative Years*. Cambridge, Harvard University Press, 1962.

Rahill, Peter J. *Catholic Indian Missions and Grant's Peace Policy, 1870-1884*. Washington, Catholic University of America Press, 1953.

Ray, Verne F. *Cultural Relations in the Plateau of Northwestern America*. Los Angeles, The Southwest Museum, 1939. Publications of the Frederick Webb Hodge Anniversary Publication Fund, Vol. 3.

Rich, E. E. *Hudson's Bay Company, 1670-1870*. 3 vols. New York, Macmillan Company, 1961. 2 vols. London, Hudson's Bay Record Society, 1959.

Roe, Frank Gilbert. *Indian and the Horse*. Norman, University of Oklahoma Press, 1955.

Ronan, Peter. *Historical Sketch of the Flathead Indian Nation from the Year 1813 to 1890*. Helena, Journal Publishing Co., 1890.

Ross, Alexander. *Fur Hunters of the Far West*. Edited by Kenneth A. Spaulding. Norman, University of Oklahoma Press, 1956.

Ruby, Robert H., and John A. Brown. *Spokane Indians*. Norman, University of Oklahoma Press, 1970.

Rushmore, Elsie Mitchell. *Indian Policy During Grant's Administration*. New York, Marion Press, 1914.

Russell, Carl P. *Firearms, Traps and Tools of the Mountain Men*. New York, Alfred A. Knopf, 1967.

Sage, Rufus B. *Letters and Papers, 1837-47*. Edited by LeRoy R. Hafen and Ann W. Hafen. 2 vols. Glendale, Arthur H. Clark Co., 1956.

Sahinen, Uuno M. *Mines and Mineral Deposits: Missoula and Ravalli Counties, Montana.* Montana Bureau of Mines and Geology, Bulletin No. 8, January, 1957.

Saum, Lewis O. *Fur Trader and the Indian.* Seattle, University of Washington Press, 1965.

Schaeffer, Claude E. *Bear Ceremonialism of the Kutenai Indians.* Mimeographed. *Studies in Plains Anthropology and History,* No. 4, Museum of the Plains Indian, Browning, Montana, 1966.

——. *Moulded Pottery among the Kutenai Indians.* Mimeographed. *Anthropology and Sociology Papers* of the University of Montana, No. 6, 1952.

Schoenberg, Rev. Wilfred P., S.J. *Jesuit Mission Presses in the Pacific Northwest: A History and Bibliography of Imprints, 1867–1899.* Portland, The Champoeg Press, 1957.

Scully, Virginia. *Treasury of American Indian Herbs.* New York, Crown Publishers, Inc., 1970.

Secoy, Frank Raymond. *Changing Military Patterns on the Great Plains.* American Ethnological Society Monographs, No. 21, 1953.

Shiner, Joel L. *Archeological Resources in the Libby and Katka Reservoirs, Northern Idaho and Northwestern Montana.* River Basin Surveys, Columbia Project, Smithsonian Institution, 1950.

——. *McNary Reservoir: A Study in Plateau Archeology.* Bulletin No. 179, Bureau of American Ethnology, 1961, pp. 149–266. *River Basin Survey Papers,* No. 23.

Shumate, Maynard. *Archeology of the Vicinity of Great Falls, Montana.* Mimeographed. *Anthropology and Sociology Papers* of the University of Montana, No. 2, 1950.

Smead, William H. *Land of the Flatheads.* St. Paul, Pioneer Press, 1905.

Stanley, George G. F. *Birth of Western Canada: A History of the Riel Rebellions.* Toronto, University of Toronto Press, 1960.

Stevens, Hazard. *Life of Isaac Ingalls Stevens.* 2 vols. Boston and New York, Houghton, Mifflin & Co., 1901.

Stevensville Historical Society. *Montana Genesis: A History of the Stevensville Area of the Bitter Root Valley.* Missoula, Mountain Press Co., 1971.

Steward, Julian H. *Basin-Plateau Aboriginal Sociopolitical Groups.* Bureau of American Ethnology, Bulletin No. 120, 1938.

Stuart, Granville. *Forty Years on the Frontier.* Edited by Paul C. Phillips. 2 vols. Cleveland, Arthur H. Clark Co., 1925.

Sunder, John E. *Bill Sublette, Mountain Man*. Norman, University of Oklahoma Press, 1959.

———. *Fur Trade on the Upper Missouri, 1840–1865*. Norman, University of Oklahoma Press, 1965.

———. *Joshua Pilcher, Fur Trader and Indian Agent*. Norman, University of Oklahoma Press, 1968.

Swadesh, Morris. "Linguistic Approach to Salish Prehistory." In Marian W. Smith, ed. *Indians of the Urban Northwest*. New York, Columbia University Press, 1949.

Swanson, Earl H., Jr. *Emergence of Plateau Culture*. Mimeographed. *Occasional Papers* of the Idaho State College Museum, No. 8, 1962.

Swanton, John R. *Indian Tribes of North America*. Bureau of American Ethnology, Bulletin No. 145, 1952.

Tabeau, Pierre-Antoine. *Tabeau's Narrative of Loisel's Expedition to the Upper Missouri*. Edited by Annie H. Abel. Norman, University of Oklahoma Press, 1939.

Taelman, Rev. Louis, S.J. *Diamond Jubilee: Founding of St. Ignatius Mission, 1855–1930*. St. Ignatius, Mont., St. Ignatius Press, 1930.

Teit, James A., Marian K. Gould, Livingston Farrand, and Herbert J. Spinden. *Folk-Tales of Salishan and Sahaptin Tribes*. Edited by Franz Boas. New York, American Folk-Lore Society, 1917.

———. *Salishan tribes of the Western Plateaus*. See government publications.

Thompson, David. *David Thompson's Narrative, 1784–1812*. Edited by Richard Glover. Toronto, The Champlain Society, 1962.

———. *David Thompson's Travels in Western North America, 1784–1812*. Edited by Victor G. Hopwood. Toronto, Macmillan of Canada, 1971.

———. *Narrative of Explorations in Western America, 1784–1812*. Edited by J. B. Tyrell. Toronto, The Champlain Society, 1916.

———. *David Thompson's Journals relating to Montana and Adjacent Regions, 1808–1812*. Edited by M. Catherine White. Missoula, Montana State University Press, 1950.

Trenholm, Virginia Cole, and Maurine Carley. *The Shoshonis, Sentinels of the Rockies*. Norman, University of Oklahoma Press, 1964.

Vaughn, Robert. *Then and Now: or Thirty-Six Years in the Rockies*. Minneapolis, Tribune Printing Co., 1900.

Voorhis, Ernest. *Historic Forts and Posts of the French Regime and British Fur Trading Companies*. Mimeographed. Ottawa, Department of Interior, 1930.

Waldron, Ellis L. *Montana Politics Since 1864: An Atlas of Elections*. Missoula, Montana State University Press, 1958.

Walker, Deward E., Jr. *Conflict and Schism in Nez Perce Acculturation: A Study of Religion and Politics*. Pullman, Washington State University Press, 1968.

Wallace, Ernest, and E. Adamson Hoebel. *The Comanches, Lords of the South Plains*. Norman, University of Oklahoma Press, 1952.

Wallace, William Stewart. *Documents Relating to the North West Company*. Toronto, The Champlain Society, 1934.

Warner, Frank W. *Montana Territory, History and Business Directory*. Helena, Fisk Brothers, 1879.

Weisel, George F., ed. *Men and Trade on the Northwest Frontier as Shown by the Fort Owen Ledger*. Missoula, Montana State University Press, 1955.

———. *Ten Animal Myths of the Flathead Indians*. Mimeographed. *Anthropology and Sociology Papers* of the University of Montana, No. 18, 1954.

White, Thain. *Battle Pits of the Koyokees*. Mimeographed. *Anthropology and Sociology Papers* of the University of Montana, No. 10, 1952.

———. *Kutenai Pipes*. Mimeographed. Lakeside, Mont., Flathead Lake Lookout Museum, No. 9, n.d.

———. *Scarred Trees in Western Montana*. Mimeographed. *Anthropology and Sociology Papers* of the University of Montana, No. 17, 1954.

———. *Tipi Rings in the Flathead Lake Area, Western Montana*. Mimeographed. *Anthropology and Sociology Papers* of the University of Montana, No. 19, October, 1959.

Woodward, Arthur. *Indian Trade Goods*. Portland, Oregon Archeological Society, Publication No. 2, 1965.

Work, John. *The Snake Country Expedition of 1830–1831*. Edited by Francis D. Haines, Jr. Norman, University of Oklahoma Press, 1971.

———. *Journal*. See Lewis and Phillips.

Wyeth, Nathaniel J. *Correspondence and Journals*. Edited by F. G. Young. *Sources of the History of Oregon*, I, Parts 3–6. Eugene, Ore., University Press, 1899.

Wyeth, John B. *Oregon*. Cambridge, John B. Wyeth, 1833.

ARTICLES

Aoki, Haruo. "Salishan Indian Languages," *Idaho Yesterdays*, Vol. XII, No. 1 (Spring, 1968), 8–11.

Barry, J. Nielson. "Spaniards in Early Oregon," *Washington Historical Quarterly*, Vol. XXIII (1932), 25–34.

Borden, Charles E. "Notes on the Pre-History of the Southern Northwest Coast," *British Columbia Historical Quarterly,* Vol. XIV (1950), 241–46.

Brockmann, C. Thomas. "Reciprocity and Market Exchange on the Flathead Reservation," *Northwest Anthropological Research Notes*, Vol. V, No. 1 (Spring, 1971), 77–93.

Burlingame, Merrill G. "Buffalo in Trade and Commerce," *North Dakota Historical Quarterly*, Vol. III, No. 4 (July, 1929), 262–91.

———. "Influence of the Military in the Building of Montana." *Pacific Northwest Quarterly*, Vol. XXIX (1938), 135–50.

Canse, Rev. John Martin. "Jason Lee: New Evidence on the Missionary and Colonizer." *Washington Historical Quarterly*, Vol. VI (1915), 251–63.

Coan, C. F. "Adoption of the Reservation Policy in the Pacific Northwest, 1853–55." *Oregon Historical Quarterly*, Vol. XXIII, No. 1 (March, 1922), 1–38.

Coates, Lawrence G. "Mormons and Social Change among the Shoshoni, 1853–1900." *Idaho Yesterdays*, Vol. XV, No. 4 (Winter, 1972), 3–11.

Craig, Joan. "Three Hundred Years of Records." *The Beaver*, Autumn, 1970, 65–70.

Criswell, Elijah Harry. "Lewis and Clark: Linguistic Pioneers." *University of Missouri Studies*, Vol. XV, No. 2 (April, 1940).

Davidson, Stanley R. "1871: Montana's Year of Political Fusion," *Montana Magazine*, Vol. XXI, No. 2 (Spring, 1971), 44–55.

Davis, Rev. William Lyle, S.J. "Peter John De Smet: the Journey of 1840." *Pacific Northwest Quarterly*, Vol. XXXV (1944), 29–43, 121–42.

Dee, Henry Drummond. "An Irishman in the Fur Trade: The Life and Journals of John Work." *British Columbia Historical Quarterly*, Vol. VII (1943), 229–70.

Driver, Harold E., and William C. Massey. "Comparative Studies of North American Indians." *Transactions*, American Philosophical Society, n.s. Vol. XLVII (1957), Part 1, 165–456.

Drury, Rev. Clifford Merrill. "Nez Perce Delegation of 1831." *Oregon Historical Quarterly*, Vol. XL (1939), 283–87.

———. "Oregon Indians in the Red River School." *Pacific Historical Review*, Vol. VII (1938), 50–60.

Dumont, Gabriel. "Account of the North West Rebellion, 1885." Edited by George G. F. Stanley. *Canadian Historical Review*, Vol. XXX (1949), 249–69.

Dusenberry, Verne. "Gabriel Nattau's Soul Speaks." *Journal of American Folklore*, Vol. LXXII (1959), 155–60.

Elliott, T. C. "Richard ('Captain Johnny') Grant." *Oregon Historical Quarterly*, Vol. XXXVI (March, 1935), 1–13.

———. "David Thompson's Journey in the Pend Oreille Country." *Washington Historical Quarterly*, Vol. XXIII (1932), 173–76.

———. "Fur Trade in the Columbia River Basin Prior to 1811." *Washington Historical Quarterly*, Vol. VI (1915), 3–10.

———. "Religion among the Flatheads." *Oregon Historical Quarterly*, Vol. XXXVII (1936), 1–8.

Ewers, John C. "Iroquois Indians in the Far West." *Montana Magazine of History*, Vol. XIII (April, 1963), 2–10.

Forbis, Richard G. "Flathead Apostasy." *Montana Magazine of History*, Vol. I, No. 4 (1951), 35–40.

———, and John D. Sperry. "An Early Man Site in Montana." *American Antiquity*, Vol. XVIII, No. 2 (1952), 127–33.

Garfield, James A. "Diary of a Trip to Montana in 1872." Edited by Oliver W. Holmes. *Frontier and Midland*, Vol. XV, No. 2 (1934), 159–68.

Garraghan, Rev. Gilbert Joseph, S.J. "Nicholas Point, Jesuit Missionary in the Montana of the Forties." *Transmississippi West*, University of Colorado, 1930.

Gibbs, George. "An Account of Indian Mythology in Oregon and Washington Territories." Edited by Ella E. Clark. *Oregon Historical Quarterly*, Vol. LVI (December, 1955), 293–325, and Vol. LVII (June, 1956), 125–67.

Grinnell, George Bird. "Coup and Scalp among the Plains Indians." *American Anthropologist*, n.s. Vol. XII (1910), 296–310.

Haines, Francis. "Where Did the Plains Indians Get Their Horses?" *American Anthropologist*, n.s. Vol. XL (1938), 112–17.

———. "Nez Perce Delegation to St. Louis in 1831." *Pacific Historical Review*, Vol. VI (1937), 71–78.

———. "Northward Spread of Horses among the Plains Indians." *American Anthropologist*, n.s. Vol. XL (1938), 429–37.

Haines, Francis D. "Western Limits of the Buffalo Range." *American West*, Vol. IV, No. 4 (November, 1967), 4–5, 8–9, 12, 66–67; and *Pacific Northwest Quarterly*, Vol. XXXI (1940), 389–98.

Harrison, Michael. "Chief Charlot's Battle with Bureaucracy." *Montana Magazine of History*, Vol. X (Autumn, 1960), 27–33.

Howard, Oliver Otis. "True Story of the Wallowa Campaign." *North American Review*, Vol. CXXIX (May, 1879), 53–64. Reply to Chief Joseph's article of April, 1879.

Jacobs, Melville. "Historic Perspectives in Indian Languages of Oregon and Washington." *Pacific Northwest Quarterly*, Vol. XXVIII (1937), 55–74.

Johnson, C. T. "Evolution of a Lament." *Washington Historical Quarterly*, Vol. II (1908), 195–208.

Joseph (Chief). "An Indian's View of Indian Affairs." *North American Review*, Vol. CXXVIII (April, 1879), 412–33.

Karlin, Jules Alexander. "Senator Joseph M. Dixon and Rocky Boy: A Documentary Postscript, 1908." Addendum to *Montana Heritage Series*, No. 3. See V. Dusenberry, *Rocky Boy Indians*.

Kehoe, Thomas F. "Tipi Rings: The Direct Ethnological Approach Applied to an Archeological Problem." *American Anthropologist*, n.s. Vol. LX (1958), 861–73.

Kingston, Ceylon S. "Buffalo in the Pacific Northwest." *Washington Historical Quarterly*, Vol. XXIII (1932), 163–72.

Kreuger, John R. "Flathead Supplement to Vogt's *Salishan Studies*." *Anthropological Linguistics*, Vol. II, No. 7 (1961), 33–38.

———. "Some Kinship Terms of the Flathead Salish." *Anthropological Linguistics*, Vol. III, No. 2 (1961), 11–18.

Larocque, Francois Antoine. "Journal." Edited by Ruth Hazlitt. *Frontier and Midland*, Vol. XIV, No. 3 (1933), 241–47, and No. 4 (1933), 332–39; Vol. XV, No. 1 (1934), 67–75, 88.

Lee, Jason, "Diary, April 20–July 16, 1834." *Oregon Historical Quarterly*, Vol. XVII (1916), 116–46.

Lewis, William S. "Francis Heron, Fur Trader: Other Herons." *Washington Historical Quarterly*, Vol. XI (1920), 29–34.

McDermott, Louisa. "Folk-lore of the Flathead Indians of Idaho: Adventures of Coyote." *Journal of American Folklore,* Vol. XIV (1901), 240–51.

McLoughlin, John. "Document among the Private Papers of Dr. John McLoughlin." *Transactions*, Oregon Pioneer Association, 1880, 46–55.

Malouf, Carling I. "Early Kutenai History." *Montana Magazine of History*, Vol. II, No. 2 (April, 1952), 5–9.

———, and Thain White. "Kutenai Calendar Records." *Montana Magazine of History*, Vol. III, No. 2 (1953), 34–39.

Meagher, Thomas Francis. "Rides through Montana." *Harper's New Monthly Magazine*, No. 209 (October, 1867), 568–83.

Mengarini, Rev. Gregory, S.J. "The Rocky Mountains: Memoirs of Father Gregory Mengarini." *Woodstock Letters*, Vol. XVII (1888), 293–309, and Vol. XVIII (1889), 25–43. Also edited by Albert J. Partoll, *Frontier and Midland*, Vol. XVIII (Spring, 1938), 193–202. There is a manuscript version in the Oregon Province Archives.

Merriam, Alan P. "Flathead Indian Instruments and Their Music." *Musical Quarterly*, Vol. XXXVII (1951), 368–75.

——. "Handgame of the Flathead Indians." *Journal of American Folklore*, Vol. LXVIII (1955), 313–24.

Morton, Arthur S. "Columbian Enterprise and David Thompson." *Canadian Historical Review*, Vol. XVII (1936), 266–88.

Nielsen, Jean C. "Donald McKenzie in the Snake Country Fur Trade, 1816–21." *Pacific Northwest Quarterly*, Vol. XXXI (1940), 161–79.

Nute, Grace Lee. "Papers of the American Fur Company: A Brief Estimate of Their Significance." *American Historical Review*, Vol. XXXII, No. 3 (April, 1927), 519–38.

O'Connor, Rev. James J. "Flathead Indians." *Records*, American Catholic Historical Society, Vol. III (1889–91), 85–110.

O'Keane, Josephine. "Church in the Valley." *Ave Maria*, n.s. Vol. LXXIII, No. 5 (1951), 148–52. Article on St. Mary's in the Bitterroot.

Parker, Rev. Samuel. "A Journey Beyond the Rocky Mountains in 1835, 1836, and 1837, Corrected and Extended in the Present Edition." *Voyages and Travels*, Vol. XX. Edinburgh, William and Robert Chambers, 1841.

Partoll, Albert J. "Blackfeet Indian Peace Council." *Frontier and Midland*, Vol. XVII, No. 3 (1937), 199–207.

——. "Duncan McDonald." *Montana Kaimin*, supplement, March 12, 1929.

——. "Flathead-Salish Name in Montana Nomenclature." *Montana Magazine of History*, Vol. I (January, 1951), 37–47.

——. "Fort Connah." *Pacific Northwest Quarterly*, Vol. XXX (1939), 399–415.

Phillips, Paul C., ed. "Family Letters of Two Oregon Fur Traders, 1828–1856." *Frontier and Midland*, Vol. XIV (1933–34), 66–75, 85. Letters of Edward Ermatinger and John Work.

——, and H. A. Trexler. "Discovery of Gold in the Northwest." *Mississippi Valley Historical Review*, Vol. IV (1917–18), 89–97.

Ray, Verne F. "Kolaskin Cult: A Prophet Movement of 1870 in Northeastern Washington." *American Anthropologist*, n.s. Vol. XXXVIII (1936), 67–75.

Ritz, Phillip. "Routes to Montana." *Walla Walla Statesman*, September 14, 1866.

Roe, Frank Gilbert. "Buffalo and Snow." *Canadian Historical Review*, Vol. XVII (1936), 125–46.

Ross, Alexander. "Journal, 1824." Edited by T. C. Elliott. *Oregon Historical Quarterly*, Vol. XIV (1913), 366–88.

Ross, Frank E. "Retreat of the Hudson's Bay Company in the Pacific Northwest." *Canadian Historical Review*, Vol. XVIII (1937), 262–80.

Rothensteiner, Rev. John, S.J. "Flathead and Nez Perce Delegations to St. Louis, 1831–1839." *St. Louis Catholic Historical Review*, Vol. II (October, 1920), 183–97.

Rothermich, Captain A. E., ed. "Early Days at Fort Missoula." See John W. Hakola, *Frontier Omnibus*.

Sanger, David. "Prehistory of the Pacific Northwest Plateau as Seen from the Interior of British Columbia." *American Antiquity*, Vol. XXXII (1967), 186–97.

Schaeffer, Claude E. "First Jesuit Mission to the Flatheads, 1840–1850." *Pacific Northwest Quarterly*, Vol. XXVIII (1937), 227–50.

Smith, Allan H. "An Ethnological Analysis of David Thompson's 1809–11 Journeys in the Lower Pend Oreille Valley, Northeastern Washington." *Ethnohistory*, Vol. VIII (1961), 309–81.

———. "Location of Flathead Post." *Pacific Northwest Quarterly*, Vol. XLVIII (1957), 47–54.

Spalding, Henry H. "Indians West of the Rocky Mountains." *Missionary Herald* (Boston), Vol. XXXIII (1837), 122, 421–28, 497.

Sperlin, O. B. "Two Kootenay Women Masquerading as Men." *Washington Historical Quarterly*, Vol. XXI (1930), 120–30.

Stenzel, Dr. Franz R. "E. S. Paxson—Montana Artist." *Montana Magazine of History*, Vol. XIII (Autumn, 1963), 50–76.

Trudeau, Jean Baptiste. "Journal." *South Dakota Historical Collections*, Vol. VII (1941), 403–74.

Turney-High, Harry Holbert. "Cooking Camas and Bitterroot." *Scientific Monthly*, Vol. XXXVI (1933), 262–63.

———. "Diffusion of the Horse to the Flatheads." *Man*, Vol. XXXV (1935), 183–85.

———. "Flathead Indians of Montana." *Memoirs*, American Anthropological Association, Vol. XLVIII (1937), 1–161.

Weisel, George F. "Animal Names, Anatomical Terms, and Some

Ethnozoology of the Flathead Indians." *Journal of the Washington Academy of Science,* Vol. XLII, No. 11 (November, 1952), 345–55.
———. "Ram's Horn Tree and Other Medicine Trees of the Flathead Indians." *Montana Magazine of History,* Vol. I, No. 3 (1951), 5–14.
Wells, Philip F. "Ninety-Six Years among the Indians of the Northwest." *North Dakota History,* Vol. XV, No. 3 (July, 1948), 169–215.
White, M. Catherine. "Saleesh House." *Pacific Northwest Quarterly,* Vol. XXXIII (1942), 251–64.
Whitman, Marcus. "Journal of Exploration in 1835 with Reverend Samuel Parker beyond the Rocky Mountains." Edited by F. G. Young. *Oregon Historical Quarterly,* Vol. XXVIII (1927), 237–57.
Williams, Glyndwr. "Highlights of the First Two Hundred Years of the Hudson's Bay Company." *The Beaver,* Autumn, 1970, 4–59.
Wood, C. E. S. "Chief Joseph, the Nez Perce," *Century Magazine,* May, 1884, 138.
Woody, Frank H. "Sketch of the Early History of Western Montana." *Contributions,* Historical Society of Montana, Vol. II (1896), 88–106.
———. "Historical Sketch of Missoula County." *Weekly Missoulian,* July 19, 1876. Little different from article in *Contributions.*

GOVERNMENT PUBLICATIONS

Armstrong, Frank C. *Condition of Reservation Indians.* 57 Cong., 1 sess. (1902), *House Doc. 406.*
"Calendar of the American Fur Company's Papers." *Annual Report of the American Historical Association, 1944.* 3 vols. Washington, Government Printing Office, 1945. 79 Cong., 1 sess., *House Doc. 207.*
Carrington, Henry Beebe. "History of Indian Operations on the Plains, 1866–67." 50 Cong., 1 sess. (1887), *Sen. Exec. Doc. 33.* Carrington's belated statement on the Fetterman massacre.
———. "Report to the Secretary of the Interior in Re Appraisement and Sale of Bitter Root Valley Lands, Authorized 1890." 51 Cong., 1 sess., *Sen. Exec. Doc. 70.*
Delano, C. "Letter from the Secretary of the Interior Communicating . . . Early Labors of Missionaries of the American Board of Commissioners for Foreign Missions in Oregon, Commencing 1836." 41 Cong., 3 sess. (1871), *Sen. Exec. Doc. 37.*
Denig, Edwin Thompson. "Of the Crow Nation." Edited by John C. Ewers, *Anthropological Papers,* No. 33, Bureau of American Ethnology, Bulletin No. 151. Washington, Government Printing Office, 1953.

Ewers, John C. *Horse in Blackfoot Indian Culture.* Bureau of American Ethnology, Bulletin No. 159. Washington, Government Printing Office, 1955.

Indian Claims Commission, Docket 61. Listed among Manuscripts.

Indian Heirship Land Study, Volume I: Analysis of Indian Opinion as Expressed in Questionnaires. 86 Cong., 2 sess. (1960), *House Committee Print 27.*

Indian Tribes of Northern Montana. 58 Cong., 2 sess. (1904), *Sen. Doc. 255.*

Jackson, Andrew. "Message of the President . . . relative to the British Establishments on the Columbia, Etc." January 24, 1831. 21 Cong., 2 sess., *Sen. Doc. 39.*

Kappler, Charles J., comp. *Indian Affairs: Laws and Treaties.* 4 vols. Washington, Government Printing Office, 1905–29.

McCammon, Joseph Kay. See *Report in Relation to an Agreement.*

Pilcher, Joshua. "Estimate of the Indian Trade." Attachment to President Jackson's message, 1831, 21 Cong., 2 sess., *Sen. Doc. 39.*

Report in Relation to an Agreement Made Between Joseph Kay McCammon . . . and the Confederated Tribes of the Flathead, Kootenay, and Upper Pend d'Reille Indians. 47 Cong., 2 sess. (1883), *Sen. Exec. Doc. 44.*

Report of a Select Subcommittee of the Senate Concerning the Condition of the Indian Tribes in the Territories of Montana and Dakota. 48 Cong., 1 sess. (March 7, 1884), *Sen. Rep. 283.*

Royce, Charles C. "Indian Land Cessions in the United States." *Eighteenth Annual Report,* Part 2, Bureau of American Ethnology, 521–997. Washington, Government Printing Office, 1899.

Sheridan, Philip H., and William T. Sherman. *Reports of Inspection Made in the Summer of 1877.* Washington, Government Printing Office, 1878.

Teit, James A. *Salishan Tribes of the Western Plateaus.* Edited by Franz Boas. Forty-fifth annual report, Bureau of American Ethnology, 1927–28. 70 Cong., 2 sess. (1930), *House Doc. 380.*

Termination of Federal Supervision over Certain Tribes of Indians: Joint Hearings on S. 2750 and H.R. 7319. Part 7: Flathead Indians, Montana, February 25–27, 1954. Pursuant to *House Concurrent Res. 108,* 83 Cong., 1 sess.

United States Bureau of Reclamation. *Project Histories and Reports . . . Flathead Project, Montana, 1909–23.* Microcopy 96, National Archives, Record Group 115.

———. *Reconnaisance Report: Clark Fork Basin, Montana.* Boise: USBR Region 1, June, 1959.

Vest, George G. See *Indian Tribes of Northern Montana* and *Report of a Select Subcommittee.*

NEWSPAPERS (published in Montana unless otherwise noted)

Anaconda Standard
Bonners Ferry, Idaho, *Kootenai Herald,* 1892
Butte Miner, 1910
Deer Lodge, *New North-West*
Fort Benton Press, 1887
Helena, *Rocky Mountain Gazette,* 1872
Helena Daily Herald
Helena Journal, 1889
Libby News, 1899
Missoula, *Missoulian,* daily and weekly
Missoula and Cedar Creek Pioneer (various titles), 1870–71
Missoula Pioneer, 1872
Polson Inter-Lake, 1891
Seattle (Washington) *Post-Intelligencer,* 1893
Virginia City and Helena, *Montana Post,* 1864–66
Virginia City and Helena, *Tri-Weekly Post*
Walla Walla (Washington) *Statesman,* 1866
Washington (D.C.) *Post*
Yakima (Washington) *Weekly Herald,* 1903
Army and Navy Journal, 1869–73
Char-Koosta, monthly, Flathead Agency, 1956–60

INDEX